# ADVANCED UNIX® USER'S

## INTERACTIVE WORKBOOK

# JOHN McMULLEN

Prentice Hall PTR
Upper Saddle River, NJ 07458
http://www.phptr.com/phptrinterative

ISBN 0-13-085456-5

90000

9 780130 854568

Editorial/production Supervision: *Kathleen M. Caren*
Acquisitions editor: *Mark L. Taub*
Development editor: *Ralph E. Moore*
Technical Reviewer: *Jeff Gitlin*
Marketing manager: *Kate Hargett*
Manufacturing manager: *Alexis R. Heyd*t
Editorial assistant: *Michael Fredette*
Cover design director: *Jerry Votta*
Cover Designer: *Anthony Gemmellaro*
Art director: *Gail Cocker-Bogusz*
Series design: *Meryl Poweski*
Web site project manager: *Eileen Clark*

Prentice Hall books are widely used by corporations and government agencies for training, marketing, and resale. The publisher offers discounts on this book when ordered in bulk quantities.
For more information, contact: Corporate Sales Department, Phone: 800-382-3419;
FAX: 201-236-7141; email: corpsales@prenhall.com
Or write: Corp. Sales Dept., Prentice Hall PTR, 1 Lake Street, Upper Saddle River, NJ   07458

Printed in the United States of America
10  9  8  7  6  5  4  3  2  1

ISBN 0-13-085456-5

Prentice-Hall International (UK) Limited, *London*
Prentice-Hall of Australia Pty. Limited, *Sydney*
Prentice-Hall Canada Inc., *Toronto*
Prentice-Hall Hispanoamericana, S.A., *Mexico*
Prentice-Hall of India Private Limited, *New Delhi*
Prentice-Hall of Japan, Inc., *Tokyo*
Prentice-Hall (Singapore) Pte. Ltd., *Singapore*
Editora Prentice-Hall do Brasil, Ltda., *Rio de Janeiro*

# DEDICATION

To all of my parents, by birth and by marriage.

# CONTENTS

# FROM THE EDITOR

Prentice Hall's Interactive Workbooks are designed to get you up and running fast, with just the information you need, when you need it.

We are certain that you will find our unique approach to learning simple and straightforward. Every chapter of every Interactive Workbook begins with a list of clearly defined Learning Objectives. A series of labs make up the heart of each chapter. Each lab is designed to teach you specific skills in the form of exercises. You perform these exercises at your computer and answer pointed questions about what you observe. Your answers will lead to further discussion and exploration. Each lab then ends with multiple-choice Self-Review Questions, to reinforce what you've learned. Finally, we have included Test Your Thinking projects at the end of each chapter. These projects challenge you to synthesize all of the skills you've acquired in the chapter.

Our goal is to make learning engaging, and to make you a more productive learner.

And you are not alone. Each book is integrated with its own "Companion Website." The website is a place where you can find more detailed information about the concepts discussed in the Workbook, additional Self-Review Questions to further refine your understanding of the material, and perhaps most importantly, where you can find a community of other Interactive Workbook users working to acquire the same set of skills that you are.

All of the Companion Websites for our Interactive Workbooks can be found at `http://www.phptr.com/phptrinteractive`.

Mark L. Taub
Editor-in-Chief
Pearson PTR Interactive

# ABOUT THE AUTHOR

John McMullen has been employed as a biologist, an actor, a bookstore clerk, an inventory clerk, a software trainer, a fiction writer, and a lumberyard guy. A couple of those jobs lasted only a few hours, but it's the principle of the thing.

However, he's been a technical writer for more than 10 years. Right now, he's the Senior Technical Writer for Softway Systems, proud makers of Interix for Windows NT (end of commercial). He's used UNIX systems since his university days, which are getting to be a long time ago.

He lives in southern Ontario, Canada, with his lovely and talented wife and his lovely and talented daughter. This is his third book; his second book, *UNIX User's Interactive Workbook*, was also published by Prentice-Hall.

# INTRODUCTION

Welcome to the *Advanced UNIX User's Interactive Workbook.* The title is somewhat daunting, so I'm glad you've looked this far. Here's what the title means:

This book is *Advanced* because it's a sequel, a follow-up to my previous book, the *UNIX User's Interactive Workbook.* If you didn't read that book (or you're not inclined to buy it), Chapter 1 of this book is a quick review of the basics. (I still think you should buy and work through my previous book first, though.)

*UNIX User's* means it's for people who use the UNIX operating system.

*Interactive Workbook* means every chapter consists of exercises for you to try. If you want to discuss your answers, there's also a Web site dedicated to this series of books, and to this book in particular. I read the discussion group associated with this book and the previous book. You can communicate with other readers or with me if you have questions or even if you (God forbid) find a mistake.

## WHO THIS BOOK IS FOR

This book is for people who want to learn more than just the basics of the UNIX computer system. You already know how to copy a file or change a directory or even use the vi editor. This book is suited for those who want to make themselves more effective with vi or use Emacs or work across a network.

Who is this book *not* for? If you're a long-time UNIX hacker, if you write Perl scripts in your sleep and dream in sed commands, you might as well put this book down; it's not advanced enough for you. Try one of the other books in the Interactive Workbook series, or other fine books by Prentice-Hall.

# WHAT YOU'LL NEED

You'll need access to a UNIX computer system. This means you need a *shell account* and access to a terminal or a computer.

You'll also need a pen or pencil and some paper. This book asks questions and expects you to answer them.

Each chapter should take you approximately an hour or two to complete.

# HOW THIS BOOK IS ORGANIZED

Each chapter contains a brief introduction and a series of labs and ends with a project ("Test Your Thinking") that makes use of the information covered in the chapter. Suggested answers to the Test Your Thinking are found on the Web site, not in the book.

Each lab is organized in a similar way. After a brief introduction, there are a set of exercises and questions. (If you do the exercises, you can answer the questions.) After the questions for the lab come the answers, which are accompanied by an in-depth discussion of what you've done and why. Following each lab's Answer section, there's a multiple-choice quiz ("Self-Review Questions") on the Lab. (Answers to the Self-Review Questions can be found in Appendix A.)

After Chapter 1, the order of the chapters is not particularly significant. In general, the later chapters build on the early ones (both Chapters 3 and 4 build on network addressing concepts discussed earlier in Chapter 2, for example). However, there are enough cross-references to allow you to read the chapters in almost any order you please.

Chapter 1, "UNIX Basics," is a non-comprehensive review of UNIX basics. It covers what you need to know to do the rest of the chapters in the book.

Chapters 2 and 3 ("Electronic Communication" and "Electronic Mail," respectively) discuss various kinds of electronic communication, both with users on your system and off.

Chapter 4, "Computer Networks," shows you a bit about computer networks: how to log in across a network and how to transfer files.

Chapter 5, "Some Useful Stuff," contains a number of useful-but-hard-to-categorize tricks, including a way to repeat commands.

If you find that vi is not to your taste and your system has the Emacs editor installed, do Chapter 6, "The Emacs Editor."

Chapters 7 and 8 ("Customizing Your Environment" and "Shell Scripts") work together to provide an introduction to shell scripting. "Shell scripting" is just a term for storing lists of commands so the computer can run them in sequence—you turn a series of commands into a single command.

Chapter 9, "More on Files and Permissions," discusses some more advanced concepts in file and permissions handling.

Chapters 10 and 11 ("Advanced vi Tricks" and "Advanced Emacs Tricks") present some more techniques for using those editors, including spell checks, running other commands, and defining new commands.

## CONVENTIONS USED IN THIS BOOK

The following typographical conventions are found in this book:

| | |
|---|---|
| `cp file1 file2` | A command you should enter into the computer. |
| `$ echo $LOGNAME`<br>`johnmc` | An example of output from the computer. This is set off from the main text. |
| *file* | A placeholder used in an example command or a command synopsis. |
| *yourname* | Either an emphasized or defined word, a placeholder, or a word you should replace with a suitable value. |

There are also some icons used in this book, as explained here:

*TIP/NOTE: This icon flags information that deserves special attention, such as an interesting fact about the topic at hand, or something the reader may want to keep in mind while programming or proceeding with the technology.*

*WARNING: This icon flags common programming pitfalls or information that, while useful, may cause unexpected results or serious frustration.*

 *WEB: This icon is used to flag passages that contain references to the book's companion Web site.*

 *ADVICE/QUOTE: This icon flags advice from teacher to student, or words of wisdom from a quoted source.*

All of the other conventions used in this book should be self-explanatory.

## ABOUT THE WEB COMPANION

This book has a companion Web site, located at:

http://www.phptr.com/phptrinteractive/

Think of the Web site as a student lounge, where you can go and find the answers to the projects or just chat with other students about the course or topics of interest. There's even a corner where the author (that would be me) presents items that didn't get into the book or answers questions or just possibly corrects a mistake.

Visit the Web site periodically to share and discuss your answers.

# CHAPTER 1

# UNIX BASICS

 *Before we can go on, we need to know where we've already been. This chapter is a whirlwind tour of UNIX basics. If you want more information on any of these topics, refer back to the* UNIX User's Interactive Workbook.

## CHAPTER OBJECTIVES

In this Chapter, you will learn about:

This book builds on the material in the previous book I wrote for the Interactive Workbook series, *UNIX User's Interactive Workbook*. Because it's possible that some people haven't read the first book, this chapter reviews some important information. This review chapter doesn't begin to cover all of the material you ought to know. However, it *does* present the basic commands you need to know in order to do the labs in this book. Some other chapters may contain a brief review lab as an introduction to that particular topic.

You need to understand the structure of a command line, you need to know how to list files and directories, how to create and edit files, and how to set and view environment variables. This chapter *doesn't* tell you how to login to your UNIX system. It doesn't talk about the different kinds of terminals you might have, or your shell.

# L A B  1 . 1

# LOGIN NAMES, USER IDS, AND GROUPS

---

### LAB OBJECTIVES

After this Lab, you will be able to:

- Identify Your Login Name and User ID
- Identify Your Group

---

You almost certainly know your login name, since you need it to use your account. Your login name is a way to identify yourself to the system, and in fact, you have *two* login identifiers: One is a number (your *user ID*), and the other is a name (your *login name*). Both are yours alone on the system. For example, on my system, I'm user `johnmc`, user number 105.

For administrative purposes, you also belong to one or more *groups*. A UNIX group is just a way of segregating permissions: If you're part of the group (the "in" crowd, if you will), you may have permissions that others don't have.

## LAB 1.1  EXERCISES

### 1.1.1  IDENTIFY YOUR LOGIN NAME AND USER ID

Enter the following commands:

```
who am I
echo $LOGNAME
id -un
```

On some older BSD systems, you may need to enter the `who am I` command as one word: `whoami`. If the `id` command on your system does not take the option `-un`, ignore the command for now.

**a)** What does the `who am i` command display?

_____

_____

**b)** What does the command `echo $LOGNAME` display? If it worked, the command `id -un`?

_____

_____

**c)** Why does each user have a unique login name?

_____

_____

## 1.1.2 IDENTIFY YOUR GROUP

Enter the following command:

```
id -a
```

(If the `-a` option doesn't work, try the `id` command without any options.)

**a)** What does the `id` command show?

_____

_____

**b)** How is the output different from the `id -un` command in the last exercise?

_____

_____

**c)** Do you belong to more than one group? (If the answer is not clear from the `id` output, try the commands `groups` and `id -a`.)

_____

_____

Enter the following commands:

```
man newgrp
man chgrp
```

(When using the `man` command, remember to press the spacebar to display more information, or press `q` to exit the `man` command.)

**d)** What is the difference between the `newgrp` and `chgrp` commands?

_____

_____

# LAB 1.1 EXERCISE ANSWERS

## 1.1.1 ANSWERS

Enter the following commands:

```
who am I
echo $LOGNAME
id -un
```

On some systems, you may need to enter the `who` command as one word: `whoami`. If the `id` command on your system does not take the option `-un`, ignore the command for now.

**a)** What does the `who am i` command display?

*Answer: The `who am i` command displays your login name. For example:*

```
$ who am I
johnmc                    /dev/pts/5        Jan 20 22:40
```

In fact, the who command displays a lot of information about the users currently on the system. With the arguments am i, it displays your login name, the name of the terminal you're logged in at, and the time and date you logged in. In this example, I'm user johnmc, logged into the terminal /dev/pts/5, and I logged in on January 20 at 22:40.

There is another command that displays your identity, the command id. The id command displays only information about you.

**b)** What does the command echo $LOGNAME display? If it worked, the command id -un?

*Answer: The command* echo $LOGNAME *displays the contents of the environment variable* LOGNAME, *which is your login name. The command* id -un *displays only your login name. For example:*

```
$ echo $LOGNAME
johnmc
$ id -un
johnmc
```

Your login name is stored in the environment variable LOGNAME for the convenience of other programs. (Some programs may create temporary files that include your login name.) The id -un command will also display your login name.

*You interact with the computer through a program called your* shell. *Your shell keeps track of information (like* LOGNAME) *for you, interprets your commands, and actually runs programs for you. Although there are different shell programs, I assume you're using the Korn Shell. (For more introductory information on shells, refer back to the* UNIX User's Interactive Workbook.)

On some systems, you can also discover your own login name with the command logname. The logname command actually exists to prevent people from trying to use echo $LOGNAME, because that only shows you the value of the LOGNAME environment variable, which may not actually be your login name. (Normally it is, but it's possible to change it on purpose or by accident.)

Why so many ways to discover your name, when you need to know your login name to, well, log in? Because modern UNIX systems contain commands inherited from more than one system. The who command is really intended to show you who's logged on, and the Berkeley people added the who am I and whoami versions. The id command is simply a standardized version of the same thing.

The id command also shows your user ID number. Internally, the UNIX system uses this number—not your login name—to set and determine the ownership of files. Programmers sometimes need to know the numeric user ID.

Why should you need to discover your own login name? Well, you might have forgotten, or you might encounter a terminal that someone has forgotten to log out from, or you might be writing a program that needs to know who's running it. (See Chapter 8, "Shell Scripts," for an introduction to shell scripts.)

**c)**   Why does each user have a unique login name?

*Answer: A user's login name identifies him or her to the computer. The name has to be unique so that the computer can distinguish between users.*

Remember that the computer has to distinguish between you and everyone else. No two people can have the same login name. (Because your password is secret, any two people might have the same password—but the operating system checks your name before it checks your password.)

## 1.1.2 ANSWERS

Enter the following command:

```
id -a
```

**a)**   What does the id -a command show?

*Answer: The id -a command displays your login name and a list of all the groups you belong to. (On older Solaris systems, the id command doesn't list all of the groups unless you give the -a option.) For example:*

```
$ id -a
uid=1010(johnmc) gid=10(R+D) groups=10(R+D), 15(Docs)
```

You can see that my user name is johnmc and my current group is R+D. I also belong to the group Docs. Each of those also has a number associated with it. The number associated with my login name is my user ID number, or "uid," and I have one *group ID*, or "gid".

On Solaris systems, the `id` command displays only one group, your *primary group*, unless you give the `-a` option. On other systems, the `-a` option doesn't work. (On Linux systems, the `-a` option is accepted but has no effect.)

**b)** How is the output different from the `id -un` command in the last exercise?

*Answer: The command displays the groups, and it also displays the numeric values for your login ID and for your groups.*

The `id -un` command displays only your login name. In this example, you can see that my *user* ID number is 1010, and my *group* ID is 10, which is the R+D group. (The root user is always user number 0.)

**c)** Do you belong to more than one group?

*Answer: This will vary for each person. You may or may not belong to more than one group.*

In the example output, I belong to two groups, "R+D" and "Docs". When I attempt to access (read or write or execute) a file, the system checks the group permissions on the file. If the group permissions apply to either Docs or R+D members *and* the permissions allow what I'm trying to do, the system lets me do it.

If you belong to more than one group (as in the example output), you'll notice that there is only one group ID (the gid) listed. That group is the *primary group*. For example, when I create a file, it belongs to my primary group. (We'll talk more about this in Chapter 9, "More On Files and Permissions.")

Your primary group is listed on the same line as the rest of your account information in the file `/etc/passwd`. The file `/etc/group` contains a list of all the groups on your system and the users in each group.

Groups are an administrative convenience. They let the administrators assign (or deny) permissions to files and directories for groups of individuals. (Other operating systems handle this kind of security in different ways; I'm sure you can imagine some.)

**d)** What is the difference between the `newgrp` and `chgrp` commands?

*Answer: The* `newgrp` *command changes your group ID for this login session; the* `chgrp` *command changes the group that a file belongs to.*

Even though you can belong to more than one group, it's convenient to think of you as "using" only one group ID at a time—that's why only one gid is shown, the group ID of your primary group. When you create a file, the group permissions apply to the group of your current group ID. In my example, any file I create will have its group permissions apply to the group Docs. If I want to create files that belong to the group R+D, I have to change my current group. There are two ways to do that: You can change *your* group with the newgrp command, or you can change the *file's* group, with the chgrp command.

The newgrp command changes your primary group for the rest of your login session (or until you give the newgrp command again). In older UNIX systems, you could only "use" one group at a time.

For example, my primary group is R+D. On an old system, I couldn't read a file that allowed only members of group Docs to read it, because Docs isn't my primary group. I would have to change my primary group (using newgrp) before I could read that file. Since most modern UNIX systems allow you to "belong" to all of your groups at once, the newgrp command isn't as important as it once was.

Only the owner of a file (or the super-user) can chgrp a file.

## LAB 1.1 SELF-REVIEW QUESTIONS

In order to test your progress, you should be able to answer the following questions.

1) Each user is identified by a unique number.
   **a)** _____ True
   **b)** _____ False

2) A user belongs to only one group at a time.
   **a)** _____ True
   **b)** _____ False

3) If you create a file, it is created with any one of your groups.
   **a)** _____ True
   **b)** _____ False

4) The user ID of the super-user is 0.
   **a)** _____ True
   **b)** _____ False

*Quiz answers appear in Appendix A, Section 1.1.*

# LAB 1.2

# COMMANDS AND COMMAND LINES

---

## LAB OBJECTIVES

After this Lab, you will be able to:

- Create Files with Output Redirection
- Explain the Parts of a Command
- Connect Commands with Pipes

---

Commands are the building blocks for using UNIX. UNIX is flexible; it allows you to build more complex commands from simpler ones. Part of this is due to the design of the commands themselves, and part of it is because of the design of your shell, the program you use to interact with the UNIX system.

In part one of this Lab, you'll learn to create files so you have something to work with in part two.

A command is just what it sounds like: It's an order to the operating system. A command starts off with an action or a verb, such as `sort`. You can modify it with options (or "adverbs") and provide the names of files or directories to be acted upon (or "objects"). The ability to modify exactly what commands do with options makes commands more flexible and reduces the total number of programs you need to know about.

Once you understand commands, you can connect them using command pipelines.

# LAB 1.2 EXERCISES

## 1.2.1 CREATE FILES WITH OUTPUT REDIRECTION

Enter the following commands:

```
echo These are the files in the directory /: > list
more < list
ls -l / >> list
more < list
```

When viewing text with the `more` command, press the space bar to display more text or press q to quit.

**a)** What does the > in the `echo` command do?

_____

_____

**b)** What does the >> in the `ls` command do?

_____

_____

**c)** What does the < in the `more` command do?

_____

_____

## 1.2.2 EXPLAIN THE PARTS OF A COMMAND

Enter the following `sort` commands. You can substitute any other text file for `list`.

```
sort list
sort -f list
sort -o sorted list
```

**a)** How do the results of the commands differ? Why do they differ?

_____

_____

**b)** According to the synopsis of the `sort` command, what parts of the `sort` command are required?

_____

_____

## 1.2.3 CONNECT COMMANDS WITH PIPES

Enter the following commands:

```
ps -f > pslist
grep $LOGNAME < pslist
ps -f | grep $LOGNAME
```

**a)** What does the | character do?

_____

_____

**b)** Can you use a pipeline on standard error?

_____

_____

**c)** Suppose you want to use `more` to display the contents of all of the files listed in the file `list`. Would a pipeline help (for example, in a command such as `cat list | more`)?

_____

_____

Enter the following command:

```
more $(cat list)
```

**d)** What does the $ (*command*) construct do?

_____

_____

# LAB 1.2 EXERCISE ANSWERS

## 1.2.1 ANSWERS

Enter the commands:

```
echo These are the files in the directory /: > list
more < list
ls -l / >> list
more < list
```

When viewing text with the `more` command, press the space bar to display more text or press `q` to quit.

**a)** What does the > in the `echo` command do?

*Answer: The > character causes the output of the* `echo` *command to be stored in the file named list.*

The `echo` command normally repeats back everything after the command. Why doesn't it repeat the "> `list`" part? The short answer is that the > character is magic. It's a *metacharacter*.

In computer-speak, the prefix "meta" usually means "of a higher kind," so "metacharacters" are characters of a higher kind. When your shell program sees a metacharacter in a command, it treats it as a "magic" instruction. These characters, such as >, >>, and < are file redirection metacharacters. (There are other kinds of metacharacters, such as $ and |. We'll discuss some of them throughout this book; for a real discussion of metacharacters in the shell, you should see the `ksh` man page or a book such as the *UNIX Shell Interactive Workbook*.)

The > character follows a command and is followed by a file name. The > character tells your shell to store the output of the command in the file. If the file doesn't exist, it's created. If the file does exist, its contents are *replaced by* the output of the command.

*If you don't want to replace the contents of files by accident, use the command* `set noclobber` *at the beginning of your login session. This prevents the shell from replacing the contents of files. (If you need to replace the contents of a shell, use >| instead of >.)*

**b)**   What does the >> in the `ls` command do?

*Answer: The >> metacharacters cause the shell to add the output of the `ls` command to the end of the file `list`.*

If you use > twice with the same file name, the contents of the file are replaced. Sometimes you don't want that; sometimes you want to append the new output to the end of the file. That's what the metacharacter construct >> is for. The output is added to the end of the file.

Metacharacters are specific to the shell program you're using. Your shell may support different additional metacharacters. (All of the UNIX shells support the metacharacters discussed in this chapter.)

We'll discuss the shell program a bit more in the next exercise, but for now remember that the shell is the program you use to interact with the computer. Metacharacters are a tool that shells provide to give you more flexibility. They're another convenience.

**c)**   What does the < in the `more` command do?

*Answer: The < causes the file `list` to be used as input for the `more` command.*

This one is subtle, and you may have missed it. On UNIX, every command has a standard place for *input* (the information coming in), *output* (information going out), and *errors* (messages to the user that aren't output). Unless you say otherwise, the standard source of input is the keyboard and the standard place to send output and error messages is the screen. The trick is that UNIX treats all of these places just as if they were files. (Your terminal screen is a file named `/dev/tty`, for example.)

Because the system already thinks that input and output are files, the > and < metacharacters just let you *redirect* these streams of information from or into different files.

If you want to redirect the standard error, the metacharacter construct is uglier (because it's used less often). It's 2>, or 2>> if you want to append the standard error to a file. The 2 indicates that this is file stream 2. (Every file stream has a number. Standard input is file stream 0, so "<" is really "0<"; standard output is 1, so ">" is really "1>". Because these two are used so often, the numbers can be left off.)

**1.2.2 ANSWERS**

Enter the command `sort`.

```
sort list
sort -f list
sort -o sorted list
```

**a)**   How do the results of the commands differ? Why do they differ?

*Answer: The first command sorts the lines in the file* `list` *and displays them on the screen (standard output). The second sorts the lines using a "folded" sort (upper- and lowercase letters are not treated differently) and displays the result on the screen. The third does a standard sort but writes the output in the file* `sorted`. *The results differ because the commands have different options.*

Compare the three commands used in this question:

```
sort list
sort -f list
sort -o sorted list
```

All three commands cause the `sort` program to do something. The first word in any command is the name of a program (a file that contains instructions for the computer). The `sort` command refers to a program file named `sort`; the `id` command refers to a program named `id`. Any other "words" (or *arguments*) in the command *modify* the command.

For example, the command `sort list` tells the `sort` command to sort the lines in the file `list`. The first word is the command, the last word is the object of the command, the file to be sorted. (In fact, the `sort` command doesn't require an object—a file—but without an object, it sorts any lines that appear on the standard input.)

This is a standard *ASCII sort.* All capital letters are sorted *before* lowercase letters. This is because `sort` sorts the characters by the numbers the computer uses to represent each character; uppercase letters are represented by the numbers 65-90, and the lowercase letters are represented by 97-122.

(This assumes you're in the U.S. In other countries, this can be complicated by the need to have other letters in the alphabet. The character Á might sort right after an A, but has a code that would go someplace else.)

The command `sort -f list` sorts the same file, but sorts it in a different way. With the `-f` option, upper- and lowercase letters are not treated differently. This sort is called a "folded" sort.

The command `sort -o sorted list` tells `sort` to perform the standard sort but to save the output in a file instead of displaying it on the screen.

These are the three common types of arguments:

- An object to the command, usually a file name, sometimes called an *operand*. This is something the command acts upon.
- An option, usually a single letter, introduced by a dash character, "-", such as `-f`. Single-letter options can usually be run together or placed in any order, so that the command `sort -f -u` is the same as the commands `sort -fu` or `sort -uf`. (Some commands use multi-letter options that cannot be run together; other commands use options that begin with "+" or with "−".) Some programs accept − as a kind of option to indicate the end of the options on the command line.
- An option with its own argument, such as `-o sorted`. The argument to the option provides additional information.

**b)** According to the synopsis of the `sort` command, what parts of the `sort` command are required?

*Answer: As reported by the command* `man sort`, *the* `sort` *command's synopsis looks like this:*

```
sort [-cmu] [-o file] [-bdfiMnr] [-t char] [-T dir] [-k
keydef] [file...]
```

*All of the arguments are optional.*

The synopsis is an abbreviated way of describing all of the options and arguments to a command. It uses a shorthand to describe what parts are essential and what arguments are needed.

- Any parts in square brackets [ ] are optional.
- Any words or letters in *italics* are placeholders. For example, the word *file* stands for the name of the file you want to sort.
- Arguments that can be repeated are often followed by three dots (...). With the `sort` command, you can provide more than one *file* name.
- Options that can be run together usually will be; it saves space.

- Sometimes you'll see vertical bars and possibly braces; these indicate mutually exclusive options. For example, if you can give option −a *file or* option −b *file*, it may be indicated like this:

**{-a *file*|-b *file*}**

The command's manual page shows a synopsis, and many commands will show a synopsis if you give a blatantly wrong option (I often use −?).

## *1.2.3* ANSWERS

Enter the following commands:

```
ps -f > pslist
grep $LOGNAME < pslist
ps -f | grep $LOGNAME
```

**a)** What does the | character do?

*Answer: The | character causes the standard output of the first command (ps) to be directed (or "piped") into the standard input of the second command (grep $LOGNAME).*

The first command runs the ps -f command and captures its output in a file named pslist. The ps command lists the commands that are currently running; the -f option produces the "full" format output, which includes your login name.

The second command uses the file pslist as standard input to grep. The grep command searches a file (or standard input) for a particular word or text pattern, in this case your login name ($LOGNAME).

The third command does exactly the same two commands, but it joins the first two together. You don't need to create pslist at all; you can send the output of ps -f directly to the input of grep.

**b)** Can you use a pipeline on standard error?

*Answer: No, or at least, not easily.*

I mention this because every once in a while I want to pipe standard *error* somewhere, usually so I can use grep to eliminate most of the error messages. Unfortunately, it's not that simple to do. The pipe symbol deals only with standard file streams zero (standard input) and one (standard output). You might think that something like "2|" would pipe the first program's standard error, but it doesn't.

Instead, use 2> to send standard error into a file and work with the error messages from there.

A second possibility would be to use *command 2>&1 | secondcommand*, which sends both standard output and standard error to the same file stream as standard output; the pipeline then accepts the standard output. This trick will work for 99 percent of the situations where you need to pipe standard error.

If you really need to pipe only standard error, there is a way to pipe standard error; it relies on a trick of the shell. I use it perhaps once a year, and I have to look it up every time, but I've placed it on the Web site accompanying this book:

**http://www.phptrinteractive.com/**

c)   Suppose you want to use more to display the contents of all of the files listed in the file list. Would a pipeline help (for example, in a command such as cat list | more)?

*Answer: No; the command* cat list | more *just displays the contents of* list.

It's easy to confuse yourself about the difference between standard output and command line arguments. I frequently make this mistake.

Suppose you've got a list of all the text files related to the current project. (Maybe it's recipes for a cookbook.) You want to read through them with more, but you hate the idea of typing all those file names. Because the file names are already in the file list, why not pipe the file names to more? After all, more reads the files named on standard input, right?

Well, no. The more command just shoves its standard input to its standard output, pausing every time the screen fills up. If you name files as command line arguments, more will open each file in turn and use the contents of those files as input.

The cat list | more command sends the contents of the file list "into" more. The more command has no idea these are file names. It just shows what comes in.

*Incidentally, if you find yourself using* `cat` *to pipe one file into another command, you're probably typing more than you need to. There's no difference between:*

```
cat list | more
and
more < list
```

*except that the second one is shorter to type. If you want to pipe the contents of two files, that's different. That's a perfectly good reason to use* `cat`. *Or if you're using command substitution, as in the next question.*

Enter the following command:

```
more $(cat list)
```

**d)**   What does the `$(command)` construct do?

> *Answer: The command substitution construct inserts the output of the command in* `$()` *into the command line.*

This is the answer to the question posed in Question c. Rather than piping the output of `cat list` into the `more` command, this inserts the output of `cat list` into the `more` *command line.*

This is a kind of output redirection. Instead of being redirected into a file, the output is redirected into the command line as arguments.

I normally use this when I need to find and edit half a dozen files in a directory that contains hundreds. For example, if I needed to edit all files that refer to the corporate headquarters in San Francisco, I might do it this way:

```
vi $(grep -l "San Francisco" *)
```

The `grep -l` command produces a list: the names of the files that contain "San Francisco." The command substitution construct `$()` inserts that list into the command line, as if I had typed:

```
vi backers.txt bios.txt ceo.txt
```

# LAB 1.2  SELF-REVIEW QUESTIONS

In order to test your progress, you should be able to answer the following questions.

1)  Identify two of the reasons why UNIX commands are so flexible:
    **a)** _____ Pipes
    **b)** _____ Options
    **c)** _____ Operands
    **d)** _____ Case sensitivity

2)  Why doesn't the command `echo $LOGNAME > /dev/null` print the "> name"?
    **a)**  The $ character is a metacharacter.
    **b)**  The > character is a metacharacter that redirects output.
    **c)**  The `echo` command prints only its first argument.
    **d)**  The file `/dev/null` is a special file; anything put into that file disappears.

3)  Some options take their own arguments.
    **a)** _____ True
    **b)** _____ False

4)  An item in [ ] brackets in a command synopsis is required.
    **a)** _____ True
    **b)** _____ False

5)  All options are single letters.
    **a)** _____ True
    **b)** _____ False

6)  Which command would sort the contents of the files `here`, `there`, and `everywhere`?
    **a)** `cat here there everywhere | sort`
    **b)** `sort $(cat here there everywhere)`
    **c)** `sort here there everywhere`
    **d)** All of the above
    **e)** (a) and (b)
    **f)** (a) and (c)
    **g)** (b) and (c)

    *Quiz answers appear in Appendix A, Section 1.2.*

# L A B   1 . 3

# FILES
# AND DIRECTORIES

---

### LAB OBJECTIVES

After this Lab, you will be able to:

- List Files and Directories
- Specify Files with Wildcards
- Create, Copy, and Remove Files and Directories
- Change Permissions on a File

---

Files are how you organize information on a UNIX system. Each file contains some information. That information may be text or it may be in a specialized format meant for a particular program. A directory is a special kind of file that can contain a file or a directory.

The collection of all files on the system is called the file system. In the UNIX file system, it's all organized as one huge hierarchy or tree. Like any good plant, it starts at the root.

## LAB 1.3 EXERCISES

### 1.3.1 LIST FILES AND DIRECTORIES

Enter the following command:

`pwd`

**a)** Explain the output.

_____

_____

**b)** What command would you use to display the contents of a directory?

_____

_____

Enter the following command:

```
ls -l
```

**c)** What information does the `ls -l` command display about files?

_____

_____

## LAB 1.3.2  SPECIFY FILES WITH WILDCARDS

Create files with the names a, `ant`, b, `bug`, `.bee`, and `fly`. You can use file redirection (for example, `pwd > a`) or any other method you want, since file content is not important in this Lab.

Enter the following commands:

```
ls a
ls ?
ls *
ls b*
ls [a-c]
ls ???
```

**a)** Of the six files you created, which are listed by each command?

_____

_____

## 1.3.3 CREATE, COPY, AND REMOVE FILES AND DIRECTORIES

Enter the following command:

```
mkdir chap01
```

**a)** What does the `mkdir` command do? (Check using `ls`.) What command does the opposite?

Enter the following command:

```
cp a ant b bug .bee fly chap01
```

**b)** What does the `cp` command do?

**c)** What would have happened if the command had been only `cp a ant`?

Enter the following command:

```
cp -R chap01 copy1
```

**d)** What does `cp` do when given the `-R` option?

Enter the following commands:

```
rm a ant b .bee fly copy1/*
rmdir copy1
```

**e)** What do these commands do?

_____

_____

## LAB 1.3.4   CHANGE PERMISSIONS ON A FILE

Enter these commands; after each `chmod` command, check the permissions on the file with an `ls -l a` command:

```
cd chap01
ls -l a
chmod 644 a
ls -l a
chmod 655 a
ls -l a
chmod ugo-x a
```

**a)** What does the `chmod 644` do to the permissions on the file a?

_____

_____

**b)** What permissions does mode 655 give that 644 does not?

_____

_____

**c)** What does the argument `ugo-x` do to the file a? What is the other symbolic way to write this command?

_____

_____

# LAB 1.3 EXERCISE ANSWERS

## 1.3.1 ANSWERS

Enter the following command:

**pwd**

**a)**    Explain the output.

*Answer: The output depends upon your directory, but it should look something like this*

**/home/john**

The pwd command prints your current working directory as an *absolute path name*. Every slash (/) separates the path name into parts, where each part is a directory name; the last part is either a directory name or a file name. (Directories are special files that can hold other files or other directories.)

The first slash (/) stands for the *root directory*. It's the big directory that holds *everything* in the UNIX file system. The name between the first slash and the second slash (home) is the name of a directory in the root directory. The root directory is its parent, and the home directory is a child directory of the root directory.

The name after the second slash (john) is a directory that is inside the home directory, a child of the home directory. (It could have been a file name, but we know it's a directory because pwd only prints directory names.)

A path name that starts at the root directory (with a slash) is called an *absolute path name* because it's a reliable, known path. Even though there may be twenty directories named john, there can be only one directory named /home/john on the system. Absolute path names always start with a slash (/).

Your working directory is the directory where you "are." Any files you refer to are assumed to be in this directory (unless you specify otherwise). If you create a file named diary, it's created in your current directory. If your current directory is /home/john, the file name diary is short for /home/john/diary. If you want to change your current working directory, use the cd command (for *change directory*). For example, the command cd /tmp makes the directory /tmp your working directory.

Having a current working directory lets you refer to files and directories by shorter names that are relative to your current location. (Not surprisingly, these shorter names are referred to as relative names.)

There are two special relative names: the directory . is the current directory, and the directory .. is the parent of the current directory. If your current directory is /home/john, then the directory . is also /home/john and the directory .. is /home. In this case, the command cd .. changes your current directory to /home. The command cd . won't change your directory at all.

If you've worked with DOS or Windows machines, you might be wondering what happens when a new disk drive is added to a UNIX machine—how is the new storage space added to the file system? (After all, on a Windows machine, you add another drive letter or two to represent the new disk.) On UNIX systems, the file system of the new disk drive is just added to the existing system as a directory and its subdirectories. Adding a new disk drive is called *mounting* it, and we'll have more to say about mounted file systems in Chapter 9, "More On Files and Permissions."

**b)**   What command would you use to display the contents of a directory?

*Answer: The* ls *command displays the contents of a directory.*

The name ls stands for "list." If you don't provide the name of a directory or file to list, ls lists the contents of your current directory.

The command has more than twenty options for specifying exactly which information is to be presented about each file. The most important are shown in Table 1.1.

### Table 1.1 ■ Important options to ls.

-a   Displays all files, including files with names that start with a dot (.); files with names that start with a dot are normally hidden.

-F   Displays the type of each file.

-l   Displays a long listing with a great deal of information about each file.

-p   Displays directory names differently from file names.

-t   Displays the files in order of time, with the newest files first. (Without this option, files are displayed in ASCII order, which is like alphabetical order except that all uppercase letters come before lowercase letters.)

Enter the following command:

```
ls -l
```

c)  What information does the `ls -l` command display about files?

Answer: *The information displayed by* `ls -l` *is summarized in Table 1.2.*

```
$ ls -l
Total 2
-rw-rw-r-- 1 johnmc pubs    219 Mar 25 18:12 archie
drwxr-xr-x 2 johnmc pubs    512 Mar 26  9:43 betty
lrwxrwxrwx 1 johnmc pubs     13 Mar 26  9:45 reggie ->
/tmp/examples
```

## Table 1.2 ■ Results of `ls -l`

| | |
|---|---|
| – | The first character (-) is the type of the file. There are six possible values:<br>A - indicates a normal file.<br>A **d** indicates a directory. *betty* in the example is a directory.<br>An **l** indicates a symbolic link. *reggie* in the example is a symbolic link.<br>A **b** indicates a "block special file."<br>A **c** indicates a "character special file."<br>A **p** indicates a pipe file or a special file type called a FIFO.<br>An **s** indicates a socket file (not found on all systems). |
| rw-rw-r— | The next nine characters describe the permissions of the file, for the file's owner, the members of the owner's group, and all others. Each user can have read permission, write permission, or execute permission. This set of permissions allows the owner and members of the owner's group to read and write the file, but not execute it. Other users may read the file but not write it or execute it. (Permissions are the topic of Exercise 1.3.4.) |
| 1 | The next number is the number of *links* to the file. A link is a name; every file and directory has at least one name and may have more. This file has only one link. |
| johnmc | The owner's login name. |
| pubs | The owner's group. |
| 219 | The size of the file in bytes. |
| Mar 25 | The date the file was last changed. |
| 18:12 | The time on that day that the file was changed. |
| archie | The file's name. If the file is a symbolic link, this will contain a pointer to the "real" file. |

This output is explained in Table 1.2.

The "Total" line that appears at the beginning of an ls –1 listing is an approximate measure of the amount of disk space used by the directories or files being listed. You can safely ignore it.

## 1.3.2 ANSWERS

**a)** Of the six files you created, which are listed by each command?

*Answer: The commands and files are listed in this table:*

```
ls  a           a
ls  ?           a, b
ls  *           a, ant, b, bug, fly
ls  b*          b, bug
ls  [a-c]       a, b
ls  ???         ant, fly
```

These commands provide a summary of the basic wildcards available in UNIX. Different shells may offer additional wildcards (the Korn Shell has an extensive set of wildcards that I find too much trouble to learn, for example), but all have these.

There are two points to make:

- None of the wildcard patterns displayed the file .bee. Neither would the command ls; a file with a name that starts with a dot is considered a *hidden* file. It can only be displayed by the –a option to ls or by a wildcard pattern that starts with a dot, such as .*.
- If *no* files match the wildcards, the command will run with the wildcards as the argument. If you're in an empty directory and you give the command ls *, you'll get back a message like this:

**ls: *: No such file or directory**

Because wildcards that don't match are passed to the command, you may occasionally create files with wildcards in their names. Use a backslash to turn off the special meaning of the wildcard. For example, to remove a file named *, use the command:

**rm \\***

If you really want to be cautious, you can use the −i option to rm, which causes rm to ask for permission before deleting each file:

```
rm -i \*
```

The common wildcard characters are summarized in Table 1.3.

## 1.3.3  ANSWERS

Enter the following command:

```
mkdir chap01
```

**a)**   What does the mkdir command do? (Check using ls.) What command does the opposite?

*Answer: The* mkdir *command creates a new directory; in this Exercise, it creates a directory named* chap01. *The command to remove a directory is* rmdir.

The mkdir command creates a new directory. If you name two directories in a path name (such as bogus/vapor) and neither one exists, the mkdir command doesn't work. If you want to create the directory bogus/vapor and neither bogus nor vapor exists, you can create both with either of these commands:

```
mkdir bogus bogus/vapor
mkdir -p bogus/vapor
```

In the first command, mkdir creates the first directory, bogus; then it creates the directory bogus/vapor. (It doesn't work if the arguments are

### Table 1.3 ■ Common Wildcard Characters

| | |
|---|---|
| ? | Matches any single character. |
| [abc] | Matches any one of the characters in the brackets (a or b or c in this example). To make ] one of the characters that matches, place it first in the set, like this: [ ]abc]. |
| [a-c] | Matches any of the characters in the range given (a or b or c in this example). To make - one of the characters that matches, place it either first or last in the set, like this: [-abc]. |
| [!ac] | Matches any single character *except* the characters in the brackets (any character except a or c). |
| * | Matches any (zero or more) characters. |

in the opposite order.) In the second version of the command, the –p option tells `mkdir` to create any intermediate directories, if necessary.

Enter the following command:

    **cp a ant b bug .bee fly chap01**

**b)** What does the `cp` command do?

    *Answer: The* `cp` *command copies files. This command copies the files* a, ant, b, bug, .bee, *and* fly *into the directory* chap01.

The `cp` command has two forms. When the last operand on the line is the name of a directory and the other operands are files, copies of those files are put into the directory. In this case, copies of the files are made in the directory chap01. The synopsis looks like this:

    **cp [-fipR] *file … directory***

The options are discussed in the next answer.

**c)** What would have happened if the command had been only `cp a ant`?

    *Answer: The command* `cp a ant` *would create a copy of the file* a *named* ant. *If the file* ant *already existed, it would be replaced by the new file.*

The other form of `cp` has only two operands of the same kind (two files or two directories).

    **cp [-fipR] *original copy***

The –i option causes `cp` to pause and ask before copying over a file with the same name (for example, if there had already been a file named fly in the directory chap01).

The –f option tells `cp` to "force" the copy, copying over the file, even if it's a read-only file. (You must be the owner of a file to copy over or remove a read-only file.)

The –p option sets the time on the copied file to be the same as on the original, as far as is possible. (Normally a copied file has the current time on it, because that's when it was last changed.)

Enter the following command:

    **cp –R chap01 copy1**

**d)**   What does `cp` do when given the −R option?

*Answer: With the −R option, the `cp` command copies directories.*

The −R option is required if the file to be copied is actually a directory. This is true for both forms of the `cp` command.

Enter the following commands:

```
rm a ant b .bee fly copy1/*
rmdir copy1
```

**e)**   What do these commands do?

*Answer: The `rm` command removes files. The `rmdir` command removes an empty directory; the reason it fails is because the directory `copy1` contains a hidden file, `.bee`.*

You cannot use `rmdir` to remove a directory that still contains files; it gives an error message. Remember that the * wildcard in the `rm copy1/*` command would not match the hidden file `.bee`. You can confirm this with the command `ls −a copy1`. After you remove the `.bee` file, you can use `rmdir` to remove the directory `copy1`.

If you're confident that the directory contains no files you might want, you can use the `rm` command to remove a directory *and all of its contents* with the −r option. Rather than remove `copy1/*` first, you could have removed the directory and its contents with the command `rm −r copy1`.

*The `rm −r` command is a very dangerous command. You can easily re-move entire sections of the file system with it. System administrators have bad dreams about typing something like `rm −rf /` and destroy-ing the entire file system. Use `rm −r` with caution.*

## 1.3.4 ANSWERS

Enter these commands; after each `chmod` command, check the permissions on the file with an `ls −l a` command:

```
ls −l a
chmod 644 a
ls −l a
chmod 755 a
ls −l a
chmod ugo−x a
```

**a)**    What does the `chmod 644` do to the permissions on the file `a`?

*Answer: It changes the permissions to read and write for the owner and read for the group and others.*

The `chmod` command changes the "mode" (permissions) on a file or directory. Every UNIX file and directory has three sets of permissions, as shown by the `ls -l` command: permissions for the owner of the file, permissions for the group of the file, and permissions for everyone else (the "others"). The synopsis of `chmod` looks like this:

> **chmod [-R]** *mode file* **...**

The `-R` option makes `chmod` recursive—if you change permissions on a directory, you're also changing permissions on every file and subdirectory in that directory. The *mode* in the synopsis is the part where you assign permissions to a file or directory. You can choose to assign permissions to a file numerically or symbolically.

**b)**    What permissions does mode 655 give that 644 does not?

*Answer: It adds execute permission for each group of permissions.*

A numerical mode is three numbers from 0 to 7. The first number is the owner's permissions, the second is the group's permissions, and the third is the other permissions. There are only three permissions (read, write, and execute), and each one has a different numerical value. Each possible combination of permissions adds to a different number, as shown in Table 1.4.

These are not the only permissions possible, but we'll discuss the others in Chapter 9, "More On Files and Permissions."

The read, write, and execute permissions show up in `ls -l` output as `r`, `w`, and `x`.

Read, write, and execute permissions are straightforward on files. On directories, they get a little bit more complicated. There are some things you should realize:

- Execute permission on a directory lets you use `cd` to make the directory your current directory. You need execute permission on *all* of the directories in the path name. For instance, if you want to `cd` into `/usr/bob/private`, you need to have `x` permission on `usr`, `bob`, and `private`.

### Table 1.4 ■ Numerical Permissions

| Number | Permission meaning |
| --- | --- |
| 0 | No permissions |
| 1 | Execute permission only |
| 2 | Write permission only |
| 3 | Write and execute permissions |
| 4 | Read permission only |
| 5 | Read and execute permissions only |
| 6 | Read and write permissions |
| 7 | Read, write, and execute permissions |

LAB
1.3

- Write permission on a directory lets a user delete files *in* the directory, regardless of the permissions on the file itself. This is why it's a bad idea to have directories with the permissions rwxrwxrwx (777).
- Read permission allows you to list the contents of the directory. If you have execute permission but not read permission, you can cd into the directory but not ls its contents. (However, if you know the name of a file in the directory, you can still have access to it, even though it's "hidden.")

When you use a numerical permission, you're setting the permissions exactly. For example, a permission mode of 744 means read, write, and execute permissions for the owner, and read permission for the group and others. If you want to adjust permissions by adding or subtracting one permission without affecting the others, you need to use symbolic permissions.

**c)**   What does the argument ugo-x do to the file a? What is the other symbolic way to write this command?

*Answer: It removes execute permission for the owner, the group, and others. It could also be written as* chmod a-x a, *because* ugo *is the same as* a *("all"), or as* chmod -x a, *because* chmod *will apply the change to all three sets of permissions if no particular set is specified.*

### Table 1.5 ■ Symbolic Permissions

| Symbol | Meaning |
| --- | --- |
| u | Modifies owner (user) permissions |
| g | Modifies group permissions |
| o | Modifies other permissions |
| a | Modifies all permissions (same as ugo) |
| r | Modifies read permissions |
| w | Modifies write permissions |
| x | Modifies execute permissions |
| + | Adds specified permissions for specified groups |
| – | Subtracts specified permissions for specified groups |
| = | Sets permissions to be only the ones specified for specified groups |

The symbolic modes are often more convenient to use than the numerical values. For one thing, you can add or subtract permissions. The symbolic mode has three parts: *whose* permissions are being changed, *how* those permissions are being changed, and *which* permissions are being changed. Possible values are summarized in Table 1.5.

# LAB 1.3 SELF-REVIEW QUESTIONS

In order to test your progress, you should be able to answer the following questions.

1) Which of the following are listed by the * wildcard?
   **a)** _____ All files in the current directory.
   **b)** _____ All files that are not hidden files.
   **c)** _____ All files with names that are one character long.

2) What is the pathname of the root directory?
   **a)** _____ /
   **b)** _____ /root
   **c)** _____ //
   **d)** _____ /unix

**3)** Identify the file names that would be matched by the pattern `.?[A-Z]*`

**a)** _____ `.profile`

**b)** _____ `TTY`

**c)** _____ `.x`

**d)** _____ `.`

**4)** Identify the command that would give you execute permission on a file you own.

**a)** _____ chmod 444 *file*

**b)** _____ chmod 677 *file*

**c)** _____ chmod u-x *file*

**d)** _____ chmod 100 *file*

**e)** _____ chmod 215 *file*

**5)** The command `mkdir $HOME/projects/advanced` will create the directory `projects` if it doesn't already exist.

**a)** _____ True

**b)** _____ False

**6)** If the command `ls projects` shows no files, the command `rmdir projects` could still legitimately fail.

**a)** _____ True

**b)** _____ False

*Quiz answers appear in Appendix A, Section 1.3.*

# LAB 1.4

# EDITING FILES

> ## LAB OBJECTIVES
>
> After this Lab, you will be able to:
>
> * Enter and Exit Vi
> * Write a File
> * Alter Text
> * Search and Replace Text

The standard text editor on UNIX systems is `vi`. Because many of the labs in this book require you to create example files, it's worth a few moments to review creating and editing files with `vi`.

Some people prefer to use Emacs (the topic of Chapter 6, "The Emacs Editor"), but Emacs is not on all UNIX systems. This Lab covers the absolute basics of `vi`. For more information on these basics, refer to Chapter 9, "The Vi Editor," of *UNIX User's Interactive Workbook*.

Chapter 10 of this book, "Advanced Vi Tricks," goes into more detail about some of the advanced features of `vi`.

## LAB 1.4 EXERCISES

### 1.4.1 ENTER AND EXIT VI

In your home directory, enter the following commands, using today's date in place of "June 1, 1999"; remember to press Enter at the end of each line.

```
vi calendar
```

Press G and then press I and then enter the line:

`June 1 1999: Finish chapter 1.`

Most commands in `vi` are not displayed on the screen, so you won't see the G or the I, though you may see their effects.

Press the Escape key and enter these two lines of commands:

`:q`
`:q!`

**a)** What file are you editing?

_____

_____

**b)** What does the G command do?

_____

_____

**c)** What does pressing I accomplish in this series of commands?

_____

_____

**d)** What does the command `:q` do? The command `:q!`?

_____

_____

## 1.4.2  WRITE A FILE

`vi ~/calendar`

Press G and then I and then enter the line:

`June 1 1999: Finish chapter 1.`

Press the Escape key and then enter the following:

`:w`

**a)** What does the `:w` command do?

_____

_____

Enter the following commands:

```
:w diary
:w
```

**b)** What does the `:w diary` command do? What name is the file saved under after the second `:w` command?

_____

_____

Enter the command:

```
:wq
```

**c)** What does the `:wq` command do?

_____

_____

## 1.4.3 ALTER TEXT

Open the file `diary` and press G and then I; now enter the following text. Press Enter at the end of each line:

```
Jan 1 New Year's Day
December 25 Christmas Day
July 4 Independence Day
02/14 Valentine's Day
04/15 Income Tax Day
10/31 Halloween
11/11 Veterans' Day
```

Press the Escape key.

Type the command `dd`.

**a)** What happens when you type `dd`?

_____

_____

Type the command `u`.

**b)** What does the `u` command do?

_____

_____

Type the commands `kx`, and then `u`.

**c)** What does the `k` command do? The `x` command? Does the `u` command have the same effect as before?

_____

_____

Save and exit the file.

### 1.4.4 SEARCH AND REPLACE TEXT

Open the `diary` file again.

Enter the following commands:

```
/Finish
fc
```

**a)** What does the `/` command do? Where does the cursor end up?

_____

_____

**b)** What does the `f` command do?

_____

_____

Enter the following commands:

```
:s/1/11
:s/1/22/g
```

**c)** What does the :s command do?

_____

_____

**d)** What is the effect of the /g at the end of the command?

_____

_____

# LAB 1.4 EXERCISE ANSWERS

*In this section, I've provided a number of tables summarizing* vi *commands. These tables are not complete; they simply cover the most common* vi *commands. For complete lists of* vi *commands, see Appendix B of the* UNIX User's Interactive Workbook, *or, of course, the* vi *man page.*

## LAB 1.4.1 ANSWERS

You started vi and entered text, then gave the commands:

```
:q
:q!
```

**a)** What file are you editing?

*Answer: The file* calendar *in your home directory.*

Any file names given on the vi command line are files to be edited. The vi editor starts with the first file loaded. (To move to the next file in the list on the command line, use the command :n, short for :next, or :n!)

If you start vi without any file names on the command line, you're creating a new file, and it doesn't have a name until the first time you save it.

**b)**  What does the G command do?

>   *Answer: It moves the cursor to the last line in the file.*

If you don't have a file named `calendar` in your home directory, or if it has only one line, the G command won't appear to do anything. It's here to ensure you add new lines at the end of the file, if you already have a `calendar` file.

In fact, the G command can move to any line in the file, just by naming the line number. For example, to move to the first line in the file, use the command `1G`. If you don't provide a line number, the G command moves to the last line.

To see what line the cursor is currently on, use the command Ctrl-G. Some other movement commands in `vi` are summarized in Table 1.6. For the definitive list, see the `vi` man page.

**c)**  What does pressing I accomplish in this series of commands?

>   *Answer: The I command enters text input mode, inserting text at the beginning of the line.*

The `vi` editor is a "modal" editor. It has different ways or modes of behaving, and the effects of a keystroke or command depend upon which mode it's in. The two important modes are *command mode* and *text input mode*. When in command mode, a capital G moves you to the last line of

### Table 1.6 ■ Basic Movement Commands in `vi`

| | |
|---|---|
| [*n*]j | Moves cursor down *n* lines (default 1). |
| [*n*]k | Moves cursor up *n* lines (default 1). |
| [*n*]l | Moves cursor right *n* characters (default 1). |
| [*n*]h | Moves cursor left *n* characters (default 1). |
| $ | Moves cursor to right end of line. |
| ^ | Moves cursor to first non-blank character on left end of line. |
| [*n*]G | Moves cursor to line *n* of file (default is end of file). |
| [*n*]w | Moves cursor to beginning of *n*th next word (default 1). |
| [*n*]b | Moves cursor to *n*th previous word beginning (default 1). |
| [*n*]Control-F | Moves cursor forward *n* screenfuls of lines (default 1). |
| [*n*]Control-B | Moves cursor backward *n* screenfuls of lines (default 1). |

the file; when in text input mode, a capital G puts a capital G into the file.

There are several different ways to enter text input mode, depending on where you want vi to start inserting the new text. In a new or empty file, it doesn't matter, but when editing an existing file, it might. The I command is one; the text input mode commands are summarized in Table 1.7.

To go from text input mode to command mode, press the Escape key.

**d)** What does the command :q do? The command :q!?

*Answer: The command :q exits vi unless there are unsaved changes to the file. The command :q! exits even if there are unsaved changes.*

For many of the commands that start with :, adding an exclamation point at the end forces the command to go on, even if there are unsaved changes in the file. For example, :n! goes to the next file on the command line, and :rewind! forces vi to return to the first file on the command line, even if there are unsaved changes in the current file.

## LAB 1.4.2 ANSWERS

You started vi and entered text; this time you entered the command:

:w

**a)** What does the :w command do?

*Answer: The :w command saves the file.*

If this is a new file without a name (that is, you started vi without any file names on the command line), the :w command doesn't save the file

### Table 1.7 ■ vi Text Input Mode Commands

| | |
|---|---|
| a | Inserts the text after the current cursor position |
| A | Inserts the text at the end of the current line |
| i | Inserts the text at the current cursor position |
| I | Inserts the text at the beginning of the current line |
| o | Inserts the text on a new line after the current line |
| O | Inserts the text on a new line before the current line |

on a Solaris system; it complains that there's no current filename. (On some systems, vi will save the file in a temporary file. Temporary file names tend to be things like "/tmp/vi.aavJad"—difficult to remember.)

By the way, if you want to see the results of your work, go to your home directory and enter the command calendar. The calendar command displays any entries from the calendar file that have today's date or to-morrow's date.

Enter the following commands:

> **:w diary**
> **:w**

**LAB
1.4**

**b)** What does the :w diary command do? What name is the file saved under after the second :w command?

*Answer: The command :w diary saves the file in a new file named "diary". The next :w command saves the file as* calendar *again.*

You're still editing the original file (calendar), but you've now saved a *copy* of the file in the file diary. If you want to edit diary from now on, instead of calendar, you need to switch from editing calendar to editing diary. You can do this by exiting vi and restarting it, or you can use the :edit command (:e for short):

> **:e diary**

Remember that you must press Enter after all commands that start with a colon (:).

Enter the following command:

> **:wq**

**c)** What does the :wq command do?

*Answer: The* :wq *command saves the current file and exits* vi.

The vi command may complain if you provided files on the command line that you haven't yet edited. You can quit anyway with :wq!. The command ZZ (two capital Zs) will also save the current file and exit vi.

## 1.4.3 ANSWERS

You entered text into the file `diary` and then typed the command `dd`.

**a)**   What happens when you type `dd`?

*Answer: The current line is deleted.*

You can combine the `d` command with any movement command. For example, the movement command `G` moves to the end of the file; the command `dG` deletes from the current line to the end of the file. The movement command `w` moves to the beginning of the next word; the command `dw` deletes to the beginning of the next word.

You can specify how many words are deleted, too. The command `2dw` will delete the next two words.

LAB
1.4

You can insert the item you deleted most recently with the `p` or the `P` commands. The `p` command inserts it *after* the cursor, and the `P` command inserts it *before* the cursor.

Other commands that can be combined with movement commands are `y` (which copies something into the same storage place as `d`, so you can copy text with `y` and `p` commands) and `c`, which changes text.

Type the command `u`.

**b)**   What does the `u` command do?

*Answer: The deleted line is restored.*

The `u` command undoes the last change. Pressing the `u` key again undoes the undo. (Some editors modeled after `vi`, such as `vim`, allow you to keep "undoing" commands. These editors may not be available on your system.)

Type the commands `kx` and then `u`.

**c)**   What does the `k` command do? The `x` command? Does the `u` command have the same effect as before?

*Answer: The `k` command moves up one line. The `x` command deletes the character under the cursor. The `u` command undoes the delete command.*

The `k` command is one of the movement commands listed under Exercise 1.4.1. The `x` command is the same as if you had typed `dl`: It deletes the character under the cursor. You can repeat the x key by specifying a number first: 5x deletes the next five characters. The u command still undoes the effects of the last command that changed text, restoring the deleted character.

Incidentally, you can repeat an insert or delete command by pressing the dot (.) key.

## 1.4.4 ANSWERS

Open the diary file.

Enter the following commands:

```
/Finish
fc
```

**a)** What does the / command do? Where does the cursor end up?

*Answer: The / command searches the file for a regular expression ("Finish" in this case). The cursor ends up at the beginning of the word "Finish."*

The / command searches forward in the file, toward the end of the file. It searches for the regular expression after the / itself. In this case, the regular expression is the word "Finish". The command to search *backward* in the file, toward the beginning of the file, is ?, and it works in the same way.

If either command can't find the pattern, it starts searching the rest of the file (at the beginning for /, at the end for ?).

To repeat a search in the same direction, you can use the command n. To search again for the same regular expression, use the command / or ? without providing a new search pattern. This is useful if you want to change the direction of your search.

**b)** What does the f command do?

*Answer: The f command searches the current line for a character ("c" in this case).*

To search to the right for a character on the line, use f. If you want to search in the *other* direction (toward the start of the line), use F. Both of these commands place the cursor on the character you're searching for; if you want the cursor to stop on the character *before*, use t and T. The t and T commands are more likely to be used in combination with delete or yank commands. For example, to delete all of the characters between the cursor up to but not including the next "<" character:

```
dt<
```

Enter the following commands:

```
:s/1/11
:s/1/22/g
```

**c)** What does the `:s` command do?

*Answer: The `:s` command replaces (substitutes) the pattern between the first two slashes ("I") with the pattern between the second and third slashes ("I I"). The line "June I Finish chapter I" becomes "June I I Finish chapter I".*

The search pattern can be any basic regular expression.

In the first version of the command, only the *first* occurrence of the pattern is replaced. To replace more, you need to add a modifier to the end of the command, after another slash.

**d)** What is the effect of the `/g` at the end of the command?

*Answer: The `/g` causes all occurrences of the search pattern to be replaced. The line "June I I Finish chapter I" becomes "June 2222 Finish chapter 22".*

To replace the pattern throughout the entire file, you need to place a percent sign (%) between the colon and the s:

```
:%s/1/22/g
```

The percent sign acts as a short form for the file's name. You could also specify a particular line number, or a pair of line numbers. For example, to replace all occurrences of "A" with "a" between lines 2 and 8, you could use this command:

```
:2,8s/A/a/g
```

There are two other modifiers to search and replace commands. Placing a c after the third slash makes `vi` ask for confirmation of each substitution. Placing a p after the third slash makes `vi` display each substituted line (this option is not often used in `vi`). You can use both modifiers. If you want to confirm each substitution of "her" for "him" throughout the file, you can use the command:

```
:%s/him/her/gc
```

## LAB 1.4 SELF-REVIEW QUESTIONS

In order to test your progress, you should be able to answer the following questions.

**1)** Pressing the u key twice in a row undoes the last two changes to the file.

    **a)** _____ True
    **b)** _____ False

**2)** Identify the vi command to move to the beginning of the file.

    **a)** _____ 1G
    **b)** _____ G
    **c)** _____ Control-G

**3)** Which vi command changes only the *first* occurrence of "AA" to "aa" for *all* lines in the file?

    **a)** _____ :s/AA/aa/g
    **b)** _____ :%s/AA/aa/g
    **c)** _____ :s/AA/aa
    **d)** _____ :%s/AA/aa

**4)** What best describes what the vi command :e! smollet does?

    **a)** _____ Moves to the end of the file.
    **b)** _____ Exits current file and edits a file named smollet.
    **c)** _____ Saves current file as smollet.
    **d)** _____ Exits current file and edits a file named smollet even if there are unsaved changes in the current file.

*Quiz answers appear in Appendix A, Section 1.4.*

# L A B   1 . 5

# ENVIRONMENT VARIABLES

---

### LAB OBJECTIVES

After this Lab, you will be able to:

- Display Environment Variables
- Set and Unset an Environment Variable

---

Every program has an *environment*, which is rather like a bulletin board. Programs are allowed to ask simple questions of their environment. Among other things, a program can ask for the type of terminal you're using, or the size of the window you're typing in, or your login name.

## LAB 1.5 EXERCISES

### 1.5.1 DISPLAY ENVIRONMENT VARIABLES

Enter the following command:

```
print LOGNAME
print $LOGNAME
env | more
```

**a)** What does the `print` command do? What's the difference between `LOGNAME` and `$LOGNAME`?

_____

_____

**b)** What does the `env` command do?

_____

_____

## 1.5.2 SET AND UNSET AN ENVIRONMENT VARIABLE

Enter the following commands:

```
MINE=me
print $MINE
env | grep MINE
```

**a)** Does the `env` command display the value of MINE?

_____

_____

Enter the following commands:

```
export MINE
env | grep MINE
```

**b)** What does the `export` command do?

_____

_____

After each of the following commands, use the `env | grep MINE` command to check if MINE is still set in the environment:

```
MINE=
set MINE
unset MINE
```

**c)** Which command removes the environment variable MINE?

_____

_____

# LAB 1.5 EXERCISE ANSWERS

## 1.5.1 ANSWERS

Enter the following command:

```
print LOGNAME
print $LOGNAME
env | more
```

**a)** What does the `print` command do? What's the difference between LOGNAME and $LOGNAME?

*Answer: The* `print` *command displays its arguments; the argument* LOGNAME *is a word, but the argument* $LOGNAME *is a reference to the value of a shell variable. In other words,* $LOGNAME *is the value stored in the variable* LOGNAME.

This is really a question about metacharacters. Remember that the $ character is a metacharacter. When a word or name starts with $, that tells your shell that the word is really the name of a variable, and it should be treated specially. "LOGNAME" is just a word, but "$LOGNAME" is a reference to a variable. (A variable is a name for a holding place for information.) Using just a $ is an old form of this *variable notation.* In some places, you'll see ${LOGNAME}. The curly brackets help the shell know exactly where the variable's name begins and ends.

The `print` command is similar to the `echo` command; the version of `print` in the Korn Shell has a few extra features that make it occasionally useful. (For instance, it's easy to print to standard error using the `print` command.)

**b)** What does the `env` command do?

*Answer: The* `env` *command displays the variables in the environment.*

Your environment is set up when you log in. (You have some control of the environment using your shell's startup files.) Every program gets a *copy* of the environment. More accurately, a program gives a copy of the environment to any program it starts. If your shell program changes the environment, every program started by your shell after that gets a copy of the changed environment.

The `env` command displays all of your environment variables.

Since the shell can also have regular shell (non-environment) variables, the difference between an environment variable and a regular shell variable is that other programs can "see" environment variables. You can turn a regular variable into an environment variable, as shown in the next section, 1.5.2.

There is a related command, set. The set command will display *all* of your shell variables. The env command will display only your environment variables.

## 1.5.2 ANSWERS

Enter the following commands:

```
MINE=me
print $MINE
env | grep MINE
```

**a)** Does the env command display the value of MINE?

*Answer: No.*

The shell keeps a large number of variables, and only some of them are in the environment. That is, only some of the variables will be given to programs started by your shell. The first line, MINE=me, creates a new variable called MINE and gives it a value, the word "me."

The second line just displays the value of MINE. When the shell interprets the command line, it sees the metacharacter $ there and replaces "$MINE" with "me" before running the command. The command it actually runs is print me.

The third line shows that, although there is a variable called MINE, it's not in the environment.

Enter the following commands:

```
export MINE
env | grep MINE
```

**b)** What does the export command do?

*Answer: The export command moves (exports) the variable MINE into the environment.*

Once the variable is in the environment, it's available for other programs.

You can also assign a variable a value and export the variable in a single line, like this:

```
export MINE=me
```

After each of the following commands use the env | grep MINE command to check if MINE is still set in the environment:

```
MINE=
set MINE
unset MINE
```

**c)** Which command removes the environment variable MINE?

*Answer: The* unset *command removes the environment variable.*

The first command just gives the variable MINE a value of nothing, but the variable, the placeholder, is still there. (A variable can exist even if it doesn't have a value; the man pages say that its value is "null.") The second option does nothing of interest. (It actually sets a positional parameter of 1 to be "MINE"; I explain positional parameters briefly in Chapter 8, "Shell Scripts.") The third command actually removes MINE from the environment.

**LAB
1.5**

# LAB 1.5 SELF-REVIEW QUESTIONS

In order to test your progress, you should be able to answer the following questions.

**1)** An environment variable can exist even if it doesn't have a value.
  **a)** _____ True
  **b)** _____ False

**2)** When you set an environment variable, the new value is accessible to programs that are already running.
  **a)** _____ True
  **b)** _____ False

**3)** Identify the command that removes an environment variable from the environment.
  **a)** _____ set
  **b)** _____ unset
  **c)** _____ export
  **d)** _____ unexport

*Quiz answers appear in Appendix A, Section 1.5.*

# CHAPTER 1

# TEST YOUR THINKING

You are setting up some training files for new employees. The original files will be stored in a single location (/docs/training) with the subdirectories tutorials/ and examples/. Beyond this, invent what you need to.

Because this is an important project, the system administrator will create new groups for you if necessary or modify the system startup files so certain environment variables are set for all new employees.

1) How are you going to make those files available to the new employees? Because you don't want to have to replace those files on a regular basis, each employee will get a copy of the files. Outline a plan for this, including:

   a) What permissions will be on the original files? (You are allowed to create new groups for this, if you need to. Try not to create too many.)

   b) How many of the files will employees need to copy? Will they need to copy the subdirectories too?

2) How are the employees going to actually copy the files? Will they read them into vi and save them under new names? Will they use the cp command? Can you make it easier for them? What command(s) would you suggest they use?

# C H A P T E R   2

# ELECTRONIC COMMUNICATION

 *As a multi-user operating system, UNIX has always provided ways for people to communicate. (After all, UNIX was created by the phone company.)*

---

## Chapter Objectives

In this Chapter, you will learn about:

---

One of the reasons that the UNIX operating system has been so successful in computer networks is that it's designed as a multi-user system. That means communication between users has been part of UNIX nearly from the beginning. By contrast, a PC is designed for one person, and it takes a lot of tinkering to provide facilities for two users to communicate.

In this Chapter, you'll learn how to find out which users are currently on the system and some ways to communicate with them. This is *not* electronic mail, which we'll tackle in the next chapter. This is more the "Hey, want to get together for lunch?" kind of communication between co-workers.

# L A B   2 . 1

# IDENTIFYING USERS

---

## LAB OBJECTIVES

After this Lab, you will be able to:

- See Who Is Out There
- Find Out About Users
- Create a .Plan File

---

Before you can communicate with a user who is logged on, you have to know that user is logged on. Without knowing who's there, you have no idea who you can talk to. The program for finding out who is on the system is called, naturally enough, `who`. It displays a list of the users logged onto the system.

The `finger` program also identifies users on the system, but it's more flexible than `who`. It will tell you about a particular user, whether or not that user is logged in, and it can often tell you about users on *other* systems. However, not all systems accept inquiries from the `finger` program.

## LAB 2.1  EXERCISES

### 2.1.1  SEE WHO IS OUT THERE

Enter the following commands and record the output:

```
who
who -H
who -s
who -T
```

**a)** What does the output of who look like? How does the -H option change it?

_____

_____

**b)** How many times does your name appear? How many times does root appear?

_____

_____

**c)** What does the -s option do, if anything?

_____

_____

**d)** What does the -T option do?

_____

_____

## 2.1.2 FIND OUT ABOUT USERS

Enter the following commands:

```
finger
finger $LOGNAME
```

**a)** What does the finger command do, without options?

_____

_____

**b)** What happens when you provide your login name (in $LOG-NAME) as an argument?

_____

_____

Enter the following commands:

```
finger @$(hostname)
finger $LOGNAME@$(hostname)
```

**c)** How does the `@$(hostname)` argument change the command's output?

_____

_____

**d)** What happens when the user name is for a user on a remote system?

_____

_____

### 2.1.3 CREATE A .PLAN FILE

Create a file named `~/.plan`. Place in it whatever text you want (but no more than five lines, for ease of reading later).

Enter the command:

```
finger $LOGNAME
```

**a)** What happens?

_____

_____

## LAB 2.1 EXERCISE ANSWERS

Both `finger` and `who` list users logged into the system. Before you can talk to people, you need to know who is available.

**2.1.1 ANSWERS**

**a)** What does the output of who look like? How does the −H option change it?

*Answer: The exact details of the* who *output depend upon the system and the options, but it always displays a list of users logged onto the system. The* −H *option adds headings to the output. On a Solaris system, the output of* who −H *looks like this:*

```
$ who
USER    LINE     WHEN           HOST
johnmc  pts/2    May 24 22:08   (thor.interix.com)
ross    pts/1    May 23 15:18   (odin.interix.com)
```

The who command lists users currently logged into the system. It won't show you a list of everyone who has an account (that's everyone listed in the file /etc/passwd), but who will show you all of the active login sessions on the system. (Of course, an active login session doesn't mean the person is present today; some people don't log out when they leave the building.)

Let's look at each column of output:

USER  The user name for each person logged in. In this case, there are only two users, johnmc (me) and ross.

LINE  This is the file name for the terminal or line the person is connected to. This is like the output of the tty command in your terminal window. In this case, both users are connected to files in /dev/pts; on Solaris, that means we were connected to "pseudo terminals." Pseudo terminals are network connections. Instead of connecting to the computer through terminals, we were connecting through other computers in the network using a command such as xterm, telnet, or rlogin. We'll talk more about telnet and rlogin in Chapter 4, "Computer Networks."

WHEN  The time when each user logged on. As you can see, I had been logged on since 10:08 PM on May 24, while Ross had been logged in since 3:18 PM the previous day. Ross may not have logged out when he went home, or he may not have gone home. (Ross is like that.)

HOST  This is a comment column, and it varies from system to system. Since we logged in over the network, it's useful to list the names of the machines we were really on. I was on a machine called thor.interix.com and ross was on a machine called odin.interix.com.

(The who command can provide much more information, depending upon the options.)

The who command has four formats, with the following synopses:

```
who [-abdHlmpqrstTu] [file]
who -q [-n x] [file]
who am I
who am i
```

The first form, the one used in this exercise, is the common one. The *file* you can provide is the name of the system file that who scans for the information. It's normally /var/adm/utmp or utmpx. If you give the file name /var/adm/wtmp (for utmp) or /var/adm/wtmpx (for utmpx), you can get a history of all of the people who have logged on since the system was last started or since the file was created, whichever is shorter.

The second form, who  -q, lists only how many users are logged on and their names. The -q stands for "quick." The -n option lets you specify how many users you want listed per line.

The commands who am I and who am i were covered in Chapter 1, "UNIX Basics"; they tell you your login name.

The who options you might find useful are -T, -H, and -s. (The other options are described in Appendix B.)

**b)**   How many times does your name appear? How many times does
        root appear?

        *Answer: Depends upon your system. Your name will appear once for each time you're logged in. The login name* root *might not appear, or it might appear many times.*

Each time you log in, the system records this with an entry in the file /var/adm/utmp; who looks in this file for the list of current users.

By the way, starting an xterm window doesn't necessarily count as logging in. An xterm window only counts if you use the -ls (for "login shell") option to xterm. (Although I have seen some systems where the logging of xterms was unreliable.)

**c)**   What does the -s option do, if anything?

        *Answer: This depends on your system. On some systems, the -s option provides a shortened display with less information; on other systems, the default output of* who *is the same as the output with* -s.

The −s option provides a shortened display. It lists only the name of each user, the terminal line (that is, the `tty` name), and the time. On some systems, the output provided by −s is the default—it's what you see if you provide no options.

**d)** What does the −T option do?

*Answer: This might vary on other systems. On Solaris, the −T option displays the user login name, the terminal line, the time, and four more fields: state, idle time, process ID, and a comment. For example:*

```
$ who -T

johnmc + pts/4  May  6 12:05   .    3765
(thor.interix.com)

ross   + pts/3  May  6 00:06 12:07 3538
(odin.interix.com)

johnmc + pts/6  May  6 12:10  0:02 3811
(thor.interix.com)
```

The default version of `who` on Solaris (that's the command file `/usr/bin/who`) offers the following fields; most of these are familiar from the `who -H` output:

| | |
|---|---|
| `johnmc` | The *login name* of the user. |
| `+` | The *state* of the terminal. If the symbol here is +, the user is allowing messages to his or her terminal. If it's −, the user is *not* allowing messages. If it's ?, the `who` command can't determine the state of the terminal. (Allowing messages is discussed in Lab 2.2.) |
| `pts/4` | The name of the *terminal line* the user is connected with. |
| `Mar 6 12:05` | The *time* the user logged in. |
| `.` | The *idle time*, the length of time since the user typed anything. A . means that the user is actively typing; a number (such as 12:07) is the number of hours, minutes, and seconds since the user did anything. The second line indicates that it's 12 minutes and 7 seconds since `ross` has typed anything. |

| | |
|---|---|
| `3765` | The *process ID* of the user's shell. |
| `(thor.interix.com)` | A *comment*. For network connections such as the ones shown here, Solaris shows the name of the machine the user is logging in from. |

You may not have all of this output. Some versions of the `who` command's default display provide less output than when used with the `-T` option; the only information the `-T` option adds is the state of the terminal. If you want to see this on Solaris, give the command `/usr/xpg4/bin/who -T`. Solaris has two versions of the `who` command. In fact, Solaris has two versions of many commands.

*For a computer system to be officially a "UNIX system," the commands must meet certain standards: They must provide certain options and behave in a certain way. The versions of the commands on Solaris (and some other UNIX manufacturers) have never behaved that way. To keep being labeled UNIX, they had to provide new versions of programs that behaved the way the UNIX standards dictated. To avoid annoying their existing customers, they tucked these new versions in a different directory. On Solaris, that directory is* `/usr/xpg4/bin`.

*If a reference other than a man page says that a command takes a certain option that yours does not, try the version supported in* `/usr/xpg4/bin`. *For example,* `/usr/xpg4/bin/id` *supports the* `-u` *and* `-n` *options, which are not supported in the regular (*`usr/bin`*)* `id` *command.*

## 2.1.2 ANSWERS

Enter the commands:

```
finger
finger $LOGNAME
finger -l $LOGNAME
```

**a)** What does the `finger` command do, without options?

*Answer: The* `finger` *command displays the list of users on the system, with additional information. On a Solaris system, the output looks something like this:*

```
Login   Name            Tty     Idle   When      Where
john    John McMullen   pts/2   -      Mon 22:08 thor.interix.com
ross    Ross Bing       pts/1   -      Sun 15:18 odin.interix.com
```

The `finger` command presents information about users. Without any arguments, it presents information about users who are currently logged in. It looks pretty much like the default `who` output, except that `finger` lists the user's full name and how long the terminal has been idle.

The idle time is presented as minutes, or as hours and minutes, or as days and hours, depending on how long the user has been inactive. If there's a single number, it's minutes; if there's a colon, it's hours and minutes; and if there's a d, it's days and hours.

**b)**  What happens when you provide your login name (in $LOGNAME) as
an argument?

*Answer: With a login name as an argument, the* `finger` *command displays information about that user, whether that user is logged in or not.*

Here's an example:

```
$finger johnmc
Login name: johnmc                In Real Life: John
McMullen
Directory: /users/johnmc      Shell: /bin/ksh
On since Mon May 24 21:41 on pts/2 from thor.interix.com
No Mail.
No Plan.
```

As you can see, this presents a certain amount of information about the user: You can discover the user's login name, real name, home directory on the system, what shell they use, when and where they last logged in (here it was a network login, but it could have been a terminal name), and whether they've read their mail recently. (In this case, I had no mail, but `finger` will also tell you if there's mail waiting that hasn't been read. This can be useful in figuring out if the person has been away for a while.)

There are some systems where `finger` with a login name only works if the user is logged on.

If you're using a BSD system, you'll see that the options to `finger` are substantially different than on a Solaris system. Check your system's man pages if you're interested in the options. For both Solaris (System V) and BSD versions, -p option keeps `finger` from printing the .plan information. (On BSD it also prevents `finger` from printing the .project file, but on Solaris and other System V systems, you'll need to use the -h option for that.)

Enter the commands:

```
finger @$(hostname)
finger $LOGNAME@$(hostname)
```

**c)** How does the @$(hostname) change the command's output?

*Answer: It lists all of the users logged into that system. For example:*

```
$ finger @asgard.interix.com
[interix.com]
Login   Name            Tty   Idle   Login Time      Office   Office
                                                              Phone
greg    Greg Fenster    p3    20:30  May  5 14:26 NY
ivy     Ivy Johnson     p1        1  May  4 18:03
ivy     Ivy Johnson     p2    19:44  May  5 08:43
ross    Ross Bing       p8    19:22  May  5 16:04
```

In the command you typed, the @$(hostname) was converted to *@name*, where *name* is the name of your computer. (We did it that way because I don't know what the name of your computer is. Normally you would type an actual machine name, as I did in my example: "@asgard.interix.com" is a machine name.) The $LOGNAME was turned into your login name.

The output format here looks slightly different because the machine asgard is not a Solaris machine. Different machines can provide finger information, and each machine can provide different information, if set up that way. Some information stays the same: login name, real name, terminal, idle time, and login time. However, the software on asgard adds fields for office number and office phone.

Since I gave the command from a machine running Solaris, you may be wondering why asgard isn't a Solaris machine. The argument "@interix.com" specifies a *machine name*. The @ symbol is used on certain types of computer networks (such as the Internet) to indicate a machine name; the name of the machine in this case is "asgard.interix.com".

You probably recognize the @ symbol as part of a lot of e-mail addresses. If I give my e-mail address as `johnmc@interix.com`, then you know that everything to the *left* of the @ symbol is my login name (`johnmc`) and everything to the *right* of the @ symbol is the name of my computer (`interix.com`). In fact, if you read @ as "at" it becomes "johnmc at interix.com". This @-addressing isn't the only format used—other networks use other formats—but this is the format used on the Internet and on most UNIX-based networks.

We'll talk more about e-mail addresses and machine names in Chapter 3, "Electronic Mail."

**d)**  What happens when the user name is for a user on a remote system?

*Answer: You see almost the same information, but for the user on the remote system.*

Again, all of this assumes that the system is running the program that answers queries from the `finger` program. (That program, incidentally, is called `fingerd`, short for "finger daemon." A *daemon* is a service program that's always running and that waits for requests; the printer daemon is an example of a daemon you've already encountered.)

System administrators can restrict the information that is sent out over the network, or even tell `fingerd` that it should not respond to requests from any other machines on the network. In that case, only local users can use `finger`.

On Solaris systems, many of the options available don't have any effect when `finger`ing users on other machines.

## 2.1.3  ANSWERS

Create a file named `~/.plan`. (Remember that `~/` at the beginning of a path name stands for your home directory.) Place in it whatever text you want (but no more than five lines, for ease of reading later).

Enter the command:

```
finger $LOGNAME
```

**a)**  What happens?

*Answer: The text of the `.plan` file is printed as part of your `finger` description.*

Let's assume you placed the following text in your `.plan` file:

```
Learn everything in chapter 2, then eat lunch.
```

When you `finger` your login name, the output is something like this:

```
$finger johnmc
Login name: johnmc        In Real Life: John McMullen
Directory: /users/johnmc     Shell: /bin/ksh
On since Mon May 24 21:41 on pts/2 from thor.interix.com
Unread mail since May 24 22:43.
Plan:
Learn everything in chapter 2, then eat lunch.
```

When someone uses the `finger` command to ask about you specifically, the `fingerd` program at your machine (or site, as it's often called) looks in your home directory for files named `.plan` and `.project`. If those files are there, their contents are added to the `finger` output as your plan and your project, respectively.

The advantage of providing this information automatically is that you don't have to send the information to anybody; anybody who wants it can go and get it using `finger`. There are two files so you can separate the information that does change often (your plan in `.plan`) from the information that doesn't change often (your project in `.project`). Suppose your boss wants to know what you're doing every day: Update your `.plan` file once a day and tell your boss to `finger` you for information.

The `.plan` file started out as a way to communicate to everyone what your short-term plan was. Nowadays it's a convenient way to communicate information to people without mailing it. For example, I have a friend who is involved with some legal cases. For the latest status on appeals and so forth, you can `finger` her login name. Some other people use their `.plan` files to distribute jokes, changing the joke each day or week.

By the way, you'll notice that the `finger` output now indicates unread mail. Mail had arrived between the time I saved the first output and the second, but I hadn't read it.

# LAB 2.1 SELF-REVIEW QUESTIONS

In order to test your progress, you should be able to answer the following questions.

1) The who command lists all users with accounts.
   a) _____True
   b) _____False

2) The who command always displays your terminal's file name as /dev/tty.
   a) _____True
   b) _____False

3) If the who -T displays someone's terminal name as - pts/9, can you send that terminal a message with write?
   a) _____Yes
   b) _____No

4) Why do some UNIX systems (such as Solaris) have two versions of commands such as who?
   a) _____To satisfy the requirements of UNIX standards without inconveniencing long-time customers.
   b) _____To allow more options; each version of the command can use all of the letters to mean different things.
   c) _____To avoid conflicts between software releases.
   d) _____To allow greater precision in setting up your PATH environment variable.

5) In "larryboy@veggie.com", identify the site name.
   a) _____larryboy
   b) _____veggie.com
   c) _____veggie
   d) _____com

*Quiz answers appear in Appendix A, Section 2.1.*

# L A B   2 . 2

# WRITING TO
# LOCAL USERS

---

## LAB OBJECTIVES

After this Lab, you will be able to:

*   Write with Write
*   Write with Talk
*   Ignore Messages with Mesg

---

Besides electronic mail, UNIX provides two other ways for users to send messages to each other. The write command sends a one-line message to a user or to a particular terminal. (The system administrator has access to a version called wall, for "write all." It's normally used to warn users of system-wide occurrences, such as a shut-down, or a slow-down caused by the start of backups.) The talk command lets you exchange messages interactively. Both talk and write only work with a user who is already logged on.

Since all of those messages can clutter your screen (especially if you have more than one xterm window open), UNIX also provides a facility for you to *block* messages sent to you. The mesg command is the equivalent of a "Do Not Disturb" sign; the messages don't get delivered.

For these labs, you'll either need two terminals or windows (two xterm windows is fine), or a willing co-worker or friend with an account.

## LAB 2.2 EXERCISES

### 2.2.1 WRITE WITH WRITE

Enter the command:

```
print hello there > /dev/tty
```

**a)** What does this command do?

_____

_____

Enter the command:

```
write $LOGNAME
```

(Here, you're writing to yourself—$LOGNAME is your login name—but normally you would write to another user's login name.)

```
hello there
```

End the message with Control-D.

**b)** What does the `write` command do?

_____

_____

If you have several terminal sessions open (either because you are using a windowing interface such as X Windows or because you are using multiple terminals), determine the device file for one of those sessions (either by using `who` or by activating that window and typing the command `tty`). Use that number for *tty*.

Enter the command:

```
write $LOGNAME tty
Hello there, from me.
```

End input with the end-of-file character (usually Control-D).

**c)** What does the additional argument do? How could you make use of this?

_____

_____

## 2.2.2 WRITE WITH TALK

If you have X Windows running, you'll need to open a second `xterm` window. If you're not running X, you'll need to log in to a second (nearby) terminal or try this with a friend. Remember that `talk` is intended for use between two people. If you're doing this with two people, then each person should initiate one `talk` session.

Like `write`, you can also specify the terminal line, so if you're doing this with two `xterm` windows, run `tty` in one window, then go to the other window and give the command:

```
talk $LOGNAME tty
```

where `tty` is the device name of the other window, as reported by `tty`.

If you're doing this with someone else, enter the command:

```
talk other
```

where `other` is the other person's login name.

**a)** What shows up on your screen? On the recipient's screen?

_____

_____

The recipient should follow the instructions on the screen.

**b)** What does the screen look like?

_____

_____

Both people can type simultaneously. Try some simple sentences, like "Hello" and "Can you read this?"

**c)** Where does your text appear on the screen? Where does the other person's text appear?

_____

_____

Enter Control-G.

**d)** What happens when you enter Control-G?

_____

_____

Each person should enter Control-D. (If Control-D doesn't do anything, try Control-C.)

**e)** What does Control-D (or Control-C) do?

_____

_____

### 2.2.3 IGNORE MESSAGES WITH MESG

Enter the command:

```
mesg
```

**a)** What is the output of the `mesg` command?

_____

_____

Enter these commands:

```
mesg n
write $LOGNAME $(tty)
The quick brown fox - well, you know the rest.
```

End input with Control-D.

**b)** What is the result of the `write` command?

_____

_____

Enter these commands:

```
who -T | grep $LOGNAME
mesg y
who -T | grep $LOGNAME
write $LOGNAME $(tty)
```

**c)** What effect does `mesg y` have?

_____

_____

# LAB 2.2 EXERCISE ANSWERS

## 2.2.1 ANSWERS

Enter the command:

```
print hello there > /dev/tty
```

**a)** What does this command do?

*Answer: It prints the words "hello there" on your screen.*

```
$ print hello there > /dev/tty
hello there
```

Remember that your terminal can be treated as a file. The display of your terminal is always the file /dev/tty, so this command redirects the output of the `print` command to the file /dev/tty.

The name /dev/tty is a convenient short form for "current terminal." In fact, because there can be many terminals on a UNIX system, each terminal has another file name which reflects that particular terminal. Terminals that exist only in software (such as `xterm` sessions) are called "pseudo terminals." You can discover the "real" file name of your current terminal with the command `tty`.

You can redirect output to a terminal "file," as long as you have write permission for that file. (A file that specifies a device such as a terminal is called a *device file*.) Let's say that I have two `xterm` windows open; we'll call them A and B. In A, I type the command `tty`, which tells me the file name of my current terminal window:

```
$ tty
/dev/pts/3
```

(On Solaris, pseudo terminals have names with `pts` instead of `tty`.) Window A can be treated as a file named `/dev/pts/3`. Now in window B, I redirect the output of my `print` command to that file:

```
$ print hello there > /dev/pts/3
```

This time, the "hello there" phrase appears in window A, not in the window where I typed the message.

You *can't* just redirect information to any terminal you want. You need to have write permission on the file. (This is the source of many practical jokes on university campuses with UNIX. You'll be sitting at your terminal with a professor or an attractive member of the opposite sex standing behind you and rude words will appear on your screen. Or, if you have an X terminal, rude pictures.)

Enter the command:

```
write $LOGNAME
hello there
```

End the message with Control-D.

**b)**   What does the `write` command do?

*Answer: This writes the message "hello there" to your terminal screen, with an introductory line something like this:*

```
Message from johnmc on thor (pts/3) [ Tue May 12 12:12:45 ]
hello there
<EOT>
```

The "<EOT>" indicates the end of transmission; on some systems, this is "EOF" instead.

This is the equivalent to redirecting a file to a terminal, except that the `write` command does these things for you:

- finds out if the user is logged on.
- finds the name of the terminal for you.
- writes to that terminal's display.

If you try sending to a user who isn't logged on or who doesn't exist, you get a message like this:

```
mark is not logged on.
```

The message can be much longer than a single line; end each line with Enter, and when you're finished, press the end-of-file character (usually Control-D) or the Interrupt character (usually Control-C).

If you're in `vi` or `more`, then the command Control-L will clear the `write` message from the screen. There's no easy way to retrieve it again once you've done that, although for users of X Windows, I offer a suggestion in the next lab.

If the other person is logged into several sessions, the `write` command will pick one session and display the message there. Normally, it displays on the first session logged in the `/var/adm/utmp` file, and `write` displays this message to the sender:

```
user is logged on more than one place.
You are connected to terminal.
Other locations are:terminal
```

You sent a message with `write $LOGNAME` *tty* (where `tty` was a terminal name).

**c)** What does the additional argument do?

*Answer: The* `tty` *argument specifies which terminal the message is displayed on.*

This is useful if someone has more than one terminal session running. The second argument can be the complete terminal name, as returned by the `tty` command, or it can be whatever is returned by the `who` command. The `write` command was written with `who` in mind.

## ■ FOR EXAMPLE

Suppose you want to send a message to `beth` but she has a dozen sessions running. (You happen to know she uses `xterm` to excess.) Since she's probably not working in all twelve simultaneously, you can choose to send your message to the terminal window with the *lowest* idle time.

After all, she's probably looking at the window she's currently typing in. So you give the command `who –T` and on a big system, you'll probably pipe it through `grep` to find all of the `beth` entries:

```
$ who -T | grep beth

beth    + pts/9        May  6 08:46  0:02    2663
(freya.interix.com)

beth    + pts/18       May  6 12:11 22:37    6521
(freya.interix.com)

beth    + pts/28       May  6 13:23 21:07    8399
(freya.interix.com)
```

Since window `pts/9` has been idle for only two seconds, you send the message to that window:

```
$ write beth /dev/pts/9

Beth, our meeting in five minutes has been moved to
2:30.
```

And end it with end-of-file (Control-D).

Because you can only send `beth` a message if she's logged in, it's likely that she has seen the message before she runs up three flights of stairs to meet you. (It's still not as certain as phoning her.)

## 2.2.2 ANSWERS

You started a `talk` session, either with another user or by using the address of a second window.

**a)** What shows up in your screen? In the recipient's screen?

*Answer: The person who started the* `talk` *session sees a message something like this:*

```
[Waiting for your party to respond]
```

Now you have to wait for the other person to start the `talk` program.

*The person who is receiving the* `talk` *request sees a message something like this:*

```
Message from Talk_Daemon@thor at 12:51 ...
talk: connection requested by johnmc@thor.
talk: respond with:  talk johnmc@thor
```

If you want to `talk` to the other person, type the `talk` command mentioned on the screen. When I start a `talk` request in my office, the other person has to give the command `talk johnmc@thor` or, if they're already logged into the same machine I am (`thor`), just `talk johnmc`.

Both people have to run the `talk` command. After the other person gives the `talk` command, the two of you can talk to each other. If the other person never gives the `talk` command, eventually the `talk` command will time out and give up.

Once the other person types `talk` *your_login*, both people see:

```
[Connection established]
```

If the network and the computers are set up correctly, *address* can be on another computer. For example, if you're on `thor` and I'm on `loki`, I could give the command `talk you@thor`—assuming your login name is you. The synopsis for the `talk` command is:

```
talk address [terminal]
```

Like `write`, `talk` allows you to specify the exact terminal, and for the same reasons. If you need to specify a particular terminal, use the `who` command.

The recipient should follow the instructions on the screen.

**b)**   What does the screen look like?

*Answer: The screen is divided into two halves, as shown in Figure 2.1.*

The `talk` command is a simple program that allows two people to communicate interactively. As I type, you see what I'm typing; I see what you're typing.

Like `finger`, your system needs to be running a particular daemon program before `talk` will work. In the case of `talk`, the daemon is named `talkd`. (You may have noticed a pattern here: `finger`, `fingerd`; `talk`, `talkd`. Generally, daemon names end in "d".)

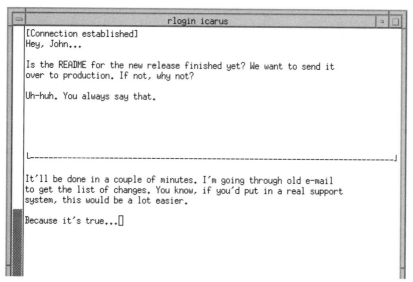

```
┌─┐                    rlogin icarus                    ┌─┐┌─┐
│─│                                                     │□││□│
│  [Connection established]                                  │
│  Hey, John...                                              │
│                                                            │
│  Is the README for the new release finished yet? We want to send it │
│  over to production. If not, why not?                      │
│                                                            │
│  Uh-huh. You always say that.                              │
│                                                            │
│                                                            │
│  L─────────────────────────────────────────────────────┘  │
│                                                            │
│  It'll be done in a couple of minutes. I'm going through old e-mail │
│  to get the list of changes. You know, if you'd put in a real support │
│  system, this would be a lot easier.                       │
│                                                            │
│  Because it's true...□                                     │
│                                                            │
└────────────────────────────────────────────────────────────┘
```

**Figure 2.1 ■ The `talk` screen is divided into two halves: one for your comments and one for the other person's comments.**

*If you try a* ps *command to see if your system is running* talkd *or* fingerd, *you probably won't see it. Network communications daemons (like* talkd *and* fingerd) *are usually started by another daemon called* inetd. *The* inetd *daemon only starts* talkd *or* fingerd *(or* telnetd *or* rlogind *or any of the others it controls) when it's needed. The easiest way to see if your system is running the appropriate daemon is to try the command.*

Both people can type simultaneously. Try some simple sentences, like "Hello." and "Can you read this?"

**c)** Where does your text appear in the screen? Where does the other person's text appear?

*Answer: Your text always appears in the top of the screen. The other person's text always appears in the bottom half. This is true whether you started the* talk *session or not.*

This makes it relatively easy to follow the conversation. You always need to read the bottom half, and what you write shows up on the top half. Programs that allow more than two users at a time (like Internet Relay Chat) need to assign names to each person. Since a talk session only has you and the other person, that's not necessary.

Enter Control-G.

**d)** What happens when you enter Control-G?

*Answer: The Control-G makes the other person's terminal beep.*

The Control-G signal is the "alert" signal. Normally it makes the terminal beep. When you use it with `talk`, it makes the *other* person's terminal beep. Some terminals aren't equipped to beep. On those terminals, the Control-G may have no effect, or it may make the screen flash.

Almost everything you type in a `talk` session is relayed to the other person; however, there are some control characters you can use to give commands. These are summarized in Table 2.1.

**e)** What does Control-D (or Control-C) do?

*Answer: The Control-D or the Control-C key combination ends the `talk` session.*

**Table 2.1 ■ Control Characters in `talk`**

| Control Character | Effect |
|---|---|
| Control-G (alert character) | Makes other person's terminal beep. |
| Control-L | Redraws your half of the screen. |
| Backspaces (erases) and line kill (normally Control-U) | Backspaces (erases) backspaces, even on the other person's display, and line kill erases from the cursor to the end of the line, even on the other person's display. |
| Control-C (interrupt) or Control-D (end-of-file or EOF) | Ends the `talk` session. Once one person has used the EOF signal (usually Control-D), the `talk` session has been ended on that side, and the person on the other side is notified that the session is over. All the other person can do is exit. According to the documentation, only end-of-file is needed, but on my Solaris system, the second person to exit has to use the interrupt signal. |
| Most printable or space characters | Displays on the other person's terminal. |
| Other non-printable characters | The `talk` program does its best to display other control characters. Most will show up as ^ followed by the appropriate ASCII character. Some characters will appear in "meta" notation, prefixed by an M. |

According to the man page, the session can be terminated by entering the end-of-file character. On most systems, Control-D is the end-of-file character and Control-C is the interrupt character. You can see the values for your system by giving the command `stty -a`. The interrupt key is indicated by `intr` and the end of file key by `eof`. Here are the relevant two lines from my system's `stty -a` output:

```
intr = ^c; quit = ^\; erase = ^h; kill = ^u;

eof = ^d; eol = <undef>; eol2 = <undef>; swtch =
<undef>;
```

When I was testing this, I found that the first person to hit end-of-file (Control-D) would end the session on his or her end, but that the other person had to type interrupt (Control-C).

## 2.2.3 ANSWERS

Enter this command:

```
mesg
```

**a)** What is the output of the `mesg` command?

*Answer: Typically the output is as follows:*

```
$ mesg

is y.
```

This means that the terminal window in which you typed the command is accepting messages.

The synopsis to the `mesg` command is:

```
mesg [y|n|-y|-n]
```

It can take no arguments, in which case the command reports on the state of the current terminal, or the argument `y` or the argument `n`. These stand for "yes" and "no." The Solaris version allows the `y` and `n` to have dashes, too, but the dashes aren't required.

The state of the terminal is whether it's accepting messages from the commands `write` and `talk`. This is the same state that was reported by who −T; you can use who −T to see if you can send someone a message with write or talk.

Enter these commands:

```
mesg n
write $LOGNAME $(tty)
The quick brown fox - well, you know the rest.
```

End input with Control-D.

**b)**   What is the result of the write command?

*Answer: The* write *command fails with the messages:*

```
Permission denied
Warning: cannot respond, set mesg -y
```

(Most systems will show only one of these messages.) The first message means that the destination terminal is not allowing messages. You'll get this message any time you try to send to a terminal that has messages turned off with mesg n.

The second message is one you'll get from write any time you try to send a write message while *your* terminal isn't allowing messages. It means that the other person can't respond to you, even if they want to.

The super-user can *always* write a message to your screen, even if you're not allowing messages. That's because the super-user has permission to write to any file, regardless of the permissions on that file.

Incidentally, the command mesg n or mesg −n has the same effect as the command chmod −w /dev/tty would have. You should be able to figure out why: the mesg command just sets the permissions on the "file" that is your terminal. (You may not be able to do it; some systems prevent you from changing permissions on /dev/tty.)

Enter these commands:

```
who −T | grep $LOGNAME
mesg y
who −T | grep $LOGNAME
write $LOGNAME $(tty)
```

**c)**   What effect does mesg y have?

*Answer: The* mesg y *command restores the ability to receive messages.*

After you've turned messages off, you need to be able to turn them on again. The `mesg y` command lets you do that.

When you login, your messages are turned on by default. Some people like to set the command `mesg n` in their startup files.

By the way, some other commands will also turn off permission for others to write to the screen in order to avoid messing up the program's output. (One that does this is `pr`.) Once the program finishes, permission is turned on again.

*If you're running X and your office is the kind where* `write` *is used often, you can control it without missing the chance to eat Thai food at lunch. Start one* `xterm` *window just for messages. In that window, make sure you type* `mesg y`. *In all other windows, type* `mesg n`. *The system will guide any messages sent to you to the "message" window and won't mess up your other displays.*

*Make sure you keep that window visible, though. The car pool might be leaving for lunch.*

# LAB 2.2 SELF-REVIEW QUESTIONS

In order to test your progress, you should be able to answer the following questions.

**1)** Since your terminal display is treated as if it were a file, you can redirect command output to a terminal.
   **a)** \_\_\_\_\_True
   **b)** \_\_\_\_\_False

**2)** Choose which control signal is sent by Control-D to end a `write` message.
   **a)** \_\_\_\_\_End-of-line
   **b)** \_\_\_\_\_End-of-file
   **c)** \_\_\_\_\_Interrupt
   **d)** \_\_\_\_\_Erase

**3)** If a user has several login sessions running, the `write` command sends the message to all of them.
   **a)** \_\_\_\_\_True
   **b)** \_\_\_\_\_False

**4)**  In a `talk` session, match the special character with its effect.

    **a)** Control-G             **i)** Ends this side of the session.

    **b)** Control-C             **ii)** Erases the last letter typed, on both displays.

    **c)** Control-D            **iii)** Interrupts this side of the session.

    **d)** Backspace           **iv)** Makes the other terminal beep.

**LAB
2.2**

**5)**  After the command `mesg n`, the super-user cannot send you a message.

    **a)** _____True

    **b)** _____False

**6)**  Who does the `wall` command send a message to?

    **a)** _____All users who belong to the same group as the sender of the message.

    **b)** _____All users logged in to regular terminals.

    **c)** _____All users logged in through network connections or `xterm` connections.

    **d)** _____All users currently logged in.

*Quiz answers appear in Appendix A, Section 2.2.*

# C H A P T E R   2

# TEST YOUR THINKING

In order to improve security at your site, you've been asked to find a way to track down users who habitually leave the building without exiting their login sessions.

1)  How can you get a record of how often people have logged in since the last time the system was rebooted?

   **a)**  Are people who have logged in a lot more likely to be logging out than people who have not logged in often?

   **b)**  Is there any way to determine people who have probably left the building?

   **c)**  Can you use information from the `finger` command to guess whether a particular person is away or not?

2)  With this information, can you be certain these people are not logging out when they leave?

# C H A P T E R   3

# ELECTRONIC MAIL

 *Electronic mail is just like postal mail, except it's faster, often cheaper, and doesn't work when the electricity's off.*

---

## CHAPTER OBJECTIVES

In this Chapter, you will learn how to:

✔ Perform Basic Mail Functions        Page 84
✔ Send Mail        Page 98
✔ Read Mail        Page 115
✔ Check for Electronic Mail        Page 129

---

Nearly everybody has electronic mail nowadays. Bright shiny e-mail programs with lots of features show up everywhere. People argue for their mail program with almost religious fervor. (We'll discuss a few of the alternatives later in the chapter.)

UNIX has been doing electronic mail for a long time, so some of the programs for sending and reading mail on UNIX are old and kind of clunky. In fact, we'll be using one of those old programs in this Chapter, for two reasons:

- First, the ideas behind electronic mail haven't changed. Once you've mastered `mailx`, you'll understand most of what you need to understand to use any mail program. The individual commands will differ, but the principles are the same.

- Second, `mailx` is on every UNIX system. You can send and receive mail with `mailx` while you're deciding which bright shiny e-mail program you want to use.

# L A B   3 . 1

# PERFORM BASIC
# MAIL FUNCTIONS

---

### LAB OBJECTIVES

After this Lab, you will be able to:

- Send a Message
- Read a Message
- Reply to a Message
- Quit Reading Mail

---

There are two parts to electronic mail: sending it and reading it. This Lab quickly shows you both. The `mailx` program behaves differently for each. (Most mail programs do.)

## LAB 3.1 EXERCISES

### 3.1.1 SEND A MESSAGE

Enter the following commands. If your system doesn't have `mailx`, try using the command `mail` instead; however, `mail` does not have all of the features that `mailx` does.

```
mailx $LOGNAME
```

If prompted for more information, enter:

```
First mail message
```

**a)** What happens after you enter the `mailx` command? Are you prompted? If so, by what prompt?

_____

_____

Start a new line and type this text as a single line. Press Enter at the end to start a new line:

```
Bob, I've got good news! You're not being laid off
after all. We got the grant money and can afford to
pay you!
```

**b)** Can you go back to the previous line by pressing Backspace?

_____

_____

Enter the command:

```
~.
```

That's a tilde (~) followed by a dot (.). Remember to press Enter after the dot character.

**c)** What does the ~ . command do?

_____

_____

## 3.1.2 READ A MESSAGE

Now that you've sent one message, send yourself another two messages: one will have the subject "Second message" and the contents will be the line:

```
From sea to shining sea
```

The next one will have the subject "Long message" and will consist of the numbers 1 through 30, one to a line, like this:

```
1
2
3
```

And so on. These will be used in Exercise 3.3.1.

Enter the command:

```
mailx
```

**a)** What does the `mailx` display look like? What parts can you identify?

_____

_____

Press 2 and then press Enter.

**b)** What happens when you press 2?

_____

_____

Enter the command:

```
h
```

**c)** What does the `h` command do?

_____

_____

## 3.1.3 REPLY TO A MESSAGE

If you exited `mailx`, start it again by entering the command:

```
mailx
```

Enter the command:

```
r 2
```

**a)** What does the `r` command do?

_____

_____

**b)** Who is the new message addressed to? Does it have a subject?

_____

_____

Write a reply (any text at all) and send the mail message.

## 3.1.4  QUIT READING MAIL

Enter the command:

`q`

**a)** What does the `q` command do?

_____

_____

Check your home directory for the file `mbox`.

**b)** What's in the file `mbox`? Use `more` or an editor to check.

_____

_____

# LAB 3.1  EXERCISE ANSWERS

## 3.1.1  ANSWERS

You sent yourself mail using the command `mailx $LOGNAME`

**a)** What happens after you enter the `mailx` command? Are you prompted? If so, by what command?

*Answer: Depends on your system. You may be prompted for a subject; on other systems, there may be no prompt. After the subject, the* mailx *command waits for you to enter the text of the message.*

The mailx command, like most mail programs, has two different operating modes: one is for sending mail and one is for reading mail. Each mode has a different way of operating—the kinds of commands you can give are different and the way mailx behaves is different. (If while reading mail you decide to send some mail, you end up in mail-sending mode.)

When you start mailx with a name or names as the argument to the command, it assumes you want to send mail to that address or addresses and puts you into mail-sending mode, which is usually called *input mode*. In this particular case, the address is your login name ($LOGNAME). Remember that the shell turns $LOGNAME into your login name before giving the argument to mailx, so if your login name is jordan, mailx $LOGNAME gets turned into mailx jordan.

On some systems, mailx asks for a subject for the mail message. This subject will appear in the display when the recipient looks at his or her list of mail. You don't need to enter a subject, but (like a memo) a subject makes it easier on the reader.

After the subject, you're in input mode. The mailx command doesn't provide a prompt to let you know you're in input mode; you just are. If mailx didn't prompt you for a subject, you're put straight into input mode.

If you start mailx without *any* arguments, or with only some of the options, it starts in mail-reading mode, which the mailx man page calls "command mode".

If you haven't already, start a new line by pressing Enter. Type:

```
Bob, I've got good news! You're not being laid off
after all. We got the grant money and can afford to
pay you!
```

**b)**   Can you go back to the previous line by pressing Backspace?

*Answer: The* mailx *command lets you edit only one line; you cannot go back to the previous line.*

First, notice that mailx doesn't automatically wrap lines when you type. Although the display shows the text continued on the next line, it's still one long line. You don't start a new line in mailx until you press Enter.

Once you press Enter, you can't back up and fix that line. In `mailx` (and most of the older mail programs) entering text is line-based. Once you press Enter, you can't back up and fix the line you just finished. There *are* ways to edit the text, but they aren't immediately obvious from reading the man page. (They aren't obvious because when you try to edit the message, you're put into the `ed` editor, which also doesn't provide any prompts and is also line-based.)

Start a new line by pressing Enter, and then enter the command:

        ~ .

Remember to press Enter after the dot character.

**c)** What does the ~ . command do?

*Answer: The ~ . command ends input and sends the message. The "~" character might not show up on screen until you press the following "." character.*

You can give commands while in input mode, but all of the commands must have a ~ character as the first character on the line. We'll cover more of these tilde escapes in the next exercise.

The command to end input is ~ . (a tilde followed by a dot). The Berkeley `mail` program uses just a single . on a line to end input, and some people have configured their `mailx` program to do the same. (When I used to get mail from people who were used to using `mail` but who had to use `mailx`, I'd often see that one lonely dot on the last line, where they tried to end the message but it didn't work.)

You can also end input with the end-of-file signal (usually Control-D).

## E-MAIL ADDRESSES

In this Exercise, the e-mail address is your login name. You've probably seen other e-mail addresses; even the president has one (`president@whitehouse.gov`).

On a regular letter, the address is a way to find a particular person at a particular house or building. An e-mail address is the same thing. Most e-mail addresses you'll see look like this:

        `name@machine.name`

(The `mailx` man page refers to this form as a "network login name.") The *name* is the login name of the person the e-mail message is going to. The *machine.name* is the name of the machine in the network of computers. (If there's no @*machine.name*, then all mail programs assume that the user is on your current machine. This is what happens when you use `$LOGNAME` as the address: The mail program knows it's going to a user with your login name on your machine; and of course that's you.) A machine address looks like this:

```
horus.kw.interix.com
```

The dots separate parts of the address. Compare that with a postal address:

```
1600 Pennsylvania Avenue
Washington, DC
USA
```

Just like a postal address, a network address goes from specific to general. "1600 Pennsylvania Avenue" is a specific building on a particular street. The street is in "Washington," which is in the District of Columbia ("DC"). The District of Columbia is in the United States of America. You've probably already seen your machine's address in your e-mail address.

In the domain address, the machine "`horus`" is part of a computer network called "`kw`." The "`kw`" network is in the computer network "`interix`," which is in the computer network "`com`." Each of these networks is called a *domain* or a *subdomain*. You may hear people talking about the dot-com domain, for example. They mean all machines and subdomains with names that end in "`.com`." The last domain in the name is referred to as the top-level domain, because it's the largest.

There are two different schemes of domain names. The address of my machine is symbolic: The "`.com`" indicates the "commercial" domain. Originally, there were six top-level domains, listed in Table 3.1.

New top-level domains have been proposed in the U.S., but these are the ones you'll see most often.

The other domain-naming scheme is strictly geographic. The top-level domains are two-letter abbreviations for countries (such as `.us` for the U.S., `.ca` for Canada, and `.jp` for Japan), and the subdomains are abbreviations for the state or province, the county or city, and so on.

## Table 3.1 ■ Top-level domains

| Name | Description |
|------|-------------|
| .com | Commercial organizations |
| .edu | Education organizations |
| .gov | Government organizations |
| .mil | Military organizations |
| .net | Network organizations |
| .org | Non-profit organizations |

Besides login names, `mailx` can also take a file name as an address, in which case the mail message is added to the end of the file. (If you want to see an example of this, try sending a mail message to the file `/dev/tty`, which is your terminal.)

## 3.1.2 ANSWERS

After mailing yourself a long message, you entered the command:

    mailx

**a)** What does the `mailx` display look like? What parts can you identify?

*Answer: A typical `mailx` display looks like the one in Figure 3.1:*

```
                                 xterm
$ mailx
mailx version 5.0 Tue Oct  6 01:11:27 PDT 1998  Type ? for help.
"/var/mail/johnmc": 3 messages 3 new
>N  1 johnmc           Sun Jun  6 23:50    6/199    First mail message
 N  2 johnmc           Sun Jun  6 23:51    6/107    Second message
 N  3 johnmc           Sun Jun  6 23:51   35/161    Long message
?
```

**Figure 3.1 ■ The `mailx` display lists each mail message you have waiting.**

When you start `mailx` to read mail, it looks in your incoming mail file for mail; if there is mail, it displays a lot of information about that mail.

The first line tells you which version of `mailx` you're using; you can ignore it. The next line identifies the mailbox file being displayed and the number of messages in it. Your incoming mail file is usually the file `/var/mail/`*yourloginname*, although on some systems it's `/usr/spool/mail/`*yourloginname*.

Below those lines, `mailx` displays a summary of the mail messages you have in your mailbox. It displays up to 18 message summaries at a time.

For each mail message, `mailx` displays a summary line like this:

```
N  1 johnmc   Mon May 31 21:22  6/199  First mail message
```

The ">" character indicates that this is the *current message*. If you give a command without specifying a particular message, `mailx` will act on this command. There is only one current message at a time. When you start `mailx`, the current message is the first *unread* message you have.

The rest of the line has these parts:

| | |
|---|---|
| `N` | The *status* of the message, whether you've read it or not. `N` means a new message; `U` means an old message that you haven't read yet (`U` stands for "unread"); `O` means an old message you've read. |
| `1` | The *message number*; this is message 1. Every message has a number, but the specific number will change every time you read mail, since some messages get deleted and new messages get added. You can specify which message you want a mail command to affect by supplying the message number. For example, you could delete message 12 with the command `delete 12`. |
| `johnmc` | The *message sender*. This is the login name of the person who sent the mail. |
| `Mon May 31 21:22` | The *message date*. The date the message was sent. |
| `6/199` | The *message size*. The first number is the number of lines in the message (6), and the second number is the number of characters in the message (199). |

`First mail message`   The *message subject*. Not all mail messages have subjects.

Press 2 and then press enter.

**b)**   What happens when you press 2?

*Answer: Message 2 is displayed. It looks something like what is shown in Figure 3.2.*

When you supply a number, the command acts on the message with that number. The default command is to display the message. (If you didn't supply a number and only pressed Enter, `mailx` would have displayed the first unread message.)

The top lines contain the message *header*. An e-mail message has two parts: a header, which like an envelope contains addressing information and the electronic equivalent of postmarks, and a *body*, which is the actual text of the message.

The "To" line contains the list of addresses the message is being sent to. A mail message can be sent to more than one person at a time, just by providing a list of addresses as arguments.

The "Subject" line is the message's subject.

```
                              xterm
$ mailx
mailx version 5.0 Tue Oct  6 01:11:27 PDT 1998  Type ? for help.
"/var/mail/johnmc": 3 messages 3 new
>N  1 johnmc           Sun Jun  6 23:50    6/199    First mail message
 N  2 johnmc           Sun Jun  6 23:51    6/107    Second message
 N  3 johnmc           Sun Jun  6 23:51   35/161    Long message
? 2
Message  2:
From johnmc Sun Jun  6 23:51:16 1999
Subject: Second message

>From sea to shining sea

?
```

**Figure 3.2 ■ The `mailx` program displays all parts of a message, including the "envelope" information and the actual text of the message. Paragraphs starting with "From" may have a > character inserted at the beginning of the first line.**

Because some mail programs use a paragraph beginning with "From" to indicate a new mail message in the mail file, a paragraph in the mail message itself may be altered slightly. In the example in the image, the mail-sending program inserted a ">" character at the beginning of the word, so other mail programs wouldn't treat the paragraph as the start of a new mail message.

*Pressing Enter is the same as giving no command at all. (Remember that all* mailx *commands must end by pressing Enter.) Without any specific command,* mailx *displays the next unread message. Pressing Enter repeatedly is a quick way to get through your unread mail.*

After you display the first message, mailx displays its prompt, a question mark. Like most UNIX commands with a long history, mailx doesn't present a lot of extraneous information.

Enter the command:

>     h

**c)** What does the h command do?

> *Answer: The* h *command displays the summary of messages in the mailbox file.*

Almost all of the mailx mail-reading commands can be abbreviated. The h command is short for headers.

Note that message 2 now has an R beside it, because it's been read.

If you're doing anything more serious than skimming your messages by pressing Enter, you'll occasionally want to see the list of messages again. The h command displays the list.

## 3.1.3 ANSWERS

Enter the command:

>     mailx

Enter the command:

>     r 2

**a)** What does the r command do?

*Answer: The r command places you in input mode to write a reply to the sender of the specified message.*

If you don't specify a number, the r (or reply) command replies to the current message, which is usually the message you just read.

Case is important; mailx has both an r command (or reply) and an R command (or Reply).

By the way, you don't have to be replying to a mail message to send mail from command or mail-reading mode. The mailx command mail *address* puts you directly into input mode as well. You can shorten the mail *address* command to just m *address*.

**b)** Who is the new message addressed to? Does it have a subject?

*Answer: The new message is addressed to you (the sender of the original mail message). The subject is "Re: second message".*

The r (or reply) command sends a response to the person who sent the message. (In this exercise, it was you.) The Reply command sends a response to the sender *and* to everybody who got the first message.

If the original message had a subject, mailx puts "Re:" at the beginning. (If the subject already began with "Re:" then it's not added.)

The meanings for Reply and reply described here are the *default* meanings for mailx.

If on your system, r replies to everybody who got the message and R replies only to the sender, then your system administrator has set an option in the system-wide startup file for mailx that "flips" or reverses the meanings of r and R.

 *Always check who's getting the message. It's very easy to reply to one person and accidentally include everyone. This can be embarrassing if you made rude comments about one of the recipients. (Never saying anything rude in e-mail helps prevent this embarrassment.)*

If you end up using mailx frequently, I recommend replying to mail using the commands replysender and replyall. They don't have short forms, but replysender always replies only to the sender, and replyall always replies to all recipients, no matter what the current settings of mailx are.

**LAB
3.1**

## 3.1.4 ANSWERS

Enter the command:

    q

**a)** What does the q command do?

*Answer: The* q *(or* quit*) command quits your* mailx *session.*

When you quit reading mail, mailx "cleans up." Messages you've deleted and messages you've saved to files get deleted from your mailbox; all of the mail messages you've read get stored in another mail file; this one is called mbox, in your home directory. You can type quit if you prefer, but q works just as well.

You can also choose to leave your mail-reading session with the exit command (abbreviated to ex or just x). When you exit using x, mailx doesn't do any cleaning up. It restores any messages you've deleted and undoes, as far as it can, any changes you've made. After you've exited with x, your incoming mailbox should be in the same state it was before you started reading mail.

Check your home directory for the file mbox.

**b)** What's in the file mbox? Use more or an editor to check.

*Answer: The file* mbox *contains mail you've already read.*

Because your read mail is automatically stored for you in a mail file, you don't have to worry too much about saving your mail messages in separate files. Your old mail is always available; all you need to do is read the mbox file.

As you can see from looking at the mbox file, mail messages are simply text. You can even edit mailbox files with an editor. Be careful if you do this: If you delete the wrong lines from the header, the mailx file won't be able to display the message.

*Because your* mbox *file contains all of your old mail, it can get very large if you use* mailx *regularly. For this reason, you should go through it regularly and delete messages you no longer want to save.*

*Some people try to avoid the problem by always exiting* mailx *with the* x *command so they keep all their mail in their incoming mailbox. That just means their incoming mailboxes get too large. It's better to save what you need and delete the rest.*

# LAB 3.1  SELF-REVIEW QUESTIONS

1) In the mail address `larry@veggieboy.com`, what's the top-level domain?
   a) _____`larry`
   b) _____`veggieboy`
   c) _____`com`

2) A mail message header is like the letter in an envelope.
   a) _____True
   b) _____False

3) A mail message body is like the letter in an envelope.
   a) _____True
   b) _____False

4) What kind of an organization has an e-mail organization with the top-level domain `.org`?
   a) _____A government organization
   b) _____A military organization
   c) _____A commercial organization
   d) _____A non-profit organization
   e) _____An American organization

5) Which of the following is *not* a valid address for `mailx`?
   a) _____`~/oldmail`
   b) _____`jordan@icarus.org`
   c) _____`/tmp/johnmc`
   d) _____`root`
   e) _____ All of the above are valid addresses

*Quiz answers appear in Appendix A, Section 3.1.*

# L A B   3 . 2

# SEND MAIL

### L<sub>AB</sub> O<sub>BJECTIVES</sub>

After this Lab, you will be able to:

- Edit a Message
- Quit a Message Without Sending
- Send a File

Unlike the `write` and `talk` programs, electronic mail can be sent to someone who isn't logged in. You don't have to answer electronic mail right away; you can wait to read it, and you can save your electronic mail in files for later reference. All of these things make e-mail a great convenience.

Unfortunately, the original e-mail programs for UNIX, which were named `Mail` and `mail`, had user interfaces that were obvious only to a computer programmer. I started using UNIX e-mail in 1981, and I still remember the frustration I felt trying to correct an error in an e-mail message. The user interfaces have improved, but the basics of e-mail developed back in the 1970s and 1980s (such as addressing and aliases) are still valid for e-mail programs today.

## INTERRUPT AND END-OF-FILE

Several of the commands in the `mailx` program itself can be ended or affected by the interrupt signal and the end-of-file signal. On most systems, the interrupt signal is sent by Control-C (although on some systems, it's sent by the Delete key), and the end-of-file (or EOF) signal is sent by Control-D.

You can check the values on your system with the command `stty -a`. In the output of that command will be values something like this:

```
intr=^C
eof=^D
```

(The exact formatting depends on your system; `stty -a` produces a lot of output.) The `intr` signal is the interrupt signal, and the ^C indicates Control-C (the ^ stands for the Control key). The eof signal is the end-of-file signal, and the ^D indicates Control-D. The characters ^? represent the Delete key.

## ALIASES

An *alias* is an alternative name for an e-mail address or a group of e-mail addresses. (On some e-mail programs, aliases are referred to by names such as "address book entries.") For example, if you have a friend whose e-mail address you cannot remember, you can set up an alias. Suzanne's e-mail address might be something awkward like "E39LANG-1STV@ plutonium.pubnames.org" but you can mail her using the address "suzanne" if you set up an alias for her.

You could also set up an alias that sends mail to a group of people. For instance, sending mail to the alias "team" might send the mail message to each person on your hockey team.

In `mailx`, aliases are normally set up in your personal `mailx` startup file, `.mailrc` in your home directory.

## MAILING A FILE AND FILE ATTACHMENTS

Mail programs only send text. A text file can be included as the mail message, but a binary file must be turned into some kind of text before you can mail it. When you mail a file using a mail program in a Web browser (such as Netscape) or other e-mail programs found on PCs, the "file attachment" mechanism turns a binary file into text and makes it part of the mail message. A program called `uuencode` is provided on all UNIX systems that converts binary files into text. (A program called `uudecode` is provided to turn the text back into a binary file.)

# LAB 3.2  EXERCISES

### 3.2.1   EDIT A MESSAGE

Enter the command:

```
mailx -sWelcome $LOGNAME
```

**a)** What does the −s option do?

_____

_____

Enter the following text as the mail message, including the mistake:

```
Welcome to your nail file
Have a pleasant stay, but beware of junk mail.
~v
```

Remember to start a new line before the ~v and to press Enter after it.

**b)** What does the ~v command do?

_____

_____

Go to the first line, change the word "nail" to "mail" and add an exclamation point at the end, so the line of text looks like this:

```
Welcome to your mail file!
```

Press Escape and exit vi with the command:

```
:wq
```

**c)** What happens when you try to exit? What is displayed?

_____

_____

Start a new line and give enter the command:

```
~p
```

**d)** What happens? What does the ~p command do?

_____

_____

Start a new line by pressing Enter and enter these commands, substituting your login name for *yourname*:

```
~c yourname
~p
```

**e)** How did the ~c command change the message?

_____

_____

Enter the ~. command again to finish the message.

An alias is an alternative name for one or more e-mail addresses. Create (or open, if it already exists) a file named .mailrc in your home directory (that is, ~/.mailrc). Add the following alias line to the .mailrc file, substituting your login name for *yourlogin*.

```
alias me yourlogin
```

Save the file and exit.

Now enter these commands:

```
mailx -s "aliased message" me
~.
```

**f)** What does the mailx command report?

_____

_____

## 3.2.2   QUIT A MESSAGE WITHOUT SENDING

Begin a mail message to yourself:

```
mailx -s Unfinished file

The true story of how I was kidnapped by space aliens
and sold to a tabloid newspaper.
```

Press the key combination to send the interrupt or intr signal (normally Control-C; you can check using the stty -a command).

**a)** What does `mailx` display?

_____

_____

Type another line of text:

> I had just finished watching the Jerry Springer show
> and the X Files

Press the interrupt signal (Control-C), then press it again.

**b)** What happens?

_____

_____

List the contents of your home directory, looking for new files.

**c)** Are there any? If so, what's in the file?

_____

_____

Start another message to yourself and interrupt it by pressing Control-C twice. Use `more` to examine the `~/dead.letter` file again.

**d)** What's in the file now?

_____

_____

### 3.2.3 SEND A FILE

Using `vi` (or the editor of your choice), create a text file named `rum.txt` and containing the text:

> Yo ho and a bottle of rum
> Fifteen men on a dead man's chest

To send the file, enter the following command:

```
mailx -s "sending a file" me < rum.txt
```

**a)** Where does this command mail the file `rum.txt`?

_____

_____

Enter the following commands. If your system doesn't have the `compress` command, try the command `gzip rum.txt`.

```
compress -f rum.txt
cat rum.txt.Z
```

If you used the `gzip` command, the file's name is `rum.txt.Z`.

**b)** What happens when you try to display the contents of the file?

_____

_____

Enter the command line:

```
uuencode rum.txt.Z rum.txt.Z
```

**c)** What does the file look like now?

_____

_____

Mail the file to yourself with the following command:

```
uuencode rum.txt.Z new.txt.Z | mailx -s "encoded
file" me
```

**d)** What does the | do in this command?

_____

_____

# LAB 3.2 EXERCISE ANSWERS

## 3.2.1 ANSWERS

Enter the commands:

```
mailx -sWelcome $LOGNAME
```

**a)**   What does the –s option do?

*Answer: The –s line provides the mail message with a subject;* `mailx` *does not prompt for a subject.*

The –s option is new in this command line. The –s option provides a subject for the mail message. (If you provide a subject with –s, `mailx` doesn't prompt you for a subject.)

Remember, if the subject contains spaces, you'll need to enclose the entire subject in quotation marks or escape the spaces in some way. Otherwise, the shell will break the subject into parts. For example, this subject contains spaces and other metacharacters, but the quotation marks allow the entire text to be used as the subject:

```
$ mailx -s "Where is that report?"
```

Without the quotation marks, `mailx` would try to send a message with the subject "Where" to the users `is`, `that`, and `report?`. If you're using an old version of `mailx`, the subject text can't be separated from the actual –s option; they should be run together as they are in the exercise text. New versions allow a space between the option and the option's argument.

You can also provide a subject while typing in the message (using ~s), so it's not critical that you remember the –s option.

Enter the following text as the mail message, including the mistake:

```
Welcome to your nail file
Have a pleasant stay, but beware of junk mail.
~v
```

Remember to start a new line before the ~v and to press Enter after it.

**b)**   What does the ~v command do?

*Answer: The ~v command places the current message in an editor.*

Normally, the ~v command places the message in the vi editor. (The ~e command is similar, but it places the message in the ed editor. The ed is a line editor, and can be quite confusing if you've never used it.)

 *If you're a fan of another editor (for example, if you love* emacs, *discussed in Chapter 6), you can specify that editor in the* VISUAL *environment variable. For example, suppose you prefer to use an editor named* pico. *In your startup file (the* .profile *file; see Chapter 7, "Customizing Your Environment"), you can set and export the environment variable* VISUAL *to point to* pico, *as shown here:*

```
export VISUAL=pico
```

*After this, when you give the ~v command, your message will be loaded into the* pico *editor.*

Other UNIX programs allow you to enter text in the same line-based way that mailx does. If you want to edit the text, they usually give you a choice of two editors to use: One command selects the editor you've named in your EDITOR environment variable (and if you haven't named one, you'll get the ed editor). The other command selects the editor you've named in your VISUAL environment variable (and if you haven't named one, you'll get the vi editor).

If you set EDITOR to be "vi," then the ~e command will also load the message into the vi editor.

Go to the first line, change the word "nail" to "mail" and add an exclamation point at the end, so the line of text looks like this:

```
Welcome to your mail file!
```

Press Escape and exit with the command:

```
:wq
```

**c)**   What happens when you try to exit? What is displayed?

*Answer: The screen is displayed as it was when you gave the ~v command, and the word "(continue)" is displayed.*

Again, the mailx interface is minimal. Once you've saved and exited the editor, mailx simply displays (continue). The text *has* been changed, but you can't see that until you display the text of the message so far, using the ~p command.

Start a new line and give the command:

```
~p
```

**d)**  What happens? What does the ~p command do?

*Answer: The ~p displays the message so far. It should look something like this:*

```
~p
-------
Message contains:
To: johnmc
Subject: Welcome

Welcome to your mail file!
Have a pleasant stay, but beware of junk mail.
 ~p
(continue)
```

The ~p command displays the message so far. It has its limitations; if your message is too long, the entire message scrolls off the screen. (Use ~v instead to view the file in an editor.)

Start a new line by pressing Enter and enter these commands; substitute your login name for *yourname*:

```
~c yourname
~p
```

**e)**  How did the ~c command change the message?

*Answer: The ~c command caused a new line to be added near the top of the message, which looks like this:*

```
~c johnmc
~p
-------
Message contains:
To: johnmc
Subject: Welcome
Cc: johnmc

Welcome to your mail file!
```

```
Have a pleasant stay, but beware of junk mail.
~p
(continue)
```

The "Cc" line is a "carbon-copy" line. Anyone named on this line will *also* receive a copy of the message. The actual name will be your login name, of course. (Since both specify your name, you'll receive two copies of this message.)

There are other header lines. For example, you can also provide a "blind Cc" or "Bcc" line. Anyone named on the Bcc: line gets a copy of the message, but nobody else knows that they did. The message just appears in your mailbox. (This feature is used a lot by people sending junk e-mail.)

The command ~? will list all of the available tilde commands. The ones mentioned here are summarized in Table 3.2, but you can find a complete list under the description of `mailx` in Appendix B.

## HOW DO I FIND SOMEONE'S E-MAIL ADDRESS?

If you want to find someone's e-mail address, the easiest way to do it is to phone him or her and ask. If that person doesn't know his or her e-mail address, give your address and ask for mail; the mail you get will have a return address in it.

If you have access to the World Wide Web, you should check the document "FAQ: How to Find People's E-Mail Addresses" at `http://www.cs.queensu.ca/FAQs/email/finding.html`. Some of these same pointers have been included on the Web site for this book, located at `http://www.phptr.com/phptrinteractive`.

**Table 3.2 ■ Some Tilde Commands in** `mailx`

| | |
|---|---|
| ~c *addresses* | Adds *addresses* to the carbon-copy (cc) list. |
| ~h | Prompts for address (to) list, subject line, and carbon-copy list. |
| ~p | Prints the message so far. |
| ~m *messages* | Reads in the specified *messages*. This is like ~f, except that the messages are all indented by one tab character. |
| ~s *subject* | Sets subject line. This replaces the current subject line. |
| ~? | Prints help text. |

Some of the commands (such as ~f or ~m) are really only useful when you started mailx to read mail, and you have decided to send a message in reply to one you've received.

You created a file named .mailrc in your home directory. It contained the line: alias me *yourlogin*

Now enter these commands:

```
mailx -s "aliased message" me
~.
```

**f)**    What does the mailx command report?

*Answer: The* mailx *command may display a message like this one:*

```
null message body; hope that's okay.
```

All versions of the mailx command will let you mail messages that contain no text and some versions may warn you about it.

The .mailrc file is the startup file for mailx. When mailx starts, it checks the .mailrc file in your home directory for commands and settings. The command here, alias, lets you create a short form for an e-mail address or a list of e-mail addresses.

The format of the line is simple:

```
alias name address ...
```

The *name* is the alias you'll type, followed by one or more addresses.

## ■ *FOR EXAMPLE*

Suppose you've been appointed to a committee and you want a convenient way to send mail to fellow committee members. Their e-mail addresses are abel@eden.edu, cain, and adam@exile.com. (Notice that cain is on your system, since there's no machine name.) To send mail to all of the other committee members, you would normally need to type:

```
mailx abel@eden.edu cain adam@exile.com
```

Instead, you can create an alias in your .mailrc file:

```
alias committee abel@eden.edu cain adam@exile.com
```

To mail the committee now, you give the alias ("committee") as the address:

```
mailx committee
```

The `mailx` command turns "committee" into the list of addresses.

Incidentally, you can include aliases you've already defined. For instance, you could define it this way:

```
alias abel abel@eden.edu
alias adam adam@exile.com
alias committee abel adam cain
```

A problem I've had with aliases is that a local user may be added with the same name as one of my aliases. For example, I had an alias `beth` for an offsite address, and then our company added a user named `beth`. To mail the local `beth` I had to give her complete address, including the host-name. Since I had to mail the local Beth more often than the offsite one, I changed the alias.

If you also want to keep a record of all committee mail, you could add a file name to the alias, too. (Remember that the address can also be a file name.) To also send mail to the file `committee.log` in your home directory, you would set up the alias like this:

```
alias committee abel@eden.edu cain adam@exile.com ~/committee.log
```

When you provide a file name as an e-mail address, you should provide an absolute pathname, or a pathname beginning with ~. On Solaris, `mailx` looks for a "/" in the address; if there's a "/" character, it's treated as a file name.

## 3.2.2 ANSWERS

You began a mail message and interrupted it with the interrupt signal (Control-C).

**a)** What does `mailx` display?

*Answer: The* `mailx` *command displays a message like this one:*

```
$ mailx -s Unfinished $LOGNAME
The true story of how I was kidnapped
by space aliens and sold to a tabloid newspaper^C
(Interrupt — one more to kill letter)
```

The `mailx` command requires you to press the interrupt key combination (normally Control-C) twice in a row before it cancels the mail. This keeps you from accidentally canceling mail messages.

If Control-C doesn't interrupt programs for you, remember that you can use the stty command to see what your current interrupt key is. Check the output of the stty -a command for the value of intr.

Type another line of text:

```
I had just finished watching the Jerry Springer show
and the X Files
```

Press the interrupt signal (Control-C), then press it again.

**b)** What happens?

*Answer: The message is canceled.*

When you cancel a message, it doesn't get sent. The mailx program saves it for you, in case you want it later, and exits; you see the shell prompt again.

You can also cancel a message using the command ~q.

*Note: These two techniques only cancel mail messages before you send them. Once a mail message is sent, there's usually no way to cancel it.*

List the contents of your home directory, looking for new files. If you find one, examine its contents using more.

**c)** Are there any? If so, what's in the file?

*Answer: There should be a new file named* dead.letter. *It contains the canceled message.*

The mailx command stores all canceled messages in the file dead.letter in your home directory. Messages canceled with ~q are also saved.

Start another message to yourself and interrupt it by pressing Control-C twice. Use more to examine the dead.letter file again.

**d)** What's in the file now?

*Answer: This answer will depend on your system. On some systems, only one message will be there; on other systems, both messages will be stored in* dead.letter.

The default behavior for mailx is to replace the existing canceled message with the new message. However, some system administrators change this by setting options in the system startup file. (Just as you have a `mailx` startup file in your home directory, there is a startup file for the whole system. `mailx` reads the system startup file, `/etc/mail/mailx.rc` before it reads yours. You can prevent `mailx` from reading the system startup file by using the –n option.)

Use the `set` command to see the list of options set for your system; you can turn off any option with the `unset` command. For example, if your system saves more than one canceled mail message, you can turn off this behavior with this command in your `.mailrc` file:

```
unset appenddeadletter
```

If your system saves only one canceled message, you can save more by adding this command in your `.mailrc` file:

```
set appenddeadletter
```

The `set` command sets a `mailx` configuration option; the `unset` command turns off that particular setting.

## 3.2.3 ANSWERS

You created a text file named `rum.txt` and mailed it with the command:

```
mailx -s "sending a file" me < rum.txt
```

**a)** Where does this command mail the file `rum.txt`?

*Answer: The file is mailed to the alias "me" which is your login name.*

When you redirect a file into `mailx`, you don't need to worry about a ~. command to end input. The `mailx` command knows when it has reached the end of the file.

Enter the following commands. If your system doesn't have the `compress` command, try the command `gzip rum.txt`.

```
compress -f rum.txt
cat rum.txt.Z
```

If you used the `gzip` command, the file's name is `rum.txt.Z`.

**b)** What happens when you try to display the contents of the file?

*Answer: You get gibberish on the screen. The file does not contain text.*

The `compress` (and the `gzip`) command shrinks files; the `-f` option forces it to create a binary file even if the new file isn't actually smaller. The purpose of `compress` in this exercise is to create a binary file.

So far, we've only sent text messages. However, the compressed file is a binary file. (Many files on your system, maybe most of them, are binary files and not text. Binary files include pictures and spreadsheets and word processor files and programs and audio files.) Binary files are difficult to mail.

The reason is that mail programs only transmit *printable characters*, such as letters and numbers and punctuation. More accurately, mail transmission across computer networks varies from one network to another. Sending a binary file may or may not work, depending upon the computers in the network. You can only be *certain* the message will be transmitted correctly if you send printable characters.

The solution that nearly everyone has adopted is to turn binary files into text. There are lots of different programs to do this. On UNIX, the standard program is called `uuencode`.

Enter the command line:

```
uuencode rum.txt.Z rum.txt.Z
```

**c)** What does the file look like now?

*Answer: The file looks something like this:*

```
begin 644 rum.txt.Z
M'YV06=Z 0",PC!LR(,* $/.&#ATV94"\,0-"3ITV"HRD,4.G3!DW(-I\E A2
2(9DR81"V,7AB#H@Q:,K,H:,

end
```

The `uuencode` program has turned the binary file `rum.txt.Z` into a set of printable characters. The first line starts with `begin`. The other information on that line, `644 rum.txt.Z`, describes the file permission mode of the file when it's decoded (that is, mode 644), and the name of the file when it's decoded.

The `uuencode` command has a slightly tricky syntax:

```
uuencode [file-name] decoded-name
```

If you provide only one argument (for example, if I typed `uuencode rum.txt.Z`), the `uuencode` program assumes the actual file is coming in on the standard input. It treats the single argument as the name that the *decoded* file should have. You have to provide two arguments, and since you usually want the decoded file to have the same name as the original, you end up typing the name twice. You don't have to. For example, if you were sending a file named `my_projections.jpg` to someone else, you might want to give it a more descriptive name when it is decoded, as in this example command line:

```
uuencode my_projections.jpg bobs_projections.jpg >
jpg.uue
```

The decoded file will have the name `bobs_projections.jpg`. Files coded with `uuencode` can be decoded with the `uudecode` program. The command to decode this file is:

```
uudecode jpg.uue
```

The `uudecode` program reads the file and decodes it, creating a new (decoded) file named `bobs_projections.jpg`, which is a copy of `my_projections.jpg`.

**Mail the file to yourself with the following command:**

```
uuencode rum.txt.Z new.txt.Z | mailx -s "encoded
file" me
```

**d)**   What does the | do in this command?

*Answer: It pipes the output of the* uuencode *command into the* mailx *command.*

You could have saved the output of the `uuencode` command in a temporary file and then mailed that file, like this:

```
uuencode new.txt.Z rum.txt.Z > rum.uue
mailx -s"encoded file" me < rum.uue
```

You can save yourself a step by using a pipeline. The output of the `uuencode` command can be the input for the `mailx` command.

Notice that when this message is decoded, it will create a file named `new.txt.Z`.

# LAB 3.2  SELF-REVIEW QUESTIONS

In order to test your progress, you should be able to answer the following questions.

1) The −s option and the input command ~s both set the subject of the mail message.
   a) _____True
   b) _____False

2) Identify the command that prints the message so far in `mailx`:
   a) _____ ~s
   b) _____ ~p
   c) _____ ~v
   d) _____ ~~
   e) _____ ~t

3) To interrupt a mail message, press the Interrupt key combination (usually Control-C) two times in succession.
   a) _____True
   b) _____False

4) The ~v command always invokes the `vi` editor, and there's no way to change that.
   a) _____True
   b) _____False

5) Which answer explains why you can*not* send binary files as binary files?
   a) The `mailx` program cannot handle binary files.
   b) Some networks cannot transmit binary files as mail, and you don't know if your mail must go through one of those networks.
   c) Binary files are too large.
   d) You can send binary files.

6) In the command `uuencode this.jpg that.jpg`, what is the name of the *decoded* file?
   a) `this.jpg`
   b) `that.jpg`

7) The ~q command retrieves and cancels a message you've already sent.
   a) _____True
   b) _____False

*Quiz answers appear in Appendix A, Section 3.2.*

# LAB 3.3

# READ MAIL

---

## LAB OBJECTIVES

After this Lab, you will be able to:

- Select a Message
- Reply to a Message
- Save and Manage Messages

---

Once you have mail, you'll want to read it. Most mail programs display a summary of your mail messages (usually displaying information such as the sender, the size of the message, and the subject), or they display a particular message. You can also choose to act on certain messages, possibly by saving them, deleting them, replying to them, or even decoding them.

> The `mailx` *mail reading commands require you to end the command by pressing Enter.*

## 3.3.1 SELECT A MESSAGE

Enter the command:

```
mailx
```

Enter the command:

```
t 1-3
```

**a)** Which message or messages is displayed?

---

---

Enter the command:

```
/long message
```

**b)** Which message or messages is displayed?

_____

_____

**c)** What happens when the long message is displayed?

_____

_____

Enter the commands:

```
set crt
/long
```

**d)** What effect did the set crt command have?

_____

_____

If the prompt at the bottom of the screen is a colon (:), press q and then press Enter. If the prompt is --More--, just press q.

Quit mailx with the q command.

## 3.3.2 REPLY TO A MESSAGE

Enter the command:

```
mailx -f ~/mbox
```

**a)** What does the -f ~/mbox option do?

To reply to the first message, enter the command:

```
r 1
```

Enter the command:

    ~m

Display the result with ~p.

> **b)** What does the ~m  command do?

_____

_____

Send the message with ~ .

## 3.3.3  SAVE AND MANAGE MESSAGES

Enter the command:

    mailx

One of these messages should be the uuencoded message you sent yourself earlier, with the subject "encoded file".

Enter the command:

    save /encoded ~/rum.uue

> **a)** What does mailx do in response?

_____

_____

Enter the command:

    | /encode uudecode

> **b)** What does mailx do?

_____

_____

Enter the commands:

```
delete /encode

h
```

**c)** What has happened to the message with the subject "encoded file"?

_____

_____

Enter the commands:

```
undelete /encode
h
```

**d)** What has happened to the message with the subject "encoded file"?

_____

_____

Exit `mailx` with the command:

```
exit
```

# LAB 3.3  EXERCISE ANSWERS

## 3.3.1  ANSWERS

Enter the command:

```
mailx
```

Enter the command:

```
t 1-3
```

**a)**   Which message or messages is displayed?

*Answer: The first three messages are displayed, scrolling rapidly off the screen.*

In Exercise 3.1.2, you specified a single message by number, but you can specify a range or a set of messages. A range (such as "1-3") performs the command on all of the messages in the range.

The t command (short for type) displays the message(s) you specify, or the current message if you don't specify one. (You can find the number of the current message by giving the h command and looking for the > character, or by giving the command =, which causes mailx to print the number of the current message.)

The actual structure of a mailx command is the command (or a short form) followed by the message or messages you want affected, then followed by other information, if necessary. (For example, if you're saving mail into a file, you need to supply the name of the file.)

**LAB**
**3.3**

Incidentally, if there are more than 18 messages in your mailbox, you'll need to move through the list of mail headers. Many people just display a message in the next 18 messages and then give the h command again, but if you want to scroll through the list of messages, you can use the commands z (to move forward through the list) and z- (to move backward toward the beginning of the list).

Enter the command:

```
/long message
```

**b)** Which message or messages is displayed?

*Answer: The message with "long message" in the subject is displayed.*

Table 3.3 lists the ways you can use to specify a message or messages in a mailx command:

**Table 3.3 ■ Specifying Messages in** `mailx`

| Specifier | Messages Specified |
|---|---|
| *n* | Message number *n*. |
| . | (A dot.) The current message. |
| * | All messages in the file. |
| ^ | The first undeleted message in the file. |
| $ | The last message in the file. |
| + | The next undeleted message. |
| − | The previous undeleted message. |
| *n-m* | The range of messages from message *n* to message *m*. "9-12" would be messages nine through twelve. |
| `login` | All the messages from the user with that *login* name. |
| `/string` | All the messages that contain the *string* in the subject; case doesn't matter. (To match messages with "FRENCH" in the subject, you can specify with "/french".) |
| `:d` | All deleted messages. |
| `:n` | All new messages. |
| `:o` | All old messages. |
| `:i` | All read messages. |
| `:u` | All unread messages. |

**LAB
3.3**

**c)** What happens when the long message is displayed?

*Answer: The entire message is displayed, leaving you with the last few lines of text.*

By default, `mailx` has no idea of the size of your screen. You need to tell it how much screen space you have available to display messages. This is done by setting a variable using the `mailx` command `set`.

Enter the command:

```
set crt
```

Enter the number for the long message again.

**d)**   What effect did the `set crt` command have?

*Answer: The command causes* `mailx` *to display messages using a pager (*`more` *or* `pg`*).*

When you set the `crt` variable, `mailx` "knows" it's supposed to display messages that are too long using a pager program.

How long is too long? That depends on the value of the `crt` variable. Since you didn't give it a value, *all* messages are displayed using a pager. If you want only messages that were, say, more than 20 lines long to be displayed using a pager, but not shorter messages, you could set the value of `crt` to be 20:

```
set crt=20
```

This is an excellent command to put in your `.mailrc` file. Once it's in the file, you can avoid the irritation that comes with suddenly encountering a long mail message.

The default pager program on Solaris is `pg`; to advance one screenful of text in `pg`, press Enter. To quit displaying a file with `pg`, press `q` followed by Enter.

The default pager program on BSD-style systems is `more`; to advance one screenful of text in `more`, press the Space bar. To quit displaying a file with `more`, press `q`.

If you want to change the pager that `mailx` uses, you can set the environment variable `PAGER` to the name of the pager you prefer. For example, if you want to display your mail messages with `less` (if `less` is on your system), you can put this line in your shell's startup file (`.profile` for the Korn Shell):

```
export PAGER=less
```

## 3.3.2   ANSWERS

Enter the command:

```
mailx -f ~/mbox
```

**a)**   What does the `-f ~/mbox` option do?

**LAB
3.3**

*Answer: The* −f *option reads mail from the specified file, instead of from your usual mailbox.*

You can use `mailx` to read any mailbox file, not just the one the system uses to store your new mail. This is useful for reading stored mail, and in this case you're looking at your already-read mail in your `mbox` file.

The display is just the same as for reading mail from your incoming mail file. The only difference when using the −f option is that mail messages you read aren't moved to another file when you quit `mailx`.

Enter the command:

```
r 1
```

Enter the command:

```
~m
```

Display the result with ~p.

**b)** What does the ~m command do?

*Answer: The* ~m *command inserts into this mail message the contents of the message you're replying to, indented by a tab.*

When you're replying to mail, it's very useful to be able to insert the text you're replying to, especially if it's a long message and you want to reply to it point by point. The ~m command is also useful when you're forwarding mail to someone else: You use the m command to start a mail message to the new recipient and use ~m to insert the file. (If you don't want to have the forwarded message indented, use the ~f command instead.)

After you insert the message, you'll probably want to use the ~v command to edit down the message.

In this case, the ~m command inserted the current message, because no other message was specified. You could (for example) specify ~m 6 and insert message 6.

There are several tilde commands which insert the message. The ~f command, as mentioned a moment ago, doesn't do the indenting, so it's better for forwarding mail.

*If you want the inserted message prefixed by something else ("&gt;" is common), set the variable* indentprefix *in your* .mailrc *file, like this:*

```
set indentprefix="> "
```

### 3.3.3 ANSWERS

You saved the message with the subject "encoded file" using the s command.

**a)**   What does mailx do in response?

*Answer:* mailx *saves the message and displays a message like this:*

```
/usr/johnmc/rum.uue [New file]
```

The s (or save) command saves the specified message(s) in a file. If the file already exists, the messages are added to the end of the file. If you give mailx a relative path name, the file is relative to your current working directory (usually the directory you were in when you started mailx).

Incidentally, when you look at the message with more or vi, you'll see that it still has the header lines, like this:

```
From johnmc Tue Mar 23 11:36:40 1999
From: johnmc@thor.softway.com
Subject: encoded file
Content-Length: 81
```

If you don't want these header lines, you can save it instead with the w command (or write). The w command saves only the body of the message with none of the header lines.

Enter the command:

```
| /encode uudecode
```

**b)**   What does mailx do?

*Answer: The* mailx *command pipes the message through the* uudecode *program.*

Remember the structure of a mail command: The first part is the command (| or the word pipe), optionally followed by a message specifier (the message number or the login name of the sender or, in this case, / followed by a word in the subject), followed by any arguments to the command. Here you're telling the pipe command to run `uudecode` on all messages that have "encode" in the subject.

Since you already saved the encoded text in a file (`~/rum.uue`), you could decode it with the command:

```
$ uudecode rum.uue
```

However, you can send the contents of the message directly into `uude-code`, which is less work for you.

## MIME ENCODING AND DECODING

Most modern mail programs don't use `uuencode` to send binary files (although many of them understand uuencoded files). They use a different coding mechanism called MIME (or just "mime"). When you send a binary file as a file attachment using a Web browser such as Netscape Communicator or Internet Explorer (on PCs), the file is turned into text using the mime-encoding.

There are command-line programs available for encoding and decoding binary files using the mime encoding. The programs are called `mpack` and `munpack`. The `mpack` program will encode and also mail the file. For example, if you wanted to mail the file `my_projections.jpg` to `cindy` using `mpack`, the command line would look like this:

```
mpack -s "The projections" my_projections.jpg cindy
```

The `-s` option specifies the subject. (The options for `mpack` and `munpack` are given in Appendix B.) Remember that `mpack` and `munpack` are **not** standard programs, but they are freely available.

If you receive a mime-encoded file attachment in a mail message, and your mail program doesn't understand mime (if you're using `mailx`, for example, or `elm` without the mime package), you can decode the attachment using the `munpack` program. Since `munpack` also understands uuencoded files, you can use it to decode uuencoded files, too. You could have decoded the message with this command:

```
| munpack
```

Enter the commands:

```
delete /encode
h
```

**c)**   What has happened to the message with the subject "encoded file"?

*Answer: The deleted message is no longer displayed in the header list.*

The `delete` command deletes files. It can be abbreviated to d.

Notice that the message numbers haven't changed, even though you've deleted a message. Deleted messages are still "there" until you quit `mailx`, but `mailx` removes them from the header list displayed by the h command. You can still save the deleted messages (if you remember the message number). You can even restore them to the mailbox using the `undelete` command.

Enter the commands:

```
undelete /encode
h
```

**d)**   What has happened to the message with the subject "encoded file"?

*Answer: The deleted message is no longer deleted.*

The message is displayed again. The `undelete` command restores messages you deleted in that `mailx` session. The `undelete` command doesn't have a short form.

You can get a summary of the commands available in command mode with either of the commands ? or `help`. Some of them (not all; `mailx` has many commands) are shown in Table 3.4. Commands that start with `set` (besides `set` itself) are normally put into the `.mailrc` file.

## SAMPLE .MAILRC FILE

Throughout this Chapter, we've made references to `mailx` commands that can be set in your `.mailrc` file. As an example, here's a commented version of my `.mailrc` file. (The e-mail addresses are all fake.)

```
# John's .mailrc file
# Lines that start with # are ignored by mailx.
# I hate writing people's entire addresses:
alias sandi sandra_mcmullen@home.com
alias bethc bcamara@frisky.dingo.com
alias jim jaguar@novel.org
alias linda lc@theatre.art.org
alias dave dtill@comedy.org
# Aliases can include aliases you've already defined.
```

## Table 3.4 ■ Some Command-Mode Commands in `mailx`

| Command | Short | Effect |
| --- | --- | --- |
| `alias` *name address* `...` | | Makes the address *name* mean the same as the list of *address*es. |
| `delete` *message(s)* | d | Deletes messages. |
| `exit` | x | Quits without changing system mailbox. |
| `headers` | h | Prints out headers of active messages. |
| `mail` *user(s)* | m | Mails to specified *users*. |
| `next` | n | Goes to and `types` next message. |
| `quit` | q | Quits, saving unresolved messages in `mbox`. |
| `Reply` *message(s)* | R | Replies to message senders. |
| `reply` *message(s)* | r | Replies to message senders and all recipients. |
| `save` *message(s) file* | s | Appends messages to *file*. |
| `set` | | Displays current settings (not used in the `.mailrc` file). |
| `set crt=`*n* | | Uses a pager to display any mail message with more than *n* lines. |
| `set flipr` | | Reverses the meaning of `Reply` and `reply` commands. |
| `set folder=`*directory* | | When saving mail, treats a path name beginning with + as if it were relative to *directory*. |
| `set indentprefix=`*string* | | Uses *string* to indent messages included with ~m instead of using a tab character. |
| `type` *message(s)* | t | Types messages. |
| `undelete` *message(s)* | | Undeletes messages. |
| `unset` *setting* | | Unsets one of the values set with `set`; for example, `unset appenddeadletter` would turn off the `appenddeadletter` option. |
| `visual` *message(s)* | v | Edits messages with `vi` or editor specified by `VISUAL` environment variable. |
| `z` | z | Scrolls forward through message headers. |

**LAB
3.3**

```
# These are the members of my writer's group.
alias writing jim linda dave
# Always ask me for the subject of the message
set asksub
# Use a pager if the message is more than 23 lines.
set crt=23
# I save my mail in the directory ~/Mail
set folder=Mail
# I want the "sent.mail" file to be in the directory
# specified by "folder"
set outfolder
# Store my outgoing mail in the file "sent.mail"
set record=sent.mail
```

## OTHER MAIL PROGRAMS

There are many mail programs available. The emacs editor contains a mail program itself. (More on Emacs in Chapter 6, "Emacs.") Most of the popular Web browsers (such as Netscape Communicator) include mail programs. Almost all of them support the same features as mailx.

Which mail program you use is a matter of taste. I'll merely mention some common ones that you can look for on your system.

- Pine is a very popular mail reader designed for beginning users. It uses its own editor (pico), which is similar to Emacs in some respects. It's text-based, although there is an X Window version.

- Elm is an older text-based mail program. It's easier to user than mailx and it's probably more common than Pine. (The name "Elm" stands for "ELectronic Mail." I think the idea of naming "Pine" for a tree comes from Elm.) I use Elm myself, so obviously I think it's useful.

- The mh and xmh mail programs are less like mail programs and more like entire operating environments. The xmh program is a shell program all by itself. I found mh intimidating when I tried it, but it appeals to a lot of users.

# LAB 3.3 SELF-REVIEW QUESTIONS

In order to test your progress, you should be able to answer the following questions.

1) Commands in command mode start with a ~ character.
   **a)** _____True
   **b)** _____False

2) All commands in command mode must be followed by pressing Enter.
   **a)** _____True
   **b)** _____False

3) Identify the `mailx` command that will save all of the messages from the user `bethany`:
   **a)** _____`s bethany ~/Mail/bethany`
   **b)** _____`bethany s ~/Mail/bethany`
   **c)** _____`s /bethany ~/Mail/bethany`
   **d)** _____`/bethany s ~/Mail/bethany`

4) If you're going to decode an encoded mail message, you must save it in a file before you run the `uudecode` message.
   **a)** _____True
   **b)** _____False

5) After you read mail messages from a file using the `-f` option, `mailx` stores the messages you've read into the file `~/mbox`.
   **a)** _____True
   **b)** _____False

6) After a message has been deleted with the `delete` command, there is no way to retrieve it.
   **a)** _____True
   **b)** _____False

*Quiz answers appear in Appendix A, Section 3.3.*

# L A B   3 . 4

# CHECK FOR
# ELECTRONIC MAIL

---

### LAB OBJECTIVES

After this Lab, you will be able to:

- Check Using `biff` or `xbiff`
- Check Using the Shell
- Check Using `mail` or `mailx`

---

Electronic mail waits for you. You don't have to be logged on when it arrives, and you can keep your e-mail messages until you're ready to respond. However, it's nice to know when new mail has arrived; it saves you the trouble of starting `mailx` every few minutes to check.

This Lab describes some of the facilities that UNIX has for notifying you of new mail:

- There are programs to check for new mail (such as `biff` and `xbiff`).
- The shell itself has facilities to check for incoming mail and to notify you.
- You can use options in `mailx` to check for mail when you first log on.

## 3.4.1   CHECK USING BIFF OR XBIFF

Enter the command:

```
biff y
```

If you're using X Windows, also enter the command:

```
xbiff &
```

**a)** What does the xbiff command do?

_____

_____

Send yourself a new message.

**b)** What happens in the terminal window where you gave the biff command?

_____

_____

**c)** What happens to the xbiff window? (You might have to wait 30 seconds to see a result.)

_____

_____

Read your new mail.

**d)** What happens to the xbiff window after you read the mail? (You might have to wait 30 seconds to see a result.)

_____

_____

## 3.4.2 CHECK USING THE SHELL

From the shell prompt, enter the command:

```
echo $MAIL
```

Make note of the value of the MAIL variable; it should be the path name of your system mail file. (If it is not, set it to the value of your system mail file.) Then enter the command:

```
MAILCHECK=0
```

Send yourself a new mail message to the alias "me" as in:

```
mailx -s "mail to the alias" me < /dev/null
```

Press Enter several times.

    **a)** What happens when the mail arrives?

_____

_____

From the shell prompt, enter the command (all as one line):

```
MAILPATH="/var/mail/$LOGNAME:~/samplemail?You have
mail to the file"
```

(If `mailx` or `$MAIL` reported a file other than `/var/mail/$LOGNAME` as your incoming mail box, use that file's name instead.)

Send a mail message to the address `~/samplemail`, then press Enter several times.

    **b)** What happens when the mail arrives?

_____

_____

Send yourself a new mail message to your login name as in:

```
mails -s "mail to myself" $LOGNAME < /dev/null
```

    **c)** What happens when the mail arrives?

_____

_____

## 3.4.3 CHECK USING MAIL OR MAILX

Send yourself a message.

Enter the following commands:

```
mailx -e
echo $?
```

**a)** What does the echo command display?

_____

_____

Enter the following multi-line command:

```
if mailx -e
then
echo You have mail!
else
echo You have no mail!
fi
```

**b)** What does the command display when you have no mail?

_____

_____

# LAB 3.4   EXERCISE ANSWERS

## 3.4.1   ANSWERS

Enter the command:

```
biff y
```

If you're using X Windows, also enter the command:

```
xbiff &
```

**a)**   What does the xbiff command do?

*Answer: The* xbiff *command displays a window with a picture of a mailbox. (See Figure 3.3.)*

Both biff and xbiff notify you of mail, but they do so in different ways. The biff command was written first and works in text terminals,

**Figure 3.3 ■ The *xbiff* command displays this mailbox, which is light when there is no new mail, and dark with the flag raised when new mail arrives.**

such as xterm; it was named for a dog named Biff who lived near the programmers. (Some books report that they named the program for the dog because he used to bark at the mailman. A couple of years ago, the programmers confessed that they made that story up because they just wanted a reason to name a program for the dog.)

Send yourself a new message.

**b)**    What happens in the terminal window where you gave the biff command?

*Answer: The terminal beeps and the screen shows the first few lines of the mail message, as is shown in Figure 3.4.*

Although the biff command works on text terminals, it has the disadvantage that it messes up the screen. On a day when you're getting a lot of mail, the biff command can be a terrible annoyance, and if you're working in a text editor (or some other program that frequently redraws the screen), you might miss the text of the message entirely.

To turn biff off, use biff n. To see whether it's on or off, give the biff command without arguments.

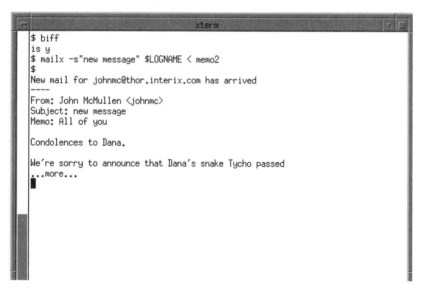

```
xterm
$ biff
is y
$ mailx -s"new message" $LOGNAME < memo2
$
New mail for johnmc@thor.interix.com has arrived
----
From: John McMullen <johnmc>
Subject: new message
Memo: All of you

Condolences to Dana.

We're sorry to announce that Dana's snake Tycho passed
...more...
```

**Figure 3.4 ■ The traditional *biff* command simply displays part of the message on your screen, which may disrupt other text.**

Just as with `mesg`, you can use `biff` to designate one terminal window as a "message window." If you use multiple terminal windows and you prefer `biff` to `xbiff`, you might want to turn `biff` off in all windows but one.

**c)**   What happens to the `xbiff` window? (You might have to wait 30 seconds to see a result.)

*Answer: The terminal beeps and the picture in the `xbiff` window changes when you get mail. (See Figure 3.5.)*

The `xbiff` command is much tidier than the `biff` command, since it doesn't disrupt any text on the screen. However, `biff` notifies you as soon as the mail arrives, while `xbiff` checks only every 30 seconds.

Read your new mail.

**d)**   What happens to the `xbiff` window after you read the mail? (You might have to wait 30 seconds to see a result.)

*Answer: Once you read the mail, the `xbiff` window returns to its previous state.*

Like most X programs, `xbiff` has a host of options. Some you might be interested in including:

| | |
|---|---|
| `-file` *filename* | Checks the file *filename* instead of your incoming mail file. |
| `-interval` *time* | Checks for mail every *time* seconds. The default is 30 seconds. Even if you're frantic for mail, I wouldn't set it lower than 15 seconds, because then the computer spends all of its time checking your mail file. |
| `-volume` *percentage* | This specifies how loudly the terminal should beep; the *percentage* is a number between 0 (no sound) and 100 (as loud as possible). The default volume is 33 percent. |

## 3.4.2   ANSWERS

You set the `MAIL` and `MAILCHECK` environment variables, then sent yourself mail.

**Figure 3.5 ■ When you have mail, the *xbiff* mailbox changes color and the flag on the mailbox goes up.**

**a)**   What happens when the mail arrives?

*Answer: The shell displays a message like this (the actual text depends upon your home directory):*

```
You have mail in /home/johnmc/samplemail
```

The `MAIL`, `MAILPATH`, and `MAILCHECK` variables tell the shell to check your mail file (or mail files). The `MAIL` variable should be automatically set to the name of your incoming mail box. (It's set by the `login` program when you log in.)

The `MAILCHECK` variable tells the shell how often to check for mail. Normally, the shell checks every ten minutes (600 seconds). For the purposes of this Lab, we set `MAILCHECK` to 0, which tells the shell to check every time it finishes a command.

In this Lab, you set the value of `MAIL` to a file's name. That's the file the shell checks every `$MAILCHECK` seconds.

When the file changes (more accurately, when the access time on the file changes), the shell displays a message at the command prompt. It only displays the message once each time the file is changed.

Note that this is for the Bourne and Korn Shells. The C Shell uses a different variable entirely.

You set the `MAILPATH` environment variable to include a file name, and then sent mail to that file.

**b)**   What happens when the mail arrives?

*Answer: The shell displays the message:*

```
You have mail to the file
```

The `MAILPATH` variable lets you specify more than one mailbox file. This is useful if you have more than one account on the system, or if you let people send mail to a particular file.

Once you set `MAILPATH`, the setting of the `MAIL` variable is ignored. Since `MAILPATH` allows you to specify more than one file name, there's no need to keep both set.

Send yourself a new mail message to your login name as in:

```
mails -s "mail to myself" $LOGNAME < /dev/null
```

**c)** What happens when the mail arrives?

*Answer: The shell displays a message something like this (depending upon your system):*

```
You have mail in /var/mail/johnmc
```

The format of the MAILPATH variable is simple. It's a list of file names separated by colons. The file names are the names to be checked. Each file name can be followed by a question mark and the message to be displayed. The default message is the one in this Exercise. (We used the question mark-message format on the file ~/samplemail to make the messages easier to distinguish.)

> *If you're using a Bourne Shell instead of the Korn Shell, it may not support these variables. If it does support them, the "?" character in MAILPATH should instead be a "%" character.*

The MAILPATH and MAILCHECK environment variables are often set in your shell startup file, .profile.

LAB
3.4

## 3.4.3 ANSWERS

Send yourself a message.

Enter the following commands:

```
mailx -e
echo $?
```

**a)** What does the echo command display?

*Answer: If you have mail in your mailbox, it should display the number 0.*

The $? variable is a special shell variable that contains the *return code* for the command that just finished. On UNIX systems, every command tells the shell whether it succeeded (the number 0) or failed (some other number). The -e option tells mailx to report 0 if there is mail in the mailbox, 1 otherwise, and report nothing else.

While this may seem like nonsense, it's like pipes: A lot of UNIX tools are built to work with this. In particular, there is the if command.

Enter the following multi-line command:

```
if mailx -e
then
echo You have mail!
else
echo You have no mail!
fi
```

**b)** What does the command display when you have no mail?

> *Answer: The command displays* You have no mail! *if you actually have no mail. The command causes* echo *to print an appropriate message based on the result of the* mail -e *command.*

The if command does one thing if the command succeeded, and another thing if it failed. This particular command can be put into your startup file (~/.profile); when you log in, it will tell you if you have mail or not.

Every UNIX command tells the shell whether it succeeded or failed. (If it succeeds, it gives the shell the number 0; if it fails, it gives the number 1.) The -e option tells mailx to "succeed" if there is mail waiting, and to "fail" if there is no mail. The rest is done by the if command. We'll address the if command in more detail in Chapter 8, "Shell Scripts."

# LAB 3.4 SELF-REVIEW QUESTIONS

In order to test your progress, you should be able to answer the following questions.

**I)** The biff command beeps if you get mail, but does nothing else.
   **a)** _____True
   **b)** _____False

**2)** The xbiff command will only check your system mailbox; you cannot make it check any other file.
   **a)** _____True
   **b)** _____False

**3)** If MAIL=/usr/spool/mail/sandi and
MAILPATH=/var/mail/sandi,
the shell will notify you when mail shows up in /usr/spool/mail/sandi.
   **a)** _____True
   **b)** _____False

**4)** If `MAILCHECK=90`, how often does the shell check for mail?

    **a)** \_\_\_\_\_Every 90 seconds.

    **b)** \_\_\_\_\_Every 90 minutes.

    **c)** \_\_\_\_\_Every time you press Enter.

**5)** All UNIX commands give the shell a return code that indicates whether they succeeded or failed.

    **a)** \_\_\_\_\_True

    **b)** \_\_\_\_\_False

*Quiz answers appear in Appendix A, Section 3.4.*

**LAB
3.4**

# CHAPTER 3

# TEST YOUR THINKING

Every week, you and 20 or so friends like to go to the movies. Fortunately, everyone has e-mail. You're responsible for notifying everyone and organizing rides. You send a suggestion to all 20 people and they reply to you; you look at all of the responses and send out lists of car pools.

1)  How would you send out the same mail message to 20 people?

    **a)**    How could you make sure the message was correct before you sent it?

    **b)**    How could you make sure the addresses were correct before you sent it?

    **c)**    How could you keep a record of all of the messages you've sent?

2)  How will you organize the mail related to the movies? (Decide if you need to keep mail for more than one week.)

# CHAPTER 4

# COMPUTER NETWORKS

*UNIX systems are easily joined together in networks. You can work with other systems over the network.*

## CHAPTER OBJECTIVES

In this Chapter, you will learn about:

✔ Displaying Machine Names        Page 142
✔ Logging In to Another System        Page 147
✔ Copying Files Between Systems        Page 158

Networking is one of the most famous attributes of UNIX systems. After all, UNIX systems made up a large part of the first Internet experiments.

A network is simply two or more computers exchanging data in some way. An internetwork is two or more computer networks joined to make one larger network. The Internet is a particular internetwork of computers connected in a certain way.

*You may not have access to these tools. Some kinds of networking are considered security risks, or are just too expensive for your system. Your system may have only `ftp` and `telnet`, or it may have only `uucp`, or it may have any combination of them. Read the labs, try them, and work through the ones you can.*

# L A B   4 . 1

# DISPLAYING MACHINE NAMES

---

**L**AB **O**BJECTIVES

After this Lab, you will be able to:

• Display Your Machine's Address

---

Every machine in a network has an address, which is a number. Besides the number, there are usually names. The most common type of name to identify a machine in a network is a *domain address*. These are the names you see in your e-mail address and in World Wide Web addresses. (There are other types of addressing; in Lab 4.3.3, "Copy Files with `uucp`," we'll discuss a different kind of addressing called *uucp addressing*, logically enough.)

Many UNIX networks will operate over phone lines. This is not surprising, considering that UNIX came out of the phone company's labs.

From your point of view, there are really three different ways to work across a network:

- First, parts of the two computers might be joined in some way to make it appear that part of the other computer is attached to yours. This is the approach of a mounted file system.
- Second, you might actually log into the other system and work. This is the approach used by commands such as `telnet`, `ftp`, and `rlogin`.
- Third, you could ask a computer program on your system to ask a computer program on the *other* system to do the chores. This is the approach used by commands such as `rcp` and `uucp`.

## LAB 4.1.1    DISPLAY YOUR MACHINE'S ADDRESS

Enter the following commands:

```
hostname
uname -n
```

**a)** What is the output of the commands? Do they produce the same output?

_____

_____

Enter the following command:

```
/usr/sbin/nslookup $(hostname)
```

**b)** What is the output of the command?

_____

_____

# LAB 4.1  EXERCISE ANSWERS

## 4.1.1    ANSWERS

Enter the following commands:

```
hostname
uname -n
```

**a)**   What is the output of the commands? Do they produce the same output?

_Answer: The answer will depend on your machine. They should look something like this:_

```
$ hostname
horus
$ uname -n
horus
```

This machine is named "horus". This name is the part of its domain name that corresponds to your machine alone. (On some systems, the commands may print the entire domain name; that is, the name would read as "horus.kw.interix.com" instead of "horus".)

The output of the two commands can be different in some cases, but it will normally be the same. Both commands print the address of your machine in the network. (The uname command will print other information about your machine, including the version of the operating system.)

If you work on a network of machines, the name of the machine you're logged onto may not be quite the same as your e-mail address. Usually, the machine's name will be longer. For example, nobody sends mail to "johnmc@horus.kw.interix.com"; they send it to "johnmc@interix.com".

That's because many organizations designate one machine to receive mail. It becomes the post office for the organization, and gets the simple e-mail address. (Rather like sending mail to "John McMullen, General Delivery, Kitchener.") When you send e-mail to any address at "interix.com" it really goes to the machine "mail.interix.com". That mail machine is responsible for sending mail around to the specific users.

One last thing about domain addresses. If you're dealing with another machine in the same domain and subdomains, you don't need to use the full address. (This is like working with files: When the files are siblings—that is, in the same directory—you don't need the full path name.) When I'm on horus.kw.interix.com and I want to contact osiris.kw .interix.com, I can just use the name "osiris" because the two computers are in the same small network (kw.interix.com).

If you're not sure, use the whole name.

Enter the following command:

```
/usr/sbin/nslookup $(hostname)
```

**b)**   What is the output of the command?

   *Answer: The output should look something like this:*

```
$ /usr/sbin/nslookup $(uname -n)
Server:   mail.interix.com
Address:  127.0.0.1
```

```
Name:     horus.kw.interix.com
Address:  127.0.0.3
```

The `nslookup` command may not work for you. Your machine must have access to a machine with a network address server. (A machine or program that provides a service, such as looking up an address, is called a *server*. A machine or program that requests that service is called a *client*.) In this case, the server is "mail.interix.com".

The `nslookup` command looks up Internet hosts. If your local network is an Internet-style network (technically, a TCP/IP network), this command will go to a server machine (the machine that stores addresses) and request the name and numeric address of the machine given as an argument. You can give the name of the machine as a symbolic name (as we did here, the output of the `hostname` command) or as a number.

Every full domain name corresponds to a number. The numbers are divided into four parts separated by dot characters: The numbers are in the opposite order from the domain parts, so the first number (127 in this example) is the top-level domain, and each number afterward is a subdomain. The last number indicates a specific machine. The number *always* has four parts but a symbolic name may not. If you send mail to me at `interix.com`, then `interix.com` is turned into a four-part number. (Even back when the company was only one computer, it was still a four-part number.)

The `nslookup` also has an interactive mode, with many more commands (for example, you can list all of the machines in a subdomain). If you're interested, you should read the `nslookup` man page.

The addresses here are fake, by the way. The number 127.0.0.1 always refers to your own machine.

# LAB 4.1 SELF REVIEW QUESTIONS

In order to test your progress, you should be able to answer the following questions.

1)  Every machine in a network has an address.
    a) _____ True
    b) _____ False

2) If your e-mail address is "dparker@constant.reader.org," what is the name of your machine in its subdomain? (Assuming your mail comes directly to your machine.)

**a)** _____dparker
**b)** _____constant
**c)** _____reader
**d)** _____org

3) If the numeric address of the machine "constant.reader.org" is 127.0.2.1, which number corresponds to the "org" top-level domain?

**a)** _____127
**b)** _____0
**c)** _____2
**d)** _____1

4) To look up the numeric address of a different internet host, use the command:

**a)** _____uname
**b)** _____hostname
**c)** _____nslookup

*Quiz answers appear in Appendix A, Section 4.1.*

# LAB 4.2

# LOGGING IN TO ANOTHER SYSTEM

---

### LAB OBJECTIVES

After this Lab, you will be able to:

- Log in with `telnet`
- Log in with `rlogin`
- Run Remote Commands with `rsh` or `rcmd`

---

One of the nice features of the Internet is that you can log in to another computer and work with that computer as if it were in your office. This feature isn't specific to the Internet, though; it's a feature of many networks. Any network that uses the same protocols for communicating (called TCP/IP) can connect using the `telnet` program. For instance, if your PC has `telnet` installed and the right kind of network, you can use `telnet` to log in to a UNIX system.

You should remember the following:

- You still need an account on the remote machine.
- Once you are logged into the other computer, you must use the correct commands for that operating system. It may not be a UNIX system, but it will have support for the Internet protocols.

There are two common commands used to log in to another machine, `telnet` and `rlogin`. You can also run commands on a remote machine with the `rsh` command (known on some systems as `rcmd`). All of these commands must be enabled by the system administrator of the remote site; he or she must set up the system so it accepts connections from those programs.

## LAB 4.2 EXERCISES

### 4.2.1 LOG IN WITH TELNET

Enter the following commands. If you know you have an account on another machine on the network, use that account information; otherwise, use your current machine's name for *hostname*, your current login name for *loginname*, and your current password for *password*.

```
telnet hostname
name: loginname
password:password
```

**a)** What happens?

_____

_____

Press the key combination Ctrl-].

**b)** What happens? What does the Ctrl-] key combination do?

_____

_____

Enter the following command:

```
help
```

Press Enter twice.

**c)** What does the `help` command do? What does `Enter` do?

_____

_____

Enter the following command:

```
exit
```

**d)** What happens?

_____

_____

### 4.2.2 LOG IN WITH RLOGIN

Enter the following command:

```
rlogin hostname
```

Use your own system's name for the *hostname*. Respond to the prompts.

**a)** What happens?

_____

_____

At the beginning of a new line, enter the following command:

```
~Ctrl-Z
```

(That's a ~ followed by the key combination Ctrl-Z.)

**b)** What happens? What does the ~Ctrl-Z command do?

_____

_____

Enter the following commands:

```
fg
exit
```

**c)** What happens?

_____

_____

### 4.2.3   RUN REMOTE COMMANDS WITH RSH OR RCMD

Enter the following commands:

```
rsh hostname ls
rsh hostname ls /tmp
```

Use your own system's name for *hostname*.

If the `rsh` command gives you an error such as "Cannot open *hostname*" or if it isn't found on the system, try `rcmd` instead. You might also want to try the command `/usr/ucb/rsh` instead of simply `rsh`.

> **a)** What does the `rsh` command do? What directory is listed in the first command? In the second command?

_____

_____

# LAB 4.2  EXERCISE ANSWERS

### 4.2.1   ANSWERS

Enter the following commands:

```
telnet hostname
name: loginname
password:password
```

**a)**   What happens?

*Answer: You are logged into the system and presented with the command prompt.*

If your login name on the remote system is not the same as your current login name, you can specify the new one with the `-l` option. A synopsis for the `telnet` command is:

```
telnet [-l username] [hostname]
```

The *hostname* can be in either the symbolic or numeric form. For example, you could have logged into your own machine with:

```
telnet 127.0.0.1
```

# ■ *FOR EXAMPLE:*

My login name is "johnmc" but on the machine "gateway" it's "john_mcmullen." I can use telnet to log in to gateway with this command:

```
telnet -l john_mcmullen gateway
```

The gateway system still asks for my password, but I don't have to type in my login name. This option is useful if you like to give aliases to often-used commands. (Aliases are discussed in Chapter 7, "Customizing Your Environment.")

The -l option is not guaranteed to work, but if it doesn't work, the other system just prompts you for your login name, as if you hadn't given the option.

The telnet command has other options, but they're rarely used. Most of them involve the underlying protocol (how the two computers talk to one another).

Press the key combination Ctrl-].

**b)**   What happens? What does the Ctrl-] key combination do?

*Answer: The prompt changes to:*

```
telnet>
```

The Ctrl-] key combination "escapes" from what telnet usually does and lets you give a command directly to the telnet program instead of the remote computer. Normally, you press Ctrl-] and type the command. Pressing Enter without a command makes the prompt go away and returns you to the normal state of the telnet program.

If you don't name a remote host on the command line, then telnet starts in this mode. The help command lists the options you have. The command open *host*, for instance, opens a connection to the remote site *host*. (By using open, you don't have to exit telnet and restart if you want to login to a different host.)

Enter the following command:

```
help
```

Press Enter twice.

**c)** What does the `help` command do? What does Enter do?

*Answer: The `help` command displays a list of telnet commands. Pressing Enter returns you to the remote computer.*

Most of the `telnet` commands have to do with the underlying workings of the telnet program, and you won't use them. (In fact, you probably shouldn't.) However, Table 4.1 lists some that can be useful.

The `z` and `!` commands are slightly different. The `z` command stops `telnet` and puts it in the background. You can then give commands on your local machine. If you try to exit your UNIX session, then you'll get a warning that you have a stopped job. To get back to your `telnet` session, you need to foreground the process with `fg`. (See the discussion of job control in *UNIX User's Interactive Workbook*, in Chapter 12, "Commands and Job Control.")

The `!` command starts a *new* shell to let you run some commands on your local machine. When you type `exit`, the new shell goes away and you're back in your `telnet` session.

Suspending the shell (`z`) means that any commands you give that affect your environment (such as changing your current directory) will still be in effect after you exit `telnet`. With a new shell (`!`), the results of commands that affect your environment go away when you exit the new shell to return to the `telnet` session.

**Table 4.1 ■ Some `telnet` commands**

| `telnet` Command | Description |
| --- | --- |
| `z` | Suspends the `telnet` session. |
| `!` | Starts a shell. |
| `quit` | Quits the `telnet` session. |
| `?` | Displays the help information. |
| `close` | Breaks a `telnet` connection without quitting the session. |
| `open` *address* `[-l` *user*`]` | Connects to the machine at *address*; used after you've started the `telnet` session. |
| Control-[ | Escapes to `telnet` session to give a `telnet` command. |

If you use `telnet` to log in to only one remote system, this interactive mode will not be useful to you. If you spend sessions "hopping" between systems, you may be interested in interactive mode. See the `telnet` man page for details on this aspect of `telnet`.

If you're actually logged into a different system, try some commands on the remote system and compare them with the same commands on your local system (using Ctrl-]). Good commands to try are:

**LAB
4.2**

| | |
|---|---|
| `date` | The time may be different on the other system. |
| `who` | The `who` command lists the users currently logged in. The remote system will probably have a different set of users logged in than the local system. |
| `uname -a` | The `uname -a` command lists information about a system. At the very least, the names of the two systems will be different. |

Enter the following command:

```
exit
```

**d)**  What happens?

*Answer: The* `telnet` *session ends.*

The `exit` command ends the session.

By the way, something to keep in mind is that different systems may have different setups. I recently had a problem interrupting a running program with Ctrl-C, and I assumed it was a problem with that system's `telnet`. On investigation, I found out that the system set the interrupt character, normally Ctrl-C, to the Delete key. (I fixed this on the remote system with a `stty` command, as described in *UNIX User's Interactive Workbook*, in Chapter 6, "Emergency Recovery.")

## 4.2.2 ANSWERS

Enter the following command:

```
rlogin yourmachine
```

Respond to the prompts.

**a)** What happens?

*Answer: You are prompted for your password; after you supply it, you are logged in.*

The `rlogin` command is a remote `login`. (The "r" at the beginning of a name often stands for "remote"—although sometimes it stands for "restricted.") Once you're logged in using `rlogin`, it's nearly identical to logging in to a local machine using `login`.

It's possible that you won't be prompted for a password. The system administrator of the remote site can designate certain machines as "trusted" machines. If your machine is trusted by the remote site, and you have an account on both sites, then you won't have to enter your password. This feature is meant to be a security feature. It's possible to run a program that looks at *all* the information going across the network ("sniffer" program). With `telnet`, you must type in your password. The sniffer program would "see" your password. With a "trusted" machine, there's no need to send your password over the network, so no program looking at network signals can see it.

If you frequently use `rlogin` to work on another machine in your network, you can set up your account on your machine as a trusted machine and account by setting up a `.rhosts` file in your home directory.

*Many system administrators consider a `.rhosts` file to be poor security, and therefore forbid them. On some systems, it's possible to prevent `rlogin` from looking at your `.rhosts` file. The convenience of a `.rhosts` file may not be worth the loss of security.*

A `.rhosts` file consists of lines of text. Each line contains the name of a host and the name of a user, separated by spaces or tabs. That user from that host is allowed to log in to your account.

My login name on the machine `horus` is `johnmc`. My login name on the machine `gateway` is `john_mcmullen`. To use `rlogin` to login to *gateway* from `horus`, I need to create a `.rhosts` file in my home directory on `gateway`. The `.rhosts` file contains this line:

```
horus johnmc
```

When I `rlogin` to `gateway`, the program that `rlogin` talks to checks that `john_mcmullen` really is a user, and it checks to see if `horus` is a trusted system. The system administrator hasn't set it up as one, but when it checks the file `~john_mcmullen/.rhosts`, the program discovers that `john_mcmullen` allows `johnmc@horus` to log in to his account.

If I want to be able to use `rlogin` to log in to `horus` from `gateway`, I need to create a `.rhosts` file in my home directory on `horus`. This `.rhosts` file contains the line:

```
gateway john_mcmullen
```

At the beginning of a new line, enter the following command:

```
~Ctrl-Z
```

**b)** What happens? What does the `~Ctrl-Z` command do?

*Answer: The ~ escapes the Ctrl-Z, so it affects the* `rlogin` *command instead of affecting a command on the remote system.* `~Ctrl-Z` *suspends the* `rlogin` *session so you can work on your local machine.*

This is the same as the command `^[z` in `telnet`. By putting the `rlogin` command to sleep for a moment, you can do work on your local machine. To reactivate the `rlogin` command, you need to use `fg`.

Again, if you're actually logged into a different system, try some commands on the remote system and compare them with the same commands on your local system (using `~Ctrl-Z`). As in the last exercise, try `date`, `who`, and `uname -a`.

Enter the following commands:

```
fg
exit
```

**c)** What happens?

*Answer: The session ends.*

You log out of an `rlogin` session in exactly the same way you log out of a normal session that starts with the `login` command.

## 4.2.3 ANSWERS

Enter the following commands:

```
rsh hostname ls
rsh hostname ls /tmp
```

**a)** What does the `rsh` command do? What directory is listed in the first command? In the second command?

*Answer: The* `rsh` *command runs a command on the remote system. The first command lists your home directory on the remote system; the second command lists the directory* `/tmp` *on the remote system.*

**LAB
4.2**

The `rlogin` command actually uses `rsh` to log you into the remote system. In order for `rsh` to work at all, the remote system must "trust" your system. That means the system administrator must have designated it a trusted system, or you must have set up a `.rhosts` file.

If you don't specify an absolute directory or file name in your command, the command uses (or works on) your home directory.

By the way, the output from `ls` is one file to a line, not in columns as it usually is. Remember that when `ls` prints files to a terminal, it prints in columns (unless you specify otherwise); when `ls` prints to a pipe or to a program, it prints one file to a line (again, unless you specify otherwise). When you run a command remotely, the output does not go to a terminal; it goes to a program that sends it to your terminal. It's a small distinction, but it can surprise you once in a while.

The `rsh` command may have a different name. On some systems, it is installed as `rcmd` (for "remote command") or `remsh` (for "remote shell"). In these cases, the `rsh` command usually starts a "restricted shell" program. If your system uses `rsh` as a restricted shell, the command line will fail with a message such as "Cannot open hostname." The command may be installed as `rcmd`.

# LAB 4.2 SELF-REVIEW QUESTIONS

In order to test your progress, you should be able to answer the following questions.

**1)** Once you have an account on one machine in a network, you can log in to all other machines.
   **a)** _____True
   **b)** _____False

**2)** You can only `telnet` into a UNIX machine.
   **a)** _____True
   **b)** _____False

**3)** Which of the following commands does not  use the `.rhosts` file?

    **a)** _____`telnet`

    **b)** _____`rlogin`

    **c)** _____`rsh`

**4)** What does an escape command do in a remote login program such as `telnet` or `rlogin`?

    **a)** _____Breaks the connection

    **b)** _____Starts a new shell so you can give commands locally

    **c)** _____Allows you to give commands to the remote login program itself

    **d)** _____Puts the remote login program to sleep

**LAB
4.2**

**5)** The ~`Ctrl-Z` command for `rlogin` is similar to which command in `telnet`?

    **a)** _____`Ctrl-] z`

    **b)** _____`Ctrl-]!`

    **c)** _____`Ctrl-]help`

**6)** The `.rhosts` file is installed on which machine:

    **a)** _____The machine calling out, where you originally logged in

    **b)** _____The machine being called, the remote machine

*Quiz answers appear in Appendix A, Section 4.2.*

# L A B   4 . 3

# COPYING FILES BETWEEN SYSTEMS

---

### LAB OBJECTIVES

After this Lab, you will be able to:

- Copy Files with `rcp`
- Copy Files with `ftp`
- Copy Files with `uucp`

---

There are several commands available to you in order to copy a file between two systems. Each is used in different circumstances, depending on the kind of network being used. Today, most networks are Internet-style networks, and people use `ftp` (and its `put` and `get` subcommands) to transfer files interactively. On local networks, the `rcp` command is used as a "remote `cp`" command.

Before the Internet became common, most network connections were done over phone lines, and files were sent in batches to minimize the time on the phone. The UUCP commands were written to work with that kind of network. The UUCP commands are not common now, although at one time they were the command set used to transfer files between most UNIX machines. Most people consider "network news" or USENET to be part of the Internet, but at one time, almost all news articles were transferred between systems using UUCP.

Although these programs originated on UNIX systems, both `ftp` and `uucp` are available on many other systems. Many PCs that connect with the Internet have the `ftp` program, for example.

# LAB 4.3 EXERCISES

## 4.3.1 COPY FILES WITH RCP

In your home directory, create the directory chap04, containing a file named transfer.test.

Enter the following command on one line:

> rcp *yourlogin@hostname*:chap04/transfer.test
> *yourlogin@hostname*:/tmp

Use your login name for *yourlogin* and your current system's name for *hostname*. (If you have a remote system you can log in to, use that system for *hostname*. Your local system is used here only because it's available to everyone.)

**a)** What happens? Is the file copied to the /tmp directory?

_____

_____

Enter the following command:

> rcp chap04/transfer.test transfer.test

**b)** What happens? Where is the file transfer.test copied to?

_____

_____

Enter the following command:

> rcp -r chap04 /tmp

**c)** What happens? What is copied into the /tmp directory?

_____

_____

## 4.3.2 COPY FILES WITH FTP

Enter the following command:

```
ftp hostname
```

Use your machine's name for *hostname*. When prompted, enter your login name and your password, and then give the following command:

**LAB
4.3**

```
pwd
```

**a)** What does the prompt look like? What directory are you in?

_____

_____

Enter the following commands:

```
cd chap04
get transfer.test ftp.get
put ftp.get ftp.put
?
bye
```

**b)** What did the `get` and `put` commands do?

_____

_____

**c)** What did the `?` command do?

_____

_____

**d)** What did the `bye` command do?

_____

_____

## 4.3.3  COPY FILES WITH UUCP

From the `chap04` directory, enter the following command:

```
uucp transfer.test hostname!~yourlogin/uucp.test.1
```

**a)** What happens? Where is the new copy created?

_____

_____

Enter the following command:

```
uucp transfer.test hostname!~/uucp.test.2
```

**b)** What happens? Where is the new copy created? (Hint: try the home directories for the users named "uucp" and "nuucp".)

_____

_____

Enter the following command:

```
uuname
```

**c)** What is the output of the `uuname` command?

_____

_____

# LAB 4.3  EXERCISE ANSWERS

## 4.3.1  ANSWERS

Enter the following command on one line:

```
rcp yourlogin@hostname:chap04/transfer.test
yourlogin@hostname:/tmp
```

**a)**  What happens? Is the file copied to the `/tmp` directory?

*Answer: The file is copied to the* /tmp *directory on your machine.*

As you might expect from the name, the rcp command copies files to or from a remote site. It looks like the cp command, except for all the extra information about the files. For each file, you can specify:

    [[*loginname@*]*hostname:*]*filename*

This identifies a file or directory (*filename*) on a host (*hostname*). The *loginname* is the name that should be used to log in to the remote host. If you leave out the *loginname*, your current login name is used. This is fine if you have the same login name on both systems. If you leave out the *hostname*, your current host is used.

By the way, because you can specify the machine for *both* files at once, you can copy files from one machine to another machine while you're actually logged into a third machine!

Enter the following command:

    rcp chap04/transfer.test transfer.test

**b)**  What happens? Where is the file transfer.test copied to?

*Answer: The file is copied to your home directory.*

Just like commands run through rsh, relative file names are taken to be relative to your home directory. (And the reason is that rcp commands are run by the same program that runs rsh commands.)

In fact, if you want to copy a file to your home directory on a machine, you can specify the target like this:

    rcp sourcefile hostname:

If you do this, you must specify the destination host's name; you cannot use just a ":" as the target to mean your home directory on your current machine.

Enter the following command:

    rcp -r chap04 /tmp

**c)**  What happens? What is copied into the /tmp directory?

*Answer: The entire directory tree is copied;* /tmp *contains* chap04 *and* chap04/transfer.test.

The -r option (for "recursive") copies an entire directory tree.

## 4.3.2   COPY FILES WITH FTP

Enter the following command:

```
ftp hostname
```

When prompted, enter your login name and your password, and then give the following command:

```
pwd
```

**a)**   What does the prompt look like? What directory are you in?

*Answer: When you log in using the* ftp *program, you start in your home directory. The login prompt of the* ftp *program looks like this:*

```
ftp>
```

Like rcp, the ftp program transfers files between two computers. But like telnet, it's an interactive program. You log in to the remote site's ftp server program and command it to transfer files.

Here's a typical login sequence:

```
Connected to osiris.kw.interix.com.

220 osiris.kw.interix.com FTP server (Version
wu-2.4(2)

Wed Jun 7 17:22:02 MDT 1995) ready.

Name (johnmc):

331 Password required for johnmc.

Password:

230 User johnmc logged in.

Remote system type is UNIX.
```

```
Using binary mode to transfer files.

ftp> pwd

/usr/johnmc
```

The "remote system type" doesn't have to be UNIX; it can be other system types as well.

The "binary mode" note indicates how files are transferred. There are two modes:

- *Binary* mode, sometimes called "image" mode, copies files exactly as they exist. Normally, this is what you want when transferring programs or data files. To put your FTP session into binary mode, give the command `binary`.
- *ASCII* mode, sometimes called "text" mode, changes files so the end-of-line character is correct for the destination operating system. This mode is useful for transferring plain text files that were created on a different operating system, such as DOS or Windows or VMS. To put your FTP session into ASCII mode, give the command `ascii`.

If you have an account on the remote system, your starting directory is your home directory. You may be able to login even if you don't have an account. The remote system may provide *anonymous ftp*.

## THE .NETRC FILE

If you do a lot of FTP transfers with a particular site, you may want to skip logging in. You can do this by setting up a file named `.netrc` in your home directory. The `.netrc` file is a set of commands for `ftp` to run when it starts up.

For each machine you want to log in to automatically, you need a line in the `.netrc` file that contains this information:

```
machine hostname login loginname password yourpassword
```

The words `machine`, `login`, and `password` are all `ftp` commands, and you can find them in the `ftp` man page. For example, if my `.netrc` file contains this line:

```
machine isis login john password ur21841f8r
```

when I give the command ftp  isis, the ftp program automatically tries to log me in using the login name johnmc and the password ur21841f8r.

 *You'll notice that the* .netrc *file contains your password for another system. This is a security risk. To minimize the risk, the* ftp *program requires the* .netrc *file to have no permissions set for anyone other than the owner. That is, you need to use* chmod *to set permissions to 600 or 400.*

Don't get confused between the .rhosts file and the .netrc file. A .rhosts file contains the names of accounts and machines you're allowing to call *in,* while the .netrc file contains the names and accounts you use to call *out.*

**L**AB
**4.3**

Enter the following commands:

```
cd chap04
get transfer.test ftp.get
put ftp.get ftp.put
?
bye
```

**b)**   What did the get and put commands do?

*Answer: The* get *command gets a file from the remote site and puts it on your site in your current directory. The* put *command puts a file from your site onto the remote site.*

There are a number of commands in ftp; you can see a list with the command ? or help, and you can get a description of any one command with help command. For example, help image displays a description of the image command.

The two most important commands are get and put. They have the following synopses:

```
get remotefile [localname]
put localfile [remotename]
```

If you don't specify a new name (either *localname* or *remotename*), the file is transferred with the same name it had before.

To cancel a transfer, use the interrupt key (usually Ctrl-C).

If you want to move more than one file at a time, you can use the commands mget and mput (for "multiple" get and put). If you use mget and mput, the ftp program asks you to confirm each file before it is transferred. (You can turn this behavior on with the command prompt y and off with the command prompt n.)

**c)** What did the ? command do?

*Answer: The ? command lists available ftp commands.*

There are many commands available in the ftp program. Table 4.2 lists some of the basic FTP commands you may find useful.

**d)** What did the bye command do?

*Answer: The bye command ends the ftp session.*

Unlike in the shell, the command is not exit.

## ANONYMOUS FTP

The administrators on some systems want to make certain files available to anyone. (This is how a lot of free UNIX software is distributed.) They set up a machine that allows *anybody* to log in using ftp. These sites are called "anonymous ftp sites."

To log in to an anonymous ftp site, use the login name "anonymous" and give your e-mail address as the password.

When you log in to an anonymous ftp site, your starting directory is /, because you don't have a home directory. (This isn't actually the root directory; to prevent people from doing damage to the system, they've "sectioned off" part of the file tree, and made it look like the root directory.)

Publicly accessible files are usually in the directory /pub.

If you need to put a file on an anonymous ftp site, new files usually go into the directory /incoming.

### 4.3.3  COPY FILES WITH UUCP

From the chap04 directory, enter the following command:

```
uucp transfer.text hostname!~yourlogin/uucp.test.1
```

**a)** What happens? Where is the new copy created?

## Table 4.2 ■ Some `ftp` Commands

| Command | Description |
| --- | --- |
| append *localfile* [*remotefile*] | Adds the file to the end of the remote file, rather than replacing the remote file. |
| ! [*command*] | Runs *command* on the local system. If no *command* is given, the ! command starts an interactive shell. |
| ascii | Sets the transfer type to "network ascii." |
| binary | Sets the transfer type to "image." |
| bye | Ends the session. |
| cd *remote-directory* | Changes directories on the remote site to *remote-directory*. |
| cdup | Changes directories on the remote site to the parent of the current directory. |
| delete *remotefile* | Deletes the file on the remote system. |
| get *remotefile* [*localfile*] | Gets the remote file and stores it on the local machine, with the name *localfile*. |
| help [*command*] | Displays help information about *command*. If you don't give a *command*, it lists all the `ftp` internal commands. |
| lcd [*directory*] | Changes your *local* working directory; files you `get` and `put` will go to and come from this directory on the local machine. If you don't specify a *directory*, your home directory becomes your local working directory. |
| ls [*remotedirectory*] [*localfile*] | Lists the contents of the remote directory. If no remote directory is given, list the contents of the current directory. If *local-file* is given, stores the contents in the local file by that name instead of displaying them on the terminal. |
| mget *remotefiles* | Gets more than one file. Wildcards can be used |
| mput *localfiles* | Puts more than one file. Wildcards can be used. |

**LAB
4.3**

## Table 4.2 ■ (continued)

| | |
|---|---|
| prompt | Turns interactive prompting on and off. |
| put *localfile* [*remotefile*] | Sends a local file to the remote machine. |

*Answer: The new file is created in your home directory with the name* uucp.test.1.

The uucp command is another copy command. It originally stood for "UNIX-to-UNIX copying." It's older than the rcp command and uses an old form of hostname addressing, usually called *UUCP addressing*. In UUCP addressing, the host's name is separated from the file name by a ! character. (Because a ! is sometimes called a "bang" by UNIX users, this form of addressing is sometimes called "bang addressing.") The actual synopsis of a uucp command is:

```
uucp [options] [host![host!…]]file [host![host!…]]file
```

If you use uucp, you'll copy from one remote host to your machine, or from your machine to a remote host. If you don't name a host (even if you put a ! but no host name), that file name is considered to be on your machine.

Although you can have UUCP connections over any kind of network, they're commonly used for dial-up connections, where one computer uses a modem to phone another. When UUCP connections were the most common kind of UNIX networking, groups of machines agreed to pass along files for each other. (This was the origin of USENET, the user's network.) E-mail addresses used UUCP addressing, for instance, and sometimes the uucp command could also be used to transfer files to and from machines that were several sites away. You could get commands with addresses like this:

```
uucp list osiris!athena!thor!~bob/johns_list
```

This meant that the file list would be sent to the machine osiris, which would send it to the machine athena, which would send it to the machine thor. On thor, the file would be copied to ~bob/johns_list. With UUCP addresses, you need to know every machine along the path to the destination. While it's still possible for a network of machines to use uucp to pass files along, most systems just use ftp and domain addressing. The addresses are easier to remember.

If you do use `uucp`, you'll almost always use it to copy a file to or from a machine that connects directly to yours, so you'll only need one *hostname!* in the address.

UUCP is quite convenient for a small computer that isn't part of a network. Instead of maintaining a connection to the network all the time, one machine phones in to another machine on a regular schedule. Some businesses use UUCP connections to transfer information nightly from branch offices to the main office.

*The UUCP commands are fundamentally different than* `rcp` *and* `ftp`. `uucp` *and its relatives are batch commands. This means that the two computer systems aren't always in contact with each other. The* `uucp` *command (and the other UUCP commands) request that files be transferred, but don't actually do the transfer. The files aren't actually copied until the next time the computers contact each other, which is typically scheduled for a regular interval. It may be tonight, tomorrow, or next week. When they do contact each other, the batch of stored file copy requests is executed. Don't use UUCP commands if you're in a hurry for the files. (Although the system administrator may configure the UUCP software to connect to the remote system as soon as the request is made, it's still not as fast as* `rcp` *or* `ftp`.)

If your system has a UUCP connection with another system and you find it useful for sending files to a user on the other machine, you should look at the `uuto` command. The `uuto` command uses UUCP to send files to a particular user on the other system. The command synopsis looks like this:

```
uuto [-mp] file ... system!user
```

The `-m` option causes `uuto` to send you mail once the file or files are copied, and the `-p` option causes `uuto` to store the files in the spool directory before they're sent.

When the files arrive on the other system, the user is notified by e-mail. To fetch the files from where they're stored, the user uses the program `uupick`. The `uupick` command lists each file that's been sent to you; you can give the following commands:

| | |
|---|---|
| a[*directory*] | Moves all of the files from this *system* to the *directory* you specified. |
| d | Deletes the file; don't save it. |
| m[*directory*] | Moves this file to the *directory* you specified. |
| p | Prints the file. |
| q | Quits uupick. |
| * | Prints a list of commands in uupick. |
| !*command* | Runs the *command* without leaving uupick. |
| Control-D | Quits uupick. |
| Enter | Goes on to next file in the list. |

Enter the following command:

```
uucp transfer.text hostname!~/uucp.test.2
```

**b)** What happens? Where is the new copy created? (Hint: try the home directories for the users named "uucp" and "nuucp".)

*Answer: The file is copied to the directory* /usr/spool/uucppublic *on the destination host, which is the home directory for the user named nuucp. On some systems it will be the home directory for the user named uucp.*

Normally, the shell sees a ~/ at the beginning of a path name and turns it into your home directory. In this case, the ~/ *isn't* at the beginning of the path name, it's in the middle, so your shell doesn't touch it. Instead, it's interpreted by the program that handles the uucp transfers for you. That program interprets ~ in path names (remember, it correctly interpreted ~*yourlogin* as your home directory), but treats ~/ as its own home directory, which is always /usr/spool/uucppublic. (Mind the spelling.) The UUCP transfer program is normally installed as a special user, named either nuucp or uucp, depending on your system.

Enter the following command:

```
uuname
```

**c)** What is the output of the uuname command?

*Answer: The* uuname *command lists the computers connected to your system through* uucp. *For example:*

```
$ uuname
osiris
```

```
isis
set
```

The `uuname` command (not to be confused with the `uname` command) lists the computers that make UUCP connections to your system.

# LAB 4.3  SELF-REVIEW QUESTIONS

In order to test your progress, you should be able to answer the following questions.

Consider the following command, and assume that these are the correct accounts and file names on those machines.

```
rcp jill@bike:/projects/notes.txt jmeyer@trike:backup/
```

1)  The command had to be given from `bike` or `trike`.
    **a)** _____True
    **b)** _____False

2)  Which of the following is the file that will be created by the copy?
    **a)** _____`/backup/projects/notes.txt`
    **b)** _____`~jill/backup/notes.txt`
    **c)** _____`~jmeyer/notes.txt`
    **d)** _____`~jmeyer/backup/notes.txt`
    **e)** _____`~jmeyer/projects/notes.txt`

3)  When logging in to an anonymous FTP site, your password should be which of the following?
    **a)** _____Your password
    **b)** _____The word "anonymous"
    **c)** _____Your login name
    **d)** _____Your e-mail address

4)  If you're transferring a text file from a UNIX system to a UNIX system, what mode should you use?
    **a)** _____Ascii mode
    **b)** _____Image mode
    **c)** _____Doesn't matter

5)  The `.netrc` file is installed on which machine:
    **a)** _____The machine calling out, where you originally logged in
    **b)** _____The machine being called, the remote machine

**6)** Batch commands such as uucp are typically:

**a)** _____Executed as soon as they're typed in.

**b)** _____Executed as soon as a certain number of requests are queued.

**c)** _____Executed on a schedule.

*Quiz answers appear in Appendix A, Section 4.3.*

# C H A P T E R  4

# TEST YOUR THINKING

You have been put in charge of a project that will involve people working on several UNIX machines linked in a network. (For convenience, the machines are named larry, curly, and moe.) There is a fourth machine, named shemp, which can use a modem and connect to moe by phone.

All of the people working on the project will need access to the main files. They will be making copies of the files, changing them, and then copying them back, assuming the system administrator has installed all of the software you need.

1) How do you want users to share files?

   a) Which machines can have file systems mounted?

   b) Which machines can use UUCP?

   c) Which machines can connect through FTP or RCP?

   d) If the system administrator cannot mount the file systems between larry, curly, and moe, how can the files be exchanged?

2) If security is very important, your system administrator may not allow `rlogin`, `rcp`, and `rsh` commands to run. How will you distribute files?

3) As project leader, you'll need to check on people's working files. If you're normally logged in to moe, how will you check on the files being used on larry? On curly? On shemp?

# CHAPTER 5

# SOME USEFUL STUFF

 *There are some things that are just nice to know, but we couldn't fit them into other chapters.*

## CHAPTER OBJECTIVES

In this Chapter, you will learn about:

Over the years, programmers have written a lot of little UNIX programs to solve particular problems. You may have the same problems that they had. Even by searching through the man pages, you may not notice the command that could help you. This section describes some of those other tools that might be useful to you at some time.

# LAB 5.1

# REPEATING COMMANDS

---

### LAB OBJECTIVES

After this Lab, you will be able to:

*   Repeat the Last Command
*   Display Previous Commands
*   Repeat an Older Command
*   Use Command Line Editing
*   Edit the History File

---

Retyping commands can be a bother. It's cumbersome and can be prone to error. (Who wants to retype long command lines a second time?)

The Korn Shell comes with a command editing feature built in, so you can repeat previous commands. This feature was first introduced in the C Shell, and was so popular that most shells written since the C Shell include some form of command editing as a feature.

In this Lab, we'll discuss only the version of command history available in the Korn Shell. To learn about command history in another shell, such as csh or bash, consult the documentation for that shell.

You'll probably find this feature useful throughout the rest of the book.

## LAB 5.1 EXERCISES

### 5.1.1 REPEAT THE LAST COMMAND

Enter the following commands:

```
pwd
r
```

**a)** What does the `r` command do?

_____

_____

## 5.1.2  DISPLAY PREVIOUS COMMANDS

Enter the following command:

    history

**a)** What does the `history` command do? What number is beside the `pwd` command?

_____

_____

## 5.1.3  REPEAT AN OLDER COMMAND

Enter the following command:

    r p

**a)** What does the command do?

_____

_____

Enter this command, substituting the number from Exercise 5.1.2 for *number*.

    r number

**b)** What does the command do?

_____

_____

Enter this command, substituting the number from Exercise 5.1.2 for *number*.

    r wd=s number

**c)** What does the command do?

_____

_____

## 5.1.4 USE COMMAND LINE EDITING

For this Exercise, you'll need an editing mode on.

Enter the following command:

```
set -o vi
```

Press Escape, then k.

**a)** What happens? What does the k key do?

_____

_____

Press k again and then j.

**b)** What does the j key do?

_____

_____

Press k until the ps command is displayed. Type 1Cwd and space, then press Enter.

**c)** What happens?

_____

_____

## 5.1.5 EDIT THE HISTORY FILE

First, set the name of the editor you want to use. You may use emacs if you want, but the examples will use vi.

Enter the following command:

```
FCEDIT=$(whence vi)
echo $FCEDIT
```

**a)** Explain the first command. What is the value it gives `FCEDIT`?

_____

_____

Enter the following command:

```
fc
```

**b)** What happens?

_____

_____

Edit the command line so it reads:

```
cd /etc
ls
cd -
```

Then save the file and exit the editor.

**c)** What happens?

_____

_____

# LAB 5.1  EXERCISE ANSWERS

## 5.1.1   ANSWERS

Enter the following commands:

```
pwd
r
```

**a)**   What does the `r` command do?

*Answer: The* `r` *command repeats the previous command.*

The shell keeps a record of all the commands you type. They're stored in the file `.sh_history` in your home directory. When you type `r`, the shell consults this history file, and runs the most recent command again.

Normally, the shell saves your last 128 commands.

## 5.1.2   ANSWERS

Enter the following command:

```
history
```

**a)**   What does the `history` command do? What number is beside the `pwd` command?

*Answer: The* `history` *command lists your most recent commands, oldest first. The number beside the* `pwd` *command varies depending on the commands you've been typing. It might look like this:*

```
$ history
161      cd /tmp
162      pax -rf week.pax
163      ls
164      rm *.txt
165      rm -f
166      ls
167      rm ./-f
168      pax -rf week.pax tuesday.txt
169      ls
170      cd -
171      pax -f week.pax
172      compress week.atr
173      compress week.tar
174      uncompress week.tar
175      ls
176      history
```

The `history` command displays the last 16 commands you typed. The number beside the command identifies it; you can use the numbers to repeat older commands.

The history file is actually the file .sh_history in your home directory. (If you delete the file, your command history goes away.) Although the history command only shows you 16 commands, the history file holds your last 128 commands.

You can change how many commands are stored in the history file by setting the variable HISTSIZE to the number of commands you want to save. It won't affect the number of commands displayed by the history command, though, just the number of commands saved in the history file.

If you want to display a different number of commands, give the history command a number as an argument:

- A positive number is the first number to be displayed. The command history 11 displays all of the commands from command 11 to the current command.
- A negative number indicates how many commands you want displayed. The command history -11 shows you your last 11 commands.

The number of commands can be more than 16.

## 5.1.3 ANSWERS

Enter the following command:

```
r p
```

**a)** What does the command do?

*Answer: It runs the* pwd *command again.*

More exactly, it runs the most recent command that started with "p". This technique is useful for re-running a recent command. It's especially good with editor commands (vi and emacs) because there aren't many other commands beginning with "v" and "e".

Enter the command, substituting the number from Exercise 5.1.2 for *number*.

```
r number
```

**b)** What does the command do?

*Answer: It runs the* pwd *command again.*

You can refer to commands by name or by number. To get the number, you need to use the `history` command. You might want to use the number if you've entered 12 `vi` commands in a row, and you want the sixth to last one.

Enter this command, substituting the number from Exercise 5.1.2 for *number*.

```
r wd=s number
```

**c)** What does the command do?

*Answer: It runs the* `ps` *command.*

You can substitute one string of letters for another in a command in the history. By replacing "wd" with "s," the `pwd` command becomes `ps`. If you leave off the *number*, then it runs the last command with the changes specified.

You can only change the first occurrence of the string. If your last command was:

```
mv chap15.txt chapter15.txt
```

you cannot replace *both* occurrences of 15 with 16. This command will not do what you expect:

```
r 15=16
```

The shell turns this into:

```
mv chap05.txt chapter15.txt
```

That is almost certainly not what you want. To replace *both* occurrences of 15, you need to edit the command, either by editing the history file or by using a command line editor.

 *If you need to rename a set of files like this, with numbers in their names (`chap1.txt` to `chapter1.txt`, and so on), you're better off using a `for` loop, which you can type at the command prompt. See Chapter 8, "Shell Scripts," for a description of the `for` loop.*

## 5.1.4 ANSWERS

Enter the following command:

```
set -o vi
```

Press Escape, then k.

**a)** What happens? What does the k key do?

*Answer: The k key displays your previous command. It goes up in the history list.*

Once you've set a command-line editing mode, you can use the editor commands to move up and down through the history file's list. If you're using the vi commands, you're not in command-line editing mode until you press Escape. If you're using the emacs mode (set -o emacs), then you don't need to press Escape.

Press k again and then j.

**b)** What does the j key do?

*Answer: The j key displays the command after the one currently shown. It goes down the history list.*

The up and down commands (k and j in vi) move up (earlier) and down (later) in the history list. Imagine that the history list is a file you're moving through. (In fact, it is—the history file.)

Incidentally, you can also search the command history with /. The command Esc /*string* retrieves the most recent command that contains *string*. For example, Esc /e retrieves the most recent command that contains an "e" somewhere in the line.

Press k until the ps command is displayed. Type 1Cwd and space, then press Enter.

**c)** What happens?

*Answer: The "s" in "ps" is replaced by "s" and the pwd command is run.*

The normal commands for editing in vi are allowed. You can move along the line, you can insert, delete, and replace text.

In this exercise, you edited the command ps to become pwd. The 1Cwd commands move the cursor one character to the right (1), change to the end of the line (C), and replace the remainder of the line with "wd". When you press Enter, the editing is done and the command is executed.

If you discover you like Emacs better as an editor (see Chapter 6, "Emacs," for a discussion of Emacs), you can use the Emacs commands instead. The command to turn on Emacs line-editing mode is:

```
set -o emacs
```

After you give this command, you can use the Emacs commands for moving through the history file and for editing command lines. For example, the sequence of commands to change the command `ps` to `pwd` is:

```
Control-P
Control-D
wd
```

This sequence of commands will make more sense after reading Chapter 6.

## 5.1.5 ANSWERS

First, set the name of the editor you want to use. You may use `emacs` if you want, but the examples given will use `vi`.

Enter the following commands:

```
FCEDIT=$(whence vi)
echo $FCEDIT
```

**a)** Explain the first command. What is the value it gives `FCEDIT`?

*Answer: The assignment sets the value of `FCEDIT` to the pathname for the `vi` editor.*

The `FCEDIT` parameter names the editor you want to use to edit the history file. The `$()` construction is replaced by the pathname of the `vi` program. (The `$()` command substitution was described in Chapter 1.)

Assigning values to parameters is discussed in Chapter 7, "Customizing Your Environment."

Enter the following command:

```
fc
```

**b)** What happens?

*Answer: Your editor starts up so you can edit a file that contains one line, the last command you entered.*

If the `FCEDIT` parameter has not been set to any value, the Korn Shell starts the editor.

**LAB
5.1**

*When* ed *starts up, it displays the number of characters in the file it
has read in. If you enter* fc *and your prompt is replaced by a small
number (probably less than 50), you may be in* ed. *You can exit* ed
*with the command* q *followed by Enter.*

From this point, you can edit the file to get the command correct. If you
want to change all occurrences of 15 to 16 (to continue the example from
the last exercise), you can use the appropriate editor command. In vi, it
would be:

```
:s/15/16/g
```

Edit the command line so it reads:

```
cd /etc
ls
cd -
```

Then save the file and exit the editor.

**c)** What happens?

*Answer: The three commands are run.*

The advantage of editing the command-line history over the r command
or over command-line editing is that it's easy to edit multiple-line commands, or to replace a single line with multiple lines. While you can do
that with command-line editing, it's much easier using fc and editing
the history file.

If you want to edit a *range* of commands, you can, but you must specify
the command numbers. The syntax of fc is:

```
fc [first [last]]
```

If you don't enter either number, you edit the most recent command. If
you enter only the *last* number, then you edit the command with that
number. If you enter both *first* and *last*, then you edit the commands between command number *first* and command number *last*; each command is edited in a separate file.

# LAB 5.1  SELF-REVIEW QUESTIONS

In order to test your progress, you should be able to answer the following questions.

1) The commands described in this Lab work for all UNIX shells.
   **a)** _____True
   **b)** _____False

2) To repeat your most recent command, which of the following commands would you use?
   **a)** _____r
   **b)** _____r p
   **c)** \_\_\_\_\_history
   **d)** \_\_\_\_\_fc -l
   **e)** \_\_\_\_\_fc

3) When command-line editing is enabled, what command displays your previous command for editing?
   **a)** _____k
   **b)** _____Ctrl-P
   **c)** _____Escape k
   **d)** _____Depends upon your command-line editing mode.

4) How many commands does the history command display?
   **a)** _____128
   **b)** _____15
   **c)** _____Depends on the setting of HISTSIZE.
   **d)** _____256
   **e)** _____Depends on the argument to history.

*Quiz answers appear in Appendix A, Section 5.1.*

# L A B   5 . 2

# COMPARING FILES AND DIRECTORIES

---

### LAB OBJECTIVES

After this Lab, you will be able to:

- Compare Two Files
- Find Lines in Common
- Compare Directory Contents

---

Often you want to know exactly how two files or directories are different. What lines were added and what lines were removed? What files are in this directory but not in that directory? Tools such as cmp, diff, and dircmp provide this information.

Before you can run this Lab, you'll need two nearly identical files. Create a directory named *chap05* and *cd* into it.

First, create the file old, which contains the following text:

```
Inventory
Grommets: 99
Insects: far too many
Pegs: 66
Ropes: 88
Tarps: 12
```

Next, create a copy of the file named new and change it as follows:

- *Add* the line "Checked July 25, 1995" after the first line.
- *Delete* the "Insects: far too many" line.
- Change the number of tarps to 11.

When you've finished this, the file new should look like this:

```
Inventory
Checked July 25, 1995
Grommets: 99
Pegs: 66
Ropes: 88
Tarps: 11
```

These two files should have the same size when you list them with `ls -l old new`.

# LAB 5.2 EXERCISES

## 5.2.1   COMPARE TWO FILES

Enter the following command:

```
cmp old new
```

**a)** What is the command's output?

_____

_____

Enter the following command:

```
diff old new
```

**b)** What is the command's output?

_____

_____

Enter the following commands:

```
cp old old2
cmp old old2
diff old old2
```

**c)** What is the output when the files are the same?

_____

_____

## 5.2.2   FIND LINES IN COMMON

Enter the following command:

```
comm old new
```

**a)** What does the output look like? What does the comm command do?

_____

_____

Enter these commands:

```
comm -1 old new
comm -2 old new
comm -3 old new
comm -12 old new
```

**b)** What do the -1, -2, and -3 options do?

_____

_____

## 5.2.3   COMPARE DIRECTORY CONTENTS

From the parent directory of the chap05 directory, use these commands to create a copy of the chap05 directory named chap05.new with some different files:

```
cp -Rf chap05 chap05.new
cd chap05; pwd > here
cd ../chap05.new; pwd > here
cd ..
```

From the parent directory of the chap05 and chap05.new directories, enter the following command:

```
dircmp chap05 chap05.new | more
```

**a)** What does the `dircmp` command do? What does the output look like?

_____

_____

Enter the following command:

```
dircmp -s chap05 chap05.new | more
```

**b)** What does the `-s` option do?

_____

_____

# LAB 5.2 EXERCISE ANSWERS

## 5.2.1 ANSWERS

Enter the following command:

```
cmp old new
```

**a)** What is the command's output?

*Answer: The output looks like this:*

```
$ cmp old new
old new differ: char 11, line 2
```

The `cmp` command compares two files and tells you if they are different. (In this case, you can't use the file size to tell if they are different, because the files are the same size.)

If the files are different, `cmp` also tells you where the two files become different. In this case, the first difference is at character 11, which is the beginning of the second line. You can use `cmp` to compare text files or binary files. Unlike checksums, both files being compared must be on the same system. (The `-l` option causes `cmp` to list every difference between the files, but I've never found that useful. You may.)

If you want to know how the two files differ, you must use a different tool, such as `diff`.

Enter the following command:

```
diff old new
```

**b)**  What is the command's output?

*Answer: The output looks like this:*

```
$ diff old new
1a2
> Checked July 25, 1995
3d3
< Insects: far too many
6c6
< Tarps: 12
--
> Tarps: 11
```

The diff command lists the differences between two files. It compares the files and provides a list of the changes you need to make to turn the first file on the command line into the second file on the command line.

Each change is presented in the same format. The first number is the line number in the *first* file that is affected, the letter is the type of change, and the second number is the resulting line in the second file. Lines from the first file are indicated with "<" and lines from the second file are indicated with ">".

The first change is:

```
1a2
> Checked July 25, 1995
```

The "1a2" means that line 2 was added after line 1, and the text of the new line is printed.

The second change is:

```
3d3
< Insects: far too many
```

The "3d3" indicates that line 3 in the first file was deleted.

The third change is:

```
6c6
< Tarps: 12
```

```
--
> Tarps: 11
```

The "6c6" means that line 6 in the first file was changed, and it is line 6 in the second file. (If a lot of lines were added or deleted, then a changed line might not have the same line number in the second file.) *Both* lines are printed, separated by "--", and it's up to you to spot the differences.

If there's a large block of lines that changed (for example, if you had changed all of the numbers on the inventory lines), diff usually prints the lines in groups.

Enter the following commands:

```
cp old old2
cmp old old2
diff old old2
```

**c)** What is the output when the files are the same?

*Answer: Neither command produces output if the files are identical.*

This is in keeping with the UNIX philosophy of not writing output when something works.

 *The* diff *command is best used on plain text files. It works on binary files, but you probably won't be able to read the output. Use* cmp *for binary files.*

## 5.2.2 ANSWERS

Enter the following command:

```
comm old new
```

**a)** What does the output look like? What does the comm command do?

*Answer: The* comm *command lists files that are common to both files. The output looks like this:*

```
$ comm old new
           Inventory
      Checked July 25, 1995
           Grommets: 99
 Insects: far too many
```

```
        Pegs: 66
        Ropes: 88
    Tarps: 11
  Tarps: 12
```

It's not at all obvious what the comm command does from its output. For one thing, you can't see that it's creating three columns, separated by tab characters. The results might be clearer if the output were reformatted into a table, as I've done here:

**LAB 5.2**

### Reformatted comm **Output**

| Column 1 | Column 2 | Column 3 |
|---|---|---|
| | | Inventory |
| | Checked July 25, 1995 | |
| | | Grommets: 99 |
| Insects: far too many | | |
| | | Pegs: 66 |
| | | Ropes: 88 |
| | Tarps: 11 | |
| Tarps: 12 | | |

The first column contains lines that are only in file 1. The second column contains lines that are only in file 2. The third column contains lines that are in both files.

This Exercise is a bit misleading because we didn't sort the file first. The comm command assumes that the two files are already in some kind of order. If the files aren't sorted, the comm command may miss some lines. Because of the simple changes here, we were able to skip the sort.

If you want to see an example, open one of the files and move the line "Pegs: 66" so it's the first line of the file, then run comm again. The line you've moved shows up in column 1 and column 2. The comm program thinks it's "only" in both files.

*Sort both files before running* comm *on them.*

Enter these commands:

```
comm -1 old new
comm -2 old new
comm -3 old new
comm -12 old new
```

**LAB
5.2**

**b)**  What do the −1, −2, and −3 options do?

*Answer: The −1 option keeps* comm *from printing column 1, the −2 option keeps* comm *from printing column 2, and the −3 option keeps* comm *from printing column 3.*

When I'm running comm, I usually only want to know which lines are really common, or I only care about one of the files. Although that information is in the default output, these options make the output much easier to read.

## 5.2.3  ANSWERS

From the parent directory of the chap05 and chap05.new directories, enter the following command:

```
dircmp chap05 chap05.new | more
```

**a)**  What does the dircmp command do? What does the output look like?

*Answer: The* dircmp *command compares two directories. The output looks like this:*

```
$ dircmp chap05 chap05.new | more -s

Jul 26 18:14 1998   chap05 only and chap05.new only
Page 1

./old                                              ./new

Jul 26 18:14 1998   Comparison of chap05 chap05.new
Page 1

directory           .
same                ./friday.txt
different           ./here
same                ./list
same                ./monday.txt
same                ./saturday.txt
```

```
same                    ./sunday.txt
same                    ./thursday.txt
same                    ./tuesday.txt
same                    ./wednesday.txt
same                    ./week.pax
same                    ./week.tar
```

(This directory has already been used for Lab 5.6.)

The Solaris version of `dircmp` formats and tabulates the information, which is why you must run it through `more`. The output on your system may be formatted differently, and you may not need to run the output through a pager to read it. In this case, we used `more -s` to eliminate most of the blank lines.

The output is largely self-explanatory. The first part (the first page, if you haven't used `more  -s`) contains two columns. The left column lists files that are only in the directory `chap05` and the right column lists files that are only in `chap05.new`.

The second part lists files that are in *both* directories. Each file is listed, along with whether the files are the same or different.

Enter the following command:

```
dircmp -s chap05 chap05.new | more
```

**b)** What does the `-s` option do?

*Answer: The `-s` option suppresses output about files that are the same.*

If all you want to know is the names of the files that differ, the `-s` option can save you some time.

# LAB 5.2 SELF-REVIEW QUESTIONS

In order to test your progress, you should be able to answer the following questions.

1) Which tool would you use on binary files?
   **a)** _____`cmp`
   **b)** _____`diff`

**LAB
5.2**

### Table 5.1 ■ Partial Output of `diff sales.yesterday sales.today`

151d150

< Ellison, Larry..........$8939.00

183c265

< Jorgenson, Klaus...$12899.00

—

> Jorgenson, Klaus.....$9219.00

---

2) What option would you give to `comm` to see only the lines that two files have in common?
   a) _____ `-1`
   b) _____ `-2`
   c) _____ `-3`
   d) _____ `-12`
   e) _____ `-13`
   f) _____ `-23`

3) Looking at the output in Table 5.1, in which file does Klaus have higher sales?
   a) _____ `sales.yesterday`
   b) _____ `sales.today`

4) Looking at the output in Table 5.1, what does the entry for Larry Ellison mean?
   a) _____Larry had no sales yesterday but did have sales today.
   b) _____Larry had sales yesterday but no sales today.
   c) _____Larry's sales changed between yesterday and today.

You have two temporary files created using `ls -lR`; each one lists all of the files in a directory and its subdirectories, like this:

```
ls -Rl dir1>listing1
ls -Rl dir2>listing2
```

5) Using temporary files created with the `ls -lR` commands above, which command could you use to get the same effect as `dircmp`? (Look at some `ls -lR` output before deciding.)
   a) _____cmp listing1 listing2
   b) _____diff listing1 listing2
   c) _____comm listing1 listing2

*Quiz answers appear in Appendix A, Section 5.2.*

# L A B   5 . 3

# CHECKING FILES

---

### LAB OBJECTIVES

After this Lab, you will be able to:

* Check a File's Sum

---

A file's *checksum* can help you determine if a file has changed in any way, either because it was damaged in transmission or because the hard drive is failing, or because someone changed it. A checksum is a number generated from the file; if the file changes, the checksum changes. You can see if a file has changed by comparing the file's current checksum with its original checksum.

When you have a problem with a transferred or copied file, the system administrator may ask you for the checksum of the file. He or she will compare it to the original to see if the files are identical.

## LAB 5.3 EXERCISES

### 5.3.1 CHECK A FILE'S SUM

Enter the following commands:

```
sum monday.txt
sum -r monday.txt
cksum monday.txt
```

**a)** What do the outputs look like?

_____

_____

Change the contents of the file `monday.txt` and run those three commands again.

> **b)** How do the outputs differ?

_____

_____

# LAB 5.3 EXERCISE ANSWERS

## 5.3.1 ANSWERS

Enter the following commands:

```
sum monday.txt
sum -r monday.txt
cksum monday.txt
```

**a)** What do the outputs look like?

*Answer: Each command prints a number (the checksum), a second number, and the name of the file. The exact numbers depend upon the contents of the file. Example output is shown here:*

```
$ sum week.pax
48239 16 week.pax
$ sum -r week.pax
48062    16 week.pax
$ cksum week.pax
3073962054     8192    week.pax
```

A checksum is a way of generating a number based on the contents of a file. The simplest form of checksum is a bit like numerology: You add the value of each character in the file and use that number as the checksum. However, in order to prevent two nearly identical files from getting the same total, the formula has to be more complicated than that.

Each of these programs produces a different number, so when you're checking the checksum of a file, make sure you know which command was used to get the original checksum. The `sum` command generates the traditional checksum found on Solaris and other System V systems, but `sum -r` is the number that would be generated on a BSD system. The `cksum` program produces yet another number.

I recommend using the `cksum` program, if you can, because the value it produces is the same whether you're on a Solaris system or a BSD system.

Change the contents of the file `monday.txt` and run those three commands again.

**b)** How do the outputs differ?

*Answer: The sums are different.*

If a file changes, its checksum changes. The most common use of a checksum is to see if a file transferred correctly. Suppose you got a copy of an archive from an FTP site, but it doesn't uncompress correctly. You contact the administrator of the FTP site and get the checksum for the file, and then run the same checksum command on your copy. If the number is the same, then you can be fairly sure it transferred correctly. If the numbers are different, it's likely there was a problem and you should transfer the file again. (Usually the problem is that the `ftp` session had the `ascii` setting on instead of the `binary` setting.)

Checksums are not always correct. Two different files *can* get the same number, and a file *can* be changed in a way that won't change its checksum. Though this is possible, it is very unlikely.

# LAB 5.3 SELF-REVIEW QUESTIONS

In order to test your progress, you should be able to answer the following questions.

**1)** What is a checksum?
 **a)** _____The sum of all the bits in the file.
 **b)** _____The size of the file.
 **c)** _____The total amount of money you have spent from your checking account.
 **d)** _____A number used to determine if a file's contents have been changed or corrupted.

**2)** To use checksums to determine if a file has been corrupted, which of the following do you need?
 **a)** _____The original size of the file and the checksum.
 **b)** _____The original checksum.
 **c)** _____The original checksum and the `sum` command.
 **d)** _____The original checksum and the command used to create it.

**3)** No two files can have the same checksum.
 **a)** _____True
 **b)** _____False
 **c)** _____False, but it's unlikely that they will

**4)** You have copied a file to another system using `ftp` with the `ascii` setting. The checksum for the original file is different from the checksum for the copy. Which action should you take to transmit a non-corrupted copy?

**a)** _____Run the checksums again.

**b)** _____Copy the file again, in case it was corrupted on the way.

**c)** _____Copy the file again, but use the `binary` setting.

**d)** _____Send the file by e-mail.

**e)** _____Either (a) or (b).

**f)** _____Either (c) or (d).

**g)** _____Either (a) or (c).

**5)** You are on a Solaris system and are transferring a file to a BSD system. You want to check the transfer using a checksum. Which commands should you use to generate the checksum?

**a)** _____`sum` on both machines

**b)** _____`cksum` on both machines

**c)** _____`sum -r` on the Solaris machine and `sum` on the BSD machine.

**d)** _____Either (a) or (b).

**e)** _____Either (b) or (c).

**f)** _____Any of the above.

*Quiz answers appear in Appendix A, Section 5.3.*

# LAB 5.4

# CALENDARS

> ## LAB OBJECTIVES
>
> After this Lab, you will be able to:
>
> - Display the Month and Year
> - Schedule and Display Reminders

Even computer programmers have appointments. Two programs are provided to help you keep track of the days and months. The `cal` program presents calendars; the `calendar` program reminds you of dates and appointments.

## LAB 5.4 EXERCISES

### 5.4.1 DISPLAY THE MONTH AND YEAR

In your home directory, enter the following command:

```
cal
```

**a)** What is displayed?

_____

_____

Enter the following command:

```
cal 98
```

**b)** What is displayed?

_____

_____

---

### 5.4.2 SCHEDULE AND DISPLAY REMINDERS

In your current directory, open or create the file `calendar` and add the following lines, substituting today's date for September 24 and tomorrow's for September 25.

```
09/24 Read Chapter 16
Sept 25 Read Chapter 7
Dec 25 Christmas
Jan 1 Happy New Year! (Don't come in to work)
```

Enter the following command:

```
calendar
```

**a)** What does the `calendar` command do?

_____

_____

Change directories and enter the `calendar` command again.

**b)** What happens?

_____

_____

## LAB 5.4 EXERCISE ANSWERS

### 5.4.1 ANSWERS

In your home directory, enter the following command:

```
cal
```

**a)** What is displayed?

*Answer: The command displays the calendar for the current month.*

You can tell it's the current month by the date at the top. Without any arguments, the `cal` command displays the calendar for the current month.

In order to display the entire year, you must add the year as an argument. If you want to look at the first half of the year, you should pipe the output through `more`.

Enter the following command:

```
cal 98
```

**LAB
5.4**

**b)** What is displayed?

*Answer: The command displays the calendar for the year 98.*

The `cal` command requires the *entire* year as an argument. If you enter only 98, it treats it as the year 98 AD.

If you want to display only a particular month, enter the month and the year. Some versions of `cal` accept month names, but the version on Solaris only accepts numbers for months.

You can only display calendars back to the year 1; trying to give `cal` a date before year 1 is an error.

The calendar used is our current calendar, the Gregorian calendar. It removes the 11 days that were taken out of September in 1752 to account for missed leap years. (Use the command `cal 9 1752` to see that calendar.)

## 5.4.2 SCHEDULE AND DISPLAY REMINDERS

In your current directory, open or create the file `calendar` and add the following lines, substituting today's date for September 24 and tomorrow's for September 25.

```
09/24 Read Chapter 16
Sept 25 Read Chapter 7
```

Enter the following command:

```
calendar
```

**a)** What does the `calendar` command do?

*Answer: The* `calendar` *command displays all entries for today and tomorrow. (On Fridays and weekends, "tomorrow" goes all the way to Monday.)*

Use the `calendar` command to remind you of appointments and deadlines. The easiest way is to set up your startup files (see Chapter 7, "Customizing Your Environment") to run the `calendar` command when you log in.

The appointment entries in the `calendar` file aren't rigidly formatted. Each entry can take up only one line, and the date must appear somewhere on that line, with the month *before* the day. Most abbreviations for the month are acceptable.

Some systems use a slightly different version of the `calendar` program that requires the date to be at the beginning of the line.

The entries in the `calendar` file don't have to be in any particular order.

Change directories and enter the `calendar` command again.

**b)** What happens?

*Answer: Nothing. There is no* `calendar` *file in the current directory.*

The `calendar` program only checks your current directory. While this means you can't check your appointments from any directory on the system, it also means you can set up project-specific reminders by creating a `calendar` file in a project directory. The system administrator can also run the `calendar` for all users; the system administrator's version can send mail to users if they have an appointment to be kept.

## LAB 5.4 SELF-REVIEW QUESTIONS

In order to test your progress, you should be able to answer the following questions.

1) Which command displays the calendar for August 1961?
   a) _____calendar August 1961
   b) _____cal August 1961
   c) _____cal 8 61
   d) _____cal 8 1961
   e) _____calendar 8 1961

**2)** Which of these lines in the `calendar` file would *not* schedule an appointment for Christmas Day?

**a)** _____Dinner at Peggy's, Dec 25,

**b)** _____december 25 dinner with peg and family 5:30

**c)** _____a bit early but peggy wants dinner dec 25

**d)** _____Christmas day (dinner with the Pegster) 5:30ish

**e)** _____12/25 Dinner, Elizabeth's, 17:30; red wine (remember her allergies)

**3)** Once you've set up a `calendar` file in your home directory, you can check it from any other directory by typing `calendar`.

**a)** _____True

**b)** _____False

**4)** Which of these commands is best for looking at the calendars for January and February of 2001?

**a)** \_\_\_\_\_cal 1 2001

**b)** \_\_\_\_\_cal 2001

**c)** \_\_\_\_\_cal 1 2 2001

**d)** \_\_\_\_\_cal 2001 | more

**e)** \_\_\_\_\_cal 1 3 2001 | head

**5)** The `calendar` file must be sorted by date (using the `sort` command).

**a)** \_\_\_\_\_True

**b)** \_\_\_\_\_False

*Quiz answers appear in Appendix A, Section 5.4.*

**LAB
5.4**

# L A B   5 . 5

# FINDING TEXT WITHIN A SUBTREE

---

### LAB OBJECTIVES

After this Lab, you will be able to:

- Use `find -exec` to Grep a Tree
- Use `xargs` to Grep a Tree

---

In the directory `chap05` (created in Lab 5.6), create a text file that contains the word "epoch." (We're using "epoch" only because it's an unusual word and unlikely to be in any other text files in your home directory. You may substitute another word if you want.)

## LAB 5.5 EXERCISES

### 5.5.1 USE FIND -EXEC TO GREP A TREE

Enter the following command:

```
find ~ -type f -exec grep -l epoch {} \;
```

**a)** What is the `-exec` operator? What does the `find` command do?

_____

_____

**b)** Why is the −1 option necessary in the grep command?

_____

_____

## 5.5.2 USE XARGS TO GREP A TREE

Enter the following command:

```
find ~ -type f -print | xargs grep epoch
```

**a)** How does the output compare?

_____

_____

**b)** Should grep be given the −1 option?

_____

_____

LAB
5.5

# LAB 5.5 EXERCISE ANSWERS

## 5.5.1 USE FIND -EXEC TO GREP A TREE

Enter the following command:

```
find ~ -type f -exec grep -1 epoch {} \;
```

**a)** What is the −exec operator? What does this find command do?

*Answer: The −exec operator runs a command (grep in this case) on each file found by the find command. This command finds all files (−type f) under your home directory and uses grep to check the file for the string "epoch."*

When running a command using -exec, the {} is a placeholder for the file name. For instance, when the command finds the file calendar, the command it runs will be grep -1 epoch calendar \;. The semicolon is needed to end the command, and the \ is needed to escape the semicolon from the shell.

The -type operator is also new. You can specify each of the file types using -type, but files (f) and directories (d) are the ones you will use most often. In this case, the type is specified to avoid running grep commands on directories.

**b)**   Why is the -l option necessary in the grep command?

*Answer: The -l option forces grep to print the file's name.*

Each grep command is run with a single file argument. When grep has only a single file argument, it doesn't print the file name. Without the -l option, the grep command would print any matching lines, but not the file's name. That would make the search less useful. (On some systems, there is a -o option to grep that forces grep to print the file name, even if there is only one argument. You could use that option instead of -l, if it's available on your system. It is not available on Solaris.) You might also want to redirect the output of grep to /dev/null.

Another way to "fool" grep into thinking there are more files on the line is by giving the name of another file that won't contain the word, /dev/null. If the command line is given as:

```
find ~ -type f -exec grep epoch {} /dev/null \;
```

Then the grep command always has two file names on the command line, and you know that /dev/null will never contain the word, since /dev/null never contains anything.

The actual options you provide to grep will depend upon what you're trying to do in your search.

## 5.5.2   Use xargs to Grep a Tree

Enter the following command:

```
find ~ -type f -print | xargs grep epoch
```

**a)**   How does the output compare?

*Answer: The output of the* xargs *command looks like this:*

```
./chap05/list
```

The xargs command exists to handle long argument lists. It adds arguments to the end of a command line. The xargs command reads a list (of arguments) from standard input, breaks it into smaller chunks if necessary, and hands those chunks to a command (grep in this case). If you try to run a command using wildcards and get an error like "Argument list too long," then you should consider using xargs.

The xargs command won't work for all commands, only for those where the file arguments come last on the command line. (For example, you can't use it to copy or move files; the cp and mv files require a target directory as the last argument on the line.) For regular users, the only common use I've seen for xargs is searching a file tree. For that purpose it works very well.

**b)**   Should grep be given the -1 option?

> *Answer: Yes, although it's not required.*

Here's why: When the xargs command gets the list of file names, you don't know how many files are in the list. When xargs breaks the list into chunks, you have no way of knowing if the last chunk will contain only one file name. If it does, then even if the pattern you're searching for is in the last file, grep won't print the file's name.

Why use xargs rather than -exec? The reason is that it takes time for the computer to start a new program. The -exec version of the search is almost always slower than the xargs version. If there are a lot of files, the system has to start grep up for *every* file it finds; with the xargs version, it starts fewer programs running grep on several groups of files.

To see this for yourself, you can use the time command. In the Korn Shell, the time command lists the time required for a command to run. Here are the results for my home directory tree, which contains 79 files:

```
$ time find ~ -type f -exec grep -1 epoch {} \;
/usr/home/johnmc/chap05/list

real    0m3.74s
user    0m0.83s
sys     0m2.58s
```

The "real" time is the total amount of time the command took. (You can ignore the other two numbers; they deal with how the time was spent.) The -exec version of the search took 3.74 seconds to search 79 files on my system.

LAB
5.5

```
$ time find ~ -type f -print | xargs grep -l epoch
/usr/home/johnmc/chap05/list

real    0m0.35s
user    0m0.12s
sys     0m0.21s
```

The `xargs` version of the search took only 0.35 seconds. It was over 3 seconds faster! That's the kind of difference that people can notice. You can imagine how much longer the `-exec` version would take over the entire file system, with thousands of files (or more).

# LAB 5.5 SELF-REVIEW QUESTIONS

In order to test your progress, you should be able to answer the following questions.

1) The `-exec` operator can be used to run any command as part of `find`.
   **a)** _____True
   **b)** _____False

2) The advantage of using `xargs` over `-exec` is which of the following?
   **a)** _____The `xargs` version handles longer file lists.
   **b)** _____The `-l` option isn't needed to get the file name in output for the `xargs` version.
   **c)** _____The `-exec` option is not supported by all versions of `find`.
   **d)** _____The `xargs` version of the command is faster.

3) Which of the following is true of the `xargs` command?
   **a)** _____It repeats its arguments.
   **b)** _____It uses its standard input as arguments to another command.
   **c)** _____It copies its arguments to standard output.
   **d)** _____It runs a command in the background.

4) Identify the mistake in this command:

   ```
   find . -name \*.txt -type f -exec grep -l {} ;
   ```

   **a)** _____The argument to the `-name` operator should be in quotation marks.
   **b)** _____The argument to the `-name` operator should be in apostrophes.
   **c)** _____The `-type` operator should come before the `-name` operator.
   **d)** _____Each parenthesis should have a backslash before it.
   **e)** _____The semicolon should be escaped.

*Quiz answers appear in Appendix A, Section 5.5.*

# L A B   5 . 6

# ARCHIVING FILES

---

**LAB OBJECTIVES**

After this Lab, you will be able to:

- Archive with `tar`
- Archive with `pax`
- Compress Files

---

Archiving is combining groups of files into a single file for storage or copying. (Common DOS or Windows programs for creating file archives are PKZip and WinZip.) The archive file might be compressed as well, to save space. On UNIX systems, these two actions are usually handled by separate programs.

Four archiving programs are common on UNIX systems. They are `cpio`, `tar`, `pax`, and `ar`.

- The `cpio` program copies all files listed on the input to its standard output or to a file. This was the System V (original UNIX) archiving program. The name stands for "*cp* *i*nput to *o*utput."

- The `tar` program copies the files named on the command line to (or from) a tape drive or a file. This was the BSD archiving program. The name stands for "*t*ape *ar*chiver."

- The `pax` program was created to standardize archives between the two types of UNIX systems. The name is supposed to stand for "*p*ortable *a*rchive e*x*change" but the arguments while `pax` was being created were fierce, and I think the name was also wish fulfillment—"pax" is Latin for "peace."

- The `ar` program also creates archives, but it's only used by programmers. It could be used to create other kinds of archives, but nobody does.

**LAB
5.6**

We will only work with `tar` and `pax` in this Lab.

Before you can archive files, you'll need some files. Create a directory named `chap05`. In it, create (or rename) some text files with the names of the week (that is, `monday.txt`, `tuesday.txt`, and so on to `sunday.txt`). The files must contain some text, but the content doesn't matter.

# LAB 5.6 EXERCISES

### 5.6.1 ARCHIVE WITH TAR

Enter the following command:

```
tar -cvf week.tar *.txt
```

**a)** What does the `tar` command do?

_____

_____

**b)** Open the `week.tar` file using an editor (`vi` or `emacs`). What do you see?

_____

_____

Enter the following command:

```
tar -tvf week.tar
```

**c)** What does the `-t` option do?

_____

_____

Enter the following commands:

```
cp week.tar /tmp
cd /tmp
tar -xvf week.tar tuesday.txt thursday.txt
```

**d)** What does the -x option do?

_____

_____


Remove your files from the /tmp directory and return to your previous directory.

## 5.6.2 ARCHIVE WITH PAX

Enter the following command:

```
pax -w -f week.pax *.txt
```

**a)** What does the pax -w command do?

_____

_____


**b)** Which file is larger, week.pax or week.tar?

_____

_____

Enter the following commands:

```
cp week.tar /tmp
cd /tmp
pax -r -f week.pax tuesday.txt
```

**c)** What does the -r option do?

_____

_____


Remove your files from the /tmp directory and return to your previous directory.

Enter the following command:

```
pax -f week.pax
```

**d)** What does the `pax` command do without the `-w` or `-r` options?

_____

_____

Change directories so you're in the parent directory of the `chap05` directory.

Enter the following commands:

```
mkdir chap05_new
pax -r -w chap05 chap05_new
```

**e)** What does the `pax` command do with both the `-w` and `-r` options?

_____

_____

### 5.6.3 COMPRESS FILES

Enter the following commands:

**LAB
5.6**

```
compress week.tar
ls
```

**a)** What happens to the `week.tar` archive?

_____

_____

**b)** How large is the `week.tar.Z` file?

_____

_____

Enter the following commands:

```
uncompress week.tar
ls
```

**c)** What happens to the `week.tar.Z` file?

_____

_____

# LAB 5.6 EXERCISE ANSWERS

## 5.6.1 ARCHIVE WITH TAR

Enter the following command:

```
tar -cvf week.tar *.txt
```

**a)** What does the `tar` command do?

*Answer: It creates an archive file named* `week.tar` *that contains all of the files with names ending in* `.txt`*.*

The archive file (also called the tar file or the tarball) is one file that contains all the other files named on the command line. The `-c` option *creates* a tar file. If a tar file already exists named `week.tar`, the `-c` option causes `tar` to replace it with a new tar file. (If you want to add files, use the `-u` option to "update" the archive instead.)

The `-f` option specifies that the tar archive is a file named `week.tar`. You need the `-f` option. Without the option, the `tar` command assumes you are creating a backup file on a tape drive, and it tries to write to a magnetic tape machine.

The `-v` option tells `tar` to be verbose, to print more messages than usual about what it is doing.

**b)** Open the `week.tar` file using an editor (`vi` or `emacs`). What can you see?

*Answer: The tar file is a text file. The contents might look something like this:*

```
friday.txt0100644000001650000144000000000007065544524470013
4440ustar00johnmcuser00001460000006Friday
Friday is my favorite day of the week.
```

The files are joined together (almost as if you had used `cat` to butt them together) but each file starts off with a line describing it: the name of the file, who owns it, what group the owner belongs to, the format ("ustar"

**LAB
5.6**

in this case), and so on. Depending on your version of `tar`, it may support several storage formats, but "ustar" is the standard format.

Tar files are not made into binary files by being tar files. They are not compressed in any way. If a tar file contains only text files, you can use `grep` on it. You can't use `grep` on a compressed file.

To create an archive with `cpio`, use `find` to get a list of files. For example:

```
find . -name \*.txt | cpio > week.cpio
```

The file `week.cpio` is an archive of all of the files listed by the `find` command, much like `week.tar`. However, `tar` cannot read `cpio` archives and `cpio` cannot read `tar` archives. (The `pax` command in Lab 5.6.2 can read both kinds of archives.) Some `cpio` archives *are* binary files (it depends upon the options). The lines at the start of each file in the archive are lines that can only be read by the `cpio` command.

Enter the following command:

```
tar -tvf week.tar
```

**c)**    What does the   `-t` option do?

*Answer: The `-t` option causes `tar` to list the table of contents for the tar file. The `-v` option causes `tar` to print more verbose output; without `-v`, `tar` lists only the file names.*

The verbose output looks like the `ls -l` output, so you should be able to figure out what most of it means:

```
tar: blocksize = 16
-rw-r--r-- 117/100     7 Jul 19 16:20 1998 friday.txt
-rw-r--r-- 117/100     7 Jul 19 16:20 1998 monday.txt
-rw-r--r-- 117/100     9 Jul 19 16:20 1998 saturday.txt
-rw-r--r-- 117/100     7 Jul 19 16:20 1998 sunday.txt
-rw-r--r-- 117/100     9 Jul 19 16:20 1998 thursday.txt
-rw-r--r-- 117/100     8 Jul 19 16:20 1998 tuesday.txt
-rw-r--r-- 117/100    10 Jul 19 16:20 1998 wednesday.txt
```

The first line describes the blocksize used in creating the archive file. You can normally ignore this; it is important only if you are actually writing to magnetic tape.

Each line presents the following information:

- The file's permissions.
- The owner's numeric user ID.
- The file's numeric group ID.
- The size of the file in bytes (you can see that these are all very small files: 7, 8, 9, and 10 bytes).
- The time and date of creation.
- The name of the file. This can be a partial path name, including subdirectories.

If you give the name of a directory in the archive, the `tar` command will print all of the files in that directory. For example, the `man.tar` archive contains a directory called `man05`, which contains manual pages:

```
$ tar tvf man.tar man05
drwxr-xr-x 117/100        0 Aug  3 23:44 1998 man05/
-r—r—r— 117/100     1738 Aug  3 23:43 1998 man05/cal.1
-r—r—r— 117/100     3956 Aug  3 23:43 1998
man05/calendar.1
-r—r—r— 117/100     2359 Aug  3 23:43 1998 man05/cmp.1
```

The command `tar tvf man.tar man` does nothing. The argument "man" has to be the entire name of the directory, not just part of the name. When `tar` gets an argument, it looks for a file or directory by that name; it doesn't match parts of names.

**LAB 5.6**

Incidentally, notice that no dash was used before `tvf` in this example. This behavior varies between UNIX systems, but most versions of `tar` treat the first argument as a "subcommand" or a "function" and don't require a dash.

To list the contents of a `cpio` archive, use the `-t` option and redirect the archive from standard input, like this:

```
cpio -t < week.cpio
```

**Enter the following commands:**

```
cp week.tar /tmp
cd /tmp
tar -xvf week.tar tuesday.txt thursday.txt
```

**d)** What does the −x option do?

*Answer: The −x option causes* tar *to extract the files named on the command line.*

The output might look something like this:

```
$ tar -xvf week.tar tuesday.txt thursday.txt
x thursday.txt, 9 bytes, 1 tape blocks
x tuesday.txt, 66 bytes, 1 tape blocks
```

Extracting all files is simple. The difficulty is in extracting only *some* files. To extract specific files, you must specify the file's name, in full. Wild-cards don't usually work. You need to provide the file's complete name. If you give a directory name, tar extracts the directory and its contents. For instance, if the tar -tv command lists backup/ as part of the file name, you can extract the entire backup directory with the command tar -xvf tarfile.tar backup.

To extract the files of a cpio archive, use the −i option, and use the archive as the command's input:

```
cpio -i < week.cpio
```

## 5.6.2  ARCHIVE WITH PAX

Enter the following command:

```
pax -w -f week.pax *.txt
```

**a)** What does the pax  −w command do?

*Answer: The* pax *command works with archives. With the* −w *option,* pax *creates ("writes") an archive named* week.pax *that contains all of the files in the directory with names ending in .txt.*

In the early days, people who used System V UNIX used the program cpio, and people who used BSD UNIX used the program tar. When the POSIX committee was trying to pick a standard program, there were terrible fights over which of the two programs should be made standard. After a great deal of arguing and name-calling by both sides, the POSIX committee decided to create a *new* program that does everything *both* of the old programs did. The new program is pax.

The pax program does everything the tar program does, but uses slightly different options. By default, it even stores files in the same format that the `tar` command does. You can usually use `pax` to extract a tar file or a `cpio` archive.

**b)** Which file is larger, `week.pax` or `week.tar`?

*Answer: The files are the same size.*

Because `pax` behaves like `tar` (unless you give the correct options), it's not surprising that the two files are the same size. In fact, if you archive the same files, the two archives are identical.

Enter the following commands:

```
cp week.tar /tmp
cd /tmp
pax -r -f week.pax tuesday.txt
```

**c)** What does the `-r` option do?

*Answer: The `-r` option causes `pax` to extract all of the files.*

In `pax`, the `-r` option reads a file, the equivalent of extracting it in `tar`, and the `-w` option writes a file, the equivalent of creating it in `tar`.

Remove your files from the `/tmp` directory and return to your previous directory.

Enter the following command:

```
pax -f week.pax
```

**d)** What does the `pax` command do without the `-w` or `-r` options?

*Answer: Without either `-r` or `-w`, `pax` lists the contents of the file.*

The `pax` command without the `-r` or `-w` options behaves like the `tar -t` command.

Sometimes you'll see two copies of the same file in an archive. This happens after you try to update an archive by using `pax -w -u` (the `-u` is for update). The problem is that `tar` was originally written to work with magnetic tape drives. With a magnetic tape, you can't replace just one file in the middle. The new file is almost always a different size than the original. If the new file's too short, you leave bits of the old file in place, and if the file's too long, you write over the next file. When `tar` was written, they decided on a different approach. When you update an archive, the `tar` command doesn't replace the original version of the file, it adds the new version to the end of the archive. The `pax` program does the same thing.

**LAB 5.6**

When the archive is unpacked, the newer version will replace the earlier version, but both versions are still in the archive. This doesn't matter a lot (unless you're replacing a *lot* of files), but it bothers some people that the older files are still in the archive, taking up space.

Change directories so you're in the parent directory of the chap05 directory.

Enter the following commands:

```
mkdir chap05_new
pax -r -w chap05 chap_new
```

**e)** What does the pax command do with both the −w and −r options?

*Answer: With both options supplied, the pax command copies a directory tree.*

I mention this only because you might accidentally include both options some day and be surprised.

This behavior comes about because the pax command was invented to replace two commands, tar and cpio. Without file operands, pax behaves like cpio. The cpio command can also be used to copy an entire directory tree. (It's like creating an archive and unpacking an archive, but without using an archive as the middle step.) The pax command can also copy the directory tree, as shown in this Exercise.

### 5.6.3 COMPRESS FILES

Enter the following commands:

```
compress week.tar
ls
```

**a)** What happens to the week.tar archive?

*Answer: The file is replaced by the compressed file, week.tar.Z.*

The compress command shrinks files. There have been several compression commands over the history of UNIX, with names like pack and unpack. The compress command seems to be the longest-lived. (However, for copyright reasons, compress is often missing from systems that are not "official" UNIX systems.)

When you compress a file, the program replaces the original file with the compressed version, and adds a .Z to the name.

**b)**   How large is the `week.tar.Z` file?

> *Answer: This varies. Text files can get quite small, while executable files don't shrink nearly as much.*

The amount of compression depends strongly on the contents of the archive. In a text-only archive, the compressed file is usually half the size, or a quarter, or less. If the archive contains binary files (such as images or spreadsheet files or programs), the compressed file tends to be 60 percent the size of the original, but it may not be. (There are some very odd files that turn out to be *larger* when they're compressed, but you're unlikely to run into them.)

Because compressed files are smaller, archived-and-compressed files are often transmitted using `ftp` or `rcp` or `uucp`. Rather than copying every file in a directory tree, it's easier to transfer a single compressed archive. When the archive is uncompressed and unpacked, the original directory tree is recreated on your system.

Enter the following commands:

```
uncompress week.tar
ls
```

**c)**   What happens to the `week.tar.Z` file?

> *Answer: The file goes away and is replaced by* `week.tar`.

Notice that you don't have to specify the `.Z` extension to the file; the `compress` program is smart enough to figure that out for itself.

Other compression programs that may be on your system are `zip` (and its counterpart `unzip`) and `gzip` (and its counterpart `gunzip`). Files compressed with `zip` have the extension `.zip` and are uncompressed with `unzip`. Files compressed with `gzip` have the extension `.gz` (or sometimes `.tgz` if it's a compressed tar file) and are uncompressed with `gunzip`.

Generally speaking, you need the same compression program to uncompress a file as you used to compress it. However, because of the copyright restrictions on `compress`, the authors of `gzip` and `gunzip` made sure that they could uncompress files that had been compressed with `compress`. And the authors of `zip` and `unzip` made sure that their programs could uncompress archives created on PCs with `pkzip` and WinZip.

**LAB
5.6**

# LAB 5.6  SELF-REVIEW QUESTIONS

In order to test your progress, you should be able to answer the following questions.

**1)** Both `tar` and `pax` compress the archives they create.
    **a)** _____True
    **b)** _____False

**2)** How do you extract or list a directory from a `tar` archive?
    **a)** _____You can specify the directory name with wildcards.
    **b)** _____You must specify the directory name exactly, but the files in that directory will be extracted.
    **c)** _____You must specify each file name precisely.

**3)** Match the option with the behavior of `pax`.
    **a)** Create an archive                **i)** `-r`
    **b)** Copy a directory tree           **ii)** `-w`
    **c)** Display the contents of an archive    **iii)** `-r -w`
    **d)** Extract files from an archive       **iv)** Neither `-r` nor `-w`

**4)** Match the file extension with the compression program.
    **a)** `compress`        **i)** `.gz`
    **b)** `zip`            **ii)** `.tgz`
    **c)** `gzip`          **iii)** `.zip`
    **d)** `tar` and `gzip`   **iv)** `.Z`

**5)** You must specify the `.Z` extension on the end of a file to `uncompress` it.
    **a)** _____True
    **b)** _____False

*Quiz answers appear in Appendix A, Section 5.6.*

**LAB
5.6**

# C H A P T E R   5

# TEST YOUR THINKING

Congratulations! You have just been assigned the task of maintaining the documentation for your group's project. You have inherited this from a co-worker, who inherited it from someone else. The first thing other workers have done is copied files from the "official" documentation directory into their home directory and changed them. Some have not bothered to put the fixed copies back in the official directory. Your job is to bring all of the official directory up to date by incorporating everyone's changes.

1) There are three stages to the problem: Finding all of the changed files, comparing them, and incorporating the changes into the official versions of the files.

   a) How will you find all of the files? Can you think of an automated way to do it?

   b) How will you compare the files? If there are two changed copies of the same file, how will you update the official version? What if someone copied the entire documentation directory into his or her home directory?

   c) How will you update the files in the official directory?

2) Before you begin, should you save a copy of the existing documentation? How?

3) Since there are commands you will be using frequently, can you think of a way to use the history file to your advantage in this process?

4) Would it be a good idea to maintain a `calendar` file in the project directory? If so, why? If not, why not?

# THE EMACS EDITOR

 *The Emacs editor is a very popular editor, and many people find it much easier to use than* vi. *Unfortunately, it's not everywhere.*

The GNU Emacs editor is a popular editor that's available for almost every platform. Besides basic editing, it does so much that many people start Emacs and never leave it. They run commands from Emacs, they read Usenet news and electronic mail in e-mail, and they may even be able to browse the World Wide Web in Emacs.

# L A B   6 . 1

# A BASIC EMACS SESSION

> ## LAB OBJECTIVES
>
> After this Lab, you will be able to:
>
> - Start Emacs
> - Add Text
> - Save the File
> - Exit Emacs

The name "Emacs" stands for "Extensible Macro" editor. The Free Software Foundation describes Emacs as "an extensible, customizable, self-documenting, full-screen editor." This makes Emacs as intimidating, in its own way, as vi. Emacs also has a set of commands that are just as quirky as those of vi. (I'm going to follow the practice of the Emacs documentation by referring to the editor as Emacs instead of emacs except when I specifically mean the command.)

On the other hand, Emacs is a modeless editor: All commands are done using special key combinations; any text you type goes into the file you're editing. An "a" is always an a; it's never a command to switch modes. Most people find Emacs easier to use than vi.

Even if Emacs is not available on the system you're using, it's highly likely there are other editors that use the same commands. (Other editors that use the Emacs command set include jed, jove, and gmacs.)

There is also no reason why you can't use both editors. If you prefer to write new text with Emacs and edit with vi, that's fine.

The basic Emacs screen has three parts: the *main buffer*, the *mode line*, and the *minibuffer*.

- The main buffer window displays the file you're editing.
- The mode line contains information about the file.
- The minibuffer is where error messages are displayed. It also displays any command over one character, as you type it.

## EMACS COMMANDS

All Emacs commands are actually words, such as "save-buffers-kill-emacs" (that's the save-and-exit command). The commonly used commands have key combinations assigned to them. (In Emacs terminology, assigning a key combination is "binding" the key combination to the command. You may see references to the key combination that a command is bound to.) Because there are so many commands, Emacs uses more key combinations than any other program I know of.

The key combinations are referred to as "Shift," "Control," and "Meta" combinations. They may be used in combination (you can have a Control-Shift combination).

The Shift key is the one you use to create uppercase letters. Hold it down while you press the other key. Shift-X is created by holding down the Shift key and pressing the X key.

The Control key is usually labeled "Control." Like the Shift key, you hold it down while you press the other key. Control-X is created by holding down the Control key and pressing the X key. (This is the same key you've been using for Control-C.)  Although the key ("X" in this case) is written in uppercase, you don't have to press the Shift key too. (You *do* have to press the Shift key to get a command like Control-@, because the only way to get an @ key on most keyboards is by pressing Shift-2. Control-@ is actually Control-Shift-2.)

The Meta key may or may not exist on your keyboard. If it does, you can generate Meta X by holding down the Meta key and then pressing the X key. It's more likely that your keyboard has no Meta key. You can still get the same effect by pressing Escape and then pressing the other key. Meta X is created by pressing Escape and then by pressing the X key. (Although the Emacs documentation writes Control and Meta combinations using uppercase letters, you don't have to use uppercase letters. You can create the Meta X combination by pressing Escape and then the x key.)

There is extensive on-line help available in Emacs, available by pressing Control-H. (On most keyboards, that's also the Backspace key.) Some people like Emacs' on-line help. Some people do not. Don't feel bad if you find the on-line help harder to understand and use than the editor.

*When you get in trouble in Emacs, you can usually get out of it by typing Control-G one or two times. The Control-G command cancels or interrupts the current Emacs command.*

## EMACS AND WINDOWS AND FRAMES

Because Emacs was written before there were graphical user interfaces like X Windows, it uses the term "window" to refer to a buffer display. The Emacs commands and documentation use the word "frame" to describe new (graphic) windows created by X Windows.

On any terminal type, you can have more than one window, but only on an X Windows display can you have more than one frame.

If you are using Emacs with X Windows, be warned that Emacs may pop up new frames for you. To go back to the original frame, click on it with your mouse. After you've clicked on the original frame, you can get rid of the extra frames with the command Control-X 1.

# LAB 6.1 EXERCISES

## 6.1.1 START EMACS

Enter the following command:

```
emacs
```

**a)** What is the name of the file you are editing? Of the buffer?

_____

_____

**b)** What mode are you in?

_____

_____

## 6.1.2 ADD TEXT

Type the following line; press Enter at the end of the line.

```
Memo: All of yor
```

**a)** What happens to the mode line?

_____

_____

**b)** Press Backspace. What happens?

_____

_____

Press Control-G, then press the Delete key.

**c)** What does the Delete key do?

_____

_____

Now press the "u" key.

## 6.1.3 SAVE THE FILE

Give the command Control-X Control-S. (Hold down Control while you press X, then hold down control while you press S.)

**a)** What happens?

_____

_____

Enter the following file name:

```
memo2
```

**b)** What happens?

_____

_____

Now add more text, as follows:

    Condolences to Dana.

Give the following command:

    Control-X Control-S

**c)** What name is the file saved under this time?

_____

_____

### 6.1.4  EXIT EMACS

Type the following text. Remember to press Enter at the end of each line.

> We're sorry to announce that Dana's snake Tycho passed
> away in a fatal vacuum cleaner incident. Long-term
> employees will remember Tycho from his lengthy stay in
> the air ducts. (Danielle still hasn't recovered from
> having Tycho drop onto her desk.) Our condolences to
> Dana.
>
> The no-pets-in-the-office rule is now withdrawn.

Give the command Control-X Control-C.

**a)** What options does Emacs provide?

_____

_____

**b)** What happens when you enter "y"?

# LAB 6.1 EXERCISE ANSWERS

## 6.1.1 ANSWERS

Enter the following command:

```
emacs
```

**a)** What is the name of the file you are editing? Of the buffer?

*Answer: The file has no name yet. The buffer is named *scratch*.*

Figure 6.1 shows the Emacs screen in this Exercise.

**Figure 6.1** ■ **The parts of the Emacs screen: window, mode line, and minibuffer.**

Just like vi, Emacs doesn't edit the file "in place." Instead, it makes a copy inside itself, in a storage area called a *buffer*. You make changes to the version in the buffer, and save them to the disk.

Usually the buffer has the same name as the file. In this case, Emacs doesn't "know" the name of the file, so it starts in a default buffer named *scratch*. Saving the file assigns the same name to the buffer.

**b)**   What mode are you in?

*Answer: You are in "Lisp Interaction Mode" or in "Fundamental Mode."*

The current mode is displayed on the mode line in parentheses. Depending on how your system is set up, you could be in any of the Emacs modes, but you are most likely to be in "Lisp Interaction Mode." If no file name is given, Emacs starts in "List Interaction Mode."

The Emacs editor uses the word "mode" in a different way than vi does. Modes in Emacs control how commands are interpreted, instead of determining if you can give commands or enter text. There are three groups of modes (there are other words that are used in different ways between Emacs and vi):

- Document modes: Modes customized for ordinary text, outlines, and some document processing languages.
- Programming language modes: Modes customized for programming languages.
- Internal modes: Modes used for specialized buffers like the help window or directory lists inside Emacs. In these modes, ordinary characters may have totally different effects. For example, in most internal modes, the "?" character provides a list of help.

These are the major modes, which can then be adjusted by any of a number of minor modes. For example, the mode to edit straight text is "text" but if you give the command that causes automatic line wrap (so you don't have to press Enter at the end of the line), that's "text fill" mode. "Fill" is the minor mode.

None of the commands discussed in this chapter are affected significantly by the mode.

## 6.1.2 ANSWERS

Type the following line; press Enter at the end of the line.

```
Memo: All of yor
```

**a)** What happens to the mode line?

*Answer: The "-----" at the beginning is replaced by "--\*\*-".*

The mode line provides information about what file you're editing, where you are in the file, and the current state of your editing session.

## THE MODE LINE

In this example of a mode line, the mode is "Fundamental" mode (this example line was shortened to fit on the page):

```
--**-Emacs: memo2          (Fundamental)--All---------
```

The "**\*\***" characters indicate that this buffer has been *modified*. If the text hasn't been modified (when you first open the file, or immediately after you save it), the "\*\*" characters are replaced by "--". If the buffer is read-only (you're not allowed to change it), the characters are "%%".

After the name "Emacs" comes the *buffer name*. Usually this is the same as the name of the file you are editing. If you haven't given a file name, it's "\*scratch\*".

The *mode name* is next. In this case, it's Fundamental mode.

The word "All" describes your current *position* in the file. It's one of "Top," "Bot" (if you're at the bottom of the file), "All," or a percentage. If you were at a point halfway through the file, it would read "50%."

Some commands will put other information in the mode line. For instance, the command Meta X `date-time` will put the current date and time in the mode line.

**b)** Press Backspace. What happens?

*Answer: The following message appears in the minibuffer:*

```
C-h (Type ? for further options)-
```

On most terminals, the Backspace key sends the signal "Control-H." The original author of Emacs felt that Control-H was the logical command for displaying help. (Remember that on the early UNIX terminals, it was the Delete key that backspaced over text. This was discussed in *UNIX User's Interactive Workbook*, Chapter 6, "Emergency Recovery.")

If you're using Emacs on an X Windows system, you probably won't have this response. On an X Windows system, the Backspace key sends the erase signal, but Control-H will still print the help message in the minibuffer.

Press Control-G, then press the Delete key.

**c)**   What does the Delete key do?

*Answer: The Delete key deletes the character before the cursor.*

Just like on the early terminals, you must press Delete in Emacs to back-space over a character.

There is a way to "swap" the Backspace and Delete keys in Emacs. It's too detailed to go into here, but you can probably get your local Emacs wizard to change it.

## 6.1.3 ANSWERS

Give the command Control-X Control-S. (Hold down Control while you press X, then hold down Control while you press S.)

**a)**   What happens?

*Answer: This prompt appears in the minibuffer:*

```
File to save in: ~/
```

The actual path name provided is your current directory when you start emacs. If you don't want to save it in that directory, you can use the Delete key to backspace over the characters and enter the new path name. Or you can just type the complete path name *after* the "~/". When Emacs sees "//" in the middle of a path name, it assumes the "real" path name starts with the second / character. So if Emacs prompted you with "~/" and you typed in "~//tmp/storage.txt", the file would be saved in "/tmp/storage.txt".

Enter the following file name:

```
memo2
```

**b)**   What happens?

*Answer: The text is saved in the file* /usr/home/johnmc/memo2, *and the buffer name changes to "*memo2*".*

The actual text displayed depends on the directory you chose to save it in. If you saved the file in your home directory, you might have noticed that the *prompt* used "~" but the response expanded the ~ character to the full path name. (Actually, sometimes Emacs won't display your home directory as "~/" but that's a separate issue. It has to do with whether your HOME environment variable is set; see Chapter 7, "Customizing Your Environment" for more information about environment variables.)

Now add more text, as follows:

```
Condolences to Dana.
```

Give the following command:

```
Control-X Control-S
```

**c)**   What name is the file saved under this time?

*Answer: The file is saved under the name* memo2.

Unless you tell Emacs to do otherwise, the name of the buffer is the same as the name of the file. It is not the path name; the buffer is "memo2", not "/usr/home/johnmc/memo2". When you're editing more than one file with the same name, Emacs adds numbers after the buffer names so you can tell them apart: A second buffer named "memo2" would be displayed as "memo2<2>", a third one as "memo2<3>" and so on.

## 6.1.4  ANSWERS

After you typed the given text, you gave the command Control-X Control-C.

**a)**   What options does Emacs provide?

*Answer: The following prompt is displayed:*

```
Save file /usr/home/johnmc/foo? (y, n, !, ., q, C-r
or C-h)
```

**L**AB
**6.1**

Table 6.1 describes each of these options and what Emacs does.

Emacs distinguishes between a response of "y" and a response of "yes"; they are not the same. When Emacs prompts "yes" or "no" (such as when it asks you to confirm that you really want to quit), you must respond with the full word.

**b)**  What happens when you enter "y"?

*Answer: Your Emacs session ends.*

Answering y to the prompt saves the file and quits.

Another way to quit a file without changing it is to tell Emacs that you didn't change the file (even though you did). The command Meta ~ (Escape, then ~) tells Emacs that you didn't really change the buffer. If you haven't changed the buffer, Control-X Control-C simply quits.

## Table 6.1 ■ Emacs Options to Quit with Unsaved Changes

| Option | Emacs... |
| --- | --- |
| y | Saves the file, then asks about the next buffer with unsaved changes (if any). |
| n | Doesn't save the file, then asks about the next buffer with unsaved changes (if any). Before finally quitting, you must enter "yes" to confirm you want to quit or "no" to cancel the quit command. |
| ! | Saves all changed buffers and exits. |
| . | Saves only the current buffer and exits. |
| q | Skips prompts for all buffers, simply asks you to confirm that you want to quit ("yes") or change your mind ("no"). |
| Control-R | Displays current buffer. |
| Control-h | Displays help summary of what these options are. |

# LAB 6.1 SELF-REVIEW QUESTIONS

In order to test your progress, you should be able to answer the following questions.

**1)** All Emacs commands are command words.
   **a)** _____True
   **b)** _____False

**2)** The Meta key is usually the Escape key.
   **a)** _____True
   **b)** _____False

**3)** In the following table, match the key combination to the results:
   **a)** Control-H                **i)** Cancel current command
   **b)** Control-G                **ii)** Save file
   **c)** Control-X Control-S      **iii)** Quit session
   **d)** Control-X Control-C      **iv)** Display help

**4)** Which item is not in the mode line when you start Emacs?
   **a)** _____The file (or buffer) name
   **b)** _____The mode
   **c)** _____Your position in the file
   **d)** _____The line number

**5)** Where would Emacs save the file `/usr/home/jake//projects/results`?
   **a)** _____`/usr/home/jake/project/results`
   **b)** _____`/project/results`
   **c)** _____`/usr/home/jake/results`
   **d)** _____`/usr/home/projects/results`

**6)** If you've changed the contents of the buffer but you don't want to save it, which command should you give to the prompt "Save file results?"
   **a)** _____y
   **b)** _____n
   **c)** _____!
   **d)** _____.
   **e)** _____q

*Quiz answers appear in Appendix A, Section 6.1.*

# L A B   6 . 2

# MOVING THE CURSOR

## LAB OBJECTIVES

After this Lab, you will be able to:

- Move the Cursor on the Line
- Move the Cursor Through the File
- Move the Cursor by Context
- Move the Screen Display

Unless you're one of those rare people who can type all of your text without ever backing up or editing, sooner or later you'll need to move the cursor. (I heard this said about one of the original creators of UNIX. He used `cat` as his editor; he would just think about what he wanted to write and when it was all complete in his head, he would type it in.)

For the rest of us, it's important to be able to move the cursor and the display.

## LAB 6.2 EXERCISES

For the Exercises in this Lab, open the file `memo2` with the command `emacs memo2`.

### 6.2.1 MOVE THE CURSOR ON THE LINE

In command mode, type the following commands:

```
Control-E
Control-B
```

```
Control-A
Control-F
```

**a)** What do each of these commands do?

_____

_____

**b)** What happens when you try to use Control-F to go past the end of a line?

_____

_____

## 6.2.2 MOVE THE CURSOR THROUGH THE FILE

Type the following commands:

```
Control-N
Control-P
```

**a)** What does each of these commands do?

_____

_____

Enter the following command:

```
Meta X line-number-mode
```

**b)** How has the mode line changed? What does the number mean?

_____

_____

Add about 20 lines to the file by holding down the Enter key until the text disappears off the screen.

Type the following commands:

```
Meta <
Control-V
Meta V
Meta >
```

**c)** What does each of these commands do?

_____

_____

Type the following command:

```
Meta X goto-line
```

**d)** What happens if you type 3 and press the Enter key when prompted?

## 6.2.3 MOVE THE CURSOR BY CONTEXT

Use the `Meta <` command to return to the beginning of the file.

Type the following commands:

```
Meta F
Meta B
```

**a)** What does each of these commands do?

`Meta F` _____

`Meta B` _____

Type the following command:

```
Meta 3 Meta F
```

**b)** How does `Meta 3` change the `Meta F` command?

_____

_____

## 6.2.4  MOVE THE SCREEN DISPLAY

Move the cursor down to line 23 and type the following commands:

```
Control-L
Meta 0 Control-L
Meta  - Control-L
```

**a)** What does each command do?

_____

_____

**b)** Does the cursor stay on the same line?

_____

_____

# LAB 6.2  EXERCISE ANSWERS

## 6.2.1  ANSWERS

In command mode, type the following commands:

```
Control-E
Control-B
Control-A
Control-F
```

**a)**  What do each of these commands do?

*Answer: Control-E moves the cursor to the end of the line.*

*Control-B moves the cursor back (left) one row.*

*Control-A moves the cursor to the beginning of the line.*

*Control-F moves the cursor forward (right) one row.*

The E indicates the end of the line and B is back. Because "b" was already taken, the command to go to the beginning of the line is Control-A, because A is the beginning of the alphabet. Control-F moves forward.

**b)**  What happens when you try to use Control-F to go past the end of a line?

*Answer: It moves to the next line.*

Because Emacs isn't a line-oriented editor, you can easily move from one line to the next using Control-F and Control-B. You cannot move past the end of the file, however.

## 6.2.2 ANSWERS

Type the following commands:

```
Control-N
Control-P
```

**a)**  What does each of these commands do?

*Answer: Control-N moves the cursor down one line.*

*Control-P moves the cursor up one line.*

"N" stands for "next"; "P" stands for "previous." If you use Control-N to go past the end of the file, Emacs will automatically add new lines to the file.

Enter the following command:

```
Meta X line-number-mode
```

**b)**  How has the mode line changed? What does the number mean?

*Answer: The line number is now displayed in the mode line, preceded by an "L".*

The `Meta X line-number-mode` is an example of an Emacs extended command. Extended commands are not associated with key combinations. When you type Meta X (Escape X), Emacs moves the cursor to the minibuffer and waits for a command name. You end an extended command by pressing the Enter key.

Incidentally, you don't need to type the "-" characters in the command names. If you type a space, Emacs will fill in the hyphen character.

*If your terminal keys don't do the "right" thing, or if you can't figure out how to press a particular key combination, you can always give the long command name. Press Escape, then X, and then enter the command name. You must press Enter at the end. The only command where this isn't really useful is Control-G.*

Add about 20 lines to the file by holding down the Enter key until the text disappears off the screen.

Type the following commands:

```
Meta <
Control-V
Meta V
Meta >
```

**c)**   What does each of these commands do?

*Answer: Meta < moves the cursor to the beginning of the file.*

*Control-V moves the display forward by one screen.*

*Meta V moves the display backward by one screen.*

*Meta > moves the cursor to the end of the file.*

You should be aware that the Emacs documentation refers to Control-V as the "scroll-up" command. The image that the author of Emacs was trying to convey was that the computer window stayed in one place, so the imaginary paper holding the text had to move *up* so you could look farther *down* in the file.

It's much easier to use than to explain.

In the same way, the Meta V command is the "scroll-down" command.

Type the following command:

```
Meta X goto-line
```

**d)**   What happens if you type 3 and press the Enter key when prompted?

*Answer: The cursor moves to line 3 of the file.*

The `goto-line` command is also not associated with a key combination. It's useful to know, however.

### 6.2.3 ANSWERS

Use the Meta < command to return to the beginning of the file.

Type the following commands:

```
Meta F
Meta B
```

**a)**   What does each of these commands do?

*Answer: Meta F moves the cursor forward by one word.*

*Meta B moves the cursor backward by one word.*

In this case, using Meta instead of Control changes the unit of movement: Instead of moving by letter, the commands move by the word. (A word is any string of letters that ends with a space character or a punctuation character.) For commands that have both a "Control" version and a "Meta" version, the Control version is normally the commonly used one or the more basic one, and the Meta version is usually somewhat more specialized.

Type the following command:

```
Meta 3 Meta F
```

**b)**   How does `Meta 3` change the `Meta F` command?

*Answer: The cursor moves forward 3 words instead of 1.*

You can repeat most Emacs commands with this technique. The number can be positive or negative. (Just Meta - means -1.) Sometimes (such as with Control-L in the next exercise), the number is taken to be an argument to the command, not a repetition.

### 6.2.4 ANSWERS

Move the cursor down to line 23 and type the following commands:

```
Control-L
Meta 0 Control-L
Meta  - Control-L
```

**a)**   What does each command do?

*Answer: Control-L redraws the screen so the line the cursor is on is in the middle of the buffer.*

*Meta 0 Control-L redraws the screen so the line the cursor is on is at the top of the buffer.*

*Meta - Control-L redraws the screen so the line the cursor is on is at the bottom of the buffer.*

The argument to the Control-L command determines where the line with the cursor appears. If there is no argument, it appears in the middle of the main buffer window. If there is a positive argument, it appears that many lines from the top. If there is a negative argument, it appears that many lines from the bottom.

**b)** Does the cursor stay on the same line?

*Answer: Yes.*

The Control-L command moves the display, it doesn't move the cursor.

The movement commands in this Lab are summarized in Table 6.2.

# Lab 6.2 Self-Review Questions

In order to test your progress, you should be able to answer the following questions.

1) In the following table, match the command to the cursor movement.
   **a)** Control-E     **i)** One character forward
   **b)** Control-F     **ii)** Beginning of line
   **c)** Control-A     **iii)** One character backward
   **d)** Control-B     **iv)** End of line

2) In the following table, match the command to the cursor movement.
   **a)** Meta <     **i)** Move one screen backward
   **b)** Meta >     **ii)** Move to beginning of file
   **c)** Meta F     **iii)** Move one word forward
   **d)** Meta V     **iv)** Move to end of file

3) What key combination do you press to run an "extended" command, such as `goto-line`?
   **a)** \_\_\_\_\_Control-X
   **b)** \_\_\_\_\_Control-Y
   **c)** \_\_\_\_\_Meta X
   **d)** \_\_\_\_\_Meta Y

### Table 6.2 ■ Movement Commands in Emacs

| Movement | Command |
| --- | --- |
| Move cursor down 1 line. | Control-N |
| Move cursor up 1 line. | Control-P |
| Move cursor right 1 character. | Control-F |
| Move cursor left *n* characters. | Control-B |
| Move cursor to right end of line. | Control-E |
| Move cursor to first row of line. | Control-A |
| Move cursor to beginning of next word | Meta F |
| Move cursor to word beginning | Meta B |
| Move cursor to end of sentence. | Meta E |
| Move cursor to beginning of sentence. | Meta A |
| Move cursor to end of paragraph. | Meta } |
| Move cursor to beginning of paragraph. | Meta { |
| Move cursor forward one screenful. | Control-V |
| Move cursor backward one screenful. | Meta V |
| Go to a specific line, by number. | Meta X goto-line |
| Redraw screen with cursor in middle. | Control-L |
| Redraw screen so line with cursor is at top. | Meta 1 Control-L |
| Move cursor to first row of first line on screen. | Meta - Control-L |

**4)**    Control-L redraws the screen.
  **a)** _____True
  **b)** _____False

*Quiz answers appear in Appendix A, Section 6.2.*

# L A B   6 . 3

# DELETING TEXT

---

## LAB OBJECTIVES

After this Lab, you will be able to:

- Delete a Character
- Undo a Change
- Delete a Line
- Delete a Region of Text
- Write Over Text

---

Sometimes it seems as though more than half of writing is removing words after putting them in.

In Emacs, there are two different ways to remove text: You can delete text, or you can kill it. Deleted text is gone (probably forever), but killed text is not. When you kill text in Emacs, the editor moves it into an internal buffer. You can retrieve killed text easily. It's more difficult to retrieve deleted text, and sometimes it isn't possible.

## LAB 6.3 EXERCISES

### 6.3.1 DELETE A CHARACTER

Type the following command:

```
Control-D
```

**a)** What does the Control-D command do?

_____

_____

**b)** What does the Delete key do (from Lab 6.1)?

_____

_____

**LAB
6.3**

## 6.3.2 UNDO A CHANGE

Enter the following command:

```
Control-X u
```

**a)** What does the `Control-X` u command do? What happens when you give the command again?

_____

_____

## 6.3.3 DELETE A LINE

Use Emacs to open the file again.

Move the cursor to the line beginning with "Memo:".

Type the following commands:

```
Control-A Control-K Control-K
```

**a)** What does the first Control-K command do? The second one?

_____

_____

## 6.3.4   DELETE A REGION OF TEXT

Move the cursor to the beginning of the word "vacuum".

Type the following commands:

```
Control-Space
Meta F
Control-W
```

If Control-Space doesn't work, use Control-@ (Control-Shift-2 on most keyboards).

**a)** What does the Control-W command do?

_____

_____

Move the cursor down three lines and give the following command:

```
Control-W
```

**b)** What does the Control-W command do this time?

_____

_____

Undo all four changes.

**c)** What does the Control-Space command do?

_____

_____

## 6.3.5   WRITE OVER TEXT

Move the cursor to the beginning of the word "mind".

Press the Insert key and type the following word:

```
wits
```

LAB
6.3

**a)** What happens?

_____

_____

**b)** What happens when you press Insert again?

_____

_____

## LAB 6.3 EXERCISE ANSWERS

### 6.3.1 ANSWERS

Type the following command:

```
Control-D
```

**a)** What does the Control-D command do?

*Answer: The Control-D command deletes the character to the right of the cursor.*

The "D" is meant to stand for "delete".

**b)** What does the Delete key do (from Lab 6.1)?

*Answer: The Delete key deletes the character to the left of the cursor.*

The Delete key does what you expect the Backspace key to do. Emacs has two different ways of removing text from the file. You can "delete" text, or you can "kill" text. Killing text is less permanent: Killed text can be retrieved. (This is how you move and copy text.) The Delete and Control-D commands actually delete text. You can undo the deletion, but you can't paste deleted text into another part of the file.

### 6.3.2 ANSWERS

Enter the following command:

```
Control-X u
```

**a)** What does the `Control-X u` command do? What happens when you give the command again?

*Answer: The* `Control-X u` *command undoes your last action. Giving the command again undoes your second-last action.*

Emacs stores a long history of your commands. The actual number of commands stored depends on the size of the changes. It keeps track of about 8000 characters worth of changes, so it can store a lot of little changes, or a few big ones. Not just deletions are stored; all changes to the text buffer are stored.

If you want to undo the undo command, you can. Give a command that has no effect on the text buffer (for instance, move the cursor one character) to let Emacs "know" you're done undoing. Then give `Control-X u` again. This time, the last command that changed the text buffer is the undo command, and Emacs undoes the undo.

On most terminals, the command Control-_ (that's Control-Shift-- on many keyboards) also runs the undo command, and on my X-terminal, the command Control-/ runs it, too.

## 6.3.3 Answers

Use Emacs to open the file again.

Move the cursor to the line beginning with "Memo:".

Type the following commands:

```
Control-A Control-K Control-K
```

**a)**  What does the first Control-K command do? The second one?

*Answer: The first command clears the line; the second removes it.*

The Control-K command clears text from the point to the end of the line. (The Control-A is just to move to the beginning of the line.)

The first command clears all of the text from the line, but leaves the "new line" character. The second time you give the command, Control-K removes the new line character as well, closing the space between lines.

 *The point is an imaginary point in the file that sits just to the left of the cursor, between it and the previous character. A lot of Emacs documentation refers to the point. The point is always near the cursor, but isn't really the cursor. Saying "the point" allows Emacs documentation to avoid phrases like "the character under the cursor."*

> *Each buffer has its own point, so if you have the same file open in several buffers, that file has several points.*

## 6.3.4 ANSWERS

Move the cursor to the beginning of the word "vacuum".

Type the following commands:

```
Control-Space
Meta F
Control-W
```

If Control-Space doesn't work, use Control-@ (Control-Shift-2 on most keyboards).

**a)** What does the Control-W command do?

*Answer: The Control-W command erases the word "vacuum".*

The Control-Space command sets a *mark* in the file. The mark is invisible. All of the file from the point to the mark is the *region*. The Control-W command kills the region. (Remember: Because the text is "killed," you can get it back.)

Every *file* has only one mark. But because a file can be in different buffers, and each buffer can have a different point, then every buffer has a different region.

Move the cursor down three lines and give the following command:

```
Control-W
```

**b)** What does the Control-W command do this time?

*Answer: The Control-W command kills the next three lines.*

The mark didn't move when you moved the point; each time you moved the cursor (and the point), you enlarged the region.

It doesn't matter if the mark is before the point or after the point to establish a region.

Undo all four changes.

**c)** What does the Control-Space command do?

*Answer: The Control-Space command sets the mark, which is one end of the region deleted by the Control-W command.*

The actual command to set the mark is `set-mark`, so if neither Control-Space nor Control-@ works on your terminal, you can still set the mark by typing Meta X `set-mark`.

## 6.3.5 ANSWERS

Move the cursor to the beginning of the word "mind".

Press the Insert key and type the following word:

```
wits
```

**a)** What happens?

*Answer: The letters "wits" replace the word "mind" and the mode changes to "Fundamental Ovwrt".*

For most keyboards, the Insert key is associated with ("bound to") the command `overwrite-mode`.

**b)** What happens when you press Insert again?

*Answer: Pressing Insert again turns off overwrite mode.*

Table 6.3 summarizes the commands covered in this Lab.

### Table 6.3 ■ Emacs Deletion, Change, and Undo Commands

| | |
|---|---|
| Control-D | Deletes the character under the cursor. |
| Delete | Deletes the character before the cursor. |
| Control-K | Kills text from the point to the end of the line. |
| Control-Space | Sets the mark. |
| Control-@ | Sets the mark. |
| Control-W | Kills the text between the mark and the cursor. |
| Control-X u | Undoes the last command that changed the file. |
| Control-_ | Undoes the last command that changed the file. |

# LAB 6.3  SELF-REVIEW QUESTIONS

In order to test your progress, you should be able to answer the following questions.

1) The region is the space between the point and the mark.
   a) _____True
   b) _____False

2) Every buffer has one point and can have more than one mark.
   a) _____True
   b) _____False

3) In the following table, match the command with the amount deleted.
   a) Delete          i)   From point to end of line
   b) Control-D       ii)  The region
   c) Control-K       iii) Character to the right of the point
   d) Control-W       iv)  Character to the left of the point

4) Which of the following commands won't set the mark?
   a) _____set-mark
   b) _____Control-M
   c) _____Control-@
   d) _____Control-Space

5) Which command *won't* undo the last command that changed the buffer?
   a) _____undo
   b) _____Control-X u
   c) _____Control-_
   d) _____Meta x u

*Quiz answers appear in Appendix A, Section 6.3.*

**LAB
6.3**

# L A B   6 . 4

# SAVING A FILE

---

### LAB OBJECTIVES

After this Lab, you will be able to:

- Save the File
- Save Under a New Name
- Save Region as a File

---

There are three different circumstances for saving a file. First, you simply want to save the file you're editing. Second, you want to save the file under a new name. Perhaps this will be a copy of the file as it is right now while you go on to make other changes or perhaps you're finished making changes to the file and you want to move it to a new name without using a mv command. Third, you may want to save only part of the file as a separate file.

All of these are possible with Emacs or with vi (or with nearly any editor). The actual process is different from vi to Emacs, of course. There are some other differences caused by the different philosophies used to design the two editors.

Which of the two editors is more comfortable for you depends on which of the two design philosophies has your sympathies.

## LAB 6.4 EXERCISES

### 6.4.1 SAVE THE FILE

Open the file memo2 and enter the following commands:

```
Control-X Control-S
```

**a)** What name is the file saved under the first time?

_____

_____

## 6.4.2  SAVE UNDER A NEW NAME

Enter the following command:

```
Control-X Control-W
```

Save it under the name `newmemo2`.

**a)** What happens to the name of the buffer?

_____

_____

## 6.4.3  SAVE REGION AS A FILE

Set the mark at the beginning of the line and move the cursor to the end of the line with Control-E.

Give the following command:

```
Meta X write-region
```

Save it in the file *oneline*.

**a)** What's the name of the buffer after you save the region?

_____

_____

Exit Emacs (or in another `xterm` window), use `cat` to display the contents of the file `oneline`.

**b)** Where does the new command prompt show up? What does this mean about the end of the line in the file?

_____

_____

# LAB 6.4 EXERCISE ANSWERS

## 6.4.1 ANSWERS

Open the file memo2 and enter the following commands:

```
Control-X Control-S
```

**a)** What name is the file saved under the first time?

*Answer: The file is saved under the name* memo2.

When you save a file, it's saved under the name associated with the buffer. If it's a new file (such as in the first Lab), you may need to provide a file name.

If the file hasn't changed since you opened the file or since you last saved it, Emacs won't save it.

## 6.4.2 ANSWERS

Enter the following command:

```
Control-X Control-W
```

Save it under the name newmemo2.

**a)** What happens to the name of the buffer?

*Answer: The buffer name changes to* newmemo2.

In vi, saving a file under a new name has no effect on subsequent saves. In Emacs, saving a file under a new name means it will continue to be saved under the new name. The Control-X Control-W command not only saves the file under a new file name, it changes the name of the buffer to match the new file.

LAB
6.4

If you supply a *directory* name instead of a file name, Emacs saves the file under the same file name in the new directory.

## 6.4.3 ANSWERS

Set the mark at the beginning of the line and move the cursor to the end of the line with Control-E.

Give the following command:

```
Meta X write-region
```

Save it in the file `oneline`.

**a)**   What's the name of the buffer after you save the region?

*Answer: The buffer name is still* `newmemo2`.

Saving a *region* doesn't change the name of the buffer. If you want to save a file under a different name just once and continue editing it under the original name, you can make the entire file the region and give the `write-region` command. In other words, move the cursor to the beginning of the file, set the mark, move the cursor to the end of the file, and then use the `write-region` command.

Exit Emacs (or in another `xterm` window), use `cat` to display the contents of the file `oneline`.

**b)**   Where does the new command prompt show up? What does this mean about the end of the line in the file?

*Answer: The new command prompt shows up at the end of the line, like this:*

```
$ cat oneline Condolences to Dana$
```

*This means that the file doesn't contain an end-of-line character.*

Remember that the point is just *before* the cursor. Because the cursor was still on the same line, the region didn't include the end-of-line character. If you want to save the end of the line, you need to move the cursor one more space, to the beginning of the next line.

## BACKUP FILES

Emacs keeps backup files for all files you change. The first time you save a file and a copy already exists, Emacs renames the older version, adding

### Table 6.4 ■ Emacs Commands to Save Files

| Effect | Key Combination | Command |
| --- | --- | --- |
| Saves file | Control-X Control-S | save-buffer |
| Saves file under new name | Control-X Control-W | write-file |
| Saves region as a file | | write-region |
| Replaces file with auto-save file | | recover-file |

"~" to the end of the file name. (You probably have the file `memo2~` in your working directory right now.)

However, Emacs *also* automatically saves files every 300 keystrokes or whenever you stop typing for 30 seconds. The auto-save files are different from the backup files, and have "#" added to the beginning and end of the file names. That is, the auto-save file for `memo2` is `#memo2#`.

When you open a file, Emacs compares the times on the file and the auto-save file (if there is one). If the auto-save file is newer, Emacs tells you:

```
Auto-save file is newer; consider M-X recover-file
```

The command `recover-file` replaces the file in the buffer with the auto-save file.

If you made a lot of changes to a file and then decided to abandon the changes without saving the file, you'll see that message the next time you open the file.

Table 6.4 summarizes the commands in this Lab.

## LAB 6.4  SELF-REVIEW QUESTIONS

In order to test your progress, you should be able to answer the following questions.

1) If the buffer's name is history<3>, what is the name of the file?
   a) _____history<3>
   b) _____history

**2)** After the command `Control-X Control-W herstory`, what is the name of the file you are editing?

    **a)** _____history<3>

    **b)** _____history

    **c)** _____herstory<3>

    **d)** _____herstory

**3)** After an Emacs session, you can safely delete files whose names begin and end with '#'.

    **a)** _____True

    **b)** _____False

**4)** Emacs saves a backup file every:

    **a)** _____10 minutes

    **b)** _____100 keystrokes

    **c)** _____30 minutes

    **d)** _____300 keystrokes

*Quiz answers appear in Appendix A, Section 6.4.*

**LAB
6.4**

# L A B   6 . 5

# SEARCHING (AND REPLACING) TEXT

---

## LAB OBJECTIVES

After this Lab, you will be able to:

- Search Incrementally
- Search for a Regular Expression
- Search and Replace with Confirmation
- Search and Replace Unconditionally

---

Because Emacs isn't organized around lines of text in the way that vi is, the searches behave differently. While vi offers commands to search on a line and to search the entire body of the file, Emacs offers only commands to search the body of the file.

The default search in Emacs does *not* use regular expressions. However, it offers an incremental search technique that often eliminates the need to use regular expressions. Regular expressions are available, if you want to use them in a search.

The search-and-replace commands in Emacs do not make use of the incremental search feature. (If you think about it, you will understand why they can't.) The default search-and-replace technique asks for confirmation of each change, and you must use a different command to replace text unconditionally. As with so many other parts of Emacs, this is the opposite of vi.

# LAB 6.5 EXERCISES

### 6.5.1 SEARCH INCREMENTALLY

Type the following command:

```
Control-S with
```

**a)** What happens after each letter? Is the search case-sensitive?

_____

_____

**b)** Press the Delete key, so you're now searching for "wit". What happens when you press Control-S again?

_____

_____

**c)** What happens when you press Control-R?

_____

_____

**d)** What happens when you try to search past the end of the file?

_____

_____

### 6.5.2 SEARCH FOR A REGULAR EXPRESSION

Go back to the beginning of the file and enter the following commands:

```
Meta Control-S wi[tl]
```

**a)** What happens when you press Control-S?

_____

_____

**b)** What happens when you press Meta Control-S again?

_____

_____

**c)** Does Emacs use basic regular expressions or extended regular expressions?

_____

_____

## 6.5.3  SEARCH AND REPLACE WITH CONFIRMATION

In the file `memo2`, to change Dana's name to Lee, move the cursor to the beginning of the file.

Now give the Meta % command.

At the prompts, enter the following:

        Dana

and

        Lee

For the first replacement, press the following:

        y

**a)** What does the `Meta %` command do?

_____

_____

At the next prompt, press

> !

> **b)** What do the y and ! commands do in a query-replace command?

_____

_____

### 6.5.4 SEARCH AND REPLACE UNCONDITIONALLY

To change Tycho's name to Newton, enter the command Meta X `replace-string`.

At the first prompt, enter the following:

```
tycho
```

At the second prompt, enter the following:

```
newton
```

> **a)** Are all occurrences changed?

_____

_____

> **b)** Are the names capitalized?

_____

_____

## LAB 6.5 EXERCISE ANSWERS

### 6.5.1 ANSWERS

Type the following command:

```
Control-S with
```

**a)**   What happens after each letter? Is the search case-sensitive?

*Answer: With each letter, Emacs searches the file for the next occurrence of the string as it is. It's not case-sensitive.*

This is the "incremental search" feature. The string "w" finds the first "w" in the file, the string "wi" finds the first "wi" in the file, and so on. This feature is tremendously useful; often, you'll find the word or phrase you want before you've finished typing it out.

This search is *not* case-sensitive. The very first "w" it finds is the beginning of the word "We're" in uppercase. The string you type is *not* a regular expression.

**b)**   Press the Delete key, so you're now searching for "wit". What happens when you press Control-S again?

*Answer: The cursor moves back to the word "withdrawn", the next occurrence of "wit" in the file.*

Pressing Control-S again repeats the last search. Emacs remembers the string you're searching for.

**LAB
6.5**

**c)**   What happens when you press Control-R?

*Answer: Emacs searches in the reverse direction.*

The Control-R command is identical to Control-S, except it searches back toward the beginning of the file.

**d)**   What happens when you try to search past the end of the file?

*Answer: Emacs beeps and prints an error message:*

```
Failing wrapped I-search: wit
```

 *Incidentally, if you press Control-S (or Control-R) a second time, the search wraps and begins again at the other end of the file.*

## 6.5.2  ANSWERS

Go back to the beginning of the file and enter the following commands:

```
Meta Control-S wi[tl]
```

**a)**   What happens when you press Control-S?

*Answer: Emacs searches for the regular expression "wi[tl]".*

Unlike the incremental search, the regular expression search doesn't happen until after you press Enter. And, did you notice that after you type the first "[" character, Emacs prints the reminder "[incomplete input]"?

**b)**   What happens when you press Meta Control-S again?

*Answer: Emacs prompts for a new regular expression.*

This is a common mistake—trying to repeat a regular expression search by giving the Meta Control-S command again. Control-S searches for the remembered search pattern, unless you enter a new one or there is no search pattern. Once you enter the regular expression "wi[tl]", it is the remembered search pattern, and Emacs searches for that each time you press Control-S.

**c)**   Does Emacs use basic regular expressions or extended regular expressions?

*Answer: Emacs uses basic regular expressions, more or less.*

Because Emacs isn't part of any standard, it doesn't have to conform to any rules. In fact, it does basic regular expressions (except for \{,\}) with the differences listed in Table 6.5.

## Table 6.5 ■ Emacs Regular Expressions in Addition to Basic Regular Expressions

| | |
|---|---|
| \{,\} | Emacs doesn't understand \{,\} regular expressions. |
| a\|b | Matches either *a* or *b*. *a* and *b* are both patterns or groups of patterns. |
| \` | Matches an empty line at the beginning of the buffer. |
| \' | Matches an empty line at the end of the buffer. |
| \b | Matches the beginning or end of a word. |
| \B | Matches anything that is *not* at the beginning or end of a word. |
| \< | Matches the beginning of a word. |
| \> | Matches the end of a word. |
| \w | Matches any character that can be part of a word. |
| \W | Matches any character that cannot be part of a word. This includes spaces, end-of-line characters, and punctuation. |

## Table 6.6 ■ Emacs Search Commands

| Effect | Key Combination | Command |
| --- | --- | --- |
| Searches forward incrementally | Control-S | isearch-forward |
| Searches backward incrementally | Control-B | isearch-backward |
| Searches forward for regular expression | Meta Control-S | isearch-forward-regexp |
| Searches backward for regular expression | Meta Control-R | isearch-backward-regexp |

The Emacs search commands described in this Lab are summarized in Table 6.6.

## 6.5.3 ANSWERS

In this Lab, you changed Dana's name to Lee using the Meta % command.

For the first replacement, press the following

    y

**a)** What does the Meta % command do?

*Answer: The Meta % command does a search-and-replace, querying for each replacement.*

The search string is like the Control-S search string: It's a case-insensitive string, not a regular expression. The Meta % key combination runs the command `query-replace`.

Search-and-replace with the Meta % command only searches from the point to the end of the file. If you want to search the entire file, move the cursor to the beginning of the file before running the command.

If you want to search and replace a regular expression, use the command `query-replace-regexp` instead of Meta %.

At the next prompt, press the following:

    !

**b)** What do the y and ! commands do in a query-replace command?

*Answer: The* y *command replaces the current instance of the string. The* ! *command replaces all of the remaining strings.*

The possible responses when you're doing a query search-and-replace are shown in Table 6.7.

## 6.5.4 ANSWERS

In this Exercise, you changed Tycho's name to Newton using the command Meta X replace-string.

**a)** Are all occurrences changed?

*Answer: Yes.*

The unconditional replace command replaces all occurrences throughout the file.

### Table 6.7 ■ Options in an Emacs Query Search-and-Replace

| Option | Key |
| --- | --- |
| Display list of possible responses | Control-H |
| Display list of possible responses | ? |
| Replace the string | y |
| Replace the string | Space |
| Skip this instance of the string | n |
| Skip this instance of the string | Delete |
| Replace this one and display the result; then edit replacement with Control-R, accept with Space, or reject with Delete | , |
| Quit without doing any more replacements | Enter |
| Replace this string, then quit | . |
| Replace all remaining instances without asking | ! |
| Display screen and ask again | Control-L |
| Go back to previous replacement; you can edit that one with Control-R, accept with Space, or reject with Delete | ^ |

**b)** Are the names capitalized?

*Answer: Yes, they are.*

The rules for capital letters in replacements look complicated, but they're quite natural when you use them:

- If the replacement string has capital letters, they will stay capitalized when inserted into the file.
- If the replacement string has lowercase letters, they will become uppercase when the equivalent letter in the string being replaced is uppercase.

If you want the search to be case-insensitive, search and replace for regular expressions, instead. The command to search and replace regular expressions unconditionally is `replace-regexp`.

The commands in this lab are summarized in Table 6.8.

# LAB 6.5 SELF-REVIEW QUESTIONS

In order to test your progress, you should be able to answer the following questions.

1) An incremental search is case-sensitive.
   **a)** _____True
   **b)** _____False

## Table 6.8 ■ Emacs Search and Replace Commands

| Type of Command | Key Combination | Command |
|---|---|---|
| Search and replace strings with query | Meta % | query-replace |
| Search and replace regular expressions with query | | query-replace-regexp |
| Search and replace strings unconditionally | | replace-string |
| Search and replace regular expressions unconditionally | | replace-regexp |

**2)** An incremental search does not use a regular expression.
  **a)** _____True
  **b)** _____False

**3)** A regular expression search is incremental.
  **a)** _____True
  **b)** _____False

**4)** To repeat the last regular expression search forward, which of the following commands would you use?
  **a)** _____Control-S
  **b)** _____Control-R
  **c)** _____Meta Control-S
  **d)** _____Meta Control-R

**5)** Which basic regular expression construct is not available in Emacs?
  **a)** _____\<
  **b)** _____\>
  **c)** _____\ (
  **d)** _____\ {

**6)** Which command does Meta % run?
  **a)** _____query-replace
  **b)** _____query-replace-regexp
  **c)** _____replace-string
  **d)** _____replace-regexp

**7)** In the following table, match the Meta % search and replace options with their results

| | |
|---|---|
| **a)** ? | **i)** Quit without doing any more replacements |
| **b)** y | **ii)** Skip this one and go on to the next |
| **c)** Space | **iii)** Display options |
| **d)** Enter | **iv)** Replace the rest without asking |
| **e)** ! | **v)** Replace this one and go on to the next |

**8)** In a Meta % command, to replace "lance" with "pike," the word "LANCe" would become
  **a)** _____pike
  **b)** _____PIKE
  **c)** _____Pike
  **d)** _____PIKe

*Quiz answers appear in Appendix A, Section 6.5.*

# L A B   6 . 6

# MOVING TEXT

---

### LAB OBJECTIVES

After this Lab, you will be able to:

- Move and Copy Text
- Insert a File

---

Copying and moving text in Emacs is done by putting a copy of the text into a buffer, and then copying text from the buffer back into the file.

## LAB 6.6 EXERCISES

### 6.6.1 MOVE AND COPY TEXT

In the file `memo2`, move the cursor to the empty line before the paragraph beginning "We're sorry to announce".

Kill the entire paragraph with Control-K commands. (It takes 9 commands to kill the paragraph.)

Now move the cursor below the line beginning "The no-pets-in-the-office rule".

Give the following command:

```
Control-Y
```

**a)** How many lines are pasted in?

_____

_____

**b)** What if you press Control-Y again?

_____

_____

Undo the last paste with Meta X undo.

Set the mark and move the cursor so you have selected a region (any region).

Give the command Meta W.

**c)** Does the region go away? What text does the command Control-Y paste now?

_____

_____

### 6.6.2 INSERT A FILE

Use the `write-region` command to save the region you have marked into a file named `temporary`.

Give the command Control-X i and enter the file name *temporary* at the prompt.

**a)** What happens?

_____

_____

**b)** What happens if you give the Control-X i command again, but *don't* specify a file name (that is, you press Enter at the prompt)?

_____

_____

# LAB 6.6 EXERCISE ANSWERS

## 6.6.1 ANSWERS

After killing the specified paragraph and moving the cursor below the indicated line, you gave the following command:

```
Control-Y
```

**a)** How many lines are pasted in?

*Answer: The entire paragraph; all of the deleted lines are pasted in.*

Emacs is smart enough to clump together a group of lines killed with Control-K as one big chunk of text. Using a bunch of Control-K commands is sometimes more convenient than marking the region. (You may not want to move the mark, for instance.)

The Control-Y command is the "yank" command. This is just one case of Emacs using the same word as vi to mean something entirely different. (Remember, in vi, "yank" means copying something *into* a storage buffer; in Emacs, "yank" means copying something *out of* a storage buffer.)

**b)** What if you press Control-Y again?

*Answer: The text is pasted in again.*

LAB
6.6

This is one way to copy text. You mark the region or use Control-K, paste the text back into its original position, then move the cursor and paste it in someplace new.

Undo the last paste with Meta X undo.

Set the mark and move the cursor so you have selected a region (any region).

Give the command Meta W.

**c)** Does the region go away? What text does the command Control-Y paste now?

*Answer: No; the region is not erased from the file with Meta W. The Control-Y command now pastes the region that was copied with Meta W.*

Instead of killing the text and yanking it back, you can use the Meta W command, which copies the region into the same buffer used by Control-Y.

## 6.6.2 ANSWERS

Use the `write-region` command to save the region you have marked into a file named `temporary`.

Give the command Control-X `i` and enter the file name `temporary` at the prompt.

**a)** What happens?

*Answer: The text of the file* temporary *is inserted at the point.*

The Control-X `i` command inserts a file into the buffer.

**b)** What happens if you give the Control-X `i` command again, but *don't* specify a file name (that is, you press Enter at the prompt)?

*Answer: The file* memo2 *is inserted into the buffer at the point.*

If you don't specify a file name, Emacs uses the name of the file associated with the buffer.

The commands in this Lab are summarized in Table 6.9.

# LAB 6.6  SELF-REVIEW QUESTIONS

In order to test your progress, you should be able to answer the following questions.

**1)** Deleted text can be yanked back with Control-Y, but killed text cannot.
   **a)** _____True
   **b)** _____False

**Table 6.9 ■ Emacs Commands for Moving and Copying Text**

| Result | Command | Key Combination |
| --- | --- | --- |
| Yanks killed text back into main buffer | yank | Control-Y |
| Copies region into yank buffer | kill-ring-save | Meta W |
| Inserts file | insert-file | Control-X i |

**2)** In the following table, match the command with its results.

**a)** Meta W            **i)** Kill region
**b)** Control-X i       **ii)** Copy region
**c)** Control-Y         **iii)** Insert file
**d)** Control-W         **iv)** Yank text

**3)** You cannot undo a paste action.

**a)** _____True
**b)** _____False

**4)** The second time you use Control-X i to insert a file during an editing session, which file does Emacs insert?

**a)** _____The same file as the last insertion.
**b)** _____The file you are currently editing.
**c)** _____The file you specify, and you must specify a file.
**d)** _____The file you specify; if you don't specify one, it inserts the same file as the last insertion.

**5)** Killing text is the same as deleting it.

**a)** _____True
**b)** _____False

*Quiz answers appear in Appendix A, Section 6.6.*

**LAB
6.6**

# L A B   6 . 7

# WORKING WITH FRAMES AND BUFFERS

---

## LAB OBJECTIVES

After this Lab, you will be able to:

- Create and Close Buffer Windows
- Create and Close Frames

---

Because the Emacs editor was written before there were fancy graphical user interfaces, it has its own way of presenting multiple buffers. Each buffer display (like the main buffer) is called a "window."

## LAB 6.7 EXERCISES

### 6.7.1 CREATE AND CLOSE BUFFER WINDOWS

In the current buffer, give the following commands:

```
Control-X 2
Control-X O
```

(That's an oh ("o"), not a zero.)

```
Control-X 1
```

**a)** What does each command do?

_____

_____

**b)** What does the command Control-X `4` `f` do? (Use `temporary` as the file name.)

_____

_____

## 6.7.2 CREATE AND CLOSE FRAMES

If you are using X Windows on your UNIX system, give the following commands:

```
Control-X 5 2
Control-X 5 O
```

(That's a capital letter O ("oh"), not a zero.)

```
Control-X 5 1
```

**a)** What does each command do?

_____

_____

**b)** What does the command Control-X `5` `f` do? (Use `temporary` as the file name.)

_____

_____

# LAB 6.7 EXERCISE ANSWERS

## 6.7.1 ANSWERS

In the current buffer, give the following commands:

```
Control-X 2
Control-X O
Control-X 1
```

**a)** What does each command do?

*Answer: The Control-X 2 command splits the current buffer window in two; each buffer contains the same file.*

*The Control-X O command moves the cursor into the other window.*

*The Control-X 1 command gets rid of the other window.*

These three commands are the basic commands for navigating through multiple buffer windows.

The Control-X 2 command splits the current window, but the new buffer window contains the same file, and the cursor doesn't automatically move to that window. This is sometimes useful if you need to read one part of the file while you're editing another part.

You can have more than two buffer windows open. The only limit on the number of buffer windows you can have open is the number of lines on your screen, because each buffer window needs at least two lines.

**b)** What does the command Control-X `4 f` do? (Use `temporary` as the file name.)

*Answer: The Control-X `4 f` command opens a new file in another window.*

**LAB 6.7**

The "4" inserted in the command indicates it should be done in a new buffer window. (Although we haven't discussed it, the Control-X `f` command opens a new file in the current buffer window.) There are a number of other commands for executing commands in new buffer windows. You can execute nearly any command in Emacs we've discussed and have the results show up in a new buffer window instead of the current buffer window.

## 6.7.2 ANSWERS

If you are working on an X Windows system, give the following commands:

```
Control-X 5 2
Control-X 5 O
Control-X 5 1
```

**a)** What does each command do?

*Answer: The Control-X 5 2 command opens a new frame; each frame contains the same file.*

*The Control-X 5 O command moves the cursor into the other frame.*

*The Control-X 5 1 command gets rid of the other frame.*

Each of these commands is the same as the "window" commands, except that the "5" is inserted.

You can also use the mouse and the entries under the Frames menu to create and remove frames.

**b)** What does the command Control-X 5 f do? (Use `temporary` as the file name.)

*Answer: The command Control-X 5 f opens a file in a new frame.*

The commands in this Lab are summarized in Table 6.10.

## Table 6.10 ■ Emacs Commands for Working with Buffers and Frames

| Result | Command | Key Combination |
| --- | --- | --- |
| Splits current buffer window into two | split-window-vertically | Control-X 2 |
| Opens a file in a new window | find-file-other-window | Control-X 4 f |
| Moves to next buffer window | other-window | Control-X O |
| Removes the current window | delete-window | Control-X 0 |
| Removes all buffer windows but active one | delete-window | Control-X 1 |
| Kills a buffer (default is current buffer) | kill-buffer | Control-X k |
| Creates a new frame containing a copy of the current frame | make-frame | Control-X 5 2 |
| Opens a file in a new frame | find-file-other-frame | Control-X 5 f |
| Goes to the next frame | other-frame | Control-X 5 O |
| Deletes frame containing cursor | delete-frame | Control-X 5 0 |

**LAB 6.7**

# LAB 6.7 SELF-REVIEW QUESTIONS

In order to test your progress, you should be able to answer the following questions.

1) Only the X Window version of Emacs has "windows."
   a) \_\_\_\_\_True
   b) \_\_\_\_\_False

2) Only the X Window version of Emacs has frames.
   a) \_\_\_\_\_True
   b) \_\_\_\_\_False

3) In the following table, match the command with its results.
   a) Control-X 0      i)   Split window into 2
   b) Control-X 2      ii)  Move cursor into other frame
   c) Control-X 5 2    iii) Open a new frame
   d) Control-X 5 0    iv)  Move cursor into other window

*Quiz answers appear in Appendix A, Section 6.7.*

LAB
6.7

# CHAPTER 6

# TEST YOUR THINKING

For these projects, us the file *ants*, shown here:

```
The aunts go marching 1 bye 1
Hoohah hoohah
The aunts g marching 1 bye 1
Hoohah hoohah
The aunts go marching 1 bye 1
The litle one stops to have sum fun
```

**1)** What commands would be required to correct the errors and resort the lines so it reads:

```
The ants go marching 1 by 1
Hoorah hoorah
The ants go marching 1 by 1
Hoorah hoorah
The ants go marching 1 by 1
The little one stops to have some fun
```

**2)** How would you go about creating the file `antsong`, which contains 5 verses with the following last lines for verses 2 through 5?

```
The little one stops to tie his shoe
The little one stops to climb a tree
The little one stops to shut the door
The little one stops to take a drive
```

# C H A P T E R   7

# CUSTOMIZING YOUR ENVIRONMENT

 *The UNIX shells allow you to customize your work environment. You can add commands, change prompts, and generally make it a more comfortable environment for yourself.*

---

## CHAPTER OBJECTIVES

In this Chapter, you will learn about:

---

UNIX is a very flexible operating environment. You can customize the appearance of your shell and the commands you use, and you can include commands in your environment that no one else uses. You can even rename common commands.

This Chapter talks about some of the basic ways to customize your environment.

*It's possible to customize your environment so thoroughly that no one else can use it, and that you feel crippled on another system. I have seen programmers who are so used to their personal environment that they cannot work on a new system until they've spent a day (or a week) customizing it.*

# L A B   7 . 1

# CHANGING SHELLS

## LAB OBJECTIVES

After this Lab, you will be able to:

*   Change Shells

All of the labs in this Chapter and the next are written for the Korn Shell. If you are not using the Korn Shell, please switch to it for the duration of these two chapters. To help, this Lab deals with changing shells.

On all systems, you can ask your system administrator to change your login shell. Some systems provide commands so that you can change your shell yourself.

Before you try to change your shell yourself, you should make sure that the Korn Shell exists on your system. The easiest way to do this is to check for the existence of a `ksh` program (the Korn Shell), with the command:

```
command -v ksh
```

If the command doesn't print a command name, then the Korn Shell isn't in your PATH. (It may still be on your system, however.) See if there's a file named `/etc/shells` on your system; on BSD-style systems, this file lists the acceptable shells. If any file ending in `ksh` (or `pdksh`) is listed, then the Korn Shell is on your system.

If you still can't find a Korn Shell, you'll need to ask your system administrator for help.

**LAB 7.1**

# LAB 7.1 EXERCISES

## 7.1.1 CHANGE SHELLS

Enter the following command:

```
grep yourlogin /etc/passwd
```

**a)** What is your current shell?

_____

_____

If it is not the Korn Shell, enter the following command:

```
/usr/sbin/usermod -s /bin/ksh
```

 *You may not have permission to run the* usrmod *command. If the command does not exist on your system, enter the following:*

```
chsh
```

**b)** Which command worked on your system, if either? What does it do?

_____

_____

# LAB 7.1 EXERCISE ANSWERS

## 7.1.1 ANSWERS

**a)** What is your login shell?

*Answer: This varies. It will be a pathname, probably ending in one of* sh, csh, ksh, tcsh, *or* bash.

The /etc/passwd file contains the list of all users on the system. (On systems that are part of a network, there may be a system-wide passwd file on one machine. Your machine will still have an `/etc/passwd` file, but it may not have all the information described here.) Because the `/etc/passwd` file contains valuable information, only the system administrator is allowed to edit it.

Below is sample output from the `grep` command in this Exercise.

```
$ grep sandi /etc/passwd
sandi:x:117:100:Sandi Bakelaar:/home/sandi:/bin/ksh
```

This line describes the user's account; there are seven fields, separated by colons:

| | |
|---|---|
| sandi | The user's login name. |
| x | A placeholder; on some systems, this field will contain an encrypted form of the user's password. |
| 117 | The user's user ID number. |
| 100 | The user's group ID number. |
| Sandi Bakelaar | The user's name and possibly other information, such as office number and phone extension. This field is sometimes called the "gecos" field, for historical reasons. |
| /home/sandi | The user's home directory. |
| /bin/ksh | The user's login shell. If there's nothing here, the user's login shell is the Bourne shell. |

Because only the system administrator is allowed to edit the file, you cannot edit the file to change your login shell yourself.

Some systems provide you with a way to change your shell; others do not. The only method that works on *all* systems is asking the system administrator to change your login shell.

If it is not the Korn Shell, enter the following command:

```
/usr/sbin/usermod -s /bin/ksh
```

**b)**   Which command worked on your system, if either? What does it do?

*Answer: On a Solaris system, probably neither command works. On a BSD system, the* `chsh` *command allows you to edit your account information.*

Solaris and other SVR4 systems provide the `usermod` command to modify a user's account, but usually restrict it to the system administrator.

**LAB
7.1**

BSD-style systems provide the `chsh` (change shell) program. They also provide a list of the acceptable shells in the file `/etc/shells`. (The command `more /etc/shells` will show you the shells that are available on your machine.)

When you give the `chsh` command, the program starts your editor; the file you are editing looks like this:

```
#Changing user database information for sandi.
Shell: /bin/ksh
Full Name: Sandi Bakelaar
Location:
Office Phone:
Home Phone:
```

After you have altered the information on the Shell line, you should save the file and exit the editor.

*You can try the Korn Shell for one session by giving the command*
`exec ksh.`

# LAB 7.1  SELF REVIEW QUESTIONS

In order to test your progress, you should be able to answer the following questions.

1) The `chsh` is normally available on Solaris systems.
   a) _____True
   b) _____False

2) Identify the information that is not in the `/etc/passwd` file:
   a) _____Login name
   b) _____Login shell
   c) _____Unencrypted password
   d) _____Login ID number
   e) _____Group ID number

3) Identify the means of changing login shells that works on all UNIX systems:
   a) _____chsh
   b) _____usermod -s /bin/ksh
   c) _____exec ksh -i
   d) _____Ask system administrator

**4)** Which of these commands is normally allowed only to the root user? Which to all users?

**a)** _____chsh

**b)** _____usermod

**c)** _____exec ksh -i

**d)** _____vi /etc/passwd

*Quiz answers appear in Appendix A, Section 7.1.*

# L A B   7 . 2

# ADDING NEW COMMANDS

---

### LAB OBJECTIVES

After this Lab, you will be able to:

- Create an Alias
- Add a Directory to Your PATH

---

UNIX is an operating system originally built by programmers for programmers. It allows you to add new commands easily. There are two meanings to "add new commands." The first is that it's easy to *create* new commands, and the second is that it's easy to make those new commands "visible" to your shell.

You can create a new command by using an alias or by writing a shell script. (Writing shell scripts is described in Chapter 8, "Basic Shell Programming.") You can make new shell scripts visible to the system by setting your PATH environment variable to include them.

## LAB 7.2 EXERCISES

### 7.2.1   CREATE AN ALIAS

Enter the following commands:

```
alias 2tmp="cd /tmp;pwd"
2tmp
```

**a)** What does the 2tmp command do?

_____

_____

Enter the following command:

```
alias
```

**b)** What does the alias command do?

_____

_____

Enter the following commands:

```
unalias 2tmp
2tmp
```

**c)** What does the unalias command do?

_____

_____

## 7.2.2 ADD A DIRECTORY TO YOUR *PATH*

Enter the following commands:

```
df
export PATH="/usr/ucb:$PATH"
echo $PATH
```

Some systems do not have a /usr/ucb directory; in this case, you will not get the expected result for Question b.

**a)** What is the result of the export command?

_____

_____

Enter the following command:

```
df
```

**b)** What happens? Why?

_____

_____

## LAB 7.2 EXERCISE ANSWERS

### 7.2.1 ANSWERS

Enter the following commands:

```
alias 2tmp="cd /tmp;pwd"
2tmp
```

**a)**  What does the 2tmp command do?

*Answer: It changes directories to /tmp and then prints the directory.*

The alias command creates an alias, an alternate name for a command or a series of commands. In this case, the alias "2tmp" is an alternate name for the commands cd /tmp and pwd. The quotation marks are needed because the first command contains a space.

*There should never be spaces around the = sign in an alias or a variable assignment. The command will not work if there are spaces.*

You could define the alias using a backslash to escape the space, as in:

```
alias 2tmp=cd\ /tmp;pwd
```

However, quotation marks are easier to type if there is more than one space.

A common alias is:

```
alias lf="ls -F"
```

Whenever you type the command `lf`, the shell turns it into `ls -F` (followed by any arguments). By using `lf` instead of `ls`, you always see the file types displayed. (Or you could use `ll` as an alias for `ls -l`.)

An alias isn't *always* translated back into its real commands, only when it's in a place where a command goes. This restriction is necessary. Suppose you had this alias to take you to the `/projects` directory:

```
alias projects="cd /projects"
```

If the word "projects" were *always* turned into "`cd /projects`" you could never use "projects" in a command. For example, the command "`ls projects`" would be turned into "`ls cd /projects`" and it wouldn't work. So aliases are only expanded when they're used as commands.

Enter the following command:

```
alias
```

**b)**  What does the `alias` command do?

*Answer: It displays the current list of aliases.*

There are a number of aliases already defined when you start the Korn Shell, including the command history commands discussed in Chapter 5, "Other Useful Stuff."

If you only want to see the definition of one alias, you can provide that alias as an argument:

```
$ alias 2tmp
cd /tmp;pwd
```

Enter the following commands:

```
unalias 2tmp
2tmp
```

**c)**  What does the `unalias` command do?

*Answer: It removes an alias.*

If you have aliases you use frequently, you may want to define them in your startup files. They will be set every time you log in.

The drawback to an alias is that it's fixed. It has no flexibility; you cannot change arguments in the middle of the alias. If you want a command to change directories and then list the contents of the new directory, you can't create it with an alias. There's no way to insert the argument (the new directory) in the middle of the alias.

**LAB
7.2**

To create this kind of new command, you need to use a shell function or a shell script. These are described in Chapter 8, "Basic Shell Programming."

## 7.2.2 ADD A DIRECTORY TO YOUR *PATH*

Enter the following commands:

```
df
export PATH="/usr/ucb:$PATH"
echo $PATH
```

**a)** What is the result of the `export` command?

*Answer: The* `export` *command sets the new value of the* `PATH` *to "the directory* `/usr/ucb` *plus the old value of the* `PATH`*."*

It's easy to add directories to the beginning or end of your `PATH` without retyping the entire `PATH`. If you use "`$PATH`" you can add new directories to the beginning or end of your current `PATH` variable.

**b)** What happens? Why?

*Answer: The* `df` *command runs, but the output is not the same. The output of the* `df` *command now looks like this (exact details will depend upon your system):*

| Filesystem<br>Mounted on | kbytes | used | avail | capacity |
|---|---|---|---|---|
| /dev/dsk/c0d0s6<br>/usr | 1582860 | 973707 | 450873 | 69% |

Because the shell searches the directories in the order they occur in the `PATH` variable, the order of directories is important. Now that `/usr/ucb` is at the beginning of your `PATH`, the shell searches the directory `/usr/ucb` first. It searches `/bin` for a command only if the command isn't in the `/usr/ucb` directory.

Because many of the commands in `/usr/ucb` directory have the same names as commands in `/bin`, you will get the BSD versions of commands instead of the SVR4 versions. The BSD commands do not always behave the same.

*Unless you have a very good reason, add new directories to the end of your* PATH. *Suppose you add a directory to the beginning of your* PATH, *and it contains a program named* rm *that does something other than the usual* rm *command (perhaps it reads memos or something). When you type* rm *to remove a file, your shell looks for the first program named* rm *it can find, and instead of removing a file, you end up reading a memo. If you add a new directory to the end of your* PATH, *this new version of* rm *won't be run by accident.*

To remove /usr/ucb from the beginning of your PATH, enter the command:

```
export PATH=${PATH#/usr/ucb:}
```

This command will be explained in Chapter 8, "Basic Shell Programming."

# LAB 7.2 SELF-REVIEW QUESTIONS

In order to test your progress, you should be able to answer the following questions.

1) What does the command export PATH="$PATH:$PATH" do?
   a) _____Adds your current directory to the beginning of your search path
   b) _____Adds your current directory to the end of your search path
   c) _____Adds your current directory to the middle of your search path
   d) _____Duplicates your search path

2) If you have set the alias ls="ls -l", then:
   a) _____It won't work, because it will always be trying to turn ls into ls -l, until you have ls -l -l -l...
   b) _____Every time you run ls, it is replaced by ls -l
   c) _____You will not be able to provide any other option to ls
   d) _____It will no longer list the current directory

3) The order of directories in your PATH is important because:
   a) _____The directories must be in alphabetical order
   b) _____The shell runs the first command it finds by a name; two commands with the same name may behave differently

**4)** The command to remove an alias called `lr` is:
  **a)** _____alias lr
  **b)** _____alias
  **c)** _____unset lr
  **d)** _____unalias lr
  **e)** _____unalias

*Quiz answers appear in Appendix A, Section 7.2.*

**LAB
7.2**

# L A B   7 . 3

# CUSTOMIZING
# YOUR SHELL

---

### LAB OBJECTIVES

After this Lab, you will be able to:

- Set Your Prompts
- Set Shell Options
- Edit Your Startup Files

---

The Korn Shell contains many options and parameters. (All shell variables are parameters, but parameters also include some special "variables" that are set up by the shell.) Shell variables include your command prompt. You can include your current directory or your login name or even the time in your command prompt.

These options, like command options, control the behavior of your shell. Two shell options have already been discussed: They are `set -o noclobber` (which prevents you from using file redirection to overwrite an existing file) and `set -o vi` (which turns on `vi`-style command line editing). There are other options as well.

Once you've tried some of these customizations and decided which you want to live with, you can include them in your shell startup files. Every time you log in, you can have the shell environment you like best.

# LAB 7.3  EXERCISES

## 7.3.1  SET YOUR PROMPTS

Enter the following command:

```
set | grep PS
```

**a)** Do you recognize the values of these variables? What are they?

_____

_____

Enter the following commands:

```
export PS1="$PWD$ "
cd /tmp
cd -
```

**b)** What happens to your prompt? Why?

_____

_____

Enter the following commands

```
export PS1='$PWD$ '
cd /tmp
cd -
```

**c)** What happens to your prompt? Why?

_____

_____

## 7.3.2  SET SHELL OPTIONS

Enter the following command:

```
set -o
```

**a)** What does the `set -o` command do?

_____

_____

Enter the following command:

```
set -o vi
```

Press Escape and then `k`.

**b)** What happens? What does the `set -o vi` command do?

_____

_____

Enter the following command:

```
set +o vi
```

Press Escape and then `k`.

**c)** What happens? What does the `set +o vi` command do?

_____

_____

## 7.3.3 EDIT YOUR STARTUP FILES

If the variable `ENV` is already set to the name of a file, use that file name here instead of `~/.envfile`. (Remember that the `~/` is turned into the name of your home directory.)

**a)** Is there a file named `/etc/profile` on your system? Is there a file named `.profile` in your home directory?

_____

_____

If `ENV` is *not* already set to a value, enter the following command:

```
export ENV=~/.envfile
```

Create the file ~/.envfile (or open the file mentioned in ENV for editing). Add the lines:

```
export PS1='$LOGNAME [!] $PWD$ '
set -o vi
set -o noclobber
export PATH="$PATH:~/bin"
```

Now start a new shell with the following command:

```
ksh -i
```

**b)** What's different about your environment in this new shell?

_____

_____

**c)** Why use two local startup files?

_____

_____

# LAB 7.3  EXERCISE ANSWERS

## 7.3.1  ANSWERS

Enter the following command:

```
set | grep PS
```

**a)** Do you recognize the values of these variables? What are they?

*Answer: They are the prompts used by the shell.*

The prompts are numbered in the frequency you see them:

- The PS1 prompt is the standard command prompt. Most users want to change their command prompt (PS1), usually to add the current working directory.
- The PS2 prompt is the prompt used to continue input when the new line character has been escaped. I can't think of a reason why you would want to change it from ">".

- The PS3 prompt is used by the shell command `select`; it asks for user input. Unless you write a lot of shell scripts, you won't need to change this prompt.

- The PS4 prompt is used when you have the `xtrace` option set. Again, unless you write a lot of shell scripts, you won't need to change this.

Enter the following commands:

```
export PS1="$PWD$ "
cd /tmp
cd -
```

**b)**   What happens to your prompt? Why?

*Answer: Your command prompt changes to the value of your current directory, but it doesn't change when you change directories.*

The reason is the quotation marks. Remember that the shell will replace a reference to a variable with the value of the variable if it's in quotation marks. If you're in the directory /home/me, the PS1="$PWD$ " is turned into "PS1=/home/me$" . It stores the value instead of the reference to the value.

Enter the following commands:

```
export PS1='$PWD$ '
cd /tmp
cd -
```

**c)**   What happens to your prompt? Why?

*Answer: Your command prompt displays your current directory in the prompt, even after you change directories.*

The apostrophes (or single quotation marks) escape the $ in the shell. The prompt is actually stored as $PWD$. The shell still replaces the $PWD with its value, but now it replaces it when it draws the prompt on the screen instead of when it stores the value of the prompt. You could also have used a backslash instead of apostrophes. Then the assignment would have been:

```
PS1=\$PWD$
```

You can also substitute commands into the prompt. In some versions, the command will be run every time the prompt is shown; in others (such as the one on Solaris), the command is run only the first time.

If you have a version that updates the commands, you can put the current time in your prompt using the `date` command. The command `date +%H:%M` displays the current time. You can include it in your prompt using *command substitution* (mentioned in Chapter 1; it was discussed more thoroughly in Chapter 12, "Commands and Job Control," in *UNIX User's Interactive Workbook*):

```
PS1='$(date +%H:%M)$ '
```

In this case, the apostrophes are to include a space after the final $ sign. I do this because I think it's easier to read. (And apostrophes were used so the prompt stores the reference to the value instead of the time when the command was given.) The prompt now looks like this:

```
19:11$
```

The exact time will vary, of course. On Solaris, this doesn't work; the prompt only reflects the time when you set the prompt.

*As a special case, a ! character in the PS1 prompt gets turned into the command's number in the command history. By adding ! to your prompt, it's much easier to use command numbers to repeat commands. If you want an exclamation mark in your prompt, use !!.*

## 7.3.2 ANSWERS

Enter the command

```
set -o
```

**a)** What does the `set -o` command do?

*Answer: The command displays the current setting for all of the shell's options.*

The output on my system is reproduced here. Many of these you can ignore; some important ones are described in Table 7.1, after the answer to Question c.

```
$ set -o
Current option settings
allexport        off
bgnice           on
emacs            off
errexit          off
gmacs            off
```

```
ignoreeof       off
interactive     on
keyword         off
markdirs        off
monitor         on
noexec          off
noclobber       off
noglob          off
nolog           off
nounset         off
privileged      off
restricted      off
trackall        off
verbose         off
vi              on
viraw           off
xtrace          off
```

Enter the command

```
set -o vi
```

Press Escape and then k.

**b)**   What happens? What does the `set -o vi` command do?

*Answer: The command turns on vi-style command-line editing.*

To activate an option controlled by `set`, use a -o followed by the option name. These options affect the *current* shell. They're often placed in your shell startup files. For instance, if you like emacs command-line editing, you can place `set -o emacs` in your `.profile` file. Every time you log in, that option will be set for you.

Enter the command

```
set +o vi
```

Press Escape and then k.

**c)**   What happens? What does the `set +o vi` command do?

*Answer: The command turns off vi-style command-line editing.*

To turn off an option that's already on, use +o followed by the option name.

Table 7.1 shows some useful options that can be set with `set -o`:

**Table 7.1 ■ set -o Options**

| Setting | | Meaning When On |
|---|---|---|
| allexport | off | If on, every variable is exported into the environment unless its name contains a dot (.). |
| emacs | off | Command-line editing is done using emacs commands. |
| ignoreeof | off | In an interactive shell, Ctrl-D will not cause the shell to exit. |
| interactive | on | The shell waits for input from standard input. Your login shell is interactive. |
| markdirs | off | When a wildcard expands to a directory name, the shell adds a / to the end. |
| noexec | off | The shell reads commands but does not execute them. This is useful for testing shell scripts. |
| noclobber | off | When using the > file redirection operator, the shell will not overwrite an existing file. To overwrite an existing file, use >| instead. |
| noglob | off | The shell does not do wildcard expansion when this is on. |
| verbose | off | The shell displays all input on standard error. Useful when you don't know what a shell script is actually doing. |
| vi | on | Command-line editing is done using vi commands. |
| xtrace | off | The shell displays every command with all of its arguments before running the command. Useful when you don't know what a shell script is actually doing. |

**LAB
7.3**

### 7.3.3 ANSWERS

**a)** Is there a file named /etc/profile on your system? Is there a file named .profile in your home directory?

*Answer: If you are using the Korn Shell as your login shell, /etc/profile will be there and .profile will probably be in your home directory.*

These are the two startup files used by the Korn Shell (and the Bourne Shell). When you log in and the Korn Shell starts, it reads the file /etc/

profile and runs any commands there, then it runs the .profile file in your home directory.

The /etc/profile file contains system-wide commands that the system administrator wants all users to run. Typically, the /etc/profile file does the following:

- Sets up the default PATH variable.
- Sets your umask (see Chapter 10, "More About Files and Permissions," for a description of the umask).
- Checks for e-mail messages you might have.
- Runs the motd (message of the day) program.

The system /etc/profile file can be quite complicated. If there are many different types of terminals connecting to your site, the /etc/ profile file might contain a lot of commands to get your TERM environment variable correct. It might run other commands that are specific to your site.

The .profile file is your personal startup file. Typically you use it to:

- Set and export variables you want set for all programs you run.
- Set options that you want to apply to your login shell only.
- Specify a script you want to run when you log out.

Instead of setting aliases and options in the .profile file (which is only run once, when you log in), you set them in *another* file, your environment file. The .profile file is run only once, when you log in, but your environment file is run every time you start an interactive shell.

For this question, you set ENV to the value "~/.envfile" and then created a file ~/.envfile, containing some shell settings and exported variables. After doing that, you started a new interactive copy of the shell with ksh -i.

**b)** What's different about your environment in this new shell?

*Answer: All of the commands in* ~/.envfile *have been executed.*

When you start a new shell, it looks at the ENV variable. If the ENV variable is set to the name of a file (the environment file), the shell runs all of the commands in that file.

Don't forget that you're now in a shell running in a shell. You might want to exit this shell before you go on. If you want the environment

file to be read the next time you log in, add the ENV setting to your
.profile file:

```
export ENV=~/.envfile
```

If you make a change to your environment file and you want to test it
right away, you can use the source (dot) command to run the contents of
the environment file in your current shell, like this:

```
. ~/.envfile
```

**LAB
7.3**

The dot command is a good way to test changes to either of the startup
files.

**c)** Why use two local startup files?

*Answer: Because not all shells read your* .profile *file.*

The Korn Shell makes a distinction between ways of starting up the shell.
The shell reads different startup files based on how it starts up.

The ones you're likely to encounter are:

- The *interactive* shell is any shell where you'll be typing commands directly. All interactive shells read the environment file,
  if there is one.
- The *login* shell is the shell you get when you log in. This shell
  reads /etc/profile and your .profile and, because it's an
  interactive shell, your environment file. The only way to get a
  login shell is to log in, using either the login command or the
  su command. (The su command lets you "act like" another
  user. If you have only one account, it isn't a very useful command. The system administrator uses it frequently to switch
  between accounts.) All login shells are interactive but not all
  interactive shells are login shells.

  Some shells will allow you to start a login shell with a
  command-line option. (The Korn Shell does not have an option like this.) For example, the Tenex C Shell is a login shell if
  you start it with the option -l.
- The *non-interactive* shell is a shell program that was started to
  run a script and then quit when the script is finished. It's the
  opposite of an interactive shell. A non-interactive shell doesn't
  read *any* startup files.

(There is also the *restricted* shell, which is intended for new users or guests. It prevents the user from changing directories, changing the ENV or PATH environment variables, running a command name with / in it, or performing file redirection. If you've successfully done all the exercises in the book so far, it's certain you're not using a restricted shell.)

Although it looks complicated, this separation of startup files lets you control what's in your environment and avoid running commands you don't need to run.

A shell script probably doesn't need your customizations. In fact, it shouldn't require them, if you expect other to people run the script as well. On the other hand, if you're going to be using the shell interactively, you probably want every customization you've included.

- The /etc/profile and .profile files contain settings you want to be true for *all* commands you run; this includes your PATH and your terminal settings.
- The environment file is intended to contain any commands and settings you want set in an interactive shell but not necessarily in a shell script.

# LAB 7.3 SELF-REVIEW QUESTIONS

In order to test your progress, you should be able to answer the following questions.

1) The shell parameters PS1, PS2, PS3, and PS4 affect the ps command.
   a) \_\_\_\_\_True
   b) \_\_\_\_\_False

2) To include your current directory in your command prompt, use:
   a) \_\_\_\_\_PS1=`$PWD$ `
   b) \_\_\_\_\_PS1=\$PWD\$\
   c) \_\_\_\_\_PS1=`$PWD`"$ "
   d) \_\_\_\_\_Any of the above

3) You can include the results of commands in your prompt.
   a) \_\_\_\_\_True
   b) \_\_\_\_\_False

**4)** To turn on the `noclobber` option, use the command:

**a)** \_\_\_\_\_`set +o noclobber`

**b)** \_\_\_\_\_`set -o noclobber`

**c)** \_\_\_\_\_`set noclobber`

**d)** \_\_\_\_\_`set`

**5)** Which variable must be set to the value of your environment file?

**a)** \_\_\_\_\_ENVIRON

**b)** \_\_\_\_\_FCEDIT

**c)** \_\_\_\_\_PS4

**d)** \_\_\_\_\_ENV

**e)** \_\_\_\_\_`.profile`

*Quiz answers appear in Appendix A, Section 7.3.*

# C H A P T E R   7

# TEST YOUR THINKING

Examine the following commands:

```
$ name=bob
$ echo $name
bob
$ name=sue echo $name
bob
```

**1)**  Why doesn't the echo command print "sue"?

Examine this .profile file.

```
set -o allexport
FCEDIT=vi
PATH=$PATH:~/bin:
VISUAL=$(whence emacs)
MACHINE=$(uname -n)
PS1="$MACHINE/$LOGNAME [!]$ "
stty erase ^h kill ^u
export TERM
alias lf = lc -F
export HISTSIZE = 256
```

**2)**  Given this .profile file, answer the following questions:

**a)**  What does each line do?

**b)**  Which lines will not work as expected?

**c)**  Which items would you put in a .profile file and which items would you put in the environment file?

 *Remember that items in your* .profile *will affect all commands you run, but items in the environment file will affect only interactive shells.*

**d)**  How will you have to change the .profile if you move some items into an environment file?

# BASIC SHELL PROGRAMMING

 *Programs do repetitive tasks for you. If you can do simple programming, you can write commands that eliminate the repetitive tasks you hate.*

This chapter is about repeating complicated commands and sequences of commands without retyping them. It will introduce you to techniques you can use from the command line and in shell scripts to perform some tasks that are tedious. The control loops can save you a lot of typing. The chapter ends with some sample shell scripts that you may find useful.

Nobody's asking you to be a programmer. However, if the information in this chapter can make your life a little easier, why not do it? This is not a complete guide to shell programming; it's not even a complete *introduction* to shell programming. If you find you write a lot of shell scripts, see the *UNIX Shell Programmer's Interactive Workbook* to learn more.

# LAB 8.1

# VARIABLES AND PARAMETERS

---

### LAB OBJECTIVES

After this Lab, you will be able to:

- Remove a Prefix from a Variable
- Remove a Postfix from a Variable
- Set a Variable's Type

---

As mentioned in Chapter 7, "Customizing Your Environment," the Korn Shell provides a number of parameters and variables. A variable is a storage location that you can refer to by name; placing a $ in front of the name means "the value this variable stores."

There are programs to change text (usually file names), and these are frequently used in shell scripts. For example, the basename command takes a path name and returns the name of the file without directories. The dirname command does the opposite: It takes a path name and returns the directory name without the file part.

However, it's slow to start a new program. So the Korn Shell includes a number of ways to change the value of a variable. These don't actually change the value stored in the variable; it's better to think of them as changes made every time the value is pulled out of the variable.

The shell parameters are useful in shell scripts. (The distinction between parameters and variables is a subtle one. All variables are parameters, but not all parameters are variables. For our purposes, if something is referred to as a parameter instead of a variable, then you cannot assign it a value.)

If you want to pass arguments to your shell scripts, you need to know some of the provided parameters. (One, $*, was discussed in Chapter 7, "Customizing Your Environment.")

# LAB 8.1 EXERCISES

## 8.1.1 REMOVE A PREFIX FROM A VARIABLE

Enter the following commands:

```
fruit=coconut
print $fruit#co
print ${fruit#co}
```

**a)** What is the output? What effect does { } have on the output? What effect does #co have on the output?

_____

_____

Enter the following commands:

```
print ${fruit#*co}
print ${fruit##co}
print ${fruit##*co}
```

**b)** Does replacing "co" with "*co" have an effect on the output? What is the output? What effect does "##*co" have on the output?

_____

_____

Enter the following command:

```
print ${PWD##*/}
```

**c)** What is the output? What effect does ##*/ have on the output?

_____

_____

### 8.1.2 REMOVE A POSTFIX FROM A VARIABLE

Enter the following commands:

```
fruit=banana
print ${fruit%na*}
```

**a)** What is the output? What effect does %na have on the output?

_____

_____

Enter the following command:

```
print ${fruit%%na*}
```

**b)** What is the output? What effect does %%na* have on the output?

_____

_____

**c)** What happens if you use "*na" as the pattern instead?

_____

_____

Enter the following command:

```
print ${PWD%/*}
```

**d)** What is the output? What effect does %/* have on the output?

_____

_____

### 8.1.3 SET A VARIABLE'S TYPE

Enter the following commands:

```
typeset -u name
```

```
name=${LOGNAME}
print ${LOGNAME} became ${name}
```

**a)** What is the output? What does the `typeset -u` command do to the value of the variable?

_____

_____

Enter the following commands:

```
typeset -l name
print ${name}
```

**b)** What is the output? What does the `typeset -l` command do to the value of the variable?

_____

_____

# LAB 8.1 EXERCISE ANSWERS

## 8.1.1 ANSWERS

Enter the following commands:

```
fruit=coconut
print $fruit#co
print ${fruit#co}
```

**a)** What is the output? What effect does { } have on the output? What effect does #co have on the output?

*Answer: The outputs are:*

```
$ print $fruit#co
coconut#co
$ print ${fruit#co}
conut
```

*The braces force the shell to treat "#co" as part of the variable or parameter name. When it's interpreted, the #co modifier removes the shortest matching pattern ("co" is the pattern) from the beginning of the variable's value.*

Up until now, all references to the values of variables and other parameters have been accomplished by placing $ at the beginning of the name. That's fine for simple references, but as soon as you start adding modifiers to the parameter name, or adding characters to the end of the variable's value, then you need a way to tell the shell where the variable name (and modifiers) end.

Without the braces, the shell examines the word after the $ sign and if the first part is a variable or parameter, expands it. Some characters, such as "#", aren't normally allowed in variable names, so the shell treats that as the end of the variable's name. (This is why "$fruit#co" turned into "coconut#co" instead of being turned into nothing, the usual value for a variable that doesn't exist.) With the braces, the shell "knows" to treat "#co" as a modifier. A dot (.) is another character that isn't normally treated as part of a variable's name.

It's a very good idea to always use braces around variable references, although many people don't. Braces make it clear that you're referring to a variable, and they make it clear how you're modifying the value of the variable.

When "#co" is treated as a modifier, it means "remove the shortest matching pattern from the beginning of this variable's value." If the value of fruit were "nococonut" then the reference ${fruit#co} would return "nococonut". The pattern "co" is not at the beginning of the value, so it doesn't get removed.

Enter the following commands:

```
print ${fruit#*co}
print ${fruit##co}
print ${fruit##*co}
```

**b)** Does replacing "co" with "*co" have an effect on the output? What is the output? What effect does "##*co" have on the output?

*Answer: Replacing "co" with "*co" doesn't have an effect when the operator is #, but does have an effect when the operator is ##. The output becomes "nut". The "##*co" modifier removes the longest matching pattern from the beginning of the variable's value.*

When you double the # character, it matches the longest matching pattern. (This is why the * was added to the pattern: The longest pattern that matches "co" is also the shortest pattern that matches "co" — it's "co".)

*Remember that these are wildcard patterns, not regular expressions.
Trying to remove "coco" from "coconut" with*
`${fruit##co*}` *won't work, because the "`*`" doesn't mean repetition in wildcard patterns.*

Incidentally, the exercises in this Lab use `print` instead of `echo`. The two commands do much the same thing, but the `print` command has some useful options that `echo` does not. Both the `print` and `echo` commands treat some characters with backslashes specially, but you can turn this behavior off with the `print` command and you cannot with `echo`. The other advantage of `print` is that it's very easy to tell `print` to write to standard error. (The command `print -u2` *arguments* copies the arguments to standard error instead of the standard output.)

The disadvantage of `print` is that it's in the Korn Shell but not in the C Shell or the Bourne Shell.

Enter the following command:

```
print ${PWD##*/}
```

**c)** What is the output? What effect does `##*/` have on the output?

*Answer: The exact text depends on your current directory. For the directory* `/home/bethany`, *the output is "bethany". The* `##*/` *modifier removes all characters up to and including the last* / *from the variable's value.*

The text after the `#` or `##` operator is a wildcard pattern. The pattern "`*/`" matches any set of characters that ends in a slash. If your current directory is `/tmp`, the value is turned into "tmp".

If the value of fruit were "nococonut", then the pattern `${fruit##[nc]o}` would be turned into "nut".

This is almost the same as the `basename` command. The command `basename $PWD` produces the same output as `print ${PWD##*/}`. The difference is that in a shell script, this version would be slightly faster than using `basename`.

Rather than include your entire current directory in your prompt, you could change your prompt to read:

```
PS1='${PWD##*/}$ '
```

If you do this, only the directory name will appear in your prompt, rather than the entire directory path. This might be useful if you do a lot of work in directories with long path names.

## 8.1.2 ANSWERS

Enter the following commands:

```
fruit=banana
print ${fruit%na*}
```

**a)**    What is the output? What effect does %na have on the output?

*Answer: The output is "bana". The %na modifier removes the shortest matching pattern ("na") from the end of the variable's value.*

Enter the following command:

```
print ${fruit%%na*}
```

**b)**    What is the output? What effect does %%na have on the output?

*Answer: The output is "ba". The %%na modifier removes the longest matching pattern from the end of the variable's value.*

**c)**    What happens if you use "*na" as the pattern instead?

*Answer: The pattern matches the entire value, and the output is an empty line.*

If you're going to use %% or ##, be aware of which end of the pattern you put the * character. In this case, "na" matches the very end of the pattern. Placing a * *before* the "na" matches everything up to the end of the variable's value.

Enter the following command:

```
print ${PWD%/*}
```

**d)**    What is the output? What effect does %/* have on the output?

*Answer: The %/* pattern removes everything after the last / in the path.*

This is equivalent to the command dirname. In Bourne Shell scripts, you will see variable assignments like this:

```
FILENAME=`basename $path`
DIRECTORY=`dirname $path`
```

Using the Korn Shell, you can write the same assignments in this way:

```
FILENAME=${path##*/}
DIRECTORY=${path%/*}
```

(You could choose not to assign the values to new variables. If you're writing a shell script, though, you should. A properly chosen variable name makes it clear what the variable contains. In six months, you may need to look at that shell script again and ${FILENAME} is much easier to understand than ${path##/*}.)

## 8.1.3 ANSWERS

Enter the following commands:

```
typeset -u name
name=${LOGNAME}
print ${LOGNAME} became ${name}
```

**a)** What is the output? What does the `typeset -u` command do to the value of the variable?

*Answer: The* `typeset -u` *command switches the contents of the variable to uppercase letters.*

The Korn Shell has a number of different variable types. This defines the kind of information that can be stored in the variable. The `typeset` command sets a variable's type. The `-u` option makes the variable's information uppercase.

Enter the following commands:

```
typeset -l name
print ${name}
```

**b)** What is the output? What does the `typeset -l` command do to the value of the variable?

*Answer: The* `typeset -l` *command switches the contents of the variable to lowercase letters.*

The `typeset -u` and `typeset -l` commands counter each other.

# LAB 8.1  SELF-REVIEW QUESTIONS

In order to test your progress, you should be able to answer the following questions.

The value of the variable `filename` is `RCS/rococo.txt,v`.

1) What is the value of `${filename##*/%,v}`?
   **a)** _____`RCS/rococo.txt`
   **b)** _____`rococo.txt,v`
   **c)** _____`RCS/rococo.txt,v`
   **d)** _____`rococo.txt`

2) What is the value of `./${filename##*/}`?
   **a)** _____`./RCS/rococo.txt`
   **b)** _____`RCS/rococo.txt,v`
   **c)** _____`./RCS/rococo.txt,v`
   **d)** _____`./rococo.txt,v`
   **e)** _____`./rococo.txt`

3) After the command `typeset -l filename`, what is the value of `${filename##RCS/}`?
   **a)** _____`rcs/rococo.txt`
   **b)** _____`rococo.txt,v`
   **c)** _____`RCS/rococo.txt.,v`
   **d)** _____`rococo.txt`

4) Which pattern is equivalent to `dirname ${filename}`?
   **a)** _____`${filename#*/}`
   **b)** _____`${filename##*/}`
   **c)** _____`${filename%/*}`
   **d)** _____`${filename%%/*}`
   **e)** _____`${filename%%*/##/*}`

*Quiz answers appear in Appendix A, Section 8.1.*

# LAB 8.2

# TESTING AND BRANCHING

---

**LAB OBJECTIVES**

After this Lab, you will be able to:

- Display the Return Code
- Branch with the if Statement
- Test Attributes with test

---

If you're writing a long chain of commands, either in a shell script or as a very long command line, how do you know if a command has failed? In fact, how do you make decisions in commands?

The UNIX system provides one way. By design, every command tells you if it succeeded or failed. It doesn't do this by writing a message to the screen. Instead, it stores the information in a parameter, and the UNIX shells provide several ways to get at this information.

To make decisions, the shell provides a programming tool called the if statement. The if statement is simply a way to choose between actions: If something is true, do this; otherwise, do that.

Because the if statement is a multi-line command, I encourage you to use command line editing to repeat the commands. (See Chapter 5, "Other Useful Stuff," for a description of command-line editing.)

# LAB 8.2 EXERCISES

## 8.2.1 DISPLAY THE RETURN CODE

Enter the following commands:

```
ls ~
print $?
```

**a)** What is the value of $?? What does it mean?

_____

_____

Enter the following commands:

```
grep ${LOGNAME} /dev/null 2> /dev/null
print $?
grep ${LOGNAME} nosuchfile
print $?
```

**b)** What are the values of $?? What do they mean?

_____

_____

Enter the following commands:

```
grep ${LOGNAME} /etc/passwd && print hello
grep ${LOGNAME} /dev/null && print hello
```

**c)** What is the output? What does the && operator do?

_____

_____

Enter the following commands

```
grep ${LOGNAME} /etc/passwd || print hello
grep ${LOGNAME} /dev/null || print hello
```

**d)** What is the output? What does the || operator do?

_____

_____

### 8.2.2 BRANCH WITH THE IF STATEMENT

Enter the following commands:

```
if ls ~
then
print success!
fi
```

**a)** What do these commands do?

_____

_____

**b)** What happens if you put "then" after the ls, on the same line?

_____

_____

Enter the following commands:

```
if ! ls ~
then
print success!
else
print failure...
fi
```

**c)** What does the command do now? What effect does the ! have?

_____

_____

**LAB
8.2**

### 8.2.3 TEST ATTRIBUTES WITH TEST

Enter the following commands:

```
dir=$PWD
if test -d .
then
    print $PWD is a directory
fi
```

**a)** What does the `test` command do?

_____

_____

Enter the following commands:

```
if ! test -f .
then
    print $PWD is not a file
fi
```

**b)** What effect does the ! have on the test?

_____

_____

**c)** What does `test -f` check for?

_____

_____

Enter the following commands:

```
if test "${PWD}" == "${HOME}"
then
    print You\'re in your home directory
fi
```

**d)** What kind of test does == do?

_____

_____

**e)** Why put quotation marks around the variable names?

_____

_____

# LAB 8.2 EXERCISE ANSWERS

## 8.2.1 ANSWERS

Enter the following commands:

```
ls ~
print $?
```

**a)** What is the value of $?? What does it mean?

_Answer: The value of $? is 0. The value of $? indicates whether the command succeeded or failed._

When a command finishes on UNIX, it gives a number to the shell, which the shell stores in the parameter ?. This return value or return code indicates whether the command succeeded or failed. A return code of 0 means the command succeeded; any other value means it failed.

Shell scripts often check the return code of a command before proceeding. You don't want to delete a file until you know that the operations you were performing have succeeded, or you might want to write an error message if the command failed.

Enter the following commands:

```
grep ${LOGNAME} /dev/null
print $?
grep ${LOGNAME} nosuchfile
print $?
```

**b)**   What are the values of $?? What do they mean?

*Answer: For the first command, the* grep *command doesn't find a match and returns a 1. For the second command, the* grep *command can't find the file, and returns a 2.*

You can rely on the fact that the return value of 0 means the command succeeded; any other value means some kind of failure. Different programs use different numbers. For example, grep has two different kinds of "failure", so it uses the numbers 1 and 2. (A 1 means it could check the file but it didn't find any matches, while a 2 means it couldn't even check the file for some reason.) The grep program defines "success" as "finding a matching line."

A value other than 0 *always* means the command didn't succeed, but you have to look on the command's man page to see what a particular number means for that command.

Enter the following commands:

```
grep ${LOGNAME} /etc/passwd && print hello
grep ${LOGNAME} /dev/null && print hello
```

**c)**   What is the output? What does the && operator do?

*Answer: The && operator runs the second command only if the first command succeeded. The output looks like this (your exact text will vary):*

```
$ grep ${LOGNAME} /etc/passwd && print hello
jordan:x:128:103:Jordan Shelbourne:/home/jordan:/bin/ksh
hello
$ grep ${LOGNAME} /dev/null && print hello
$
```

The && operator is another command that the shell understands and that joins two commands together (just as ; and | join commands together). The && operator checks the return value of the *first* command; if and *only* if it succeeded, it runs the second command. This saves you the trouble of checking the value of $?. You can think of it as similar to being in a restaurant: If the restaurant has pistachio ice cream (the first command is true), then you will eat it (the second command is true). If the restaurant doesn't have pistachio ice cream, there's no reason to try to eat it.

Suppose you are copying files to a backup directory. You want to rename the original files in the current directory to indicate that the file is backed up, but only if the copy command actually worked. You can use a command like this:

```
cp workfile backup/ && mv workfile savedfile
```

Obviously those names are artificial. (You wouldn't type each command, either; this is better done in a command loop, like a `for` loop.)

**Enter the following commands:**

```
grep ${LOGNAME} /etc/passwd || print hello
grep ${LOGNAME} /dev/null || print hello
```

**d)**  What is the output? What does the `||` operator do?

*Answer: The `||` operator runs the second command only if the first command failed. The output looks like this (your exact text will vary):*

```
$ grep ${LOGNAME} /etc/passwd || print hello
jordan:x:128:103:Jordan Shelbourne:/home/jordan:/bin/ksh
$ grep ${LOGNAME} /dev/null || print hello
hello
```

The `||` operator is the opposite of the `&&` operator. It joins two commands together, but it runs the second command *only* if the first command fails. It's often used in shell scripts to exit the shell script if an important command has failed or to print error messages.

Going back to the restaurant, you may decide that if the restaurant *doesn't* have pistachio ice cream, you're going to write a strongly worded letter. This is an action that's only important if the first command (your attempt to order pistachio ice cream) fails.

## ■ FOR EXAMPLE

You're backing up files again, but this time you only want to know if the copy failed:

```
mv workfile backup/ || print workfile didn\'t get
moved!
```

Again, this is a command that works better in a control loop, because when you're typing one command at a time, you know if the command didn't work.

In shell scripts, you'll sometimes see || used in this way:

```
cd ${workdir} || exit 1
```

In this case, the shell script will exit with a return code of 1 if the cd command doesn't work.

The && and || operators do similar things, but which operator you use depends on what you want to accomplish.

Often when you're using grep or some other search commands, you don't care about the exact line that matches, you just want to know if the grep command succeeded. You can make the output of the grep command a little more friendly by using a longer command that discards grep's regular output. For example, you could do something like this:

```
$ grep ${LOGNAME} /etc/passwd >/dev/null || print
${LOGNAME} not in /etc/password file
```

This way you don't see the output of the grep command, just the print statement if grep doesn't find ${LOGNAME}.

## 8.2.2 ANSWERS

Enter the following commands:

```
if ls ~
then
print success!
fi
```

**a)**   What do these commands do?

*Answer: If the* ls *command succeeds, it prints "success!" on the screen.*

This is the most basic if statement. If the command succeeds (if its return code is 0), then it performs the commands between the then and the fi.

The basic syntax of the if command is:

```
if condition
then
   commands
[else
   commands]
fi
```

The `then` and the `fi` mark the beginning and end of the commands you want to run if the `ls` command succeeds. There's only one command in this example, but you could have 6 or 60. This set of commands is sometimes called a *clause* or a *branch*. The command in this Exercise is equivalent to:

```
ls && print success!
```

However, the `if` command can go beyond the `&&` operator by offering you two (or more) choices. These are the commands in the `else` clause.

**b)**   What happens if you put "`then`" after the `ls`, on the same line?

*Answer: The command doesn't work. It prints an error message:*

```
ksh: syntax error: `fi' expected
```

The `if` command is normally a multi-line command. Because there's no way for the shell to "know" what the command will be after the `if`, the shell relies on `then` being a new command, starting on a new line.

For a very simple `if` command, you can use semicolon (;) instead of starting new lines. The semicolon was described in the *UNIX User's Interactive Workbook*, in Chapter 12, "Commands and Job Control." The command might look like this:

```
if ls ; then print success!; fi
```

The tricky part is that you *don't* need a new line after the `then`. You can put complicated sequences of commands on a single line using the semicolon, but it's hard to read and not worth the mental energy. If you start a new line for `then` and `fi` and each command between the two, you'll be fine.

Enter the following commands:

```
if ! ls ~
then
print success!
else
print failure...
fi
```

**c)**   What does the command do now? What effect does the `!` have?

*Answer: The command prints the contents of your home directory and then prints "`failure  . . .`" The `!` character made the `if` treat the `ls` as if it had failed.*

There are actually two new items here: the ! character and the else clause. We'll deal with the else clause first.

The else clause provides a second choice. It describes what you will do if the command doesn't succeed. To return to our restaurant, you can now describe *both* of your actions: If the restaurant has pistachio ice cream, then you will eat it; otherwise, you will write a strongly worded letter.

**LAB 8.2**

In this context, the ! character is called a *negation* operator. It reverses the meaning of the test. Even though the ls command succeeded, the ! character reversed the meaning of the return code, and the if command behaved as though the command had failed.

*When you're using a command after the if command, remember that the command gets run. This is important if the command has a serious effect, such as deleting files.*

The negation operator is important when you're checking for some conditions. Perhaps you want to print an error message if a file doesn't exist or if a command fails. You *could* do it with an else clause (this grep command sends both output and error messages to /dev/null; all we care about is the result code):

```
if grep ${LOGNAME} /dev/null 2>/dev/null
then
    false
else
    print grep did not find the name
fi
```

(The false command is a special command that always returns non-zero as its return code. There's also a true command, which always returns zero.)

It's simple to type and to read using the negation operator:

```
if ! grep ${LOGNAME} /dev/null
then
    print grep did not find the name
fi
```

## 8.2.3 ANSWERS

Enter the following commands:

```
dir=$PWD
if test -d .
then
    print $PWD is a directory
fi
```

**a)**  What does the `test` command do?

*Answer: The* `test` *command performs a test and returns 0 if the test is true and 1 if the test is false. The output is (your directory name will vary):*

```
/home/johnmc/chap08 is a directory
```

The `test` command was written to take advantage of return codes. All it does is test something and return 0 or 1, depending on whether the test succeeded or failed. This test checks to see if the argument is a directory (`-d`). Because . is always a directory, you know this test will succeed.

There are two kinds of tests:

- The first (and simplest) test is to test the properties of an object, such as a file. If the object has the property, the test returns true; if it doesn't, the test returns false. This is the kind of test used in this Exercise. This test has the form:

  ```
  test option objectname
  ```

- The second test compares two objects. You need to specify the two objects and the relationship between them. If the relationship is true, the test returns true; if it isn't, the test returns false. This test has the form:

  ```
  test object1 relationship object2
  ```

The *relationship* can be checking to see if the two objects are equal (for instance, do two files have the same name?) or if one is bigger than the other, or if one is newer than the other. The `test` command provides many tests, and it's worth checking some time.

Enter the following commands:

```
if ! test -f .
then
```

```
      print $PWD is not a file
fi
```

**b)**  What effect does the ! have on the test?

*Answer: The ! negates the meaning of the test.*

This is the same as in the previous Lab: The ! before the test reverses the meaning of the test. Notice that the ! comes *before* the test command. Some of the relationships for test include a ! character, so it's easy to get confused.

**c)**  What does test -f check for?

*Answer: The test -f command checks to see if an object is a file.*

The most common properties that test is used for are in Table 8.1.

There are many more tests. If you want to test for something else, it's worth looking at the test man page.

 *Instead of writing the command* test, *you can also surround the arguments to test with square brackets. The test* test -f $HOME *can also be written as* [ -f $HOME ]. *Remember that you have to have an opening and a closing bracket, and that there must be spaces on each side of the brackets. This is usually how shell scripts use* test, *it makes the shell script look much more like other programming languages.*

Enter the following commands:

```
if test "${PWD}" == "${HOME}"
then
    print You\'re in your home directory
fi
```

### Table 8.1 ■ **Properties Checked by** test

| Property | Option |
| --- | --- |
| The file exists | -a *file* |
| The file exists and is a directory | -d *file* |
| The file exists and is a regular file | -f *file* |
| The file exists and is readable | -r *file* |
| The file exists and is writable | -w *file* |

**d)** What kind of test does `==` do?

*Answer: It compares two strings to see if they're the same.*

This is one of the most confusing tests. There are two equals signs, not one, and they test words or strings, and not numbers. For numerical comparisons, use `-eq` instead of `==`. The common comparisons done by test are shown in Table 8.2.

LAB
8.2

**e)** Why put quotation marks around the variable names?

*Answer: If a variable has not been set, this prevents an error.*

To demonstrate, take out the quotation marks and suppose the comparison were not to PWD, which always has a value, but to some other variable that might not have been set—say, MYDIR.

If MYDIR has a value (we'll use / because it's short), then the comparison becomes:

```
if test / == /home/mine
```

These two are obviously not equal, and the test returns failure. That is, the `test` command works, but it returns a code of failure.

Now suppose that you forgot to set MYDIR. It doesn't exist. Variables that don't exist get turned into nothing, so the test is now:

```
if test == /home/mine
```

This is an error; there's nothing on the left side of the `==` signs. The `test` program doesn't know what to do with a test like this, so it gives up. It doesn't report failure (because that might make a script do the wrong thing!) but instead it just quits.

**Table 8.2 ▪ Comparisons Done by** `test`

| Comparison | Syntax |
|---|---|
| Are two strings the same? | *string1* `==` *string2* |
| Are two strings different? | *string1* `!=` *string2* |
| Is one number equal to another? | *num1* `-eq` *num2* |
| Is the first number less than the second? | *num1* `-lt` *num2* |
| Is the first number greater than the second? | *num1* `-gt` *num2* |

Now put quotation marks around `MYDIR`. The `MYDIR` still doesn't exist, so the shell turns it into "". To the shell, that means "empty" and the test becomes:

```
if test "" == /home/mine
```

Because there's now some value on the left side of the equality operator (even if it's empty quotation marks), the syntax of the `test` command is satisfied, and there's no error. The command still won't work correctly (the test will never return success), but it won't suddenly quit in an unexpected and possibly inexplicable way.

# LAB 8.2  SELF-REVIEW QUESTIONS

In order to test your progress, you should be able to answer the following questions.

**1)**  All UNIX programs return a return value.
   **a)** _____True
   **b)** _____False

**2)**  Which of the following is true if you have two commands joined by `&&`?
   **a)** _____The second command gets run only if the first command fails.
   **b)** _____The second command gets run only if the first command succeeds.
   **c)** _____Both commands get run, no matter what.
   **d)** _____Neither command gets run.

**3)**  Which of the following is true if you have two commands joined by `||`?
   **a)** _____The second command gets run only if the first command fails.
   **b)** _____The second command gets run only if the first command succeeds.
   **c)** _____Both commands get run, no matter what.
   **d)** _____Neither command gets run.
   **e)** _____Output from the first command is used as input for the second.

**4)**  The return code of a command is 2. What does this mean?
   **a)** _____The options were wrong.
   **b)** _____A file could not be opened.
   **c)** _____Command succeeded.
   **d)** _____Depends upon the command.
   **e)** _____`grep` could not find a match.

**5)**  Given this command, which of the following is true?

```
if ! ls /lost+found
then
```

```
    cd /lost+found
else
   print oops
fi
```

**a)** \_\_\_\_\_The `ls` command doesn't get run, because it's negated.

**b)** \_\_\_\_\_The `ls` command doesn't get run if you don't have permission to list the directory.

**c)** \_\_\_\_\_The command prints "oops" if you have permission to list the directory.

**d)** \_\_\_\_\_The command prints "oops" if you don't have permission to list the directory.

**6)** What test can be used to see if you have permission to read the directory `/lost+found`?

**a)** \_\_\_\_\_`test -f /lost+found`

**b)** \_\_\_\_\_`test -d /lost+found`

**c)** \_\_\_\_\_`test -r /lost+found`

**d)** \_\_\_\_\_`test -w /lost+found`

**e)** \_\_\_\_\_`test -a /lost+found`

*Quiz answers appear in Appendix A, Section 8.2.*

# L A B   8 . 3

# REPEATING COMMANDS WITH LOOPS

---

### LAB OBJECTIVES

After this Lab, you will be able to:

- Repeat Commands on Items in a List
- Run Commands on Lines of a File

---

One of the greatest assets of computers is *automation*. You can make a computer do a boring, repetitive task as many times as you want, and you can be assured that the hundredth time it does something, it will do it exactly as it did the first time.

A loop is a programming construct that repeats commands. Although there are several different commands in the Korn Shell to create loops, we'll look at only two.

In the first case, the for loop, you have a list of items (usually files) and you want to run the same set of commands on each item in the list. One example might be renaming all of the files in the directory. Perhaps you copied an archive file from another site using ftp and when you unpacked the archive, all of the files had names that where in uppercase.

In the second case, the while loop, you have information in a file, and you want to use that information in other commands. For example, you might have a list of file names and you want to read the list of file names and check that each file exists. A while loop just executes commands, and every time it starts the block of commands it tests to see if it should run the commands again. Combined with the read command, a while loop can read each line in a file and use it in other commands.

## 8.3.1   REPEAT COMMANDS ON ITEMS IN A LIST

Enter the following commands:

```
for x in a b c d e f
do
    print $x
done
```

**a)** What does the `for` command do? Does it work without the `do` line?

_____

_____

**b)** What happens to the value of `x` each time?

_____

_____

**c)** What happens if you assign a new value to `x` right after the `print` line?

_____

_____

## 8.3.2   RUN COMMANDS ON LINES OF A FILE

Enter the following commands:

```
while read line
do
    print "$line"
done < ~/.profile
```

**a)** What does this command do? What does the `while` command do?

_____

_____

**b)** What does the `read` command do?

_____

_____

**c)** When does the `while` command end?

_____

_____

**d)** Why put quotation marks around "`$line`"?

_____

_____

# LAB 8.3 EXERCISE ANSWERS

## 8.3.1 ANSWERS

Enter the following commands:

```
for x in a b c d e f
do
     print $x
done
```

**a)**    What does the `for` command do? Does it work without the do line?

*Answer: The command prints out each item in the list. You must have the* `do` *and* `done` *lines, or the command will not work.*

The `for` command takes a variable (x in this case) and a list (a b c d e f). It assigns the variable the first value in the list and then executes all the commands between `do` and `done`. Then it assigns the variable the second value in the list and executes all of the commands between `do` and `done`, and so on. The syntax is:

```
for variable in list
do
    commands
done
```

The do *has* to be there; so does the done. They mark the beginning and end of the list of commands to be executed. You should always put them on new lines. (There are ways to get around that, but it's easier just to do it.)

By the way, I've indented the commands inside the do and done commands because it makes the file easier to read. The shell doesn't care, as long as new lines start in the right places. With indenting, I can look at the command and see which commands are part of this loop and which commands are outside of it.

 *Use indenting to identify subordinate sections of your commands and scripts.*

**b)** What happens to the value of x each time?

*Answer: The value of x is assigned to each of the items in the list.*

The *list* can be anything. It doesn't even have to be related to the commands; you can use the list simply as a counting mechanism.

## ■ FOR EXAMPLE:

Suppose you need five random numbers (perhaps you're running a numbers racket, or you're going to use your computer as the world's most expensive die). One of the parameters in the shell is RANDOM, which is just a random number. (It's value is different every time you check.) You can generate five numbers quickly with this command:

```
for n in . . . . .
do
    print $RANDOM
done
```

In this case, the list is just five dots.

**c)** What happens if you assign a new value to x right after the print line?

*Answer: There's no visible effect.*

When the shell goes back to the top of the loop, the value of x gets set to the next value in the list, replacing the value you just gave to x.

## ■ *FOR EXAMPLE:*

If you have a set of files with the extension TXT and you want to change the file extension to text, you can type a simple for loop to handle it:

```
for x in *.TXT
do
      mv $x ${x%TXT}text
done
```

**LAB
8.3**

## 8.3.2 ANSWERS

Enter the following commands:

```
while read line
do
    print "$line"
done < ~/.profile
```

**a)**   What does this command do? What does the while command do?

*Answer: The command writes the contents of your* .profile *command to the standard output.*

The while command repeats a set of commands while some condition or test is true. This is one of the most common uses. (The other common use is to repeat actions a certain number of times, but we'll describe that one in a later exercise.) The syntax of the while command is:

```
while condition
do
      commands
done
```

This exercise demonstrates one other feature of while loops (and other loops): You can redirect their input and output. This command would also work if it were typed:

```
cat ~/.profile | while read line
do
      print "$line"
done > newprofile
```

In this version, the input is read from the pipe, taken from cat, and is redirected into the file newprofile.

**b)**   What does the read command do?

*Answer: The* read *command reads a line of text from standard input, and stores it in a variable or variables.*

If you're not thinking of shell scripts, you may wonder what the point of read is. This is a command that only makes sense in the context of shell scripts. The read command gives you a way to read input and store it in a variable or variables.

The read command takes one or more arguments, which are variable names. The first word is put into the first variable, the second word is put into the second variable, and so on; if there are more words than variables, the remaining words are all placed together in the last variable.

## ■ *FOR EXAMPLE:*

To put a person's first and last names into variables, you could use the commands:

```
print Enter your first and last name:
read first last
print Your first name is ${first}
print your last name is ${last}
```

If the user types "John McMullen," then the variable first contains "John" and the variable last contains "McMullen." If the user types "Bartleby Q. Scrivener," then the variable first contains "Bartleby" and the variable last contains "Q. Scrivener."

**c)**   When does the while command end?

*Answer: The command ends when the condition is no longer true, when* read *returns false.*

When the read command comes to the end of the file, it returns false, and the while loop ends.

## ■ *FOR EXAMPLE:*

Some of my projects at work require me to create hundreds of files. I can easily forget one or two, so I keep a list of the files that are supposed to be in each project. Then, when I think I'm done, I run a little loop like this:

```
while read filename junk
do
    if [ ! -f $filename ]
    then
            print $filename is missing!
    fi
done < manifest
```

The `read` command reads a line and puts the first part in the variable `filename`; the `junk` variable is there in case I wrote a note beside the file name. (I do that sometimes and forget to take them out.) The `if` test checks to see if the file is not there (the `!` reverses the meaning of the test). If the file doesn't exist, I print out a message. If the file does exist, I go on. The `manifest` file is the list of files.

The `test` command here has the same meaning as if I had typed:

```
if test ! -f $filename
```

**d)** Why put quotation marks around "`$line`"?

*Answer: Without the quotes, all of the white space that comes before the first charac-ter is not printed.*

Suppose the value of `$line` is " This line starts with two spaces." Without quotation marks, the `print` command is:

```
$ print   This line starts with two spaces.
This line starts with two spaces.
```

The spaces are ignored, just as if you had typed two extra spaces in the command. With the quotation marks, any spaces at the beginning of the line become part of the arguments to print:

```
$ print "  This line starts with two spaces."
  This line starts with two spaces.
```

# LAB 8.3  SELF-REVIEW QUESTIONS

In order to test your progress, you should be able to answer the following ques-tions.

**1)** A `for` loop checks the value of the variable every time it loops.
   **a)** _____True
   **b)** _____False

**2)** How many times does this `for` loop run?

```
for x in 1 2 3 4 5
do
    x=$x+1
    print ${x}
done
```

**a)** _____3 times.
**b)** _____5 times.
**c)** _____8 times.
**d)** _____10 times.

LAB
8.3

**3)** What does this loop do?

```
for x in *
do
    grep -l tomato $x | sort > tomato.list
done
```

**a)** _____Creates a sorted list of all files containing the word "tomato".
**b)** _____Creates a file containing the name of the last file in the directory that contains the word "tomato".
**c)** _____Creates a sorted list of the lines that contain the word "tomato".
**d)** _____Nothing; it has an error in the `for` loop.

**4)** If the file `newemployees` contains a list of names of new employees, what does this command do?

```
while read input moreinput
do
    mkdir /home/${input}
done < newemployees
```

**a)** _____Creates new directories, each with an employee's first name.
**b)** _____Creates new directories, each with an employee's full name.
**c)** _____Creates new directories, each with an employee's last name.

*Quiz answers appear in Appendix A, Section 8.3.*

# L A B  8 . 4

# SHELL SCRIPTS AND FUNCTIONS

| LAB OBJECTIVES |
| --- |
| After this Lab, you will be able to: |
| • Write a Shell Script |
| • Write a Shell Function |

Shell scripts and functions are the second way to add new commands to your system (after aliases). A shell script is simply a set of commands stored in a file. Adding a shell script to your system is like adding a new program. When you type the name, the shell looks for an executable file with that name in each directory in your PATH. When it finds the file, it runs it.

A shell function is like a shell script but is usually smaller. The reason it's usually smaller is that it stays in your shell's environment. Shell functions run faster because the shell doesn't have to read them from the file system; they've already been read.

## LAB 8.4 EXERCISES

### 8.4.1 WRITE A SHELL SCRIPT

Create a file named CD, which contains the following lines:

```
cd /tmp
ls
```

Enter the following command:

```
./CD
```

**a)** What happens? Why?

_____

_____

**b)** Why is the `./` necessary?

_____

_____

Enter the following commands:

```
chmod 770 CD
./CD
```

**c)** What happens?

_____

_____

Change back to the directory containing the file `CD` and edit it, replacing "`/tmp`" with "`$*`", and adding a first line that starts with #. The file should now read:

```
# Change to a directory and then list its contents
cd $*
ls
```

Enter the following command:

```
./CD /etc
```

**d)** What happens?

_____

_____

## 8.4.2  WRITE A SHELL FUNCTION

Enter the following commands:

```
function repeat
{
    print $*
}
repeat hello, ${LOGNAME}
```

**a)** What happens?

_____

_____

Enter the following commands:

```
function repeat
{
    print $1
}
repeat hello, ${LOGNAME}
```

**b)** What happens?

_____

_____

Enter the following commands:

```
function math
{
print -R $(($*))
}
math 9 + 5
math 11/2
```

**c)** What happens?  What does the `math` function do?

_____

_____

# LAB 8.4 EXERCISE ANSWERS

## 8.4.1 ANSWERS

Enter the following command after creating the file CD:

```
./CD
```

**a)** What happens? Why?

*Answer: The command doesn't execute, because the file is not executable.*

In order for the shell to "know" that the script is to be executed, it needs to have the executable permission set on it. Use the chmod command to add this permission.

A shell script is a list of commands for the shell to run. Like an actor's script, it's one instruction after another. This shell script contains only two commands: cd and ls.

**b)** Why is the ./ necessary?

*Answer: The ./ is needed so the shell can find the CD program.*

When a command name has no slashes in its name, the shell searches each directory in the PATH looking for that file. In this instance, if your PATH doesn't contain the current directory, then the shell won't find the CD script. Adding the ./ at the beginning of the command name, the command becomes a path name that includes a slash and the shell doesn't look through the PATH directories for that file.

If you want to create your own personal set of scripts, the usual procedure is to create the directory ~/bin and add it to your PATH. Then put your personal scripts in ~/bin.

Once you've done this and moved CD into ~/bin, you will no longer need to use ./CD to run the CD script.

Enter the following commands:

```
chmod 770 CD
./CD
```

**c)** What happens?

*Answer: The commands in the script are run, but after it finishes, your current directory hasn't changed.*

Once the execute permission is set, the shell runs the commands in the script.

However, your current shell doesn't run the commands. Instead, your shell starts a new shell to run the script. Because the current working directory is part of your environment, the new shell (running the script) starts in your current directory, changes directories, runs `ls`, and then finishes—but it hasn't affected the environment of your current shell. In other words, "you" haven't moved directories at all; it was a different shell that changed directories.

If you really want to change directories in a script and have that change take effect in your current environment, you need to get your current shell to run the commands in the script itself instead of starting another shell to do the work. There are three ways to get your current shell to run the commands:

1. Use an alias instead of a script. This may not work if the commands need arguments (see the next question).
2. Use a *function* instead of a script. A shell function is a tiny script that's stored in memory so the shell can run it any time.
3. Use the *source* command to force the shell to run the script itself.

## ■ FOR EXAMPLE:

The source command is a dot, followed by a script's name. Here's how it might look:

```
$ . ./CD
mail.debug  nuc.start   snmpd.pid   xdm-errors
$ pwd
/tmp
$
```

*After editing the file CD, enter the following command:*

```
./CD /etc
```

**d)** What happens?

*Answer: The script now lists the contents of the /etc directory.*

The # character is a *comment* character. Anything that comes after # on the line is ignored, so you can write comments about what the script does or what a particularly tricky line is trying to accomplish. In this script, the shell ignores the entire first line. (The #! pair is an exception which has a special meaning when it begins the first line in the file.) The comment at the top of the script will remind you of what the script does.

It's *always* a good idea to comment on your scripts. No matter how clear the script seems today, in six months it won't be clear at all.

The $* is a parameter designed to be used in shell scripts and functions. When the shell script runs, the $* is turned into the complete list of arguments to the command. (If there are no arguments, $* turns into "" or nothing.)

This is one of the advantages of shell scripts and functions over aliases. With a shell script or a function, you can provide different arguments. Your custom command can be more flexible.

## WHICH SHELL RUNS THIS SCRIPT?

Because there are several different shells on the system, each with different capabilities and built-in commands, which shell runs the script?

The script is run by the user's shell. If you use the Korn Shell, this script is run by another copy of the Korn Shell, /bin/ksh. If you use the Bourne Shell, then the script will be run by a copy of the /bin/sh program. Because this is an introductory example, we don't worry about which shell will run it: cd and ls are the same, no matter which shell you use. If, however, the script contains built-in commands, it matters which shell runs it.

Fortunately, there's an answer. Most shell scripts you see on UNIX systems start with the line:

```
#!/bin/sh
```

This is a line of "magic" text that the shell reads. If the first two characters are #!, then the rest of the line is the program that should run the script, no matter what the user's shell is. (Some old shells don't actually understand this magic, but the Korn Shell and the C Shell do.) In this case, the script will be run by the Bourne Shell.

Should you use this magic line of text in your scripts? Yes, if you think anyone else will be using the script from a different shell. (Remember to use /bin/ksh to indicate the Korn Shell.)

## 8.4.2 ANSWERS

Enter the following commands:

```
function repeat
{
    print $*
}
repeat hello, ${LOGNAME}
```

**a)** What happens?

*Answer: The shell prints "*`hello,`*" followed by your login name.*

A shell function is almost the same as a script, except that once it's been read, it stays in the memory of the shell program. When you run the function, the shell doesn't have to search for it, it already "knows" what commands you want to run. (Programmers use shell functions in shell scripts to organize their scripts and avoid typing the same commands more than once.)

The syntax for creating a shell function is:

```
function name
{
    commands
}
```

The *name* is the function's name; it becomes the command you call. When you type the function's name, the commands are executed.

This function doesn't do anything that the `print` command doesn't do. It could easily be replaced by an alias:

```
alias repeat=print
```

The power of functions and shell scripts come with multiple arguments and multiple commands. Instead of writing a script for the CD command, you could have typed the commands directly into the shell as a function:

```
function CD
{
    cd $*
    ls
}
```

When you type CD, the commands are run. If you have a copy of the CD script in your PATH and you create a function by the same name, the script will not get run. If a program or shell script and a function have the same name, the function gets run instead of the program.

If you load up too many functions, then you can actually reduce the performance of your system. Use a function instead of a script if:

- The command will be called very often.
- Speed of execution is very important.

You can remove a function from memory by using the command unset.

Enter the following commands:

```
function repeat
{
    print $1
}
repeat hello, ${LOGNAME}
```

**b)** What happens?

*Answer: The command prints "hello," but doesn't print your login name.*

The $* parameter is the list of arguments to a shell script or function, but sometimes you don't want to use the entire argument list, or you want to do different things to each argument. The shell breaks up the argument list into *positional parameters*, which you refer to by number. The parameter $1 refers to the first argument, $2 refers to the second argument, and so on, up to $9. (The parameter $# contains the number of arguments in total.)

You may find this useful when trying to handle the arguments to your functions and scripts. (Programmers call this *parsing* input.)

Enter the following commands:

```
function math
{
        print -R $(($*))
}
math 9 + 5
math 11/2
```

**c)**   What happens?  What does the `math` function do?

> *Answer: The `math` function does simple arithmetic. It doesn't provide for fractions at all.  It can do 8/2 = 4, but not 8/3 = 2.6666666.*

This function introduces the `(())` operators, which are unique to the Korn Shell. Normally, the values of all variables are treated as strings. Even though you may assign a variable the value "1," it's really the character 1, not the number 1. (Remember that inside, the computer stores them differently.)

Inside double parentheses, the Korn Shell treats everything as numbers. If a variable contains a number (such as 1), it is treated as if it is a number. (If it contains a word, like "chocolate," then it's an error. The Korn Shell doesn't know what to do.)

The `print` command prints the value of whatever's in the double parentheses. (The `$` means "the value of" for variables and parameters; it also means "the value of" what's in the double parentheses.) The `$*` turns into the list of arguments to the math function. When you type `math 9 + 5`, here's what happens:

- The shell turns it into `print $((9 + 5))`
- The numbers in the `(())` are added.
- The `print` command prints the value of what's in the double parentheses, or 14. The `-R` option to `print` keeps `print` from treating negative numbers as an option.

The Korn Shell ignores fractions, both in the answers and in the numbers you enter.  For example, `math 10.5/1.5` gives the result 10; both fractions are ignored.

Arithmetic in the Korn Shell handles addition (+), subtraction (–), multiplication (*), division (/), and the modulus operator (%). The modulus operator gives you the remainder from division. Two goes into eleven five times with one left over. In the Korn Shell, 11/2 gives you five, and 11%2 gives you the remainder, 1. The operations are done in this order: multiplication, division, and modulus, and then addition and subtraction. You can use parentheses to group operations, but with the `math` function, you may have to escape the parentheses.

## ■ *FOR EXAMPLE:*

If you want to convert 78 degrees Fahrenheit to Celsius, the conversion is (Fahrenheit –32) *5 / 9. You need the parentheses to prevent the Korn

Shell from trying to do 32*5/9, and then subtracting that from 78. However, when you type in (78 – 32) * 5 / 9, you'll get a syntax error. You need to escape the parentheses and any asterisks.

To type this into math would be:

```
$ math \(78 - 32\) \* 5 / 9
25
```

You can use (()) from the command line, in shell scripts, and in shell functions.

## ■ FOR EXAMPLE:

Suppose you want to print 100 random numbers instead of the five in a previous example. You can use a while loop to count the number you've printed. (The test operator is -le for "less than or equal to," and it treats its objects as numbers, too.)

```
x=1
while [ $x -le 100 ]
do
    print $RANDOM
    ((x=x+1))
done
```

You must start by giving x a value; otherwise the test fails because x doesn't exist. When x is 1, the test will return true (because 1 is less than or equal to 100), so the shell will execute the commands. First, the shell prints the value of $RANDOM. Second, it adds one to the value of x, and then it goes back to the test in the while command.

It's much easier to type this loop than to type 100 dots as the list in a for loop.

## LAB 8.4 SELF-REVIEW QUESTIONS

In order to test your progress, you should be able to answer the following questions.

1)   A shell script is a series of commands.
     **a)** _____True
     **b)** _____False

**2)** What must you do to a shell script to make it executable?
   **a)** _____Place it in a directory mentioned in your PATH
   **b)** _____Start it with the line #!/bin/ksh
   **c)** _____Run it with ./ at the beginning of its name
   **d)** _____Turn on execute permissions
   **e)** _____All of the above

**3)** What does the source command (.) do?
   **a)** _____Runs scripts in the current directory
   **b)** _____Runs a script in the current shell's environment
   **c)** _____Loads a shell function into memory
   **d)** _____Runs a script in another shell's environment

**4)** A #! as the first two characters of a file is which of the following?
   **a)** _____An indication that the file is a script
   **b)** _____The beginning of a comment
   **c)** _____A negation operator
   **d)** _____Automatically replaced with the history number of the command

*Quiz answers appear in Appendix A, Section 8.4.*

# L A B   8 . 5

# EXAMPLE SCRIPTS

---

**LAB OBJECTIVES**

After this Lab, you will be able to:

- Make a File Name Lowercase
- Create a Temporary Trashcan

---

These scripts make use of nearly everything we've covered in the last two chapters. The point of this Lab is to look at scripts and understand them, and to think through what they do. These scripts are not necessarily finished; you can improve them yourself.

Most people write shell scripts a bit at a time. What usually happens is that you have a set of commands you type repeatedly, so you decide to store them in a shell script. It works fine for a while, and then you run across a circumstance you didn't anticipate, so you fix the shell script to handle that. Then you give the script to someone else who has to do the same thing, and they discover a circumstance you didn't anticipate.

Programmers are told to avoid this sort of incremental growth. For non-programmers, I think it's the only reasonable way to develop shell scripts. Try to keep to the following rules:

- If something can fail (not work), test it first, or check to see if it did work.
- Include comments.
- Don't make drastic changes to your `.profile` and environment files; save functions in a different file and source them by hand with . until you're sure they work the way you want.
- Keep your shell scripts short. One shell script can call another, so you don't have to write one huge script.

# LAB 8.5 EXERCISES

## 8.5.1 MAKE A FILE NAME LOWERCASE

Examine this script. You may want to type it in and run it.

```
#! /bin/ksh
# A script to rename files so their names are all
lowercase
typeset -l name
for x in $*
do
    name=$x
mv $x junk.$$ && mv junk.$$ $name
done
```

**a)** What does the `typeset -l` command do?

_____

_____

**b)** What does the `mv` command do?

_____

_____

**c)** How could this script go wrong? What tests could be added?

_____

_____

## 8.5.2 CREATE A TEMPORARY TRASHCAN

Examine these functions. You may want to type them in and source the file.

```
function Rm
{
   for f in $*
   do
```

```
        mv ${f} ~/.trashcan/${f##*/}
    done
}

function Unrm
{
    for f in $*
    do
            if [ -f ~/.trashcan/${f##*/} ]
            then
                    mv $TRASH/${f##*/} .
            else
                    print -u2 The file ${f} isn\'t in the
trash
                    exit 1
            fi
    done
}
function Empty
{
    rm -f ~/.trashcan/*
}
```

**a)** What does each function do? What do these three functions provide?

_____

_____

**b)** In which file would you put these functions?

_____

_____

**c)** What happens if you try to Rm a directory and then Unrm it?

_____

_____

**d)** What happens if .trashcan doesn't exist? How would you make sure it exists?

_____

_____

# LAB 8.5 EXERCISE ANSWERS

## 8.5.1 ANSWERS

As part of the script, you typed:

```
typeset -l name
```

**a)** What does the typeset -l command do?

*Answer: The* typeset -l *command makes the contents of the* name *variable lowercase.*

**LAB 8.5**

The rest of the script is fairly straightforward. For each argument, it saves the file name in name. Then it moves the original file to a temporary file (named junk.$$) and then moves junk.$$ to the new lowercase file name. (It renames the file twice because some remote file systems are case-insensitive. If you try a command such as mv README readme, the remote file system reports that they're the same file, and the mv command fails.) The reason that we name the temporary file junk.$$ instead of just junk is that the file "junk" may already exist. Naming the file junk.$$ makes it more likely that the file will not exist. "$$" is the current process ID number, which changes for each program or shell script run.

**b)** What does the mv command do?

*Answer: The* mv *command renames the current file* junk *and if that works, then it renames* junk *to the value of* name.

**c)** How could this script go wrong? What tests could be added?

*Answer: There are several ways it could go wrong. A discussion follows.*

Here are some possible problems with the script:

What if no files are provided as arguments? Do you want to give the user information about how the command should be used, or just let it run and do nothing? If you want to fix it, you'll have to add a check for the number of arguments.

What if there is already a file named junk in the current directory? The first mv command will replace it. You could check for a file named junk.$$ before you start, or you could pick some other temporary file name.

What if a file or directory in the current directory already has a lowercase version of the argument file's name? You could check to see if $name already exists. Or maybe you only care if $name exists and is a directory, since the script will then move the file junk.$$ into the directory.

What if one of the mv commands in the middle of the list fails? Do you want the whole script to quit, or just that one?

These are only a few possibilities. You should be able to come up with others. Thinking about a shell script involves figuring out what the odd cases are, and what your needs are. It's possible to put too many fixes into a script. If you know that there are no case-insensitive file systems in your file tree, maybe the double mv command is too complicated.

In that case, maybe you want a script like this:

```
#! /bin/ksh
typeset -l name
for x in $*
do
    name=$x
    if [ -d $name ]
    then
            print $name exists and is a directory
    else
        mv -i $x $name
    fi
done
```

By using mv -i, you don't have to check to see if a file exists; you only have to check if a directory exists.

You can probably think of other improvements to make yourself.

## 8.5.2 ANSWERS

Examine these functions. You may want to type them in and source the file.

```
function Rm
{
    for f in $*
    do
            mv ${f} ~/.trashcan/${f##*/}
    done
}

function Unrm
{
    for f in $*
    do
            if [ -f ~/.trashcan/${f##*/} ]
            then
                    mv $TRASH/${f##*/} .
            else
                    print -u2 The file ${f} isn\'t in the
trash
                    exit 1
            fi
    done
}
function Empty
{
    rm -f ~/.trashcan/*
}
```

**a)**  What does each function do? What do these three functions provide?

*Answer: The* Rm *function moves a file into a hidden directory called* .trashcan. *The* Unrm *function moves a file or files from* .trashcan *into the current directory. The* Empty *function removes all files from the* .trashcan *directory. These three functions provide "undelete" capability.*

These three functions give you the ability to store deleted files in a temporary trashbin. This allows you to retrieve files you've deleted accidentally. (This idea was described in the *UNIX User's Interactive Workbook*, in Chapter 6, "Emergency Recovery.")

**b)**  In which file would you put these functions?

*Answer: These functions would go in your environment file.*

These are functions you would want in all your interactive shells. They aren't necessary for non-interactive shells, so they shouldn't go into your ~/.profile file.

If the Rm function were named rm, typing rm would run the function instead of the rm program. The shell only searches for programs in the PATH if there are no aliases or shell functions with the same name. However, it's not a good idea to write commands that have the same names as standard commands but behave differently. You might get confused some day on a different system and delete files you don't want to delete. At least if the command is named Rm, you'll get a "command not found" message on a different system, and you won't have deleted files you don't want to delete.

**c)**   What happens if you try to Rm a directory and then Unrm it?

*Answer: It will report "The file isn't in the trash."*

You can't use Unrm to restore a directory. Even if the directory exists in the .trashcan directory, the test on line 13 checks to see if the argument is a file. You can fix this by changing the test -f to be a test -e.

**d)**   What happens if .trashcan doesn't exist? How would you make sure it exists?

*Answer: If ~/.trashcan doesn't exist, the mv command in Rm will fail. You can make sure it exists by testing for the existence of ~/.trashcan in the environment file before you load the functions. You can create it then if it doesn't exist.*

You should be able to write the test that checks for the directory. It might look like this:

```
[ -d ~/.trashcan ] || mkdir ~/.trashcan
```

If the test for the directory fails, it creates the directory. You could put this line in the Rm function.

Of course, that still doesn't account for the possibility that there might be a *file* named .trashcan. It's up to you whether you want to add an additional check for the file. You may decide it's not worth the effort. (These are the kinds of decisions programmers make.)

As these questions have shown, these functions aren't perfect. You can certainly change them to behave the way you want them to behave.

# LAB 8.5  SELF REVIEW QUESTIONS

In order to test your progress, you should be able to answer the following questions.

1) Which of the following should you do when writing shell scripts?
   a) _____Leave out comments.
   b) _____Make small changes, so you can see their effects.
   c) _____Try to get it right before testing it.
   d) _____Try to fit everything into one script.

2) You should always test the result of a command.
   a) _____True.
   b) _____False.
   c) _____Usually, but it depends on the situation.

3) The name `junk.$$` was used instead of `junk` for which of the following reasons?
   a) _____The file extension `.$$` is reserved for temporary files.
   b) _____The `$$` is converted to the process ID for the job, and a file by that name is less likely to exist than a file named `junk`.
   c) _____The `$$` is interpreted by the shell as a unique number, guaranteeing that no file by that name exists.
   d) _____The name "`junk.$$`" is less likely to exist than the name `junk`.

4) Which of the following is good practice when writing a shell script?
   a) _____Think about how it could go wrong.
   b) _____Consider who is going to use it; a command only you will use has different requirements from one that many people will use.
   c) _____Use comments to make the logic obvious.
   d) _____(a) and (b).
   e) _____(b) and (c).
   f) _____(a), (b), and (c).

*Quiz answers appear in Appendix A, Section 8.5.*

# CHAPTER 8

# TEST YOUR THINKING

Use the following script for the first four Projects:

```
#!/bin/ksh
if [ $# -ne 1 ]
then
    print -u2 One argument, please
    exit 1
fi
if ! "$BPDIR"
then
    if [ -d $HOME/bp ]
    then BPDIR=$HOME/bp
    else
        print -u2 No boilerplate directory named.
        print -u2 Please set BPDIR or create
        $HOME/bp
        exit 1
    fi
else
    if ! [ -d $BPDIR ]
    then
        print -u2 $BPDIR isn\'t a directory!
        exit 1
    fi
fi
if ! [ -f $1 ]
then
    print -u2 $1 doesn't exist!
    exit 1
else
    cat $BPDIR/$1
fi
```

**LAB
8.5**

1) Looking at this script:

   **a)** What does this script do?

**b)** What happens if the environment variable BPDIR isn't set?

**c)** What happens if the directory $HOME/bp doesn't exist?

**d)** How can you improve it?

Now examine this script:

```
#! /bin/ksh
returnvalue=0
for f in *
do
     if grep -s "^$f$" manifest > /dev/null
     then
            if [ "$f" -nt manifest ]
            then
                 print "$f" is newer than the manifest
                 returnvalue=1
            fi
     else
            print $f is not in the manifest
            returnvalue=1
     fi
done
exit returnvalue
```

**LAB 8.5**

**2)** Looking at this script:

**a)** What does this script do?

**b)** What happens if the working directory contains a subdirectory?

**c)** How could you fix this?

**d)** When will it return an error (a 1) for the return value?

**e)** What happens if you update the manifest file before updating a file?

**f)** Where can this script go wrong? How could you fix it?

**3)** One problem with the trashcan commands presented here is that you still need to remember to empty the trashcan. Read the man page for the trap command and see if you can figure out how to change your .profile so that an Empty function or script gets called when you logout.

**a)** Is this the best way to automatically empty the trashcan?

**b)** Can you think of other ways?

# C H A P T E R   9

# MORE ON FILES AND PERMISSIONS

All of the information you create or use on the computer is organized by files, either plain files or special files (such as terminal displays). Although the *UNIX User's Interactive Workbook* covered files and file permissions in some detail in Chapters 4 and 5, it won't surprise you that there is still more.

In this Chapter, we'll talk about some more specialized ways to look at files, some rather specialized file permissions and some ways to accomplish occasional tasks, and we'll look at remote file systems, one of the ways you can share information across a computer network without using any of the tools covered in Chapter 4, "Computer Networks."

# L A B   9 . 1

# FILES AND TYPES

---

### LAB OBJECTIVES

After this Lab, you will be able to:

- Identify a File's Type
- Display a File's Contents with od

---

The `ls` command can give you some information about the type of a file by using either the `-l` flag or the `-F` flag. It can tell you the *kind* of file—whether the file is a directory or a plain file, a symbolic link, or a pipe or a special device. Often, you want to narrow it down more than that. However, once you've identified a file as being actually a file, what next? Is it a program, a picture, a word processing file, a shell script, or simply a text file?

The two commands in this Lab help identify what type a particular file is. The first is the `file` command, which tries to guess what a file is. The second is the `od` command, which can be thought of as `more` for binary files, in that it displays their contents in a readable way.

### 9.1.1 IDENTIFY A FILE'S TYPE

In your home directory, type the command:

```
file * /bin/* | more
```

**a)** What does the output of the `file` command look like?

_____

_____

Create an empty file named `sampletext`.

Give the command:

    `file sampletext`

    **b)** What is the output of the command?

_____

_____

Add this line to `sampletext`:

    `#`

    **c)** What does `file sampletext` report now?

_____

_____

Make the file executable with the command:

    `chmod u+x sampletext`

    **d)** What does the command `file sampletext` report now?

_____

_____

## 9.1.2  DISPLAY A FILE'S CONTENTS WITH **od**

Enter the command:

    `od sampletext`

    **a)** What does the output of the `od` command look like?

_____

_____

Now enter the command:

```
od -c sampletext
```

**b)** How does the output of od -c differ from the output of od?

_____

_____

# LAB 9.1 EXERCISE ANSWERS

## 9.1.1 ANSWERS

In your home directory, type the command:

```
file * /bin/* | more
```

**a)** What does the output of the file command look like?

*Answer: The exact text will vary depending on the contents of your home directory, but on a Solaris system, it should look something like this (this text has been shortened):*

```
$ file * /bin/*
ch03.doc.1        text
chap09:   directory
dead.letter     English text
mbox:      ascii text
printit.1 [nt]roff, tbl, or eqn input text
printit.c:      c program text
/bin/acctcom:  ELF 32-bit LSB executable 80386 Ver-
sion 1, dynamically linked, stripped
/bin/admintool: cannot open: Permission denied
/bin/appletviewer:   executable /bin/ksh script
/bin/arch:       executable /usr/bin/sh script
```

I've edited the output from my directory to show some of the different responses file can give.

The file command examines a file and tries to classify it. File identifies all of the file types that ls -F does, and it tries to classify regular files in additional categories. For example, a number of files in the example output are classified as "ascii text" files. In fact, file sometimes attempts to guess what language the file is in. For example, some of the files in the output are identified as "English text" although `file` is much less successful at guessing other languages.

For programs, `file` tries to tell you what kind of machine the program is intended for. An "ELF 32-bit LSB executable 80386 Version 1, dynamically linked, stripped" file is a kind of program (you can tell by the word "executable"). The BSD version of `file` (which is a publicly available version, so it may be on other systems as well) has a much more extensive list of file types than the Solaris version.

**Create an empty file named** `sampletext`.

**Give the command:**

```
file sampletext
```

**b)** What is the output of the command?

*Answer: It should look something like this:*

```
sampletext: empty file
```

The `file` command can identify an empty file. On some systems, the message simply reads "empty". The `file` command is one way to find all of the empty files in a directory. You already know commands to find them in three other ways.

## ■ *FOR EXAMPLE*

If I want to identify all of the empty files in a directory, I find it easier to write the command:

```
file * | grep "empty file"
```

than to write any of these others, which will also find empty files in different ways:

| | |
|---|---|
| Sorting `ls -l` output | `ls -l | sort -r -k 5` |
| Testing the size of each file | `for x in * ; do` |
| | `if [ ! -s $x ] ; then` |
| | `echo $x` |
| | `fi` |
| | `done` |
| Using the `-size` test in `find` | `find . -size 0c -print` |

Each of these techniques has its own advantages and disadvantages. For example, the first one produces a lot of extraneous output, but because the sort is reversed (-r), all of the zero-length files are easily seen at the end of the list. The second and third techniques print only the empty files. Only the third one can be used to find all of the empty files on the file system, but it's likely to be the slowest, because find recursively descends into subdirectories.

Which technique you use depends upon what you're trying to do. If you want to automatically remove those files (perhaps using xargs and rm), using ls output or file output won't work, because the output isn't suitable for an rm command line.

Add this line to sampletext:

```
#
```

**c)** What does file sampletext report now?

*Answer: It now reports this line:*

```
sampletext: ascii text
```

The file command identifies files by looking at the beginning of the file and comparing it to a list in a file called /etc/magic (or /usr/share/misc/magic on BSD-style systems). The magic file contains a list of characteristics that different file types have. For example, all files meant for a PostScript printer start with the characters "%!"or "%! PS-Adobe".

However, file is just "guessing." The less information there is in the file, the less likely it is that file will make a correct guess. The default categories, if file can make no other matches, are "text" and "data". (A "text" file is readable and contains end-of-line characters but no binary information. Anything else is "data.")

Make the file executable with the command:

```
chmod u+x sampletext
```

**d)** What does the command file sampletext report now?

*Answer: It now reports this line:*

```
sampletext: commands text
```

The `file` command also checks the permissions on the file. If the file is executable and a text file, it's reported as "commands text."

The synopsis for the `file` command looks like this:

```
file [-h] [-f listfile] file ...
```

(There are two other options to `file`, but they're only important if you're creating new `magic` files.)

The `-h` option affects how `file` treats a symbolic link. Normally the `file` program reports the type of the file the link points to, but the `-h` option causes it to tell you that the file is a symbolic link.

Suppose the file `symbol` is a symbolic link to `realfile`:

```
$ file realfile symbol
realfile: English text
symbol:   English text
$ file -h realfile symbol
realfile: English text
symbol:   symbolic link to realfile
```

The `-f` option allows you to name all the files you want described in another file rather than listing them on the command line. If `listfile` contains the lines:

```
realfile
symbol
```

then the command `file -f listfile` produces this output:

```
realfile: English text
symbol:   English text
```

## 9.1.2 ANSWERS

Enter the command:

```
od sampletext
```

**a)** What does the output of the `od` command look like?

*Answer: The* od *command produces output like this:*

```
$ od sampletext
0000000 005043
0000002
```

If the numbers in the first output look radically different from your results, don't worry. What's important is that the second (od –c) output looks the same.

The od command prints out the contents of any file as numbers. Remember that all information is actually stored inside the computer as numbers. Letters and digits are also stored as numbers (the ASCII codes). The letter "A" for example is stored as the number 63.

As text, the file sampletext contains two characters. However, as numbers, those two characters are stored as 005043. The numbers along the left side of the screen (0000000 and 0000002) tell you how far into the file you are.

(Don't try to look up the ASCII values for "#" and a new line and match those to the raw od output. There's more to it than just a simple comparison.)

Now enter the command:

```
od -c sampletext
```

**b)** How does the output of od –c differ from the output of od?

> *Answer: The* od –c *output looks like this:*

```
0000000    #   \n
0000002
```

When you add the –c option, the od command interprets the file as if it contained characters (even if it doesn't, really). Because the sampletext file really is characters, it becomes understandable with the –c option. The new line character is displayed as "\n". (A tab character would be displayed as "\t".)

Why would you want to use this command? You would use it to identify binary files. Remember that not all files are text files. There are some types of files that contain lots of text but are binary files, such as word processor files. On some systems, I've run across word processor files that couldn't be displayed using more or vi because one or more lines were too long to be displayed.

### The Whole Truth

The name od stands for "octal dump" because the program normally displays all the numbers as *octal numbers*. What does that mean?

Technically speaking, the default od display shows 2 byte half-words in octal format, or base 8. A half-word is just 16 bits; there are 8 bits to a byte, and 4 bytes to a word. A bit is a single piece of information—a yes or a no, a 1 or a 0—but the computer reads them in chunks, or bytes, and assembles them into larger chunks, called words. (There are no computer paragraphs.) So what's octal?

Normally numbers are shown in *decimal*. It goes by tens: 0, 1, 2, 3, 4, 5, 6, 7, 8, 9—and then you've run out of numerals and have to use two digits: 10, 11, 12 and so on to 19. There are only 10 different numerals used to represent numbers. (That's why it's called "base 10," because it's based on ten numerals.)

In octal counting, the computer uses eight digits: 0, 1, 2, 3, 4, 5, 6, and 7. Once you count past 7 (using octal counting), you've run out of numerals and have to use two digits: 10, 11, 12, and so on to 17. (You might recognize that the file permission modes can be treated as octal numbers.) A decimal 15 is one ten and five ones; an octal 15 is one eight and five ones (or decimal 13).

Octal counting is very convenient for programmers. It's more convenient for programmers to convert numbers between the format

It's also possible for the act of displaying a binary file to confuse your terminal display. (I discussed this briefly in the *UNIX User's Interactive Workbook*, in Chapter 6, "Emergency Recovery," in Lab 6.4, "Clearing Your Display.") By displaying the file with od -c and more, you avoid that possibility.

The od command doesn't have that limitation. So if you discover (for example) a data file and you want to examine it, you can use a command like this one:

```
$ od -c unknownfile | more
```

You can also examine files using more -v, which handles binary characters properly for display.

**LAB
9.1**

# LAB 9.1 SELF-REVIEW QUESTIONS

In order to test your progress, you should be able to answer the following questions.

1) The `file` command identifies different types of files.
   a) _____True
   b) _____False

2) The `file` command is always right.
   a) _____True
   b) _____False

3) One of the advantages of using `od` is that you don't risk confusing your display by trying to display a binary file.
   a) _____True
   b) _____False

4) You have a list of 200 files in the file `filelist`; identify which of these commands will tell you which of those files are executable shell scripts.
   a) _____ `file -f filelist | grep 'executable.*sh script'`
   b) _____ `file $(cat filelist) | grep 'executable.*sh script'`
   c) _____ `file -m filelist | grep 'executable' | grep 'script'`
   d) _____ Answers (a) and (b)
   e) _____ Answers (b) and (c)
   f) _____ Answers (a), (b), and (c)
   g) _____ None of the above

5) Identify the meaning of "\t" in `od -c` output.
   a) _____ A new line character
   b) _____ An alarm character (the terminal beeps)
   c) _____ A backslash
   d) _____ A tab character

*Quiz answers appear in Appendix A, Section 9.1.*

# L A B   9 . 2

# PERFORMING SOME SPECIALIZED FILING TASKS

---

## LAB OBJECTIVES

After this Lab, you will be able to:

- Understand Default Permissions
- Display Special Permissions
- Delete Almost All Files

---

When you want to set the permissions of a file, you use the chmod command, as explained in Chapter 1, "UNIX Basics." When you want to see the permissions on a file, you use the ls -1 command. However, when you create a file (using an editor or with file redirection), what are the permissions on that file?

What special permissions does the login program need in order to start your shell as you—instead of as root—the user who started the login program?

And, in a more practical sense, how do you remove all but one file in a large directory? Wildcards don't help.

## 9.2.1   UNDERSTAND DEFAULT PERMISSIONS

Enter the command:

```
umask
```

**a)** What is the output of `umask`?

_____

_____

Enter the following command:

```
mkdir chap09
```

**b)** What are the permissions on the directory? (You can check with
`ls -ld chap09`.)

_____

_____

Enter the commands:

```
chmod 700 chap09; cd chap09
```

Now create a file named `default`:

**c)** What are the permissions on the file?

_____

_____

**d)** What group does the file belong to?

_____

_____

## 9.2.2   DISPLAY SPECIAL PERMISSIONS

In the directory `chap09`, enter the following commands:

```
chmod 1777 chap09
ls -ld .
```

**a)** What are the permissions of the directory now?

The next three questions require another user's help, so you may not be able to do them fully. If you have root privilege, you could create a second login to simulate another person.

Create files in the `chap09` directory and set the permissions on them:

```
chmod a+w *
```

**b)** Ask another user to try to delete the files. What happens?

Enter the command:

```
ls -l /usr/bin/login
```

**c)** What's unusual about the permissions on `login`?

Create a file named `perms0` and enter these commands:

```
chmod u+s perms0
cp perms0 perms1
cp -p perms0 perms2
ls -l perms?
```

**d)** Compare the permissions on `perms1` and `perms2` and explain the effect of the `cp -p` command.

## 9.2.3 DELETE ALMOST ALL FILES

In the current directory, which contains several files including `sampletext`, enter the following commands:

```
ls | grep sampletext
ls | grep -v sampletext
```

**a)** What does the `grep -v` command do?

_____

_____

Enter the command:

```
rm $(ls -d * | grep -v sampletext)
```

**b)** What does the command do?

_____

_____

**c)** How would you change the command to remove all but two of the files (`sampletext` and `perms0`)?

_____

_____

# LAB 9.2  EXERCISE ANSWERS

## 9.2.1 ANSWERS

Enter the command:

```
umask
```

**a)**   What is the output of `umask`?

*Answer: This varies, but is probably 002 or 022.*

Your umask or "user mask" is a set of permissions you want to keep from people. When you create a file or a directory, UNIX blocks (or masks) the file or directory from having the permissions in your umask. If you think of permissions as numbers, it's a *subtraction*. The permissions in your umask are subtracted from the permissions of the new file or directory.

Some people use a umask of 027, subtracting all permissions from people other than yourself and your group.

Enter the following command:

```
mkdir chap09
```

**b)**   What are the permissions on the directory? (You can check with `ls -ld chap09`.)

*Answer: The answer will vary, but permissions on your new directory will probably be either 775 (rwxrwxr-x) or 755 (rwxr-xr-x).*

The default permissions on a new directory are 777, minus your umask (that's "user mask"). If your umask is 000, then the permissions on the new directory are 777 (777-000). If your umask is 002, your directory permissions are 777-002, or 775. For now, we'll assume your umask is set to 022, so the permissions on the directory are 777-022, or 755: read, write, and execute permission for you, read and execute permission for your group and the world.

As another example, if your umask is 027, the permissions on the directory will be 750.

Enter the commands:

```
chmod 700 chap09; cd chap09
```

Now create a file named `default`:

**c)**   What are the permissions on the file?

*Answer: The answer will vary, but permissions on the new file will probably be either 664 (rw-rw-r--) or 644 (rw-r--r--).*

Even though the permissions on the directory are 700, the file you create has the permissions of 666 minus your umask.

**d)**   What group does the file belong to?

*Answer: The file belongs to the same group as the directory.*

**LAB
9.2**

The group on the directory will be the same as your current group, which you can display with the command id. If you belong to more than one group, the directory will belong to the group displayed by id. (Even if you belong to more than one group, on Solaris, the id command only displays your current group ID, unless you give the -a option.)

On most UNIX systems now, a file has the same group as the user who creates it. However, on some systems (such as Solaris) this is configurable, which can cause some confusion. You might discover that in some directories, a file belongs to your primary group, while in other directories, the file belongs to the same group as the directory.

## 9.2.2 ANSWERS

Enter the following commands:

```
mkdir chap09
ls -ld chap09
chmod 1777 chap09
ls -ld .
```

**a)**   What are the permissions of the directory now?

*Answer: The permissions on the file are now displayed as:*

```
-rwtrwxrwx
```

There are three special permissions on most UNIX systems, the *sticky bit*, the *locking bit*, and the *set UID* or *set GID bit*. The t permission represents the sticky bit. The 1777 permission has the sticky bit (the 1) and read, write, and execute permission for the owner, the group, and the world (the 777). (The sticky bit permission can also be given symbolically as t, but for this exercise it's necessary to make sure that the permissions on the directory are 777.)

The word *bit* refers to how these permissions are actually done deep in the operating system. When one of these permissions is on, we refer to that bit being "set". The chmod command in this Lab sets the sticky bit.

The next three questions require another user's help, so you may not be able to do them. If you have root privilege, you could create a second login to simulate another person.

Create files in the chap09 directory and set the permissions on them:

```
chmod a+w *
```

**b)** Ask another user to try to delete the files. What happens?

*Answer: The user cannot remove the files.*

Remember what happens normally in a directory: Permission to remove a file depends on the permissions on the *directory*, not on the permissions on the *file*. If you have write permission on the directory, you can remove the files in that directory. (If you don't have write permission, rm will ask you if you really want to remove the file.)

When you set the sticky bit on a directory, only the owner of a file in that directory (and the super-user) can remove the file. (The super-user has permission to do anything.)

The sticky bit is very useful for maintaining security. Your home directory may have the sticky bit set; the /tmp directory usually has the sticky bit set so no one but you can delete your temporary files.

The sticky bit permission can be applied to a directory or a file; it has a different meaning applied to a file and only the super-user can apply the permission to a file. Originally, the sticky bit was developed for files, and it affected how fast a program started. On most modern systems, it's not necessary for files, but it is useful on directories.

Enter the command:

```
ls -l /usr/bin/login
```

**c)** What's unusual about the permissions on login?

*Answer: The* login *program has an unusual permission bit, "s":*

```
-r-sr-xr-x   1 root     bin         27996 Oct  6  1998
login
```

When this permission is in the user position (the first three permission characters), it is called the *set user ID bit*, or the *set-UID bit*. It's represented symbolically by s or by adding 4000 to the permissions mode. For example, the mode here is 4555: set-UID, and read and execute permissions for each of the owner, the group, and other.

Normally, a program runs as the person who started it. When I run a command as johnmc, the program runs as if it were me, with my permissions. The set UID bit causes the program to run as if its *owner* were running it instead. It's acting as an agent or a surrogate for the owner.

A number of important programs are set-UID programs, such as the mail delivery program. It needs to be able to copy files into directories that only the root user can touch, but any user can run the program.

A set-UID program is usually safer than creating a special group for those permissions. For one thing, the effects of a program are usually limited: The system administrator knows exactly what a file will do. A good example would be a backup program that copies files to a special device owned by the root user; any user could use the program to back up files, but no user needs to know the root password in order to do it.

You may be thinking that you could write a shell script that added progress messages to a particular log file in your home directory, and then make it set-UID for yourself. Then you could set permissions on the file so only you could write to it, but anyone who used the script could add a progress message. On Solaris and all UNIX systems you're likely to encounter, that's considered a security risk. Set-UID permission can only be applied to binary programs, not to shell scripts.

## ■ FOR EXAMPLE

You can try this series of commands to see the effect of the set-UID bit. First, copy the `id` command (the one that returns the identity of the person who ran it) to your current directory and set the set-UID bit:

```
cp /usr/bin/id .
chmod u+s,+rx id
```

Now have some other user run your version of the `id` command. If I do it, as user `johnmc` and then ask user `beth` to run the command, Beth gets this result:

```
$ echo $LOGNAME
beth
$ id
uid=1010(johnmc) gid=10(R+D) groups=10(R+D), 15(Docs)
```

Instead of running as `beth`, the program runs as `johnmc`. This user identity is called the program's *effective user ID*, because the program is effectively run by me.

If the same permission appears in the *group* permissions, then it's called a set-GID bit, and it causes the program to run as a different group rather than your group. For example, the `/usr/bin/passwd` command lets you update the file /etc/passwd, which is restricted to the root user or to other privileged users.

On a directory, the set-GID bit can have different effects. On Solaris (and other SVR4) systems, the set-GID bit on a directory changes the default group on files you create. Here's a little summary:

| | | |
|---|---|---|
| BSD system | | New files are in your primary group (the group of your group ID). |
| Older System V system | | New files are in the same group as the directory is. |
| Solaris and SVR4 systems | Set-GID bit is *not* set | New files are in your primary group, just like BSD |
| | Set-GID bit *is* set | New files are in the same group as the directory, just like older System V systems. |

You copied a file named perms0 twice, once using cp and once using cp –p.

**d)** Compare the permissions on perms1 and perms2 and explain the effect of the cp -p command.

*Answer: The permissions on* perms1 *are the default permissions for the directory; the permissions on* perms2 *are the same as on* perms0. *The* –p *flag causes* cp *to preserve the original permissions and timestamps, if it can.*

Besides preserving the permissions, the –p option causes cp to try and keep everything the same in the file, at least as far as the permissions allow, including owner and times. This can be a useful option when you want to copy a file but don't want to change the time and date on it.

## 9.2.3 ANSWERS

In the current directory, which contains several files including sampletext, enter the following commands:

```
ls | grep sampletext
ls | grep -v sampletext list
```

**a)** What does the grep –v command do?

*Answer: The* `grep -v` *command finds all lines in the file except those that match the pattern.*

Normally, `grep` displays the lines of the file that match a regular expression ("sampletext" in this example). The `-v` reverses that and `grep` only displays the lines that *don't* contain a match.

Enter the command:

```
rm $(ls -d | grep -v sampletext)
```

**b)** What does the command do?

*Answer: The command removes all of the files except* `sampletext`.

This is a three part command. The pipeline in `$( )` creates a list of all of the files in the directory *except* the file `sampletext`. The first part (`ls -d`) lists all of the files in the directory, including `sampletext`; the `-d` keeps `ls` from listing the contents of any directories. The `grep -v` command *removes* `sampletext` from the list.

**c)** How would you change the command to remove all but two of the files (`sampletext` and `perms0`)?

*Answer: Use* `egrep` *instead of* `grep`.

The `egrep` command allows you to use extended regular expressions to pick out the files you don't want to delete. The | operator in an extended regular expression chooses either of the two words you supply. So, for example, if you wanted to delete all of the files except for `sampletext` and for `perms0`, you could use this command:

```
rm $(ls -d | egrep -v 'sampletext|perms0')
```

Because you can supply more than two alternatives using |, this technique allows you to specify any number of files.

# LAB 9.2 SELF-REVIEW QUESTIONS

In order to test your progress, you should be able to answer the following questions.

**I)** Your umask helps determine the default permissions on files you create.

    **a)** _____True

    **b)** _____False

**2)** If your umask is 034 (for whatever reason), what are the permissions on a file you create?

    **a)** \_\_\_\_\_664

    **b)** \_\_\_\_\_666

    **c)** \_\_\_\_\_636

    **d)** \_\_\_\_\_632

**3)** Which bit is set when `ls -l` displays the permissions `-rwTrwxrwx`?

    **a)** The sticky bit

    **b)** The set-UID bit

    **c)** The set-GID bit

**4)** When the sticky bit is set on a directory, the following people can remove files in that directory:

    **a)** Only the owner

    **b)** Only the super-user

    **c)** Anyone with write permission on the directory

    **d)** Anyone with write permission on the file

    **e)** Only the owner and the super-user

*Quiz answers appear in Appendix A, Section 9.2.*

**LAB
9.2**

**LAB**
**9.2**

# LAB 9.3

# MOUNTED FILE SYSTEMS

---

### LAB OBJECTIVES

After this Lab, you will be able to:

*   Show Mounted File Systems

---

In Chapter 1, "UNIX Basics," we briefly mentioned the fact that file systems can be added to a UNIX system. These file systems are said to be "mounted" on the UNIX file tree. The file systems can be an additional disk drive, or they can be files on another computer.

If the new file system is just a hard drive, or if it's the files on a UNIX system, then the files and directories in that file system look just like UNIX files (because that's what they are). On most networks, that's all you need to know.

However, if the rules on that file system are different, you need to know. For example, one of the standard formats for CD-ROMs requires file names to be all in uppercase and have a maximum length of 11 characters: 8 for the file name and 3 for the extension. If you're working with a CD-ROM, you need to know this.

## LAB 9.3 EXERCISES

### 9.3.1 SHOW MOUNTED FILE SYSTEMS

Enter the following command:

```
/usr/sbin/mount -v
```

If you're on a BSD system, enter the following command:

```
more /etc/fstab
```

**a)** What is a mounted file system?

_____

_____

**b)** What types of file systems are mounted on your system?

_____

_____

# LAB 9.3 EXERCISE ANSWERS

## 9.3.1 ANSWERS

**a)** What is a mounted file system?

*Answer: A mounted file system is a file system added (or "mounted") to your computer's file tree.*

The `mount -v` command shows the list of file systems that have been mounted. This includes extra disk drives (or "partitions") mounted locally and remote file systems. On a BSD system, you must look at the `/etc/fstab` file; the third column of information shows the type of each file system.

Not all file systems are remote. File systems with the types `nfs`, `afs`, and `Samba` are remote file systems; most of the others are local. (There may be file system types I haven't discussed here.)

Why discover the types of mounted file systems? Normally, you won't. Under most circumstances, it doesn't matter what type of file system a file is on. However, if a mounted file system is on another computer, creating and copying files happens according to the rules of that computer's file system. More importantly, accessing files across a network is slower than accessing files on your machine.

For example, your network may consist of MS-DOS or Windows machines and UNIX machines. One big Windows machine holds all the project files for a particular group. By mounting that machine's file system, you can look at (or even change) the files on that machine. However, they're still on a Windows file system.

For removable file systems such as CD-ROMs and floppy disk drives, your system may have special commands. Those file systems can come from other operating systems, so they may operate by different rules. Solaris offers a floppy disk formatting program called `fdformat`, for example, which can format floppies as MS-DOS file systems. Use of the floppy disk drive may be restricted to the system administrator.

**b)** What types of file systems are mounted on your system?

*Answer: The answer varies. You should see at least something like the following:*

```
$ mount -v
```

or

```
$ /usr/sbin/mount -v

/dev/dsk/c0d0s0 on / type ufs read/write/setuid on
Tue Aug 25 20:59:42 1998

/dev/dsk/c0d0s6 on /usr type ufs read/write/setuid on
Tue Aug 25 20:59:42 1998

/proc on /proc type proc read/write/setuid on Tue Aug
25 20:59:42 1998

fd on /dev/fd type fd read/write/setuid on Tue Aug 25
20:59:42 1998
swap on /tmp type tmpfs read/write on Tue Aug 25
20:59:43 1998
```

Each line describes a mounted file system. For example, the second line describes the device `/dev/dsk/c0d0s6`, which appears in the file system as `/usr`. It's a UFS file system with the actions "read," "write," and "setuid" available, and it was mounted on Tuesday, August 25. For our purposes, the only information that's important right now is the file type. These types, and others, are explained in Table 9.1.

The most common networking system for connecting remote computers is NFS, the Network File System. NFS is similar to other networked file systems. First, all of the computers must be connected by an actual network. Each machine that is going to share its file system has a server run-

## Table 9.1 ■ File System Types

| Type | Description |
| --- | --- |
| afs | Andrew file system. Developed at Carnegie Mellon University and freely available. The Andrew file system has some special features; see your system administrator for details. |
| cdrom | CD-ROM drive. If your UNIX system has CD-ROM drives, they will be identified with this. |
| mfs | Memory file system. These are for system administrators only. |
| nfs | Network file system. NFS is one of the most common remote systems for sharing file systems. |
| proc | The process file system is a listing of all processes on the system. This is the information that ps retrieves and a debugger could use. It's arranged as if it were a file system, even though there aren't real files involved. |
| Samba | Networked file system generally used to connect with Microsoft (DOS and Windows) machines. |
| s5 | The original UNIX file system type. Now replaced by UFS or vxfs. |
| swap | Swap areas. These are for system administrators only. |
| tmpfs | Temporary file system, usually used for the /tmp subtree. |
| ufs | The Unix File System (also known as the Berkeley Fast File System). This is the default type for a local system. |
| vxfs | Veritas journaling file system. An alternative file system type that offers good file recovery. |

**LAB 9.3**

ning. Remember that the server provides a service; a program that asks for that service is called a client.

Let's say that the machine edison is going to share its files with the other machine in the network, tesla. If you're logged into tesla, your system administrator has already arranged for edison's files to be mounted, to look like part of your file system. When you do anything that asks for a file on edison (you try to use vi on the file /nfs/edison/notes/great_novel, for example), a special client program on tesla notices you're asking for a file from edison. The client asks the server on edison to get the file; the server does and hands the file to the client on tesla, which hands it to vi. You look at the file.

If you save the file, then the client program on tesla asks the server on edison to make these changes to the file, and the server does them.

You should never see these intermediate steps. They're invisible to you (unless something goes wrong). However, all of this extra work is why accessing files over a network is slower than accessing files on your machine.

Computers running other operating systems can also run servers. For instance, there are NFS clients and servers available for Windows NT machines. A Windows NT machine running an NFS client can get files from a UNIX machine running an NFS server; conversely, a UNIX machine running an NFS client can get files from a Windows NT machine running an NFS server. Many networks today are "heterogeneous" networks, meaning they connect machines running different operating systems.

**LAB 9.3**

# LAB 9.3 SELF-REVIEW QUESTIONS

In order to test your progress, you should be able to answer the following questions.

1) A mounted file system is always on another computer.
   **a)** \_\_\_\_\_ True
   **b)** \_\_\_\_\_ False

2) Which of the following is the command to display the types of mounted file systems on a Solaris system?
   **a)** _____mount
   **b)** _____df
   **c)** _____mount -v
   **d)** _____more /etc/fstab

3) Beside each file system type, indicate whether files will necessarily behave in the same way as local, real UNIX files (yes or no).
   **a)** \_\_\_\_\_afs
   **b)** \_\_\_\_\_cdrom
   **c)** \_\_\_\_\_ufs
   **d)** \_\_\_\_\_Samba

4) To use a mounted file system, you must log in to a second computer.
   **a)** \_\_\_\_\_ True
   **b)** \_\_\_\_\_ False

*Quiz answers appear in Appendix A, Section 9.3.*

# CHAPTER 9

# TEST YOUR THINKING

A programmer has just completed a new timesheet program (called `timesht`) and left for vacation. It's your job to set the program up on every system in the NFS network. The `timesht` program creates a timesheet file for each user, and stores it in the directory `/usr/share/times`. For security reasons, everyone needs to write in the directory but only the owner of a file should be allowed to delete it.

1) How will you structure the permissions on `/usr/share/times`?

2) Should timesheet files be recognizable by `file`? Why or why not?

There is also a program for administrators called `gettimes`, which goes through all of the timesheet files and generates billable hours for the staff.

3) Do you have to install `gettimes` on every machine? Why or why not? (Hint: Symbolic links will help here.) Describe your final plan for setting up the programs and directories.

# ADVANCED vi TRICKS

<table>
<tr><td colspan="2" align="center">**CHAPTER OBJECTIVES**</td></tr>
<tr><td colspan="2">In this Chapter, you will learn about:</td></tr>
<tr><td>✔ Running Programs Inside vi</td><td>Page 394</td></tr>
<tr><td>✔ Changing Upper- and Lowercase</td><td>Page 407</td></tr>
<tr><td>✔ Creating Your Own Commands</td><td>Page 414</td></tr>
<tr><td>✔ Options and Startup Tricks</td><td>Page 425</td></tr>
<tr><td>✔ Some Useful vi Tricks</td><td>Page 434</td></tr>
</table>

Both vi and emacs have capabilities far beyond simple editing. This Chapter is about some of those extra capabilities available using vi. Some of them will be useful to you, and you will start to use them every day; others won't fit into the way you work, but you might need them some day in the future. If you know these capabilities exist, you can look them up again if you need them; if you've never heard of them, you can never use them.

Before you complete this Chapter, you may find it useful to refer back to Chapter 9 of the *UNIX User's Interactive Workbook*, "The vi Editor."

# L A B   1 0 . 1

# RUNNING PROGRAMS INSIDE vi

---

### LAB OBJECTIVES

After this Lab, you will be able to:

- Run a Command on a Line
- Run a Command on a Paragraph
- Run a Command on a File

---

Most interactive commands in UNIX have something called a "shell escape" that allows you to run a command using the shell while you're using that interactive command. (We examined shell escapes as part of rlogin.) The command doesn't really affect the interactive session you're running; running ls while you're in an rlogin session has no effect on the rlogin session.

However, both vi and emacs allow you to run a command on the file you're editing, or even on a portion of the file you're editing, and replace text with the results of the command. For example, you can sort the entire file (or a portion of it) by running the sort command on the file.

Remember that movement commands can often be used to define the *context* for a vi command. The contextual movement commands are shown in Table 10.1:

### Table 10.1 ■ Contextual Movement Commands

| | |
|---|---|
| ) | Moves to the end of the current (or next) sentence. |
| } | Moves to the end of the current (or next) paragraph. |
| ]] | Moves to the end of the current (or next) section. |
| ( | Moves to the beginning of the current (or previous) sentence. |
| { | Moves to the beginning of the current (or previous) paragraph. |
| [[ | Moves to the beginning of the current (or previous) section. |
| % | When inside parentheses (such as a comment in text or in shell or C programs) beginning with (, {, or [, goes to the matching parenthesis or bracket. |

# LAB 10.1 EXERCISES

## 10.1.1 RUN A COMMAND ON A LINE

Start vi without any file argument. Enter the command:

```
:!ls
```

**a)** What happens?

_____

_____

Press Enter to clear the screen.

Use the a (append) command and type the letter 'a' on the line in lowercase letters, like this:

```
aaaaaaaa
```

Then press Escape to end input, and move the cursor to the beginning of the line with the ^ command.

Enter this command:

```
!!tr a B
```

**b)** What happens?

_____

_____

**c)** What does the `tr` command do?

_____

_____

## 10.1.2  RUN A COMMAND ON A PARAGRAPH

In `vi`, create a file called `rhymes` that contains these three paragraphs, ending each line where shown:

```
Mary had a little lamb
Its fleece was white as snow
And everywhere that Mary went
The lamb was sure to go

Jack and Jill went up the hill
To fetch a pail of water
Jack fell down and broke his crown
And Jill came tumbling after

Old Mother Hubbard went to the cupboard
To fetch her poor dog a bone
When she got there the cupboard was bare
And so her poor doggie had none
```

Enter the commands:

```
1G
}
}
}
```

**a)** Where does the cursor move after each } command?

_____

_____

Enter the command

```
:set all
```

**b)** What does the entry beside "paragraphs" say?

_____

_____


Move the cursor to the start of the second verse ("Jack and Jill") and enter the command:

```
!}sort
```

**c)** How does the command appear on the bottom line of the vi display?

_____

_____


**d)** What does the command do?

_____

_____


**e)** What happens when you press the u key (the undo command)?

_____

_____


Move the cursor to the next-to-last line ("When she got there") and enter the command:

```
!}fmt
```

**f)** Which lines are affected?

_____

_____

Enter the command

    :1,4!sort

**g)** Which paragraph is changed?

_____

_____


Save the file and exit.

### 10.1.3 RUN A COMMAND ON A FILE

Open the file rhymes again. Enter the command:

    :%!sort

**a)** What happens? What does the :% indicate?

_____

_____


Undo the sort with the u command and move the cursor to the beginning of the file with 1G. Enter the command:

    !Gfmt

**b)** What happens? What does the !G mean?

_____

_____


# LAB 10.1 EXERCISE ANSWERS

### 10.1.1 ANSWERS

Start vi without any file argument. Enter the command:

    :!ls

**a)** What happens?

*Answer: The contents of your current directory are displayed.*

There are two different ! commands in vi. This one is a shell escape, like the one you've seen with rlogin and telnet. It begins with a colon (:), runs a command (ls in this case), and displays the results on the screen. To get your normal vi display back, press Enter.

*You can insert the results of a command into the current buffer by using the :r (or :read) command; for instance, to insert the current time and date, enter :r !date.*

There is also the *filter* command. A vi filter command runs a command (usually a filter command, such as sort or fmt) on some or all of the file you're editing and replaces that text with the filtered text. (Filter commands were discussed in the *UNIX User's Interactive Workbook*, in Chapter 2, "The Command Line.") The vi filter command usually begins with ! rather than :!.

*Remember that vi is really two editors in one, the line editor ex and the one that displays multiple lines, vi. The commands that begin with : are commands for ex. The vi editor is added on to ex and makes use of ex commands where it can.*

The filter command in vi begins with !.

You can run any command line using ! or :!, not just any single command. The escaped command line can contain pipes or parentheses or semicolons—it can be as complex as any single command line in the shell.

Press Enter to clear the screen.

Use the a (append) command and type the letter 'a' on the line in lowercase letters, like this:

```
aaaaaaaa
```

Then press Escape to end input and move the cursor to the beginning of the line with the ^ command.

Enter this command:

```
!!tr a B
```

**b)** What happens?

*Answer: All of the 'a' characters are transformed into 'B' characters.*

The tr command changed them. What's important to look at is the structure of the filter command. There are two ways the ! filter command can be given to run a command (shown here as *shellcommand*):

```
!! shellcommand
! movement shellcommand
```

(I've separated the parts of the command with spaces to make it easier to read.) You might recognize this as being similar to the d (delete) and y (yank) commands. If you want the filter command to affect the current line only, use !!. If you want the filter command to affect some region of text, use a single ! followed by a movement command that moves the cursor to the end of the region of text.

You can also repeat the command several times by placing the number of repetitions before the command. To run this command on the next four lines, you can enter it as:

```
4!! shellcommand
!4! shellcommand
```

Either form will work to repeat the command four times.

In theory, you could apply a command against only a current word using a command such as *!wshellcommand*. To filter from the cursor to the next letter "w" in the line, you would use *!fwshellcommand*. In practice, the versions of vi I tested only run filters on lines of text, not on individual words.

**c)** What does the tr command do?

*Answer: The* tr *command transforms one letter into another. In this command, it turned every 'a' into a 'B'.*

The tr command is a very specialized substitution command. It substitutes or deletes characters in the input according to its options and arguments. The usual format is to provide two strings of characters as arguments; every time tr sees the first character in the first string, it turns it into the first character in the second string, and so on. If the command line was:

```
tr abcde 12345 < before > after
```

Every 'a' in `before` would be turned into a '1', every 'b' into a '2', every 'c' into a '3', 'd' into a '4', and 'e' into '5'. The transformed result would be stored in `after`. This is sometimes used to change a file into all lower-case, for example:

```
tr ABCDEFGHIJKLMNOPQRSTUVWXYZ abcdefghijklmnopqrstu-
vwxyz
```

Some versions of `tr` let you use character classes, which makes this much easier to type:

```
tr `[a-z]' `[A-Z]'
```

You can also use `tr` to delete certain characters by using the -d option. For example, DOS and Windows files end a line with the characters for a carriage return followed by a new line character; UNIX files end a line with only the new line character. When you open a DOS file in vi, all the lines end in ^M (the carriage return character). While you can get rid of those ^M characters with the vi command (where ^ indicates holding down the Control key with that character; ^V is Control-V):

```
:%s/^V^M/
```

You can also do it from the command line with `tr`. The carriage return character can be represented as \r, so you can convert a DOS text file to UNIX format with this command:

```
tr -d `\r' < dosfile > unixfile
```

Some other useful filter programs are listed in Table 10.2. Some will be familiar to you already.

Of course, you might have other needs. I used `grep` in a filter once when I was trying to get information from a file that was several thousand lines long.

Your site may have specialized shell scripts (called `sed` or `awk` or `perl`) you can use. These depend on the work you're doing and the people at your site.

## Table 10.2 ■ Some Filter Programs

| | |
|---|---|
| column | Organizes text into columns; found on BSD systems. |
| fmt | Formats text in paragraphs. |
| fold | Folds long text lines to make them shorter. |
| nl | Numbers lines. |
| pr | Formats for printing and other purposes. |
| uniq | Removes duplicate lines. |
| sort | Sorts files. |
| tr | Transforms or deletes characters. |

## 10.1.2 ANSWERS

In vi, you created a file called rhymes that contained three paragraphs, then moved to the beginning of the file and ran the } command three times.

**a)** Where does the cursor move after each } command?

*Answer: After the first and second } commands, it moves to the blank line between paragraphs; after the third, it moves to the last character of the last line.*

The } and { commands move the cursor by *paragraph*. The } command moves to the end of the current paragraph, and the { command moves to the beginning of the current paragraph. The question is, what is a paragraph? Where does one begin and end? Obviously, vi considers a blank line to be the end or beginning of a paragraph, and the beginning and end of the file also mark the beginning and end of the first and last paragraphs.

Enter the command

```
:set all
```

**b)** What does the entry beside "paragraphs" say?

*Answer: This may vary on different systems, but the usual entry looks something like this:*

```
paragraphs="IPLPPPQPP LI"
```

The :set all command displays all of your current settings for vi. The paragraphs setting controls what vi thinks is a paragraph, but it's not particularly useful.

Besides a blank line, vi also looks for lines that begin with a dot followed by one or two characters. (The reason for this has to do with a formatting program called troff, which is normally used to create man pages.) The paragraphs setting is a list of pairs of characters that will mark a paragraph. With the setting shown here, a new paragraph starts with a blank line or a line starting with any of .IP, .LP, .PP, .QP, .P or .LI. (The "P" gets translated as .P.)

Changing the setting of paragraphs is only useful if you're working with text files that use formatting lines that start with a dot. You may find it useful if some day you are forced to work in troff.

Move the cursor to the start of the second verse ("Jack and Jill") and enter the command:

```
!}sort
```

**c)** How does the command appear on the bottom line of the vi display?

*Answer: The } does not appear, so the line looks like this:*

```
!sort
```

The ! appears and the command appears, but the movement command doesn't. This can surprise you. (If the movement command *does* appear, you've either typed it twice or you're typing a colon command, like : !.)

**d)** What does the command do?

*Answer: The command sorts only that paragraph, so it looks like this:*

```
And Jill came tumbling after
Jack and Jill went up the hill
Jack fell down and broke his crown
To fetch a pail of water
```

What's important to note here is that *only* the paragraph was sorted. The rest of the file was not affected.

**e)** What happens when you press the u key (the undo command)?

*Answer: The sort is undone.*

The u (undo) and :undo commands will undo filter commands as well as undoing other vi commands.

Move the cursor to the second-to-last line ("When she got there") and enter the command:

```
!}fmt
```

**f)**    Which lines are affected?

*Answer: Only the last two lines of the file are reformatted.*

Remember that the command only works upon the lines covered by the movement command. If the cursor starts in the middle of a paragraph, the } command moves from the middle of the paragraph to the end of the paragraph. The filter command doesn't automatically affect the whole paragraph.

If you want to format the entire paragraph, you can give a { command first, which moves the cursor to the beginning of the paragraph:

```
{!}fmt
```

Enter the command:

```
:1,4!sort
```

**g)**    Which paragraph is changed?

*Answer: The first paragraph (lines 1-4) is sorted.*

Normally, the :! command (the `ex` version of the filter command) is a shell escape: It runs the command and then displays the results. However, if you supply an address (a range of lines), those lines are *filtered* through the command. In this example, you specified the line numbers for the first paragraph.

To change only one line, you could use the address dot (.), which stands for the current line. The `tr` command in 10.1.1 would instead be:

```
:.!tr a B
```

If there are only certain lines you want to change, you can also use a regular expression to specify the lines.

## ■ FOR EXAMPLE

I have a script I wrote called `center` that centers lines of text. Suppose I want to center all of my section headings in a big text file. (All of the section headings always start with a number like the ones in this book, such as 10.1 or 8.3.)

I could search through the file for each line starting with a number using the regular expression:

```
/^[0-9][0-9]*\.[0-9][0-9]* /
```

This matches a line starting with one or more numbers followed by a dot, followed by one or more numbers, followed by a space.

As I found each line, I would then have to run the center command on it:

```
!!center
```

By using the ex colon command, I can combine both steps into one command:

```
:/^[0-9][0-9]*\.[0-9][0-9]* /!center
```

Remember that *only* the lines matching the regular expression will be run through the center command.

## 10.1.3 ANSWERS

Open the file rhymes again. Enter the command:

```
:%!sort
```

**a)**   What happens? What does the : % indicate?

*Answer: The entire file is sorted. The : % indicates a : command that affects the current file (%).*

Remember the % as an address is a short form for the current file. You can also use a regular expression. Suppose I had a huge document stored as a text file, and I wanted to make sure that all of the chapter headings were in cap. (There are other ways to capitalize text, which we'll describe later in this Chapter.)

Undo the sort with the u command and move the cursor to the beginning of the file with 1G. Enter the command:

```
!Gfmt
```

**b)** What happens? What does the `!G` mean?

*Answer: The file is formatted into three paragraphs. The `!` command indicates that this is a filter command and the `G` is a movement command that moves the command to the end of the file. Since you started at the beginning of the file, this command takes in the entire file.*

You could also change the entire file by giving the address `:1,$!`.

# LAB 10.1 SELF-REVIEW QUESTIONS

In order to test your progress, you should be able to answer the following questions.

1) The command `:/dingo/!tr d b` will act as a shell escape and not as a filter command.
   **a)** _____ True
   **b)** _____ False

2) Which of these commands will run the filter command `fold` on *only* the current line?
   **a)** _____ `:.! fold`
   **b)** _____ `!! fold`
   **c)** _____ `!1! fold`
   **d)** _____ All of the above
   **e)** _____ None of the above

3) How much text will the command `!}fmt` format?
   **a)** _____ To the beginning of the next sentence
   **b)** _____ To the beginning of the next paragraph
   **c)** _____ To the beginning of the next section
   **d)** _____ Only the current line
   **e)** _____ The entire file

*Quiz answers appear in Appendix A, Section 10.1.*

# LAB 10.2

# CHANGING UPPER-
# AND LOWERCASE

---

### LAB OBJECTIVES

After this Lab, you will be able to:

- Change Case on a Line
- Ignore Case in Searches
- Change Case in Substitutions

---

A perpetual problem (for me, anyway) is that text in files never seems to be capitalized correctly. If a line is ALL CAPS, I need it capitalized Like This, or I need it all lowercase; if it's already capitalized, I probably need it all lowercase. On large files, it's just not possible for me to retype all of the lines where I have to change the capitalization. And after I've changed the case, it's difficult to search for a word that might be spelled "unix," "Unix," or "UNIX"—it requires either three different searches or that I use the regular expression [Uu][Nn][Ii][Xx].

The vi editor offers different tools for dealing with changing the case. There is a command for directly changing the case of text, a way to ignore case in searches, and tools for changing the case of text in search-and-replace operations.

## LAB 10.2 EXERCISES

### 10.2.1 CHANGE CASE ON A LINE

Open the file rhymes again.

Press the ~ key repeatedly until you are at the end of the line.

**a)** What does the ~ key do?

_____

_____

## 10.2.2  IGNORE CASE IN SEARCHES

Enter the command:

```
/mary
```

**a)** What happens?

_____

_____

Enter the command (you may have to press Enter again to clear the screen):

```
:set ignorecase
```

Enter the command:

```
/mary
```

**b)** What happens this time?

_____

_____

Turn off the setting with the command:

```
:set noignorecase
```

## 10.2.3  CHANGE CASE IN SUBSTITUTIONS

With the cursor on the "Jack and Jill" line, enter the command:

```
:s/J/\lJ/
```

The "l" in "\l" is a lowercase L, not the number 1.

**a)** What happens?

_____

_____

Now enter the commands:

```
:s/../\u&/
:s/../\U&/
:s/../\L&/
```

**b)** How does the effect of \u differ from \U?

_____

_____

Enter the commands:

```
:s/\(jack\) and \(Jill\)/\U\2\e and \1/
```

**c)** What does the output look like? What effect does the \e have?

_____

_____

# LAB 10.2 EXERCISE ANSWERS

## 10.2.1 ANSWERS

Open the file rhymes again.

Press the ~ key repeatedly until you are at the end of the line.

**a)** What does the ~ key do?

*Answer: The ~ key reverses the case of the letter under the cursor; uppercase letters become lowercase and lowercase letters become uppercase.*

You can use this feature to "flip" the case of text on a line because after you've pressed ~, the cursor moves to the next character. This is useful when you need to change a specific word once in the file. You can also alternate ~ commands with movement commands to capitalize words or sentences. For example, repeating w~ several times will capitalize the words; repeating )~ is a quick way to capitalize sentences.

However, the ~ command doesn't move the cursor to the next line after you've reached the end of the current line. Another problem is that if the text was already capitalized, you get "reverse capitalization" with words like "mARY." It can be awkward holding down the ~ key and then stopping in time to "step over" the capitalized letter using the l command.

## 10.2.2 ANSWERS

Still editing rhymes, enter the command:

```
/mary
```

**a)** What happens?

*Answer: The search doesn't find anything.*

Searches and substitutions in vi are normally case-sensitive. A search for an "M" doesn't match an "m".

Enter the following command (you may have to press Enter again to clear the screen):

```
:set ignorecase
```

Enter the command:

```
/mary
```

**b)** What happens this time?

*Answer: The search expression "mary" now matches "Mary".*

One of the options in vi that affects searches is called ignorecase. By default, ignorecase is *off* (that is, it's set to noignorecase) and vi performs case-sensitive searches. The :set command is used to set and unset these options. (Lab 10.4 deals with :set and options.)

## 10.2.3 ANSWERS

With the cursor on the "Jack and Jill" line, enter the commands:

```
:s/J/\lJ/
```

**a)** What happens?

*Answer: The \l causes the replacement character to be lowercase, so "Jack" be-comes "jack".*

By itself, this isn't useful at all; if you had wanted to replace "J" with "j" it would have been easier to type :s/J/j/. However, this becomes more powerful when you start to use the replacement metacharacters such as & and \1.

Remember that & in the replacement string causes vi to insert whatever text matched. The command to replace any uppercase letter with itself would be:

    :s/[A-Z]/&/

The & gets turned into whatever letter matched, whether it was an A, B, or any uppercase letter to Z. You don't have to know which letter it was.

At this point, it becomes clear how \1 can be useful. If the replacement command had been :s/[A-Z]/\1&/, *any* uppercase letter in the line would have been replaced by its lowercase equivalent.

# ■ FOR EXAMPLE

If you have a line of text that's all uppercase or upper- and lowercase, and you want it to be all lowercase, you can give this command:

    :s/./\l&/g

The . matches any single character in the search half of the command. In the replacement, the \l makes the replacement character lowercase and the & character makes sure it's the same letter that matched. The g (for "global") after the last / *repeats* the replacement over every character that matches (that is, globally across the line).

If the letter that matches is already lowercase, then \l doesn't affect it (unlike the ~ command).

Because \l makes letters lowercase, you might suspect that \u makes characters uppercase. It does.

Now enter the commands:

    :s/../\u&/

```
:s/../\U&/
:s/../\L&/
```

**b)** How does the effect of \u differ from \U?

*Answer: The* \u *affects only the first letter in the substituted text; the* \U *affects all of the letters in the substituted text. Here's what the first word ("jack") looks like after each command:*

```
Jack
JAck
jack
```

The \u and \l metacharacters affect only the first letter in the substitution. (This wasn't evident when you were working with only a single character in the replacement pattern.) If you have a line of text that's all in lowercase letters, you could capitalize each word with this command:

```
:s/\([^ ]*\)/\u\1/g
```

The group in \(\) characters is any string of zero or more characters that are not a space. (We'll assume that's a word; you could make the regular expression fancier if you wanted.) This group or subexpression is represented in the substitution half by \1. The \u makes the first character of the word an uppercase letter.

Enter the commands:

```
:s/\(jack\) and \(Jill\)/\U\2\e and \1/
```

**c)** What does the output look like? What effect does the \e have?

*Answer: The* \e *turns off or ends the effect of the* \U. *The output should look like this:*

```
JILL and jack went up the hill
```

Remember that the \2 is replaced by the *second* grouped subexpression (\(Jill\)), just as \1 is replaced by the *first* one.

The \e will also turn off \L. You can also use \E to turn off the effects of \U or \L; both \e and \E have the same effect.

# LAB 10.2 SELF-REVIEW QUESTIONS

In order to test your progress, you should be able to answer the following questions.

1)  Match the character/command with its effect.

    **a)**_____ ~

    **b)**_____ \u in the replacement part of a substitute command

    **c)**_____ & in the replacement part of a substitute command

    **d)**_____ \e in the replacement part of a substitute command

    **i)** Makes next character uppercase

    **ii)** Makes character under the cursor flip case

    **iii)** Ends a \U or \L command

    **iv)** Inserts the matched text

2)  Searches in vi are normally case-insensitive

    **a)** _____True

    **b)** _____False

3)  What will the command :s/./\L&/g do?

    **a)** _____ Capitalize all letters on the line

    **b)** _____ Lowercase all letters on the line

    **c)** _____ Capitalize the first letter on the line only

    **d)** _____ Lowercase the first letter on the line only

    **e)** _____ Capitalize the first word on the line

4)  What will the command :%s/\([^ ]*\)/\U\1/ do?

    **a)** _____ Capitalize all letters on the line

    **b)** _____ Lowercase all letters on the line

    **c)** _____ Capitalize the first letter on the line only

    **d)** _____ Lowercase the first letter on the line only

    **e)** _____ Capitalize the first word on the line

*Quiz answers appear in Appendix A, Section 10.2.*

# LAB 10.3

# CREATING YOUR OWN COMMANDS

---

## LAB OBJECTIVES

After this Lab, you will be able to:

- Create (and Remove) an Abbreviation
- Create (and Remove) a Macro
- Run a Buffer as a Command

---

You can create your own commands and short forms in vi. There are really only two different ways to create a command: You can create an abbreviation, which is a short form that gets expanded to a different word, and you can create a macro, a series of commands.

When you delete or yank text in vi, it's stored in a buffer, a temporary holding place. There are also buffers with names. Text stored in a named buffer can be run as if it were a series of commands typed into vi. (For this work, the text in the buffer should be valid ex commands.)

Remember that in vi the Control-V character is the special escape character that prevents the *next* character typed from having its usual meaning (just as backslash on the command line prevents a character from having its usual meaning).

# LAB 10.3 EXERCISES

## 10.3.1 CREATE (AND REMOVE) AN ABBREVIATION

Open `vi` and enter the following command:

```
:ab b UNIX
```

Now enter text entry mode and type the following line:

```
I am in a glib b book. b? b!
```

**a)** What does the line look like after you've typed it?

_____

_____

Exit text entry mode and enter the command:

**b)** What does the `:ab` command do, without arguments?

_____

_____

Enter the command:

```
:unab b
```

In text entry mode, enter the line of text again.

```
I am in a glib b book. b? b!
```

**c)** What does the `:unab` command do?

_____

_____

## 10.3.2 CREATE (AND REMOVE) A MACRO

Open the file `rhymes` in `vi` and enter the following command (^V means Control-V):

```
:map fp !}fmt^V
```

Press Enter twice at the end of the command; the ^V should become a ^M and then the command line vanishes.

In command mode, type:

```
fp
```

**a)** What happens when you type `fp`?

_____

_____

Enter the command:

```
:map
```

**b)** What happens when you type `:map`?

_____

_____

Enter the commands:

```
:unmap fp
:map
```

**c)** What has happened to the `fp` macro you created?

_____

_____

### 10.3.3 RUN A BUFFER AS A COMMAND

Open the file `rhymes` in `vi` and go to the end of the file. Add this line at the end:

```
:%s/\([MJmj][^ ]\{3,3\}\) /\U\1 /g
```

(There are spaces after the ^, after the ), and after the 1.)

**a)** What would this line do, if executed as a command?

_____

_____

Now exit text mode by pressing the Escape key. With the cursor on the last line, enter the command:

    "add

**b)** What does this command do?

_____

_____

Enter the command:

    @a

**c)** What happens?

_____

_____

# LAB 10.3  EXERCISE ANSWERS

## 10.3.1  ANSWERS

Open `vi` and enter the following command:

    :ab b UNIX

Now enter text entry mode and type the following line:

    I am in a glib b book. b? b!

**a)**  What does the line look like after you've typed it?

*Answer: The line looks like this:*

    I am in a glib UNIX book. UNIX? UNIX!

The :ab command creates abbreviations or short forms for words. When the abbreviation is typed, vi replaces the abbreviation with the long form. Notice that if the abbreviation appears in the middle of a word, it isn't replaced. An abbreviation is only replaced if there is white space *before* it (a space, a tab character, a new line, or the start of the file) and if there is white space or punctuation *after* it.

The abbreviation command is described this way in the vi man page:

```
:ab[breviate] lhs rhs
```

You can give the command as :abbreviate or as :ab. The *lhs* is the vi man page term for "left-hand side" and *rhs* is "right-hand side." The left-hand side is often limited to ten characters; the right-hand side can be much longer. You *must* have a right-hand side; you can't abbreviate a word to nothing.

Exit text entry mode and enter the commands:

```
:ab
```

**b)**   What does the :ab command do, without arguments?

*Answer: The :ab command lists all of the abbreviations you have defined.*

It's useful to see all of the abbreviations you currently have defined.

Abbreviations can be very frustrating if you need to type the abbreviation as a word. For example, the abbreviation "b" for "UNIX" would drive you mad if you were typing a file with a lot of lists in it that contained "b)" because vi would change them to "UNIX)". For this reason, try not to define abbreviations that are actually words.

Enter the command:

```
:unab b
```

In text entry mode, enter the line of text again.

```
I am in a glib b book. b? b!
```

**c)**   What does the :unab command do?

*Answer: The :unab command removes a defined abbreviation.*

If you've forgotten about an abbreviation and you want to undo it, you must go into command mode. (Abbreviations only occur in text input mode.) You can remove the offending text with d or x commands, or you can use a substitute command (such as :s/UNIX/b/) to reverse the effects of the abbreviation.

In the worst case, you can remove the abbreviation with :unab and retype the line.

*You can use abbreviations to correct your most common typing mistakes. I have "teh" defined as an abbreviation for "the" so that when I type "teh"* vi *inserts "the", the word I really wanted. (I place these in my* vi *startup file.) Try not to define abbreviations that are themselves words, though.*

## 10.3.2 ANSWERS

Open the file rhymes in vi and enter the following command (^V means Control-V):

```
:map fp !}fmt^V
```

Press Enter twice at the end of the command; the ^V should become a ^M and then the command line should vanish.

In command mode, type:

```
fp
```

a)    What happens when you type fp?

Answer: *The current paragraph is filtered through the* fmt *command*

Whenever the name of a macro is typed (fp  in this example), vi behaves just as if the rest of the line had been typed. A user-defined sequence of commands invoked by a single name is called a *macro*. The :map command in this exercise creates a macro named fp which runs the filter command to format the current paragraph.

The Control-V (^V) is the vi escape character (just as backslash, \, is the escape character for the shell). If you typed fmt and then pressed Enter, the Enter would end the :map command. When you ran the macro, it would end with the word fmt and you would have to press Enter to make the command run.

By typing ^V after the fmt command, you are able to escape the special meaning of the Enter key and insert the Enter key into the macro. (The

^M that appeared is the signal that the Enter key sends, and sometimes you will see ^M used to indicate pressing the Enter key.) You might want to try creating the same macro without the ^V to see the difference.

Enter the command:

```
:map
```

**b)**   What happens when you type `:map`?

*The `:map` command without arguments causes `vi` to display a list of your currently defined macros.*

The synopsis of the `:map` command in the `vi` man page looks like the synopsis for the `:ab` command:

```
:map[!] [lhs rhs]
```

Without any argument, `:map` displays your current list of macros.

The *lhs*, left-hand side, is restricted to a maximum of ten characters in most versions of `vi`. If you want to run your macro from the function keys on your keyboard (the keys F1-F10), you can specify the function keys as #1, #2, and #3 through #0. For example, to map the `fmt` command to the function key F10 instead of to the name "fp" you could define it as:

```
:map #0 !}fmt^V^M
```

I use the ^M here to represent the Enter key.

The *rhs*, right-hand side, can be longer. The `fp` macro only works in command mode; you can write "fp" in text input mode without worrying about the paragraph being formatted. If you include the ! after `:map` (as in `:map!`) you create a macro that works in text input mode. (I've never found much use for this feature, but you might.)

Enter the commands:

```
:unmap fp
:map
```

**c)**   What has happened to the `fp` macro you created?

*Answer: It's been removed.*

I don't create macros every day; for something I need just for today, I often use the buffer technique in the next exercise. However, I have several macros I use regularly and that I put into my `vi` startup file. One centers text on a line (it's not as general as the `center` script, but it works for the most common line length I use). Another formats the current paragraph. A third one inserts a random quotation into the current file; I use it when I write mail messages.

If you find yourself repeating a certain task or command in `vi`, consider writing it as a macro.

LAB
10.3

## 10.3.3 ANSWERS

Open the file `rhymes` in `vi` and go to the end of the file. Add this line at the end:

```
:%s/\([MJmj][^ ]\{3,3\}\) /\U\1 /g
```

(There are spaces after the ^, after the ), and after the 1.)

**a)** What would this line do, if executed as a command?

*Answer: This command makes all four-letter words that start with "M", "J", "m", or "j" uppercase.*

This question is really a review of regular expressions and substitute commands. Remember that most characters in regular expressions match themselves. The exceptions are the metacharacters—(^, $, ., *, and [)—and the special metacharacters—\{, \}, \(, and \). This regular expression is mostly metacharacters.

A substitute command has four parts:

- The `:%s` is the substitute command itself with the range of lines it will affect. In this case, it affects the entire file (`%`).
- The second part is between the first two slashes (/); that is, the regular expression you're searching for.
- The third part is between the second and third slashes; that is the text that will replace whatever was matched by the regular expression.
- The fourth part consists of flags to modify how the substitute command behaves; here we have the `g` flag, which makes the substitute command affect all matching patterns on a line.

The \( and \) metacharacters group part of the expression together, and are used here so that text can be inserted in the replacement text (using \1). The character class [MJmj] matches any one of the letters "M", "J", "m", or "j". The [^ ] is a character class that matches any single character except a space (the ^ at the beginning makes the character class exclude the space rather than include it). The \{3,3\} matches three in a row of the previous character (that is, any three non-space characters in a row).

The replacement text is almost all special metacharacters. The \U ensures that the replacement text will be uppercase. The \1 stands for the text that matched the part of the expression in the \( \) characters.

This regular expression is enough to match the names in this file, but wouldn't work for every file. Words might be separated by tabs, for example, or the names might come at the end of a line, and none of those would be matched by this expression.

*You can use any punctuation character instead of slashes to delimit a substitution command, but it has to be the same punctuation character for the whole command. You could have written the substitute command as:*

```
:%s!\([MJmj][^ ]\{3,3\}\) !\U\1 !g
```

*This is useful when the regular expression contains / characters.*

Now exit text mode by pressing the Escape key. With the cursor on the last line, enter the command:

```
"add
```

**b)** What does this command do?

*Answer: This command deletes the current line (dd) and stores it (using the " command) in the buffer "a" instead of in the normal buffer.*

Normally, when you delete a line in vi using the d or dd commands (or when you yank a line with y or yy), it's stored in a buffer that has no name; you can put the contents of that buffer back in the file with the p and P commands.

The next time you delete or yank a line or lines, it's stored in the buffer without a name, and the text that *was* in the buffer without a name is moved into *another* buffer without a name. If there was text in that one, it gets shifted to another. The `vi` program actually saves the last *nine* things you deleted or yanked.

You *can* get them back. Even though these are buffers without names, you can use numbers to get them back. To get back the last lines of text you deleted or yanked, give the command:

    "1p

To get back the second-to-last set of lines you deleted or yanked, give the command:

    "2p

And so on, up to `"9p`. (Of course, this also works with the `P` command.)

You can't deliberately choose to store something in a particular unnamed buffer. For that, `vi` has buffers with names. There are 26 of them, named for each letter of the alphabet, buffers a through z. The command to get to a buffer is `"` followed by the buffer letter, then followed by the yank, delete, or put command. To put the contents of buffer "a" back into the file, give the command:

    "ap

If you have a particular piece of text you need to insert in many places, put it in a named buffer. Normal deletions and yanks will go into the buffer with no name (referred to in the `vi` documentation as the *unnamed buffer*).

Although there are actually 26 named buffers, it's difficult to keep track of what's in more than five or six of them.

Enter the command:

    @a

**c)** What happens?

*Answer: The substitute command in buffer "a" is run as a command.*

The `@` command makes `vi` run any text in the buffer as if it were a series of colon commands. (You can't use this trick with commands that don't start with a colon.)

*Running text in a buffer is an excellent way to avoid retyping long and complicated regular expressions. If you don't get the expression quite right, you can put it back in the file, edit it, and then store it in the buffer to run it again.*

Macros and buffers run as macros are treated as a single command by `vi`, so a single `u` (undo) command undoes a single macro.

On many versions of `vi`, the `*` character has the same effect as `@`: In this example, `*a` would do the same thing as `@a`.

# LAB 10.3 SELF-REVIEW QUESTIONS

In order to test your progress, you should be able to answer the following questions.

1)  An abbreviation is replaced as soon as you type the short form.
    **a)** _____ True
    **b)** _____ False

2)  Which command lists your currently defined macros?
    **a)** _____ `:abbreviate`
    **b)** _____ `:map`
    **c)** _____ `:unab`
    **d)** _____ `:unmap`

3)  To map a macro to the F10 key, which of the following would you use as the left-hand side of the `:map` command?
    **a)** _____ `#10`
    **b)** _____ `F10`
    **c)** _____ `^[[10`
    **d)** _____ `#0`
    **e)** _____ `#F0`

4)  Identify the command that escapes a character in `vi`
    **a)** _____ Control-L
    **b)** _____ Control-N
    **c)** _____ Control-A
    **d)** _____ Control-V
    **e)** _____ \

*Quiz answers appear in Appendix A, Section 10.3.*

# LAB 10.4

# OPTIONS AND STARTUP TRICKS

> ### LAB OBJECTIVES
>
> After this Lab, you will be able to:
>
> * Setting vi Options
> * The Startup File

Previous Labs described some of the commands for setting options and customized macros. If you've gone to the trouble of setting options and creating macros, it's a nuisance to type them in again every time you need them.

Fortunately, `vi` provides two mechanisms for setting options and loading macros at startup.

## LAB 10.4 EXERCISES

### 10.4.1 SETTING VI OPTIONS

Open the file `rhymes` in `vi` and enter the command:

```
:set all
```

**a)** What are the results of the command?

_____

_____

Enter the commands:

```
:set number
:set
```

**b)** What does the number option do?

_____

_____

**c)** What command will turn off the number option?

_____

_____

## 10.4.2  THE STARTUP FILE

Open the file ~/.exrc (create it if it doesn't already exist). Remember that to enter ^V you need to type Control-V *twice*; to enter ^M you need to type Control-V and then press Enter.

Enter the following text:

```
" vi startup file
"
set number
set showmode
map #1 !}fmt^V^M
ab teh the
```

Start vi and enter several lines of text, including typing the word "teh" for "the".

**a)** How has the behavior of vi changed? (You may want to give the :map and :ab commands as well.)

_____

_____

**b)** What does each of these lines do?

_____

_____

Exit vi and at the command prompt, enter the command:

```
export EXINIT="set wm=50|set nonumber"
```

Start vi again and check the settings.

**c)** Are the settings in vi a combination of the ones in EXINIT and in your .exrc file, just the EXINIT settings, or just the .exrc settings?

_____

_____

# LAB 10.4 EXERCISE ANSWERS

## 10.4.1 ANSWERS

Open the file rhymes in vi and enter the command:

```
:set all
```

**a)**   What are the results of the command?

_Answer: vi displays the list of current settings._

When I type :set all in vi on my Solaris account, this is the list of options displayed:

| | | |
|---|---|---|
| noautoindent | nomodelines | noshowmode |
| autoprint | nonumber | noslowopen |
| noautowrite | nonovice | tabstop=8 |
| nobeautify | nooptimize | taglength=0 |
| directory=/var/tmp | paragraphs=IPLPPPQPP Lipplpipnpb | tags=tags /usr/lib/tags |
| noedcompatible | prompt | tagstack |
| noerrorbells | noreadonly | term=xterm |

| | | |
|---|---|---|
| noexrc | redraw | noterse |
| flash | remap | timeout |
| hardtabs=8 | report=5 | ttytype=xterm |
| noignorecase | scroll=12 | warn |
| nolisp | sections=NHSHH HUuhsh+c | window=24 |
| nolist | shell=/bin/ksh | wrapscan |
| magic | shiftwidth=8 | wrapmargin=0 |
| mesg | noshowmatch | nowriteany |

This list is in alphabetical order, more or less. These 45 options are a minimum; most implementations of vi will have most of these. Some have more options; the nvi command, found on many systems instead of vi, has 76 options.

A few of the options are described in Table 10.3, "Some vi Settings." This is not all of the settings, by any means; however, it may help you fine-tune vi to your needs.

Some options (such as term and shell) are set automatically from your environment.

Enter the commands:

```
:set number
```

**b)** What does the number option do?

*Answer: The* number *option causes* vi *to display line numbers beside the text.*

There are two types of settings. One type is on or off (sometimes referred to as *Boolean* setting). Examples of this are ignorecase and number. To turn on an on/off or Boolean option, you enter the command :set *optionname.*

The other type of setting has a value. When you set the wrapmargin with the command :set wm=8 or :set wrapmargin=8, you're assigning a value to the option. After you type :set wm=8, the value of the wrapmargin option is 8. (When the text gets within 8 characters of the right-hand side of the screen, vi will insert a line break to wrap the text to the next line.)

**c)** What command will turn off the number option?

*Answer: The command* :set nonumber *turns off the* number *option.*

## Table 10.3 ■ Some `vi` Settings

| Setting | Effect when on or set |
| --- | --- |
| `autoindent` | Automatically indents lines to match the indentation of the previous line. Pressing Control-D will move out one tabstop of indentation; pressing Control-T will move in one tabstop of indentation. |
| `autowrite` | Automatically writes modified files when changing files. |
| `exrc` | If there's a file named `.exrc` in the current directory, it reads it when starting up. |
| `ignorecase` | Ignores the case of letters when searching. |
| `list` | Displays lines with `$` at the end of the line. |
| `magic` | Allows full extent of regular expression metacharacters. When on, regular expressions behave as normal. When `magic` is off (`:set nomagic`) only the regular expression metacharacters `^`, `$`, and `\` are still special, unless you put a `\` character in front of them. That is, the expression `[a-z]` only matches a square bracket followed by "a-z" followed by another square bracket. If you want to use a character class when `nomagic` is set, you need to type it this way: `\[a-z]`. |
| `mesg` | Allows messages to be displayed (just as the `mesg` command does); if the terminal is set to `mesg n`, then setting the `vi` option `mesg` on has no significant effect. |
| `number` | Numbers lines along the left margin. |
| `novice` | Turns on settings suitable for beginning users. (Only on SVR4 systems such as Solaris.) |
| `readonly` | Makes the file you're editing read-only; doesn't allow writing the file. |
| `showmatch` | When you type a closing `)`, `]`, or `}` character, briefly moves the cursor to the matching opening `(`, `[`, or `{` character. |
| `showmode` | Displays the current mode on the bottom line. |
| `wrapmargin=n` | Automatically inserts a line break if the text comes within *n* characters of the right-hand margin. |
| `wrapscan` | When a search reaches the end or beginning of the file, automatically wraps around to start searching again from the other end. |

**LAB
10.4**

To turn off a Boolean option, you enter the command `:set nooption-name`. To return to the normal search mechanism, you turn off `ignore-case` with the command `:set noignorecase`.

You can't turn off an option that takes a value; however, you can set options such as `wrapmargin` to zero.

## 10.4.2 ANSWERS

You created a ~/.exrc file and entered some text, then saw the effect it had on vi.

**a)**    How has the behavior of vi changed? (You may want to give the :map and :ab commands as well.)

*Answer: The commands in the file have been executed: The settings* number *and* showmode *are on. The FI key is mapped to the command* !}fmt *and the letters "teh" are an abbreviation for "the."*

The `.exrc` file in your home directory is the vi and ex startup file. When starting up, the vi program reads the commands in a global startup file, `/etc/exrc`, and then looks in your environment for the environment variable `EXINIT`. If `EXINIT` doesn't exist, the program looks in your home directory for the file `.exrc`. If `.exrc` exists, vi runs the ex commands in that file.

Only ex commands (colon commands) can be used. The startup file is normally used to set options and to define macros and abbreviations.

**b)**    What does each of these lines do?

*Answer: Following is a description of the startup file.*

The first two lines start with the double quotation mark, `"`. When reading files of commands, vi ignores lines starting with `"`, so it's used to putting comments in the file. The first line is a title line and the second line (containing only `"`) adds a blank line to make it easier to read.

The next two lines turn on the `number` and `showmode` options. (I chose these because they're very visible when you start vi; you actually may not want to have them defined.)

*In a vi command file such as* `.exrc`*, you don't need to put the* `:` *at the beginning of commands.*

The next line maps the F1 key to the "format paragraph" command shown earlier. There's one important difference: The ^V is not added in the same way as when you define the same command during a `vi` session.

In a `vi` session, you press Control-V once and then press Enter (Control-M). In the `.exrc` file, you need to enter characters so that what `vi` reads out of the file is the same as Control-V Control-M. That means entering an actual Control-V (by pressing Control-V twice) and then entering a Control-M (by pressing Control-V Enter).

The last line defines "teh" as an abbreviation for "the".

By the way, you can save your current `vi` settings into a file with the command `:mkexrc` *filename*. Suppose I'm editing a lot of man pages, and I'm creating special macros and abbreviations to deal with problems unique to man pages. After I've created all of those special `map` commands in `vi`, I can save the current settings in a file called `manmacros.ex` (the `.ex` file extension is to remind me; it's not required by any software) with this `vi` command:

```
:mkexrc manmacros.ex
```

I can reload this file of `ex` commands as if it were a startup file by using the `:source` command. When working with man pages, I can load all of these specialized macros with the command:

```
:source manmacros.ex
```

This can eliminate a lot of tedious retyping.

Exit `vi` and at the command prompt, enter the command:

```
export EXINIT="set wm=50|set nonumber"
```

Start `vi` again and check the settings.

**c)**   Are the settings in `vi` a combination of the ones in `EXINIT` and in your `.exrc` file, just the `EXINIT` settings, or just the `.exrc` settings?

*Answer: The options set in* `EXINIT` *take precedence over the ones set in* `.exrc`.

If the `vi` program finds a valid environment variable named `EXINIT`, it uses the contents of that environment variable as the startup commands, not the `.exrc` file.

*If there is a valid setting for* EXINIT, vi *doesn't even look in the* ~/.exrc *file. If questions (a) and (b) didn't work for you, check to see if your normal working environment has* EXINIT *defined.*

Since EXINIT is an environment variable and not a file, it needs to have a way to fit more than one command on a single line. EXINIT uses the | character to separate lines (similar to how the shell uses the ; character). When vi reads the contents of the EXINIT line, it treats every | character as if it started a new line. This line:

```
set wm=50|set nonumber
```

is treated the same as if it were two lines in a file:

```
set wm=50
set nonumber
```

You can use | in this way in the .exrc file, too. (On a couple of old versions of vi, you need to do this; the program only reads the first line of the .exrc file and expects that line to be exactly like an EXINIT environment variable.)

If you need to insert an actual | character in your EXINIT line, you can put a backslash in front of it:

```
export EXINIT='map \| set number|set'
```

Some vi documentation claims that if there is a conflict between the EXINIT variable settings and a startup file, the file takes precedence. Since it doesn't read your ~/.exrc file if EXINIT is set to commands, the file referred to is the system startup file, /etc/exrc.

# LAB 10.4 SELF REVIEW QUESTIONS

In order to test your progress, you should be able to answer the following questions.

1)  If your ~/.exrc file contains the command :set number and your
    EXINIT variable contains the command :set nonumber, your vi
    session will start with number set.
    a) _____ True
    b) _____ False

**2)** The command : set displays all of your options.
    **a)** _____ True
    **b)** _____ False

**3)** What does the " command do in the first column of a startup file?
    **a)** Marks a buffer
    **b)** Moves to another location in the file
    **c)** Makes vi ignore the rest of the line
    **d)** Turns on all options

**4)** To turn on the showmode option in your startup file, which command should you use?
    **a)** :set showmode
    **b)** set showmode
    **c)** Either (a) and (b)
    **d)** Neither (a) nor (b)

*Quiz answers appear in Appendix A, Section 10.4.*

LAB
10.4

# LAB 10.5

# SOME USEFUL
# vi TRICKS

**LAB
10.5**

---

### LAB OBJECTIVES

After this Lab, you will be able to:

- Repeat Last Command
- Run Commands as a Script
- Append to a Buffer
- Mark a Place

---

This last section covers a few more incidental vi commands that may prove useful.

vi provides the ability to easily repeat the last command that changed the file or to run commands other than set, ab, and map automatically. You can add text to a buffer rather than replacing the existing text, and you can mark places in the text to make it easier to navigate through a file.

## LAB 10.5 EXERCISES

### 10.5.1 REPEAT LAST COMMAND

Open the file rhymes again. Go to the end of the file and enter the following commands:

```
dd
.
```

**a)** What does the . command do?

_____

_____

Enter the commands:

```
3~
.
10.
```

**b)** How many characters are affected by each of these commands?

_____

_____

Move to the line beginning with "Old" and enter the commands:

```
:%s/[A-Z]/#/
&&k&
```

**LAB
10.5**

Remember that the k in the command will move the cursor up one line.

**c)** What is the effect of the & command?

_____

_____

Exit without saving the changes to `rhymes`.

## 10.5.2 RUN COMMANDS AS A SCRIPT

Create a file called `script` that contains the following lines:

```
:%s/Mary/Bo Peep/
:%s/lamb/sheep/
:w sheep
:q
```

At the command prompt, enter the commands:

```
ex rhymes < script
ls
more sheep
```

**a)** What does the ex command do?

_____

_____

## 10.5.3   APPEND TO A BUFFER

There should now be a file named sheep; open the file sheep using vi. Move the cursor to the beginning of the second verse ("Jack and Jill"). Enter the commands:

```
"add"add"ap
```

**a)** How many lines are restored from buffer "a" by the "ap command?

_____

_____

Enter the commands:

```
"add"Add"Add"ap
```

**b)** This time how many lines are restored from buffer "a" by the "ap command?

_____

_____

## 10.5.4   MARK A PLACE

Open the file sheep using vi. Change the second line of the file in some way and then move the cursor to the end of the file with the G command.

Enter the command:

```
' '
```

(Those are two apostrophes, not a quotation mark.)

    **a)** What does the ' ' command do?

_____

_____

Move the cursor to the capital B in the second line of the file and enter the command:

    mz

Now move the cursor to the end of the file using G.

Enter the command:

    'z

    **b)** Where does the cursor move?

_____

_____

Move the cursor to another line.

Enter the command:

    'z

(The ' character is often found on the same key as the ~ character.)

    **c)** Where does the cursor move?

_____

_____

**LAB
10.5**

# LAB 10.5 EXERCISE ANSWERS

## 10.5.1 ANSWERS

Open the file `rhymes` again. Go to the end of the file and enter the following commands

```
dd
.
```

**a)**   What does the `.` command do?

*Answer: The `.` command repeats the* `dd` *command.*

In fact, the `.` command repeats any command that deleted or inserted text. Suppose you use the `o` command to insert a line of text that says "This line intentionally left blank" and then press Escape. The `.` command will insert that line of text again.

The `.` command will *not* repeat substitution commands.

Enter the commands:

```
3~
.
10.
```

**b)**   How many characters are affected by each of these commands?

*Answer: The first and second commands affect three characters each; the third command affects 10 characters.*

For many `vi` commands, you can specify a number of repetitions. The `3~` command means to repeat the `~` command 3 times. (This only works for the `vi` commands; it doesn't work for the `ex`-style commands that start with a colon.)

When you repeat a command, you repeat the entire command. The first `.` command repeats the entire `3~` command, affecting three characters.

If you specify how many times the `.` command should be repeated (as it was when you gave the command `10.`), then the number of repetitions you provide for `.` is used instead of the "existing" number of repetitions. (This is really the only possible option. It wouldn't work very well if the two numbers were multiplied together or if they were added.)

Move to the line beginning with "Old" and enter the commands:

```
:%s/[A-Z]/#/
&&k&
```

Remember that the k in the command will move the cursor up one line.

**c)**   What is the effect of the & command?

*Answer: The & command repeats the last substitution command, on the current line.*

You can repeat a substitution command by typing :s (or :%s). However, if that's too much to type, you can also repeat the substitution with the command &.

This repeated substitution has some limitations. First, it's only effective on the current line; there's no way to specify particular addresses or the entire file. Second, any option flags you placed at the end of the original substitute command (such as g or y) don't get repeated.

**LAB
10.5**

## 10.5.2 ANSWERS

You created a file called script that contained ex commands and then ran these commands:

```
ex rhymes < script
ls
more sheep
```

**a)**   What does the ex command do?

*Answer: The* ex *command here edits the file* rhymes *using the commands in* script, *and creates the file* sheep.

If you are editing a lot of files and performing the same changes to each file, create a script and edit the files more automatically.

This command line works because the standard input is redirected. The editor (vi acting as ex) reads instructions from the file script rather than from the keyboard.

There are some limitations:

- You can only use the ex-style commands (the ones that start with a colon).

- Think very carefully about what you want the script to do. If something goes wrong, it can be hard to detect.
- Always end the script with `:q!`. This ensures that the ex command will end, whether it worked or not. (Since ex doesn't provide a full-screen display, trying to exit ex can be difficult if you're not already familiar with it.)
- I prefer to use the ex command because it reminds me to use the ex-style commands, but you don't have to. The `-e` option to `vi` will cause it to behave like ex. (Without the `-e` option, `vi` won't read a script.) You could write the command as:

```
vi -e rhymes < script
```

## 10.5.3 ANSWERS

Open the file `sheep` using `vi`. Move the cursor to the beginning of the second verse ("Jack and Jill"). Enter the commands:

```
"add"add"ap
```

**a)** How many lines are restored from buffer "a" by the `"ap` command?

*Answer: Only one line is restored.*

Each time you add text to the buffer with a new `"add` command, it replaces the text that was there before.

Enter the commands:

```
"add"Add"Add"ap
```

**b)** This time how many lines are restored from buffer "a" by the `"ap` command?

*Answer: Three lines are restored.*

If you specify the name of the buffer as an uppercase letter, the new text is *added* to the buffer instead of replacing it. This can be useful if you're gathering together lines from throughout a file.

## 10.5.4  ANSWERS

Open the file sheep using vi. Change the second line of the file in some way and then move the cursor to the end of the file with the G command.

Enter the command:

    '  '

(Those are two apostrophes, not a quotation mark.)

**a)**   What does the '  ' command do?

*Answer: The '  ' command moves the cursor back to the line where you changed the text.*

Any change in text counts, whether you inserted text, deleted it, or substituted text with a :s command. The '  ' is actually a special case of a general "move to a marked place" command, the ' character.

Using the ' character twice ('  ') will also move the cursor to the last place where you changed the file.

Move the cursor to the capital B in the second line of the file and enter the command:

    mz

Now move the cursor to the end of the file using G.

Enter the command:

    'z

**b)**   Where does the cursor move?

*Answer: The cursor moves to the beginning of the second line of the file.*

The m command (or mark) puts a placeholder or a bookmark in the file. The name of the bookmark is a lowercase letter (z in this case).

Move the cursor to another line.

Enter the command:

    'z

(The ' character is often found on the same key as the ~ character.)

**c)** Where does the cursor move?

*Answer: The cursor moves to the capital B on the marked line.*

The ' character makes the cursor move to the *beginning* of the line with the bookmark; the ` character makes the cursor move to the same place it was when the mark was made. In this case, the mark was made while the cursor was at the letter "B".

If you've changed the line since you made the mark (perhaps you deleted the word where the mark was), the cursor will move to the same position on the line.

# LAB 10.5 SELF-REVIEW QUESTIONS

In order to test your progress, you should be able to answer the following questions.

1)  Identify the commands that will be repeated by the . command.
    **a)** \_\_\_\_\_ `Iburgundy` **Escape**
    **b)** \_\_\_\_\_ `:%s/burgundy/chardonnay/g`
    **c)** \_\_\_\_\_ `3x`
    **d)** \_\_\_\_\_ (a) and (b)
    **e)** \_\_\_\_\_ (b) and (c)
    **f)** \_\_\_\_\_ (a) and (c)
    **g)** \_\_\_\_\_ (a), (b), and (c)

2)  If mark a is placed on line 8 and mark b on line 12, which is the command to delete lines 8-12?
    **a)** \_\_\_\_\_ `:'a,'bd`
    **b)** \_\_\_\_\_ `:"a,"bd`
    **c)** \_\_\_\_\_ `'a,'bd`
    **d)** \_\_\_\_\_ `"a,"bd`

3)  Identify the command that can*not* be used in an `ex` script.
    **a)** \_\_\_\_\_ `:substitute`
    **b)** \_\_\_\_\_ `ZZ`
    **c)** \_\_\_\_\_ `:wq`
    **d)** \_\_\_\_\_ `:next`
    **e)** \_\_\_\_\_ `:rewind`

*Quiz answers appear in Appendix A, Section 10.5.*

# C H A P T E R   1 0

# TEST YOUR THINKING

**1)** In the early days of Usenet news and on some mailing lists, messages containing dirty jokes or other objectionable material were sometimes encrypted using `tr` in what was called "rot13" or rotate 13 encryption. It was done with a `tr` command like this:

```
tr '[a-m][n-z][A-M][N-Z]' '[n-z][a-m][N-Z][A-M]'
```

    **a)** Explain what this command does.

    **b)** Map this command to the F5 key, so you can encrypt and decrypt.

    **c)** Set this up in your `.exrc` file.

# ADVANCED EMACS TRICKS

As I mentioned in Chapter 6, "The Emacs Editor," Emacs is more than an editor. It's an entire operating environment, complete with a programming language. (That's not true for most of the Emacs-like editors, such as Jove, so most of the information in this Chapter doesn't apply to those editors.)

This chapter will cover only a few of the extra features in Emacs. There's a sophisticated command history that allows you to repeat and edit your Emacs commands. There are specialized commands for editing text. There are also facilities for running shell commands, customizing Emacs, and there's even a mode (dired mode) for working with files: listing them, moving them, and deleting them.

Before you begin this chapter, you may find it useful to refer back to Chapter 6, "The Emacs Editor."

# L A B  1 1 . 1

# USING TEXT MODE

> ## LAB OBJECTIVES
>
> After this Lab, you will be able to:
>
> - Fill Text
> - Sort Files
> - Check Spelling
> - Create Abbreviations

Emacs has a number of modes. A mode in Emacs is a special setting for a buffer that adds new commands or re-defines some old ones. One of the modes is Text mode, which provides special commands for handling text.

Emacs has many commands available for handling text. Most of these commands are available in any Emacs mode, including Fundamental mode, but some are available only in Text mode.

## LAB 11.1 EXERCISES

### 11.1.1 FILL TEXT

Open Emacs and then visit (Control-X Control-F) the file `rhymes`, which you created in Chapter 10, "Advanced `vi` Tricks." The cursor should already be in the first verse. Enter the command:

```
Meta-Q
```

**a)** What happens?

_____

_____

Move the cursor to the first "w" in "white". Enter the commands:

```
Control-X f
Meta-Q
```

**b)** What is displayed in the minibuffer after the first command? What happens this time after the Meta-Q command?

_____

_____

Move the cursor to the last line of this verse and enter the command:

```
Meta-X center-line
```

**c)** What happens to the line?

_____

_____

Undo the changes with `Meta-3 Control-X u`.

## 11.1.2  SORT FILES

Move to the beginning of the second verse and set the mark (Control-@ or Control-Space). Move the cursor to the end of the file (Meta->) and enter the command:

```
Meta-X sort-lines
```

**a)** What happens?

_____

_____

Now move the cursor to the top of the file, set the mark, and move to the end again (Meta-< Control-Space Meta->). Enter the command:

```
Meta-X sort-paragraphs
```

**b)** How is this sort different from the last one?

_____

_____

Set the mark at the beginning of the last paragraph, then move to the end of the last line of text. Enter the command:

```
Meta-6 Meta-X sort-fields
```

**c)** How is the paragraph sorted now?

_____

_____

## 11.1.3 CHECK SPELLING

Move the cursor to the "m" in "tumbling" and delete it (with Control-D). Enter the command:

```
Meta-X spell-word
```

**a)** What happens?

_____

_____

Press Control-G to avoid correcting the word. Enter the command:

```
Meta-X ispell-word
```

(This command will not work if your system does not have `ispell` installed.)

**b)** What happens?

_____

_____

Once again, use Control-G to avoid correcting the spelling. Enter the command:

```
Meta-$
```

(Normally that's Escape followed by Shift-4.)

> **c)** Which command does Meta-$ invoke on your system, `spell-word` or `ispell-word`?

_____

_____

The following command only works in text mode. Enter the command:

```
Meta-X text-mode
```

Move to the end of the file and start a new paragraph. Type the following letters and then enter the Meta-`Tab` key command:

```
ebMeta-Tab
```

> **d)** What happens? What's the name of the new buffer?

_____

_____

### 11.1.4 CREATE ABBREVIATIONS

You can create mode or global abbreviations in Abbreviation mode. The word *before* the point becomes the expansion; you type in the abbreviation. You can do it the other way around, too.

Move the cursor to the "b" in "cupboard" and enter the command:

```
Control-X a g
```

At the prompt, enter:

```
c
```

**a)** What does the prompt say? What happens when you type "c."

_____

_____

Move to the end of the file and type:

        c.

Enter the command:

        Meta-X abbrev-mode

Type:

        c.

**b)** What happens this time?

_____

_____

Now move the cursor to the end of the word "Hubbard" and enter the command:

        Meta-3 Control-X a l

At the prompt, enter:

        omh

Create a new buffer with Control-X B named "abbrevs" and turn on Abbreviation mode. Then type the following line:

        My c overfloweth, but omh had to go shopping.

**c)** What's the mode of the new buffer? Which abbreviations were expanded?

_____

_____

Enter the command:

```
Meta-X list-abbrevs
```

**d)** What is displayed?

_____

_____

# LAB 11.1 EXERCISE ANSWERS

## 11.1.1 ANSWERS

Open Emacs and then visit (Control-X Control-F) the file rhymes, which you created in Chapter 10, "Advanced vi Tricks." The cursor should already be in the first verse. Enter the command:

```
Meta-Q
```

**a)** What happens?

*Answer: The text looks like this:*

```
Mary had a little lamb.  Its fleece was white as
snow.  And everywhere
that Mary went The lamb was sure to go.
```

The Meta-Q command (fill-paragraph) acts much like the fmt command. It formats the paragraph, breaking long lines and pushing together short ones until it comes to the end of a paragraph. The end of a paragraph is generally indicated by an empty line or a line that contains only white space (spaces and tabs), although different modes recognize other characters as the start of a paragraph.

If you want the text to format automatically when you type a line that's too long, you need to put Emacs into "auto fill mode." To do this, give the command Meta-X auto-fill-mode.

Move the cursor to the first "w" in "white." Enter the commands:

```
Control-X f
Meta-Q
```

**b)** What is displayed in the minibuffer after the first command? What happens this time after the Meta-Q command?

*Answer: The minibuffer displays this text:*

```
fill-column set to 40
```

*The Meta-Q command still reformats the paragraph, but the line length is now 40 characters, so it looks like this:*

```
Mary had a little lamb.   Its fleece was
white as snow.   And everywhere that Mary
went The lamb was sure to go.
```

Fill-column is the name of the variable in Emacs that stores the current line length for formatting purposes. When you give the command Control-X f (or Meta-X set-fill-column), the fill column is set to the right of the point (effectively the cursor).

Unfortunately, the meaning of the term "fill-column" is not immediately obvious. If you can't quite remember the command to fill the paragraph and you use Control-X f (because you think "f" stands for "fill", as I often do), you are certain to be surprised when you actually use Meta-Q.

If you give the command a numeric argument, the line length is set to that value, no matter where on the line the cursor is. For example, to set the current line length to 72 characters for formatting, use the command Meta-72 Control-X f.

Move the cursor to the last line of this verse and enter the command:

```
Meta-X center-line
```

**c)** What happens to the line?

*Answer: The last line is centered, but it's centered on a line length of 40 characters, so the verse now looks like this:*

```
Mary had a little lamb.   Its fleece was
white as snow.   And everywhere that Mary
        went The lamb was sure to go.
```

The center-line command is another command that relies on the value of fill-column. If you want to center more than one line at a time, give the command an argument: To center 8 lines, use Meta-8 Meta-X center-line.

Another useful Emacs feature when filling paragraphs is the "fill prefix." The fill prefix is some text that's supposed to go before every line in the paragraph, such as "#" at the beginning of a comment in a shell script. Move the cursor to the end of that common text and set it as the fill prefix.

## ■ FOR EXAMPLE

Suppose you are preparing a response to a mail message and each line of the original message starts with "> ". Move the cursor to after the space and enter the command Control-X . (or Meta-X `set-fill-prefix`). When you give the Meta-Q command, the "> " text is inserted before all of the lines in the paragraph.

New paragraphs that *don't* start with "> " aren't affected; they format normally.

The text commands in this section are summarized in Table 11.1, "Some Emacs Text Commands."

### Table 11.1 ■ Some Emacs Text Commands

| Effect | Keys | Command |
|---|---|---|
| Centers the current line. | | center-line |
| Enters auto-fill mode. | | auto-fill-mode |
| Enters text mode. | | |
| Fills (formats) the entire region, ignoring paragraph breaks, as if it were one paragraph. | | fill-region-as-paragraph |
| Fills (formats) the paragraph that contains the point. | Meta-Q | fill-paragraph |
| Fills the entire region, each paragraph separately, and indents paragraphs to match their first lines. | | fill-individual-paragraphs |
| Fills the region, each paragraph separately. | | fill-region |
| Sets line length for fill mode and for centering lines. | Control-X f | set-fill-column |
| Sets the fill prefix to the portion of the current line preceding the point. | Control-X . | set-fill-prefix |

**11.1.2 ANSWERS**

Move to the beginning of the second verse and set the mark (Control-@ or Control-Space). Move the cursor to the end of the file (Meta->) and enter the command:

```
Meta-X sort-lines
```

**a)** What happens?

*Answer: The lines in the region (the second verse) are sorted.*

This is an ASCII sort, so all of the uppercase letters come before any of the lowercase letters. In fact, the sort-lines command is the same as running the text in the region through the sort command on the command line.

All of the sort commands in this Lab act upon the region, the text between the mark and the point.

Now move the cursor to the top of the file, set the mark, and move to the end again (Meta-< Control-Space Meta->). Enter the command:

```
Meta-X sort-paragraphs
```

**b)** How is this sort different from the last one?

*Answer: The paragraphs in the region are sorted but the lines in each paragraph stay in the same order.*

This is an extremely useful sort when you're working with text lists that take up more than one line. In vi, the only way to do this is to turn each paragraph into one long line and then run the file through sort.

Set the mark at the beginning of the last paragraph, then move to the end of the last line of text. Enter the command:

```
Meta-6 Meta-X sort-fields
```

**c)** How is the paragraph sorted now?

*Answer: The paragraph is now sorted according to the sixth word on each line.*

This is the same as running the region through the command sort -k 6.

Some of the Emacs sort commands are listed in Table 11.2, "Emacs Sort Commands."

## Table 11.2 ■ Emacs Sort Commands

| Command | Effect |
|---|---|
| `sort-lines` | Sorts the lines in the region by ASCII order. |
| `sort-paragraphs` | Sorts the paragraphs in the region by ASCII order. A paragraph is separated by blank lines. |
| `sort-fields` | Sorts the lines in the region according to some field; the number of the field is specified by the argument (Meta-*number* or `Control-u` *number*). |
| `sort-numeric fields` | Sorts the fields as if they were numbers. |

## 11.1.3 ANSWERS

Move the cursor to the "m" in "tumbling" and delete it (with Control-D). Enter the command:

```
Meta-X spell-word
```

**a)** What happens?

*Answer: The following text appears in the minibuffer:*

```
`tubling' not recognized; edit a replacement: tubling
```

You can edit "tubling" in the minibuffer; when you press Enter, Emacs will ask for confirmation, and after you confirm, Emacs will replace "tubling" with the corrected word. To do the correction, Emacs runs the `replace-regexp` command, so "tubling" will actually appear as \btubling\b. The \b is the Emacs regular expression for the end of a word.

The command `spell-word` runs the UNIX `spell` command on the word that contains the point. The `spell` command simply reports whether a word is in the dictionary or not, so Emacs reports this result; if the word is incorrect, Emacs offers you the opportunity to replace the word.

Press Control-G to avoid correcting the word. Enter the command:

```
Meta-X ispell-word
```

**b)** What happens?

*Answer: Emacs opens a new buffer and displays a list of possible words.*

The `ispell` command is a command that's available on many systems. Instead of simply checking a dictionary and reporting on misspelled words, `ispell` is interactive (that's the "i" in `ispell`). For each misspelled word, it presents a list of possible corrections, and you select the word from the list.

Once again, use Control-G to avoid correcting the spelling. Enter the command:

```
Meta-$
```

**c)** Which command does Meta-$ invoke on your system, `spell-word` or `ispell-word`?

*Answer: This will vary between systems.*

On some systems, Meta-$ is configured for `ispell-word`, but on older systems, it may be configured for `spell-word`. If your system has both `spell` and `ispell`, you can set which command Meta-$ runs by binding the key combination Meta-$ to the command you want. See Lab 11.3.2, "Alter Key Bindings," for more information.

The following command only works in text mode. Enter the command:

```
Meta-X text-mode
```

Move to the end of the file and start a new paragraph. Type the following letters and then enter the Meta-Tab key command:

```
ebMeta-Tab
```

**d)** What happens? What's the name of the new buffer?

*Answer: Emacs opens a new buffer named \*`options`\* and displays a list of words beginning with "eb".*

Text mode is specialized for handling text. It's a *major mode* in Emacs. (There are also *minor modes*; a minor mode adds some extra commands or features, but can be added to almost any of the major modes.)

Each word displayed has a character before it, starting with (1) through (0), then moving on to punctuation, then capital letters, then lowercase letters. To select a word and insert it in the file, press the appropriate character. For example, if you wanted the word "ebullient," you would press the Q key. (Your list may be slightly different because your dictionary isn't the same as mine.)

*Don't press "a" or "A"! Notice that "a" and "A" aren't offered as options; they cause* `ispell` *to accept the current spelling, and will cause Emacs to insert "Local word: eb" into the file (or whatever text you've typed).*

The Emacs spelling commands are summarized in Table 11.3.

## 11.1.4 ANSWERS

Move the cursor to the "b" in "cupboard" and enter the command:

```
Control-X a g
```

At the prompt, enter:

```
c
```

Now type:

```
c.
```

**a)** What does the prompt say? What happens when you type "c."?

*Answer: The prompt is shown as follows; after this command, when you type "c.", it remains a "c".*

```
Global abbrev for "cup":
```

## Table 11.3 ■ Emacs Spelling Commands

| Effect | Keys | Command |
|---|---|---|
| Asks for a word and then checks its spelling. | | spell-string |
| Checks and corrects spelling of word under point. | Meta | spell-word<br>ispell-word |
| Checks and corrects spelling of words in buffer. | | spell-buffer |
| Checks and corrects spelling of words in region. | | spell-region |
| Completes the word under the point. | Meta-Tab | ispell-complete-word |

In Emacs, you must type the full word in the editing buffer and then place the point *after* the word (or words). In this case, the point was after the "cup" in "cupboard" so the text being abbreviated is "cup". If the point had been after the "d", the entire word would have been abbreviated.

After you give the Control-X a g command, Emacs asks you for the abbreviation you want to use.

In Emacs, you can create abbreviations that apply to the current mode (called *local* abbreviations) or abbreviations that apply to all modes in this editing session (called *global* abbreviations). The Control-X a g command creates a global abbreviation. (The Control-X a l command creates a local abbreviation.) Not all modes let you create a local abbreviation.

You can always *create* an abbreviation, but Emacs will only expand abbreviations if you turn on that feature (by turning on abbreviation mode, abbrev-mode). At this point, abbreviation mode isn't on, so a "c" remains a "c". Abbreviation mode is a minor mode; you can add it to a major mode. Auto-fill is also a minor mode; you can add auto-fill to a major mode, such as Fundamental mode.

Enter the command:

```
Meta-X abbrev-mode
```

Type:

```
c.
```

**b)** What happens this time?

*Answer: The letter "c" is replaced by "cup".*

Another difference between Emacs and vi is that Emacs recognizes more situations in which an abbreviation should be expanded. The vi command wouldn't expand this abbreviation because it starts with a punctuation character (the string typed over the two questions is ".c.c"), but Emacs happily expands it.

To create an abbreviation for more than one word, give the number of words as an argument to the command to create the abbreviation, as shown in the next exercise.

After defining the abbreviation "omh" for "Old Mother Hubbard" you created a new buffer and entered the line:

```
My c overfloweth, but omh had to go shopping.
```

**c)** What's the mode of the new buffer? Which abbreviations were expanded?

*Answer: The new mode is in Fundamental mode. Only the "c" abbreviation was expanded, because it was global.*

The global abbreviation affects all buffers; the "omh" abbreviation is local to text mode buffers. To make the "omh" abbreviation apply to the current buffer, you would have to put it in text mode.

A local buffer affects *all* buffers of that type or mode, not just the one where the abbreviation was created.

If you try to create a local abbreviation in Fundamental mode, you'll get the error message:

```
No per-mode abbrev-table
```

This message means that Fundamental mode doesn't have a special entry in the table of abbreviations.

Enter the command:

```
Meta-X list-abbrevs
```

**d)** What is displayed?

*Answer: Emacs opens a buffer window that displays all of your currently defined abbreviations.*

This buffer is actually displaying the abbrev-table mentioned in the error message. If you move the cursor into this buffer (with Control-X o), you can scroll down and see all of the different modes that support local abbreviations. Under Text Mode, the "omh" abbreviation is listed.

You can edit existing abbreviations with the command `edit-abbrevs`; this command creates the same buffer that `list-abbrevs` does, but it also makes this the current buffer. To remove a single abbreviation, delete it. Once you've edited the abbreviations in the buffer that `edit-abbrevs` displays, you can have your changes take effect with the command `edit-abbrevs-redefine`, or Control-C Control-C.

Some of the Emacs abbreviation commands are listed in Table 11.4, "Emacs Abbreviations Commands."

# LAB 11.1 SELF-REVIEW QUESTIONS

In order to test your progress, you should be able to answer the following questions.

1) Emacs works with all files in Text Mode.
   **a)** _____True
   **b)** _____False

2) In Emacs, `fill-column` is the command to reformat a paragraph.
   **a)** _____True
   **b)** _____False

## Table 11.4 ■ Emacs Abbreviations Commands

| Effect | Keys | Command |
|---|---|---|
| Defines global abbreviation for text in buffer. | Control-X a g | add-global-abbrev |
| Defines global expanded text for an abbreviation in the buffer. | Control-X a I g | inverse-add-global-abbrev |
| Defines local abbreviation for text in buffer. | Control-X a l | add-mode-abbrev |
| Defines local expanded text for an abbreviation in the buffer. | Control-X a I l | inverse-add-mode-abbrev |
| Edits current abbreviations. | | edit-abbrevs |
| Lists current abbreviations. | | list-abbrevs |
| Loads the edited abbreviations buffer; the key combination only works in that buffer. | Control-C Control-C | exit-abbrevs-redefine |
| Reads and loads abbreviations from a file. | | read-abbrev-file |
| Saves abbreviations in a file; you are prompted for the file name, but the name ~/.abbrev_defs is common. | | write-abbrev-file |
| Undefines all abbreviations. | | kill-all-abbrevs |

**3)** Match the command with the effect.

   **a)** _____Formats or fills paragraph

   **b)** _____Sets line length for formatting

   **c)** _____Adds a global abbreviation

   **d)** _____Checks spelling of the word under the point

   **i)** Meta-$

   **ii)** Control-X a g

   **iii)** Meta-Q

   **iv)** Control-X f

**4)** What is the meaning of the error message `No per-mode abbrev-table`?

   **a)** _____You have not loaded your abbreviations file

   **b)** _____You have not saved the abbreviations in a file

   **c)** _____You are trying to create a local abbreviation and the mode won't allow it

   **d)** _____None of the above

**5)** In an ASCII sort (such as the one done by `sort-lines`), what is the sorting order of A b C d?

   **a)** _____A b C d

   **b)** _____b d A C

   **c)** _____A C b d

   **d)** _____d C b A

**6)** You want to create an abbreviation for the word "antidisestablishmentarianism" which you've already typed in the text buffer. Where should the cursor be to create the abbreviation?

   **a)** _____Anywhere in the word

   **b)** _____At the beginning of the word

   **c)** _____On the last character of the word

   **d)** _____Immediately after the last character of the word

*Quiz answers appear in Appendix A, Section 11.1.*

# L A B   1 1 . 2

# RUNNING SHELL COMMANDS IN EMACS

---

### LAB OBJECTIVES

After this Lab, you will be able to:

- Use a Subshell
- Run Commands Against the Buffer

---

Because Emacs has so very many commands, it's often not really necessary to run a shell command against a buffer. However, one of the neat features of Emacs is its ability to run a shell *within* one of the buffer windows. If you're on a terminal where you can't create new windows, this is very handy.

## LAB 11.2 EXERCISES

### 11.2.1 USE A SUBSHELL

Enter the command:

```
Meta-!
```

**a)** What prompt appears in the minibuffer?

_____

_____

Enter the command:

```
ls
```

**b)** Where do the results appear?

_____

_____

Enter the command:

```
Meta-X shell
```

**c)** What's the name of the new buffer?

_____

_____

Enter some shell commands (such as cd /tmp, ls, and cd -). Now enter the commands:

```
Meta-P
Meta-P
Meta-N
```

**d)** What does Meta-P do? Meta-N?

_____

_____

## 11.2.2 RUN COMMANDS AGAINST THE BUFFER

Mark the entire buffer as the region (Meta-< Control-Space Meta->) and enter the command:

```
Meta-|
```

At the prompt, enter:

```
sort -k 5
```

**a)** What happens?

_____

_____

**b)** How would you replace the current file with these results?

_____

_____

# LAB 11.2 EXERCISE ANSWERS

## 11.2.1 ANSWERS

Enter the command:

```
Meta-!
```

**a)** What prompt appears in the minibuffer?

*Answer: The minibuffer displays this prompt:*

```
Enter shell command:
```

Enter the command:

```
ls
```

**b)** Where do the results appear?

*Answer: The output appears in a buffer named *Shell Command Output*.*

If the command doesn't produce any output (for example, if you had entered the command `rm my_tempfile`), then Emacs doesn't create a new buffer. If you enter another shell command, Emacs re-uses the same shell output buffer, replacing the old output with the new output.

If you really need to save the output, you can save the contents of the buffer as though it were a file, or you can rename the buffer so that Emacs creates a new buffer named *Shell Command Output* to store the output. (The command to rename a buffer is `rename-buffer`.)

Enter the command:

```
Meta-X shell
```

**c)** What's the name of the new buffer?

*Answer: The new buffer is named *Shell*.*

You can edit commands in the subshell using the normal Emacs commands (such as Control-D).

This subshell is nearly identical to a normal shell, but there are some differences. One is that you don't have to wait for a command to finish before you switch back to another window in Emacs. (You can also run a command in the background in the subshell.)

Another important difference is that control characters (such as end-of-file, normally Control-D) don't mean the same thing in this Emacs subshell. For example, if you wanted to send an end-of-file signal to a regular shell, you would type Control-D. To interrupt a command, you would type Control-C. Inside Emacs, Control-D and Control-C have different meanings.

Instead, in an Emacs subshell type Control-C *first* and then type the control character. To send an end-of-file inside the subshell, type Control-C Control-D. To send an interrupt to a program, type Control-C Control-C.

If you give the shell command again, you're returned to this buffer. If for some reason you really need to have a second subshell open, you can: You need to change the name of this buffer (with the rename-buffer command) and then give the shell command again.

Enter some shell commands (such as cd /tmp, ls, and cd -). Now enter the command:

```
Meta-P
Meta-P
Meta-N
```

**d)** What does Meta-P do? Meta-N?

*Answer: The Meta-P command scrolls backward through the command history list in the subshell. The Meta-N command scrolls forward through the command history list in the subshell.*

Once you've pulled up an old command, you can edit it using the normal Emacs editing commands; press Enter to run the command.

There are also two commands that let you search through the command history list in the subshell, Meta-R (for searches back through the history) and Meta-S (for searches forward through the history). Both commands prompt you for a regular expression and search through the history list.

These three commands (Meta-N, Meta-R, and Meta-S) only work *after* you've entered Meta-P. The Meta-P command is the one that puts you into the command history.

This behavior is similar to what you get by setting `set -o emacs` in your Korn Shell. In the Korn Shell's version, you use Control-P, Control-N, Control-S, and Control-R to edit the command history and not the Meta-versions. Also, the Korn Shell's Control-R and Control-S commands search with incremental searches and not regular expressions.

## 11.2.2 ANSWERS

Mark the entire buffer as the region (Meta-< `Control-Space` Meta->) and enter the command:

```
Meta-|
```

At the prompt, enter:

```
sort -k 5
```

**a)**  What happens?

*Answer: Emacs opens a new buffer named* `*Shell Command Output*` *and places the sorted output there.*

Like Meta-!, this command opens a buffer named `*Shell Command Output*` but it uses the text in the region as its input.

**b)**  How would you replace the current file with these results?

*Answer: Save the buffer *Shell Command Output* as the file* `rhymes`.

You could also choose to copy the output you need from the `*Shell Command Output*` buffer into the original file buffer. (Since the region is already defined, it's easy to delete.)

# LAB 11.2 SELF-REVIEW QUESTIONS

In order to test your progress, you should be able to answer the following questions.

1) Running the shell command `rm tmpfile` will cause Emacs to create an output buffer named `*Shell Command Output*` (assuming there is such a file).
   a) _____True
   b) _____False

2) If you're working in an Emacs subshell (started with the `shell` command), and you need to signal end-of-file, which key combination will work on most systems?
   a) _____Control-C
   b) _____Control-D
   c) _____Control-C Control-C
   d) _____Control-C Control-D

3) It's not possible to cut and paste shell command output in Emacs as if it were ordinary text.
   a) _____True
   b) _____False

4) In an Emacs subshell, which key combination searches for previous commands in the command history?
   a) _____Meta-P
   b) _____Meta-R
   c) _____Control-P
   d) _____Control-S

5) In an Emacs subshell, you cannot run commands in the background.
   a) _____True
   b) _____False

6) The Emacs subshell is not connected with the Korn Shell `set -o emacs` command.
   a) _____True
   b) _____False

*Quiz answers appear in Appendix A, Section 11.2.*

# L A B   1 1 . 3

# CUSTOMIZING EMACS

> ## LAB OBJECTIVES
>
> After this Lab, you will be able to:
>
> - Create a Macro
> - Alter Key Bindings
> - Edit the Startup File

Like the UNIX shells, Emacs is very flexible. It can be programmed using a programming language (the language is called Lisp), so people have, at different times, written Emacs modules to read mail and Usenet news, to display Web pages, and to play games. (Try the extended command `doctor`.)

In some ways, this flexibility has worked against Emacs: The Emacs programmers assume that anyone who wants a sophisticated customized command will write the appropriate Lisp code. The macro facilities, for example, are not necessarily as powerful as `vi`'s.

Rather than teach you Lisp, this Lab will cover some of the easier customizations: macros, redefining keys, and some things you can put in your startup file, `.emacs`.

## LAB 11.3 EXERCISES

### 11.3.1 CREATE A MACRO

Enter the commands (printed here one to a line for easy reading):

```
Control-X (
Control-A
```

```
Control-Space
Control-E
Control-X Control-U
```

If you get a help buffer explaining that Control-X Control-U is a "disabled command," press the Space bar and continue.

```
Control-X )
```

**a)** What does this series of commands do?

_____

_____

Visit the file `rhymes`, if you haven't already got it in a buffer. Place the cursor on the first line and enter the command:

```
Control-X e
```

**b)** What does the Control-X e command do?

_____

_____

Now define the macro again, but use the command Control-X Control-L instead of Control-X Control-U. Now enter the command:

```
Control-X e
```

**c)** Which macro is executed—the first one or the second one?

_____

_____

Enter the command:

```
Meta-X name-last-kbd-macro
```

At the prompt, enter:

```
lower-line
```

Move the cursor to a line containing text and enter:

```
Meta-X lower-line
```

**c)** What does the `lower-line` command do?

_____

_____

Visit the file ~/.emacs and move to the end of the file. Enter the command:

```
Meta-X insert-kbd-macro
```

At the prompt, enter:

```
lower-line
```

**d)** What does the inserted text look like?

_____

_____

Save the changed ~/.emacs file.

## 11.3.2 ALTER KEY BINDINGS

Visit a text file and enter the command:

```
Meta-X global-set-key
```

At the first prompt, enter:

```
Control-C Control-L
```

At the second prompt, enter:

```
lower-line
```

Now move the cursor to a line of text and enter the command:

```
Control-C Control-L
```

**a)** What happens?

_____

_____

Enter the commands:

```
Control-H k Control-C Control-L
```

**b)** What information is displayed in the help window?

**LAB
11.3**

_____

_____

## 11.3.3   EDIT THE STARTUP FILE

Open the file ~/.emacs. Enter the following lines at the beginning of the file:

```
(define-key global-map "\C-x?" 'help-command)

(define-key global-map "\C-h" 'backward-delete-
char-untabify)

(define-key text-mode-map "\C-c\C-l" 'lower-line)
```

Type two ;; characters at the beginning of the fset command that defines the lower-line **macro**.

Start Emacs. Type some text, then press the Backspace key.

**a)** What happens?

_____

_____

Enter the lower-line macro command Control-C Control-l.

**b)** What happens?

_____

_____

Enter the key command Control-X ?.

    **c)** What happens?

_____

_____

Exit Emacs and start it again with the command-line option -q. Type some text and then press Backspace.

    **d)** What happens? What does the -q option do?

_____

_____

# LAB 11.3 EXERCISE ANSWERS

## 11.3.1 ANSWERS

You created a macro.

**a)** What does this series of commands do?

*Answer: These commands define a macro that converts a line to uppercase.*

A macro in Emacs is just a recorded series of keystrokes. You can use a macro to repeat a complex series of commands or to insert some text you must repeat frequently. The Ctrl-X ( and Ctrl-X ) commands start and end the macro; anything you type in between those two brackets are the commands in the macro.

Some commands in Emacs are *disabled*. These commands are still available, but because they might cause problems or confuse new users, Emacs asks for confirmation before running them. (I often run into it by accidentally hitting the Escape key twice.) When you issue a disabled command, Emacs asks for one of these responses:

- If you don't want it to be disabled any more, type y. Emacs then asks if you want it enabled just for this editing session or forever; in either case, the command is enabled for this editing session.

- If you didn't really mean to type that command, type n. The command remains disabled and isn't run.
- If you want to run it just this once, press the Space bar. The command remains disabled, but Emacs runs it.

In this case, you pressed Space.

Notice that if you had pressed y instead, the macro would not have worked correctly. Because the macro plays back the keys you type, replaying or running the macro would have included the answers to the prompts; a "yy" or a "yn" would be inserted into your text buffer.

Visit the file rhymes, if you haven't already got it in a buffer. Place the cursor on the first line and enter the command:

```
Control-X e
```

**b)**   What does the Control-X e command do?

*Answer: The Control-X e command runs the macro you've defined.*

The Control-X e command (or `call-last-kbd-macro`) runs the last command you defined with the Ctrl-X ( and Ctrl-X ) commands.

Now define the macro again, but use the command Control-X `Control-L` instead of `Control-X Control-U`. Now enter the command:

```
Control-X e
```

**c)**   Which macro is executed—the first one or the second one?

*Answer: The second (or most recent) macro.*

This macro is known as the "anonymous macro" because it has no name. Because you (and Emacs) can't distinguish between two macros without names, there can be only one anonymous macro.

If you need to run two macros concurrently, the solution is to give them names. You can run a named macro as if it were a command. Type Meta-X to give the extended command and then enter the name of the macro. You can even assign a macro to a key combination.

Enter the command:

```
Meta-X name-last-kbd-macro
```

At the prompt, enter:

```
lower-line
```

Move the cursor to a line containing text and enter:

```
Meta-X lower-line
```

**c)** What does the `lower-line` command do?

*Answer: The* `lower-line` *command runs the macro you just defined.*

Once you've given a macro a name, it's stored in Emacs for the rest of the session. You can store lots of named macros in an Emacs session.

If you discover that you're defining the same macros time and time again, you may want to store them in a file. (Emacs lets you store macros in a file and load them from a buffer.) Normally, you store them in your `.emacs` file, since that file is loaded every time you start Emacs.

Visit the file ~/`.emacs` and move to the end of the file. Enter the command:

```
Meta-X insert-kbd-macro
```

At the prompt, enter:

```
lower-line
```

**d)** What does the inserted text look like?

*Answer: It looks like this:*

```
(fset 'lower-line
    "\C-a\C-@\C-e\C-x\C-l")
```

This is actually a little bit of Lisp code for programming Emacs. Fortunately, you don't have to know how to write macros as Lisp code because Emacs does it for you.

## 11.3.2 ANSWERS

You assigned the macro lower-line to the key combination Control-C Control-L.

```
Meta-X global-set-key
```

At the first prompt, enter:

```
Control-C Control-L
```

**LAB
11.3**

At the second prompt, enter:

```
lower-line
```

Now move the cursor to a line of text and enter the command:

```
Control-C Control-L
```

**a)** What happens?

Answer: *The key combination runs the lower-line macro.*

You can assign any command name to a key. In Emacs, this is called *binding* the command to the key. The entire set of keys and commands is called a *keymap*.

Because Emacs already has a lot of commands bound to keys, you want to make sure that the key you're assigning to a command isn't already assigned to one you'll use. You can display the list of key combinations currently bound to keys with the help command describe-bindings. (The key combination for describe-bindings is Control-H b.)

Enter the commands:

```
Control-H k Control-C Control-L
```

**b)** What information is displayed in the help window?

Answer: *The help buffer displays this information:*

```
lower-line:
keyboard macro.
```

Emacs is smart enough to update some of the help information when you map a key. The key is updated in the describe-bindings information; and so is the where-is command's information. (The where-is is the inverse of the describe-bindings command: When you give it the name of an Emacs command, it tells you what key combination the command is assigned to. The key combination for where-is is Control-H w.)

There are some keys and key combinations you can't assign commands to. Any key that is the first part of a set of key combinations (such as Control-X) isn't available, although you could assign a command to Control-X *something*.

*The Emacs programmers reserve all key combinations starting with Control-C for users. When assigning commands to keys, you should generally restrict yourself to key combinations starting with Control-C.*

You've probably figured out that the `global-set-key` assigns a key for all modes. There is an equivalent command for assigning a key to your current mode only, the command `local-set-key`.

## 11.3.3  ANSWERS

Open the file ~/.emacs. Enter the following lines at the beginning of the file:

```
(define-key global-map "\C-x?" 'help-command)

(define-key global-map "\C-h" 'backward-delete-char-
untabify)

(define-key text-mode-map "\C-c\C-l" 'lower-line)
```

Type two ;; characters at the beginning of the `fset` command that defines the `lower-line` macro.

Start Emacs. Type some text, then press the Backspace key.

**a)**   What happens?

*Answer: The Backspace key deletes the previous character instead of running the help command.*

These two lines are the startup file version of global key maps, written as Lisp. They look quite different from the interactive versions in the previous exercise.

The first one assigns the Emacs command `help-command` to the key combination Control-X ?. The "\C-" stands for "control." (A "\M-" stands for "meta," if you need to bind something to a Meta-key combination.)

The second one assigns the Emacs command `backward-delete-char-untabify` to the Control-H combination. The backspace key sends the Control-H combination.

The third one assigns Control-C Control-L to the `lower-line` macro, but only in text mode.

These lines really run the `define-key` command. The command has three arguments: the mode (global or a particular mode), the character string (usually in quotation marks), and a single apostrophe followed by the name of an Emacs command. (The apostrophe is rather like the $ in a shell variable name. The $ tells the shell to look at what's in the variable rather than treating the variable as an object itself; the apostrophe tells Emacs to look at the variable as an object instead of looking inside it. The difference is because, by default, the shell always treats a variable name as an object; by default, Emacs always looks inside a variable.)

In some startup files, you'll see key combinations in [ ] brackets instead of in quotes, like this:

```
(define-key global-map [?\C-x?] 'help-command)
```

These are different ways of expressing sequences of characters in Lisp. Both `"\C-x"` and `?\C-x` refer to Control-X. The ? is a way to refer to a single character without putting it in quotation marks. This particular key definition assigns the command `help-command` to the key sequence Control-X ?.

For now, it's enough to know that the [ ] notation allows you to specify more keys and signals. You need to use the [ ] notation if you're going to bind commands to things like mouse clicks and function keys, or specifying the backspace key directly. (There's information on this in the Emacs manual, if you're interested in doing this.)

Enter the lower-line macro command with Control-C Control-L.

**b)** What happens?

*Answer: The terminal beeps and Emacs displays this message in the minibuffer:*

```
Symbol's function definition is void: lower-line
```

Although the Control-C Control-L key combination is still mapped to a command, the command `lower-line` is no longer valid because it's been commented out. The ; character starts a comment; everything after ; on the line is not interpreted by Emacs.

Most `.emacs` files you see will have comments set apart by a pair of ; characters, like this:

```
;; John's .emacs file
;; Mostly stolen from other people.
```

When you edit your `.emacs` file, it's important to keep track of the relationships. If you remove a function, you should also remove any key bindings that refer to that function.

Enter the key command Control-X ?.

**c)**   What happens?

*Answer: Emacs runs the help command.*

I didn't try binding the help command to the Delete key; that's considered to be a bad idea. Part of the reason is that some modes assign new meanings to the Delete key; if you had made the Delete key the help key, you couldn't get help in those modes.

Some modes (such as Emacs Lisp mode and Lisp Interaction mode and C mode) will still have the old mapping for Backspace and Delete. You can correct this by adding these extra lines; however, I'm in no sense an Emacs wizard, and there may be situations I haven't discovered yet.

```
(define-key lisp-interaction-mode-map "\C-h" 'back-
ward-delete-char-untabify)

(define-key emacs-lisp-mode-map "\C-h" 'backward-
delete-char-untabify)

(define-key c-mode-map "\C-h" 'backward-delete-char-
untabify)

(setq search-delete-char ?\b)
```

Exit Emacs and start it again with the command-line option -q. Type some text and then press Backspace.

**d)**   What happens? What does the -q option do?

*Answer: The Backspace key once again starts help. The -q option prevents Emacs from loading startup files.*

The -q option prevents Emacs from loading any `.emacs` files, including the system-wide one and yours.

An interesting command-line option is the -u *username* option; it loads the Emacs startup file of another user (the one whose login name is *username*). A lot of Emacs customizations are spread by cutting and copying from other startup files. (This is easier than learning Lisp.)

## OTHER CUSTOMIZATIONS

There isn't really enough space to discuss all of the possible customizations. Here are some simple customizations you may want to make.

First, to avoid system-wide customizations (perhaps the system administrator has set some option that keeps getting in your way), you can place this line at the beginning of your `.emacs` file:

```
(inhibit-default-init t)
```

In Emacs startup files, a `t` sets a value to "true." (If you want to set something to false, you don't use "f", you must use the word `nil`.)

Some other useful snippets you can put into your `.emacs` file:

| | |
|---|---|
| Unsets a particular global key (here, Control-X Control-V). | `(global-unset-key "\C-x\C-v")` |
| Always starts text mode with line filling on. | `(add-hook 'text-mode-hook '(lambda () (auto-fill-mode 1)))` |
| Sets the line length for text filling to 72 characters. | `(setq fill-column 60)` |
| Makes searches case-sensitive by default. | `(setq-default case-fold-search nil)` |
| Makes text mode the default mode for new buffers. | `(setq default-major-mode 'text-mode)` |

# LAB 11.3 SELF-REVIEW QUESTIONS

In order to test your progress, you should be able to answer the following questions.

1) Define a keyboard macro in Emacs.
   **a)** _____ A way of setting a particular Emacs variable to true
   **b)** _____ A disabled command
   **c)** _____ A key binding
   **d)** _____ A recorded series of keystrokes

2) How many anonymous macros are there in Emacs?
   **a)** _____ 1
   **b)** _____ 2

**c)** _____ 0

**d)** _____ Depends upon the version of Emacs you're using.

**3)** Which command runs a macro?

    **a)** _____ Control-X e

    **b)** _____ Control-X (

    **c)** _____ Control-X )

    **d)** _____ Meta-X followed by the macro's name.

    **e)** _____ (a), (b), and (c)

    **f)** _____ (a) and (d)

**4)** To set a key binding in your `.emacs` file, you must set it interactively first.

    **a)** _____ True

    **b)** _____ False

**5)** When defining a key binding in your `.emacs` file, you can specify the mode the key binding will affect.

    **a)** _____ True

    **b)** _____ False

**6)** Identify the startup file key reference that refers to the key combination Meta-Q!

    **a)** _____ "\C-q!"

    **b)** _____ [\M-q-!]

    **c)** _____ "\M-!"

    **d)** _____ "\M-q!"

**7)** In a startup file, what is the effect of the line:

```
;; (setq fill-column 72)
```

    **a)** _____ Sets the fill column to 72 characters

    **b)** _____ Binds the keys Meta-X 7 2 to the `set-fill-column` command

    **c)** _____ No effect; the semi-colon comments out the line

    **d)** _____ Formats the paragraph to a line length of 72 characters

*Quiz answers appear in Appendix A, Section 11.3.*

# LAB 11.4

# USING THE DIRED MODE

> ## LAB OBJECTIVES
>
> After this Lab, you will be able to:
>
> - List Directories
> - Load File In Dired Mode
> - File Operations in Dired Mode

Emacs contains a specialized mode intended for directory listings and file operations, which is called Dired mode. (Dired means "directory edit.") In Dired mode, you can copy, move, and delete files.

Many of the commands in Dired mode are different than other modes, so working in Dired mode can sometimes be confusing. Once you're used to it, however, Dired mode can be a convenient way to clean up directories, especially to remove Emacs backup files and autosave files.

## LAB 11.4 EXERCISES

### 11.4.1 LIST DIRECTORIES

Start Emacs, if you haven't already. Enter the following command:

```
Control-X d
```

At the prompt, press Enter.

**a)** What's displayed?

_____

_____

Enter these commands:

```
Control-A
Control-N
Control-P
Control-E
```

**b)** What do these commands do?

_____

_____

Press the ? key.

**c)** What's displayed?

_____

_____

Press the q key.

**d)** What happens?

_____

_____

## 11.4.2 LOAD FILE IN DIRED MODE

In Emacs, start Dired mode again. Specify a directory that has some autosave files or backup files in it. (A good place would be the directory where you performed Lab 11.1.)

Move the cursor to the line containing the directory . . . Press the f key.

**a)** What does the f key do when the cursor is on a directory line?

_____

_____

Exit the new buffer with the q command. Select a file in your directory and press f again.

**b)** What does the f key do when the cursor is on a file line?

_____

_____

Kill the buffer containing the new file (Control-X k). Once you're back in Dired mode, press the o key.

**c)** What does the o key do?

_____

_____

## 11.4.3 FILE OPERATIONS IN DIRED MODE

Move the cursor to one of your backup files (the files with names starting and ending in #).

Press the d key.

**a)** What does the d key do?

_____

_____

Press the u key.

**b)** What does the u key do?

_____

_____

Press the # key.

**c)** What does the # key do?

_____

_____

Press the x key. (Enter `yes` at the prompt.)

**d)** What does the x key do?

_____

_____

Move the cursor to select another file.

Press the m key.

**e)** What does the m key do?

_____

_____

Press the C key (it's important to make it a capital C). Type `newname` at the prompt and press Enter.

**f)** What does the C key do?

_____

_____

Exit Dired mode by pressing `q`.

## LAB 11.4 EXERCISE ANSWERS

### 11.4.1 ANSWERS

Start Emacs, if you haven't already. Enter the following command:

```
Control-X d
```

At the prompt, press Enter.

**a)** What's displayed?

*Answer: A new buffer opens labeled Dired. An example of a Dired buffer is shown in Figure 11.1.*

The display looks like `ls -l` output; that's because it is `ls -l` output, and you read it in exactly the same way. Each file or directory is shown on a single line, with its permissions, number of links, owner, group, size, date of last modification, and the file's name.

When you give commands in Dired mode, they usually affect the file or directory on the line with the cursor.

Enter these commands:

```
Control-A
Control-N
Control-P
Control-E
```

**b)** What do these commands do?

*Answer: These commands move the cursor from line to line and within a line, just as they do in regular Emacs buffers.*

```
/usr/home/johnmc:
total 2953
-rw-r--r--   1 johnmc  user      380 May  4 15:54 #rhymes#
drwxr-xr-x   9 johnmc  user     2048 Jun  9 14:43 .
drwxr-xr-x  33 root    wheel    1024 Feb 15 17:22 ..
-rw-r--r--   1 johnmc  user      635 Jun  5  1996 .Xmodmap
-rw-r--r--   1 johnmc  user      808 Jun  5  1996 .Xresources
-rw-r--r--   1 johnmc  user     1070 Jun  5  1996 .Xresources-colors
-rw-r--r--   1 johnmc  user      139 Jun  5  1996 .Xresources-conf
-rw-r--r--   1 johnmc  user     3128 Jun  5  1996 .Xresources-fonts
-rw-r--r--   1 johnmc  user     2724 Jun  5  1996 .Xresources-mosaic
-rw-r--r--   1 johnmc  user     2580 Jun  5  1996 .Xresources-xterm
-rw-r--r--   1 johnmc  user      367 Apr 30 12:56 .abbrev_defs
-rw-r--r--   1 johnmc  user     1253 Jun  5  1996 .cshrc
drwx------   2 johnmc  user      512 Sep 11  1996 .elm
-rw-r--r--   1 johnmc  user      241 May  3 01:48 .emacs
-rw-r--r--   1 johnmc  user      272 Jan 18 16:51 .environ
-rw-r--r--   1 johnmc  user     1951 Jun  5  1996 .fvwmfmgr
-rw-r--r--   1 johnmc  user    15476 Jun  5  1996 .fvwmrc
-rw-r--r--   1 johnmc  user     8584 Jun 11 22:29 .history
-rw-r--r--   1 johnmc  user       11 Dec  5  1997 .ispell_english
-rw-r--r--   1 johnmc  user      258 Jun  5  1996 .login
--%%-Dired: ^                    (Dired by name)--Top----------------
Reading directory /usr/home/johnmc/...done
```

**Figure 11.1 ■ You can look at any directory using Dired, but the default is the current directory for Emacs. (That's normally the directory where you started Emacs.)**

The major movement commands (the ones you tried here as well as Meta-> and Meta-<) move the cursor through the Dired buffer just as they do in a regular Emacs buffer. The Control-S and Control-R (incremental search) commands also work.

Pressing the Space bar or the n key will also have the same effect as `Control-N`.

*The case of commands is important in Dired mode. Pressing n has a different effect than pressing N. (In fact, pressing N will do nothing.)*

Press the ? key.

c)   What's displayed?

*Answer: Emacs displays the following text down in the minibuffer:*

```
d-elete, u-ndelete, x-punge, f-ind, o-ther window, R-
ename, C-opy, h-elp
```

The ? key displays a brief summary of the most important commands in Dired. The case of the letter is important: D has a different effect than d. This little summary is usually enough to accomplish what you want. Remember that renaming a file is the same as moving it.

If you want *more* help, press the h key. Emacs opens a *\*Help\** buffer containing a lengthier description of the different commands available in Dired mode. You can either make the *\*Help\** the active window and scroll through it, or you can scroll through it as the "other" window using Meta-Control-V to scroll down. To remove the *\*Help\** window, move the cursor back to the Dired buffer and press Control-X 1.

Press the q key.

d)   What happens?

*Answer: The Dired buffer disappears.*

You can also exit Dired by killing the Dired buffer (Control-X k). The two methods of exiting result in different behaviors the next time you enter Dired mode in this editing session.

Exiting by killing the buffer destroys the information in the buffer; the next time you open Dired on the same directory, it will read the contents of the directory, just as it did this first time. That can be slow in a directory that contains hundreds of files.

Exiting with q *hides* the Dired buffer but doesn't eliminate it. If the directory has changed since the last time Emacs read the contents of the directory (for example, if you've changed any files), Emacs warns you the next time you enter Dired mode for that directory and asks if you want to update the listing (with the Dired g command).

## 11.4.2 ANSWERS

In Emacs, start Dired mode again. Specify a directory that has some autosave files or backup files in it. (This would be the directory where you performed Lab 11.1.)

Move the cursor to the line containing the directory . . . Press the f key.

**a)** What does the f key do when the cursor is on a directory line?

*Answer: The f command opens a new Dired buffer listing the contents of the directory in your current window.*

The f command corresponds to the `find-file` command in Emacs. If you open a directory, Emacs and Dired mode are clever enough to display the contents of that directory. Normally, each directory gets its own Dired buffer. If you want to replace the contents of the current Dired buffer with a listing of the directory, use the i command instead.

Exit the new buffer with the q command. Select a file in your directory and press f again.

**b)** What does the f key do when the cursor is on a file line?

*Answer: The f command loads the file into a new Emacs buffer in your current window.*

If you want to look at the file as a read-only file, use v to view it.

Kill the buffer containing the new file (Control-X k). Once you're back in Dired mode, press the o key.

**c)** What does the o key do?

*Answer: The o command opens a new buffer and window (just as f does), but it also splits the screen and places the cursor in the new window.*

Because it splits the screen, the o command is useful for browsing a directory, showing you both the directory listing and the contents of the file you've just opened.

## 11.4.3 ANSWERS

Move the cursor to one of your backup files (the files with names starting and ending in #).

Press the d key.

**a)**   What does the d key do?

*Answer: The d key causes a letter D to appear beside the file's line, at the left of the screen.*

To work a command on more than one file at a time, Dired mode lets you mark the files for a particular action before you actually perform the action. Since the most common action is deleting files, file deletions have their own key to mark them, the d key. (When you mark a file specifically to be deleted, the Emacs documentation refers to it as *flagging* a file, instead of marking it.)

A file marked with d is not deleted immediately. (If you want to delete the file immediately, use D.)

Press the u key.

**b)**   What does the u key do?

*Answer: The u key removes the letter D beside the file's line.*

The u command removes the mark from the current line and moves to the next line. (Pressing the Delete key removes the mark and moves to the previous line.)

Press the # key.

**c)**   What does the # key do?

*Answer: The # key marks all backup files in the directory with the letter D.*

The # key is a convenience to allow you to mark all of the backup files for deletion. The ~ command marks all autosave files (the ones whose names end in ~).

There is a command that marks all files that match a regular expression (%d); you could get the same effect as the # key by specifying files that match the regular expression #.*#. (that's a regular expression, not a wildcard match, so the . is necessary before the *).

Press the x key. (Enter yes at the prompt.)

**d)** What does the x key do?

*Answer: The x key deletes all of the files marked with a D.*

Once you've marked the files for deletion, you can delete them (or "expunge" them) with the x key. For both the x command and the D command, you must confirm the file deletion by entering yes; simply typing y isn't enough.

Move the cursor to select another file.

Press the m key.

**e)** What does the m key do?

*Answer: The m key causes the file's line to be marked with an asterisk (\*).*

The * is a regular mark, as opposed to the D flag-to-delete. Some of the commands (such as C for copy) can work on more than one file at a time. (Imagine you're copying files into a directory, for example.)

To run those commands on more than one file, you can repeat the command many times or you can mark all of the files you want to be affected.

If you decide to delete a set of marked files, you can delete them with the D command, which works on marked files instead of flagged files.

If you mark a directory, all of the files in that directory are marked. If you unmark a marked directory (with u), all of the files in the directory are unmarked.

Press the C key (it's important to make it a capital C). Type newname at the prompt and press Enter.

**f)** What does the C key do?

*Answer: The C key copies the file to a file named* newname. *The prompt looks something like this, assuming your file is named* myfile.

```
Copy [-p] myfile.txt to: ~/
```

If you specify a directory name as the target, Dired copies the files into the directory. If you mark several files to be copied, the destination must be a directory, or the copy will fail.

The command to *move* a file is R, and it works in the same way as the c command.

The dired mode commands discussed here are summarized in Table 11.5, "Dired Mode Commands."

# LAB 11.4 SELF-REVIEW QUESTIONS

In order to test your progress, you should be able to answer the following questions.

1) "Dired" stands for "directory edit."
   **a)** _____True
   **b)** _____False

2) The d command deletes files.
   **a)** _____True
   **b)** _____False

3) The f command is for files and will not work on directories.
   **a)** _____True
   **b)** _____False

### Table 11.5 ■ Dired Mode Commands

| Effect | Command |
| --- | --- |
| Deletes all files flagged with #, ~, and d. | x |
| Deletes all marked files. | D |
| Flags all files that match a regular expression to delete them. | %d |
| Flags auto save files to delete them. | # |
| Flags backup files to delete them. | ~ |
| Flags file to delete it. | d |
| Marks all files that match a regular expression. | %m |
| Marks file for marked operations. | m |
| Opens a file as read-only. | v |
| Removes the mark and moves down one line. | u |
| Removes the mark and moves up one line. | Delete |

**4)** Identify the command to copy files.

    **a)** `m%`

    **b)** `c`

    **c)** `C`

    **d)** `f`

*Quiz answers appear in Appendix A, Section 11.4.*

# L A B   1 1 . 5

# USING THE COMMAND HISTORY

---

### LAB OBJECTIVES

After this Lab, you will be able to:

- Repeat the Last Complex Command
- Display Command History
- Repeat an Older Command
- Modify an Older Command

---

The vi editor lets you repeat any insertion or deletion of text with the command . (dot). The Emacs editor has a command history feature that you can use, but it's not as comprehensive as the vi history.

Instead, the Emacs command history records all of the *minibuffer* commands you have given during your session. If the command makes use of the minibuffer, it's recorded. This includes all extended commands. (Remember that the extended commands are the ones you give with Meta-X.) Any command where you have to respond to a prompt makes use of the minibuffer.

## LAB 11.5 EXERCISES

### 11.5.1 REPEAT THE LAST COMPLEX COMMAND

Open the file rhymes again with Control-X Control-F.

Enter the command Meta-% to replace "Jack" with "Bill", and replace the first occurrence of "Jack" with "Bill". (Press . at that replacement to make only that substitution.)

Enter the command:

```
Control-X Esc Esc
```

**a)** What does the Control-X Esc Esc command do?

_____

_____

Press Enter.

**b)** What happens when you press Enter?

_____

_____

## 11.5.2  DISPLAY COMMAND HISTORY

Enter the command

```
Meta-X list-command-history
```

**a)** What does the list-command-history command do?

_____

_____

## 11.5.3  REPEAT AN OLDER COMMAND

Enter the commands:

```
Control-X Esc Esc
Meta-P
Meta-N
```

**a)** What do the Meta-P and Meta-N commands do?

_____

_____

Enter the command:

```
Meta-R list
```

**b)** What does the Meta-R command do?

_____

_____

### 11.5.4  MODIFY AN OLDER COMMAND

**LAB
11.5**

Go back through the command list until you get to the query-replace of "Jack" to "Bill".

Use `Control-B` and `Control-D` to edit the line, changing "Jack" to "Jill" and "Bill" to "Jane", then press Enter.

**a)** What happens after you press Enter?

_____

_____

## LAB 11.5  EXERCISE ANSWERS

### 11.5.1  ANSWERS

Open the file `rhymes` again with Control-X Control-F.

Enter the command Meta-% to replace "Jack" with "Bill", and replace the first occurrence of "Jack" with "Bill". (Press . at that replacement to make only that substitution.)

Enter the command:

```
Control-X Esc Esc
```

**a)** What does the Control-X Esc Esc command do?

*Answer: The command causes Emacs to display this line in the minibuffer:*

```
(query-replace "Jack" "Bill" nil)
```

This is how the `query-replace` command is stored in Emacs—as a Lisp function. Although it may not be the way you expect the command to appear, it's fairly easy to read: The entire command line is in parentheses; the first word is the command itself, followed by the arguments; and you can ignore the `nil` part.

**b)** What happens when you press Enter?

*Answer: Emacs runs the command again.*

When you press Enter, Emacs runs the command in the minibuffer, just as you'd expect.

If you want to display the second-to-last command, give the numeric argument 2:

```
Meta-2 Control-X Esc Esc
```

**LAB
11.5**

An argument of 3 displays the third-to-last command, and so on through the command history list.

Past two or three commands, you'll probably need to display the list of commands so you know how far back a particular command is. To do that, you need to list the command history.

## 11.5.2 ANSWERS

Enter the command:

```
Meta-X list-command-history
```

**a)** What does the `list-command-history` command do?

*Answer: It lists your complex commands in a separate buffer, the most recent commands at the top of the list.*

The buffer is read-only, so you can't easily edit the commands in that buffer. Still, it can be useful for seeing what you've done in the session. If you give a numeric argument to Control-X Esc Esc, such as 3, then that's the command that will be displayed in the minibuffer.

You can run the command on a particular line by moving the cursor to that line and entering the command `command-history-repeat`.

The `list-command-history` command isn't in the buffer, by the way, although it is in the command history list you can get with Control-X Esc Esc.

## 11.5.3 ANSWERS

Enter the commands:

```
Control-X Esc Esc
Meta-P
Meta-N
```

**a)**  What do the Meta-P and Meta-N commands do?

*Answer: The Meta-P command displays the previous command in the history list, and the Meta-N command displays the next command in the history list.*

**LAB 11.5**

These two commands let you move up and down the history list. They only work after you display the previous command with Control-X Esc Esc.

Enter the command:

```
Meta-R list
```

**b)**  What does the Meta-R command do?

*Answer: The Meta-R command asks for a regular expression and then searches backward through the command history for the next command that matches.*

Once you're in the command history, you can also search forward using Meta-S.

## 11.5.4 ANSWERS

Go back through the command list until you get to the query-replace of "Jack" to "Bill".

Use Control-B and Control-D to edit the line, changing "Jack" to "Jill" and "Bill" to "Jane", then press Enter.

**a)**  What happens after you press Enter?

*Answer: Emacs runs a query-replace command, substitution "Jane" for "Jill".*

You can edit previous commands in the minibuffer, just as you'd edit any command you were typing in.

 *Don't remove the parentheses surrounding the expression; when Emacs runs a command from the command history, it expects the command to be in Lisp format.*

The different command-history commands described here are summarized in Table 11.6, "Complex Command History."

# LAB 11.5 SELF-REVIEW QUESTIONS

In order to test your progress, you should be able to answer the following questions.

1) Only complex commands are stored in the command history
   a) _____True
   b) _____False

## Table 11.6 ■ Complex Command History

| Effect | Keys | Command |
|---|---|---|
| Displays most recent command in minibuffer. | Control-X Esc Esc | repeat-complex-command |
| Displays previous command in minibuffer. | Meta-P | |
| Displays next command in minibuffer. | Meta-N | |
| Searches backward through history for command matching regular expression. | Meta-R | |
| Searches forward through history for command matching regular expression. | Meta-S | |
| Lists the command history. | | list-command-history |
| Runs command on current line in command history buffer. | | command-history-repeat |

2) Complex commands are only commands that are preceded by Meta-X.
   **a)** _____True
   **b)** _____False

3) The commands for moving through the history of complex commands are the same as the commands for moving through the command history in an Emacs subshell.
   **a)** _____True
   **b)** _____False

4) You can use regular Emacs line-editing commands to change the commands before you run them again.
   **a)** _____True
   **b)** _____False

   *Quiz answers appear in Appendix A, Section 11.5.*

# C H A P T E R   1 1

# TEST YOUR THINKING

For the first project, use the following `.emacs` file.

```
(setq inhibit-startup-message t)
(setq default-major-mode 'text-mode)
(setq fill-column 72)
(setq make-backup-files nil)
(setq text-mode-hook 'turn-on-auto-fill-mode)
(fset 'mark-buffer
    "\M<\C@\M>")
(define-key c-mode-map ":" 'self-insert-command)
(global-set-key "\C-xg" 'goto-line)
```

**1)** Describe what's happening in the sample `.emacs` file. You may need to use the Emacs help facility to find out what some of the lines mean.

**2)** Emacs fans claim that Emacs is more than an editor, it's an operating environment. You can read e-mail in Emacs, Usenet news in Emacs, use Dired mode for cleaning up directories, and for any commands that aren't already in Emacs, you can run a subshell. The die-hard Emacs user starts Emacs upon loading up and doesn't really exit Emacs until it's time to log out.

Emacs critics (who are often `vi` fans) claim this is rationalization; this is how Emacs fans justify a big program that's slow to start. They claim that Emacs is loaded down with extra bells and whistles only a fraction of the user population uses.

**a)** Which position do you agree with? Why?

# APPENDIX A

# ANSWERS TO SELF-REVIEW QUESTIONS

## LAB 1.1 SELF-REVIEW ANSWERS

1) a  Your login ID number is unique, just as your login name is unique on your system. You are the only user who has that name.

2) b  On all modern UNIX systems, you can belong to more than one group at a time.

3) b  A file you create is always created with your current group. You can change your current group with the `newgrp` command.

4) a  The super-user always has the login ID number 0.

## LAB 1.2 SELF-REVIEW ANSWERS

1) a, b  Options allow commands to be flexible and pipes allow commands to be linked in a variety of ways. "Operands" (c) might be considered, but operands are required on all systems I know of, so I wouldn't class them as part of the UNIX model.

2) b  Although nothing printed to `/dev/null` is ever displayed, the real reason is that *anything* redirected into a file with > doesn't display on the screen. (Unless the file is also a screen, which is discussed in Chapter 2.)

3) a  Options such as the `-o` option to `sort` require more information, which has to be supplied as an argument.

4) b  An item in [ ] brackets is optional.

5) b  Usually, options are single letters, but many commands (such as GNU utilities from the Free Software Foundation and X Window commands) use multiple-letter options.

6) f  Commands (a) and (c) will work. In command (b), the contents of the files are placed on the *command line* of the `sort` command; the `sort` program will try to open each word on the command line as a file.

## LAB 1.3 SELF-REVIEW ANSWERS

1) b    Hidden files aren't listed.

2) a    The root directory is always /.

3) c    The pattern matches a file whose name starts with dot and has at least one more character (the ?). If there are more letters, they are all capitals (the [A-Z]*). Only .x matches that.

4) d    Of these examples, only (d) gives you execute permission (which is a 1). This command doesn't give you read or write permission, and it gives no permissions to anyone else. Answer (c) actually *removes* execute permission from the file.

5) b    By default, the mkdir command doesn't create intermediate directories. Use the -p option if you want to do that.

6) a    If there are hidden files in the directory, the rmdir command will not work.

## LAB 1.4 SELF-REVIEW ANSWERS

1) b    The vi editor only undoes one change; pressing u again undoes the undo. (But see Lab 10.3 in Chapter 10, "Advanced vi Tricks," for information about retrieving deleted lines.)

2) a    The G command moves to a particular line. The first line in the file is line 1.

3) d    The %s specifies all lines in the file; without the command /g at the end, the command changes only the first occurrence of "AA".

4) d    The ! after the command means that it will be carried out even if there are unsaved changes in the current file.

## LAB 1.5 SELF-REVIEW ANSWERS

1) a    A variable that exists without having a value is still said to be "set." This is called a "null value."

2) b    An environment variable's value is only accessible to programs that start running *after* it is set.

3) b

# LAB 2.1 SELF-REVIEW ANSWERS

1) b     The who command lists all users with accounts who are currently logged in. It doesn't list users who aren't logged in.

2) b     The tty command lists the specific file name of your terminal; /dev/tty is the "generic" name for your current terminal. If you login to three different terminals, each will have a different name (returned by tty), but for convenience, in each terminal window you can refer to it as /dev/tty.

3) b     The – before the terminal name indicates that messages are not accepted at that terminal.

4) a     Rather than change the existing (default) programs to match the UNIX standard, Solaris and some other manufacturers chose to provide a second set of programs.

5) b     The site name always comes *after* the @.

# LAB 2.2 SELF-REVIEW ANSWERS

1) a     In fact, your terminal is the standard place for output to be sent ("standard output" or stdout).

2) b     On most systems, Control-D sends the end-of-file signal. This can be set with the stty command.

3) b     The message is only sent to one terminal session.

4) a-iv b-iii c-i d-ii

5) b     The super-user can always send you a message with write, regardless of the state of your terminal.

6) d     The wall command stands for "write all" so it's a write command that automatically sends to all users logged in.

# LAB 3.1 SELF-REVIEW ANSWERS

1) c     The top-level domain is the *last* part of the name.

2) b     The header is like the writing on the envelope: it contains postmarks and other delivery information.

3) a     The message body is like the letter in the envelope.

4) d     Non-profit organizations typically have domain names ending in .org.

5) e     Remember that mailx can send to files, too.

# LAB 3.2 SELF-REVIEW ANSWERS

1)     a     Either one can be used to set the subject of a mail message in `mailx`.

2)     b     The ~p command prints the message so far; the others have different effects.

3)     a     You only need to press the interrupt key combination twice; pressing it three times would work, but only because you have to press twice before you can press three times.

4)     b     The ~v command starts the editor named by your VISUAL environment variable; only if no editor is named there (or if the editor it names is `vi`) does the ~v command start `vi`.

5)     b     The files could be damaged by some intermediate computer in the network. Also, the header lines added by `mailx` might affect the binary file.

6)     b     When two names are provided on the `uuencode` command line, the first is the file to be encoded and the second is the name when it's decoded. If only one name is provided, it's the decoded name.

7)     b     There are no commands in `mailx` that will cancel a command you've already sent.

# LAB 3.3 SELF-REVIEW ANSWERS

1)     b     Only input mode commands start with a ~ character, not command mode commands.

2)     a     Note that most of the input mode commands also require you to press Enter. (The exception is ~~, although you could argue that's not a command at all.)

3)     a     A `mailx save` command has the command first, then the argument that specifies which messages, then the name of the file. A login name by itself specifies messages from that user; the /bethany specifier specifies all messages with "bethany" in the subject.

4)     b     You can run the `uudecode` command directly on the message with the `pipe` or | command.

5)     b     When you read mail from a file using –f *file*, `mailx` doesn't move the read messages to ~/mbox.

6)     b     You can restore any deleted message using the `undelete` command until you exit the `mailx` session.

# LAB 3.4 SELF-REVIEW ANSWERS

1)   b   The `biff` command also displays the first few lines of the message on your screen.

2)   b   You can specify which file it will check by giving it the `-file` option.

3)   b   Once `MAILPATH` is set, the Korn Shell ignores the contents of the `MAIL` variable. Make sure you include the directory indicated by `MAIL` as one of the directories in `MAILPATH`.

4)   a   The `MAILCHECK` variable specifies the number of seconds.

5)   a   A return code of 0 indicates the command succeeded.

# LAB 4.1 SELF-REVIEW ANSWERS

1)   a   Every machine in a network has an address.

2)   b   In a symbolic name, the machine's name is the first component (after the @ in an e-mail address). Of course, some UNIX sites have more complicated mail delivery schemes than that, so your e-mail address doesn't always reflect the name of your machine.

3)   a   The order of a numeric address is the opposite of the order in the symbolic name. The top-level identifier comes first.

4)   c   The other two commands will return your current machine's symbolic name.

# LAB 4.2 SELF-REVIEW ANSWERS

1)   b   Each machine may have its own passwords and user lists. On some networks, you will be able to log into all other machines, though; ask your system administrator.

2)   b   You can telnet into any network machine that is running a telnet server, assuming you have an account, of course.

3)   a   The `telnet` command does not use the `.rhosts` file.

4)   c   The escape command allows you to give commands to the remote login program itself.

5)   a   The `~Ctrl-Z` command for `rlogin` and `Ctrl-]` z for `telnet`; both put the remote login program to sleep.

6)   b   The `.rhosts` file is installed on the remote machine, the machine being called.

# LAB 4.3 SELF-REVIEW ANSWERS

1)    b    The command specifies both machines, so it could be given from a third machine in the network. (It's unlikely, but possible.)

2)    d    The destination name is relative to the home directory of `jmeyer`; since the target is a directory name, the file `notes.txt` is copied into that directory.

3)    d    When logging in to an anonymous FTP site, your password should be your e-mail address.

4)    a or c    It doesn't matter for text. If you're finicky, you might want to use ascii mode, but there should be no difference.

5)    a    The `.netrc` file is on the machine calling out, where you originally logged in.

6)    c    Batch commands such as `uucp` are typically executed on a schedule.

# LAB 5.1 SELF-REVIEW ANSWERS

1)    b    The commands described in this Lab are specific to the Korn Shell.

2)    a    The `r` command repeats your most recent command.

3)    d    In `vi` mode, Escape k will display your previous command; in `emacs` mode, Control-P will display it.

4)    e    The default is 16 commands if you don't specify one.

# LAB 5.2 SELF-REVIEW ANSWERS

1)    a    The `diff` output is difficult to read with binary files and may not be useful.

2)    d    To see only the third column, you need to suppress the first and second column of output.

3)    a    The line beginning with < is from the first file in the command, `sales.yesterday`.

4)    b    There is no entry for Larry today, so `diff` interprets it as meaning Larry's line was deleted.

5)    c    Using `comm` is the closest you'll get. By the way, some versions of `diff` have options that allow `diff` to compare directories.

# LAB 5.3 SELF-REVIEW ANSWERS

1)     d     The actual mechanism used is more complicated than adding all of the bits together.

2)     d     Since there are different ways to calculate checksums, you need to know how the original checksum was calculated.

3)     c     It's certainly unlikely that two slightly different files will have the same checksum, and that's the condition checksums are meant to detect.

4)     f     Even if the file is a text file, the changes made by `ftp` in `ascii` mode mean that a text file may have a different checksum after transmission. If you send the file using `uuencode` with `ftp` in `binary` mode, the files should come through without change.

5)     e     The Solaris `sum -r` command is intended for exactly this purpose, to give the same number as the BSD `sum` command.

# LAB 5.4 SELF-REVIEW ANSWERS

1)     d     The command is `cal`, the month must be a number, and the year 1961 must contain all four digits.

2)     d     The month and date must be specified; `calendar` has no idea what "Christmas day" means.

3)     b     The `calendar` command checks the current directory for a calendar file.

4)     d     The command in (b) will scroll off the screen; the commands in (c) and (e) have the wrong number of arguments. The command in (a) will only display January.

5)     b     There's no need to sort your `calendar` files.

# LAB 5.5 SELF-REVIEW ANSWERS

1)     a     The `-exec` operator can be used to run any command as part of `find`.

2)     d     The `xargs` version of the command is faster.

3)     b     It uses its standard input as arguments to another command.

4)     e     The semicolon should be escaped.

# LAB 5.6 SELF-REVIEW ANSWERS

1)  b                      Neither `tar` nor `pax` compress the archives they create.

2)  b                      To extract or list a directory, name the directory as an argument. Its contents will be extracted or listed.

3)  a-ii b-iii c-iv d-i

4)  a-iv b-iii c-i d-ii

5)  b                      You don't need to specify the `.z` extension to the `uncompress` command.

# LAB 6.1 SELF-REVIEW ANSWERS

1)  a                      Trick question. All Emacs commands are command words. Some of them have alternate forms that are key combinations.

2)  a                      The Meta key is usually the Escape key.

3)  a-iv b-i c-ii d-iii

4)  d                      If you want the line number displayed, you must add it with the command `line-number-mode`.

5)  b                      Emacs interprets the `//` in the middle of the pathname as meaning `/`, the root directory.

6)  c or b                 If you gave n, you would have to confirm it by typing `yes`.

# LAB 6.2 SELF-REVIEW ANSWERS

1)  a-iv b-i c-ii d-iii

2)  a-ii b-iv c-iii d-i

3)  c

4)  a                      Specifically, it redraws the screen with the point in the center of the screen (the command `recenter`).

# LAB 6.3  SELF-REVIEW ANSWERS

1)  a       The region is the space between the point and the mark.

2)  b       A *buffer* can have only one mark; a file can have more than one mark, by having more than one buffer devoted to it.

3)  a-iv b-iii c-i d-ii

4)  b

5)  d       Meta-X u isn't actually a standard Emacs command.

# LAB 6.4  SELF-REVIEW ANSWERS

1)  b       The <3> indicates this is the third buffer open on this file. The name history<3> would be a valid file name on UNIX, but it would be a nuisance to type.

2)  d

3)  a       These are backup files.

4)  d       The default is 300 keystrokes or 30 seconds.

# LAB 6.5  SELF-REVIEW ANSWERS

1)  b       An incremental search is not case-sensitive.

2)  a       An incremental search does not use a regular expression.

3)  b       Regular expression searches in Emacs are not incremental.

4)  a       If you type Meta Control-S, it will prompt you for a new regular expression.

5)  d

6)  a       This is a search-and-replace, querying for each replacement.

7)  a-iii b-v    Trick question. Space and y do the same thing; the command
    c-v d-i     to do "skip this one and go on to the next" choice (ii) is either
    e-iv        n or the Delete key.

8)  c       Emacs capitalizes the replacement word because LANCe is capitalized.

# LAB 6.6 SELF-REVIEW ANSWERS

1) b    It's the other way around: Killed text can be yanked back, but deleted text cannot.

2) a-ii b-iii
   c-iv d-i

3) b

4) b    The Control-X i command doesn't "remember" the name of the last file you inserted.

5) b    Killing text and deleting it are different in Emacs.

# LAB 6.7 SELF-REVIEW ANSWERS

1) b    Trick question. Both versions of Emacs refer to windows. Only the X Window version has frames.

2) a    The X Window version uses the word "frames" to mean X windows instead of buffer windows.

3) a-iv b-i
   c-iii d-ii

# LAB 7.1 SELF-REVIEW ANSWERS

1) b    The chsh command is normally available on BSD systems.

2) c    Your password isn't saved in an unencrypted form. That would be a security risk.

3) d    The only reliable way is to ask the system administrator.

4) root: b,d    The only tricky one is d; although any user is allowed
   all: a,c    to view the passwd file with vi, only the root user can change it, which is the point of this Lab.

# LAB 7.2 SELF-REVIEW ANSWERS

1) d    The command export PATH="$PATH:$PATH" duplicates your search path.

2) b    The shell is smart enough that it doesn't keep trying to expand an alias.

3)　　b　　The shell runs the first command it finds by a name; the order is important because two commands with the same name may behave differently.

4)　　d　　The command to remove an alias called `lr` is `unalias lr`.

## LAB 7.3 SELF-REVIEW ANSWERS

1)　　b　　The shell parameters `PS1`, `PS2`, `PS3`, and `PS4` set prompts used by the shell.

2)　　d　　Any of them will work. The most important part is escaping the $ at the beginning of `$PWD`.

3)　　a

4)　　b　　To turn on an option, use `-o`. To turn it off, use `+o`.

5)　　d

## LAB 8.1 SELF-REVIEW ANSWERS

1)　　d　　The ##*/ removes everything from the beginning to the last / in the name and %,v removes the last ,v in the name.

2)　　d　　Without the `%,v`, the ",v" stays on the end.

3)　　a　　The `typeset -l` command changes the "RCS" to "rcs". The `##RCS/` string matches only uppercase characters.

4)　　c or d　　The `dirname` command removes the last component of a file name. For this value of `filename`, either (c) or (d) will work because there's a single / character. If `filename` were an absolute path name, then only (c) would work; (d) would remove *everything* in the path name.

## LAB 8.2 SELF-REVIEW ANSWERS

1)　　a　　All UNIX programs return a return value.

2)　　b　　The second command gets run only if the first command succeeds.

3)　　a　　The second command gets run only if the first command fails.

4)　　d　　Only the return code 0 has a specific meaning (success). All non-zero values mean failure of some kind, but the exact meaning for a number depends upon the command.

5)　　c　　This is an example only; don't try to make your `if` tests this hard to comprehend.

6)　　c　　The `test -r` test checks for read permission.

# LAB 8.3 SELF-REVIEW ANSWERS

1)   b   The `for` loop shown in this Lab never checks the variable, it just goes through the list.

2)   b   There are five items in the list. The reassignment of `x` in the body of the loop doesn't matter in a `for` loop.

3)   b   The trick is that the redirection operator is inside the loop; each time it `grep`s a file, it overwrites the existing `tomato.list` file. If you want all of the files that contain "tomato," place the `| sort > tomato.list` after the `done`.

4)   a   The directory is created from the variable `input`; the value of `input` is the first word on a line. If the argument `moreinput` weren't there, it would be the employee's full name.

# LAB 8.4 SELF-REVIEW ANSWERS

1)   a   A shell script is a series of commands.

2)   d   To make a shell script executable, turn on execute permissions.

3)   b   The source command (`.`) runs a script in the current shell's environment instead of starting a subshell.

4)   a   A `#!` as the first two characters of a file is an indication that the file is a script.

# LAB 8.5 SELF-REVIEW ANSWERS

1)   b   The rest are fine examples of things *not* to do.

2)   c   Usually, but it depends on the situation. It's a good idea to test the results of commands, but every time you test a command, you add lines to your script. It's a compromise between the strength of your script and its readability.

3)   b   Using the variable `$$` (the process ID for the job) is a trick. You know that the process ID for a job is unique at that moment, so it's useful for creating unique names.

4)   f   All three are good ideas.

# Lab 9.1 Self-Review Answers

1) a

2) b   The `file` command can only make a guess based on the first 512 bytes of the file.

3) a

4) a   The `-f` file specifies a file containing a list of file names.

5) d

# Lab 9.2 Self-Review Answers

1) a   The value of your umask is subtracted from the default mode of your files or directories.

2) d   The default value of a file is 666, and your umask is subtracted from that: 666-034=632.

3) a   The sticky bit is represented by `t` or `T`. The capital `T` means that the sticky bit is set, but you do not have execute permission.

4) e   The super-user can remove files anywhere on the system.

# Lab 9.3 Self-Review Answers

1) b   "Mounting" just adds a file system to your computer; the file system being added may be on another device (that is, another disk driver) or it may be on another computer.

2) c   The `-v` option is necessary to display the type of the mounted file system.

3) a-n b-n c-y d-n   The tricky one is the Andrew file system, `afs`. One could argue whether its files "look" like regular UNIX files or not. The CD-ROM may be formatted for a different operating system type, and Samba is a networked drive and may be on another computer.

4) b   Remember, the mounted file system looks as though it's on your computer.

# LAB 10.1 SELF-REVIEW ANSWERS

1)     b     When an address is specified, the `:!` command acts as a filter; the `/dingo/` address specifies all lines that contain the word "dingo".

2)     d     All of them will run the filter command on the current line.

3)     b     It filters the lines covered by the movement command `}`, which moves to the beginning of the next paragraph.

# LAB 10.2 SELF-REVIEW ANSWERS

1)     a-ii b-i
           c-iv d-iii

2)     b     Searches are normally case-sensitive.

3)     a     The `g` affects all matching characters on the line, and every character matches the `.` regular expression.

4)     e

# LAB 10.3 SELF-REVIEW ANSWERS

1)     b     Trick question. The abbreviation is replaced as soon as `vi` knows the abbreviation isn't part of a larger word, so it's replaced when you type a space or punctuation character or when you press Enter.

2)     a     If you don't specify an abbreviation, the `:abbreviate` command lists all abbreviations you have defined.

3)     e

4     d     To escape a control character, use Control-V.

# LAB 10.4 SELF-REVIEW ANSWERS

1)     b     If there is a valid setting for the `EXINIT` variable, `vi` doesn't look in the `.exrc` file.

2)     a

3)     c     The `"` character marks a comment line in a `.exrc` file.

4)     c     In the startup file, the `:` isn't necessary before the commands, but it doesn't hurt.

# LAB 10.5 SELF-REVIEW ANSWERS

1)   f   Only insert and delete commands are repeated by ., not substitute commands.

2)   a   This kind of addressing requires a colon command, so it must begin with a colon; the " is used for the contents of buffers, not for marks.

3)   b   This is a visual command, so it can't be used in a script.

# LAB 11.1 SELF-REVIEW ANSWERS

1)   b   Different files have different modes.

2)   b   The command to reformat a paragraph is `fill-paragraph`. The `fill-column` variable determines how wide a paragraph is allowed to be.

3)   a-iii
     b-iv c-ii
     d-i

4)   c   The mode of this buffer doesn't support abbreviations.

5)   c   Uppercase letters come before lowercase letters.

6)   d   This is because the point is immediately to the *left* of the cursor, and the abbreviation expands to the text from the beginning of the word to the point.

# LAB 11.2 SELF-REVIEW ANSWERS

1)   b   Emacs only creates the buffer `*Shell Command Output*` when there is output from the command; the `rm` command normally doesn't produce output.

2)   d   Remember that you must press Control-C before your usual end-of-file key combination.

3)   b   Text in the output buffer can be cut and pasted just as if it were ordinary text.

4)   a   The Meta-P command shows the previous command in the history, and enters command-editing mode.

5)   b   You can run commands in the background.

6)   a   They are separate commands.

# LAB 11.3 SELF-REVIEW ANSWERS

1)    d

2)    a    There is only one anonymous macro.

3)    f    The Control-X e command runs the anonymous macro, and Meta-X followed by the macro's name runs any named macro.

4)    b    It's easier if you set it interactively first, but you can set key bindings in your startup file without setting them interactively.

5)    a    If the define-key statement has a local-mode-map in it, the key binding will only affect a specific mode.

6)    d    The [\M-q-!] has the wrong structure (it's missing a ?), and the \M-! is missing the "q".

7)    c    The semi-colons comment out the line. If they weren't there, then (a) would be the correct answer.

# LAB 11.4 SELF-REVIEW ANSWERS

1)    a

2)    b    The d command marks files for deletion, but doesn't delete them.

3)    b    The f command opens a directory as well as a file; it simply works differently on directories than on files.

4)    c    The C command copies files.

# LAB 11.5 SELF-REVIEW ANSWERS

1)    a

2)    b    A complex command uses the minibuffer.

3)    a

4)    a

# A P P E N D I X  B

# COMMANDS

This Appendix contains descriptions for most of the commands in this book. Each command synopsis is listed, along with a brief description of the command and a summary of the options. There have been omissions: Options that only the system administrator can use have been left out.

This list is meant as a convenience, not a definitive reference; see your man pages if the description doesn't apply to your version of the program. Where there are several different versions of a program, the one described is the standard version on Solaris. The shell described is the Korn Shell.

The commands described in Chapter 1 (such as `ls` and `cd`) are not described here because they are covered in Appendix B of the previous book, the *UNIX User's Interactive Workbook*.

The commands `vi`, `emacs`, and `mailx` are not fully described here either, for reasons having to do with space. Complete books have been written about `vi` and `emacs`, and `mailx` could have a small book written about it. All I've done here is present some of the command-line options and some of the internal commands.

## alias—SET A SHELL ALIAS

```
alias [-tx] [name[=command]]
```

This is a shell built-in. It assigns the *command* to be executed when the alias *name* is given. If no *name* is given, the `alias` command lists all of the aliases that match the option given. If no option is given, all aliases are listed. See Chapter 7, "Customizing Your Environment," for more information.

-t     Makes *name* a tracked alias. The shell stores the full path name of a tracked alias, so it is found more quickly.

-x     Exports the alias so it can be used in shell scripts and subshells.

## basename—STRIP DIRECTORIES FROM PATHNAME

```
basename file [suffix]
```

The basename command removes the directory part of a path name and prints only the file portion. If you provide a *suffix*, then the suffix is also removed, if present. For example:

```
$ basename /usr/home/records.txt
records.txt
$ basename /usr/home/records.txt .txt
records
```

Useful in shell scripts for getting the file name of the script file.

## biff—NOTIFY YOU OF MAIL

```
biff [y|n]
```

Without arguments, biff reports on whether mail notification is enabled ("y") or disabled ("n"). An argument of y enables mail notification; an argument of n disables mail notification. Some versions of biff accept −y and −n as the arguments.

See Chapter 3, "Electronic Mail."

## cal—DISPLAY CALENDAR

```
cal [[month] year]
```

The cal command displays the calendar for the current month. If you specify a *year* as a number, it displays the entire year. If you specify a *month* (as a number) and a *year*, it displays only that month for that year. The *year* must be complete; using 98 as a year produces a calendar for 98 AD, not 1998.

See Chapter 5, "Other Useful Stuff."

## calendar—DISPLAY SCHEDULED APPOINTMENTS

```
calendar
```

The calendar command displays all of the appointments scheduled for today and tomorrow. (If today is a Friday, "tomorrow" includes until Monday.) The appointments are taken from a file named calendar in the current directory. An appointment takes up one line in the calendar file, and has the date somewhere in the line. This is a useful command to have in your .profile file.

See Chapter 5, "Other Useful Stuff."

## cd—CHANGE DIRECTORIES

```
cd [directory]
cd -
cd [old new]
```

The cd command changes your current working directory. If you don't provide any arguments, you move to your home directory (the directory named by the HOME environment variable). If you do name a *directory*, that directory becomes your current directory. The *directory* name can be an absolute path name or a relative path name.

If you give the argument -, you go back to your *previous* directory.

If you specify two arguments, the cd command replaces *old* in your current directory with *new*, and changes you to that directory. For example, if you are in the directory /tmp/work, and you give the command cd tmp projects, the cd command puts you in the directory /projects/work. It creates the name of the target directory by replacing the first argument (in the current directory) with the second argument.

## chgrp—CHANGE A FILE'S GROUP

```
chgrp [-R] group file ...
```

The chgrp command changes the group of the specified *file* to *group*. Unless you are the super-user, you must own the file and you must belong to *group*.

-R If any of the *files* is a directory, recursively applies the change in group to all files and subdirectories in that directory.

## chmod—CHANGE FILE PERMISSIONS

```
chmod [-R] mode file ...
```

The chmod command changes the permissions on a file. You can only change permissions on a file you own.

-R    If any of the *files* is a directory, recursively applies the change in *mode* to all files and subdirectories in that directory.

The *mode* can be specified as a symbolic mode or as a numeric mode.

A symbolic mode can *add*, *subtract*, or *assign* permissions to the user, group, or other, in the form `[ugoa][+-=][rwx]`.

| Symbol | Meaning |
| --- | --- |
| u | User permissions. |
| g | Group permissions. |
| o | Other permissions. |
| a | All (user, group, and other). |
| + | Adds the specified permissions to the specified category. |
| - | Subtracts the specified permissions from the specified category. |
| = | Assigns exactly the specified permissions to the specified category. |
| l | The locking bit (see the description of mode 20*n*0 in the next table). |
| r | Read permission. |
| w | Write permission. |
| x | Execute permission. |
| t | Sticky bit permission. |
| s | Set-UID permission. |

Symbolic modes may be joined by commas, so the mode `u+x,g=rw, o-wx` adds execute permission for the owner, sets the group permissions to read and write (exactly), and subtracts write and execute permission from the other permissions.

In a numeric mode, the numbers assign all of the permissions. The number is three digits, with the first digit being the owner's permissions, the second digit being the group's permissions, and the third digit being everyone else's permissions

| Number | Permission meaning |
| --- | --- |
| 0 | No permissions. |
| 1 | Execute permission only. |

| 2 | Write permission only. |
| 3 | Write and execute permissions. |
| 4 | Read permission only. |
| 5 | Read and execute permission only. |
| 6 | Read and write permissions. |
| 7 | Read, write, and execute permissions. |
| 1000 | Turns on the sticky bit. |
| 20$n$0 | If the permission in the place of $n$ is one of 7, 5, 3, or 1 (a number that includes execute permission), this sets the set group ID permission. If that permission does not include execute permission, this enables the locking bit. The locking bit prevents two programs from reading the file at the same time; this is useful for files that might be accessed and changed by many people nearly simultaneously, like database files. |
| 4000 | Turns on the set user ID permission. |

See Chapter 9, "More About Files and Permissions."

## chown—CHANGE FILE OWNERSHIP

```
chown [-R] user [:group] file ...
```

The chown program changes the ownership of the specified files or directories to *user* in the named *group*. Normally this is restricted to the super-user, but on some systems it's possible for you to give your files away.

-R    If any of the *files* is a directory, recursively applies the change in ownership to all files and subdirectories in that directory.

## chsh—CHANGE YOUR LOGIN SHELL

```
chsh [user]
```

The chsh program is provided on some systems to allow you to change your login shell. The command asks for your password and the name of the new shell. Only the super-user can supply the *user* argument to change someone else's login shell.

## cksum—DISPLAY A FILE'S CHECKSUM

```
cksum [-o 1 | -o 2] file ...
```

The cksum calculates a file's checksum and its size.

-o 1   Calculates the checksum as if using the command sum -r or the BSD version of sum.

-o 2   Calculates the checksum as if using the command sum.

See Chapter 5, "Other Useful Stuff."

## cmp—COMPARE TWO FILES

    cmp [-l|-s] *file1 file2*

The cmp command compares *file1* with *file2*. If they are the same, the command exits without printing a message. If they are different, cmp prints the line and byte where the first difference occurs.

-l     Lists all differences, and for each difference, prints the byte number as a decimal number and the two different bytes as octal numbers.

-s     Silently compares them, and indicates differences in the return codes.

       Files are identical: 0

       Files are different: 1

       Files can't be compared for some reason: 2

See Chapter 5, "Other Useful Stuff."

## comm—DISPLAY LINES IN COMMON

    comm [-123] *file1 file2*

The comm command compares two sorted files and prints three columns of output. The first column contains lines that are only in *file1*, the second column contains lines that are only in *file2*, and the third column contains lines that are in both files. Except in very special circumstances, you should use sort on both files before running comm.

-1     Doesn't print lines only in *file1*.

-2     Doesn't print lines only in *file2*.

-3     Doesn't print lines found in both files.

See Chapter 5, "Other Useful Stuff."

## command—RUN A SIMPLE COMMAND

```
command [-pvV] command
```

This is a Korn Shell built-in. Normally it runs the *command* line given as an argument, but it *never* runs an alias or a shell function (that is, if you have a shell function named ls and a program named ls, the command command ls will always run the program).

-p   Finds the *command* using a special default PATH instead of the PATH currently set.

-v   Doesn't run the *command* but displays information about where the command is and what type of command it is.

-V   Like -v, but with more words.

## compress—COMPRESS A FILE

```
compress [-cfv] [-bn] [file ...]
```

The compress command shrinks a file's size. It replaces the original file (or each *file* on the command line) with a compressed version; the compressed version of the file has the extension .z added to its file name.

-bn   Uses *n* bits in the encoding; the default is 16. The lower the value of *n*, the less compression.

-c   Writes the compressed file to the standard output instead of replacing the original file.

-f   Forces compression; does not prompt before overwriting existing compressed files.

-v   Prints the percentage of size reduction for each file.

See Chapter 5, "Other Useful Stuff."

## cp—COPY A FILE

```
cp [-ipR] old new
cp [-ipR] file ... directory
```

The cp command copies files and directories. There are two forms. In the first form, you specify the name of the file or directory (*old*) and the name of the new copy (*new*). In the second form, you name one or more files or directories that will be copied into another *directory*.

-i    Prompts for confirmation before overwriting a file.

-p    Preserves times and modes on the copied file.

-R    Recursively copies a directory.

## diff—SHOW DIFFERENCES BETWEEN FILES

```
diff [-bitw] [-c | -e | -f | -h | -n] file1 file2

diff [-bitw] [-C num] file1 file2

diff [-bitw] [-D def] file1 file2

diff [-bitw] [-c | -e | -f | -h | -n] [-l] [-r] [-s]
[-S file] directory1 directory2
```

The diff command compares *file1* to *file2* and displays a list of the changes required to turn *file1* into *file2*. The first three forms of the command deal with incompatible options; the fourth form given here compares two directories.

-b    Ignores spaces and tab characters at the ends of lines and treats sequences of space and tab characters as equivalent.

-c    Normally, diff provides only the lines that contain changes. This provides three lines of context (before and after changed lines) and changes output slightly. Lines that have been added have a + before them and lines removed have a - before them, while changed lines have !.

-C *num*    Like -c, except it provides *num* lines of context instead of 3.

-D *def*    Creates a merged version of *file1* and *file2* so that the C preprocessor can be used to create either *file1* or *file2*. (The C preprocessor is a programming tool.)

-e    Produces the output in a form that the editor ed can use as a script to change *file1* into *file2*.

-f    Produces a script similar to the one produced by -e, but in the opposite order. This script cannot be used by ed.

-h          Does a faster but half-hearted job. This misses some kinds of changes and cannot be used with the -e and -f options.

-i          Ignores the case of letters, so changing an uppercase letter to a lowercase (or vice versa) does not count as a difference.

-l          Produces long format output. Each text file is sent through pr before they are compared.

-n          Produces a script similar to the one produced by -e but in the opposite order and with a count of the lines changed on each add or delete command.

-r          Compares common subdirectories and files in those subdirectories.

-s          Reports files that are identical; normally they are not mentioned.

-S *file*   Compares two directories, but skips some files, beginning with the one named *file*.

-t          Converts tab characters in output to spaces. Normal output adds characters to the beginning of the line, which can make tab-aligned columns look bad. This option can correct the appearance.

-w          Ignores all space and tab characters when comparing lines.

The diff command returns 0 if no differences were found, 1 if some differences were found, and a number greater than 1 if there was an error.

See Chapter 5, "Other Useful Stuff."

## dircmp—COMPARE TWO DIRECTORIES

        dircmp [-ds] [-wn] *directory1* *directory2*

The dircmp command compares file names in *directory1* to *directory2*. It lists the files that exist only in each directory; it also lists file names the directories have in common. With the -d option, it runs diff on files with the same name.

-d      Runs diff on files with the same name.

-s      Doesn't print messages about files that are the same.

-wn   Sets the width of the line to *n* characters. (Normally dircmp uses a line of 72 characters.)

See Chapter 5, "Other Useful Stuff."

## dirname—STRIP FILE FROM PATHNAME

```
dirname path
```

The dirname command removes everything after the last / in *path*. It's often used in shell scripts to store the directory a file is in.

## echo—REPEAT ARGUMENTS

```
echo [-n] [arguments...]
```

The echo command is a shell built-in that repeats its arguments on standard output. It's useful in shell scripts or for discovering how the shell interprets a command line or finding the value of a shell variable or parameter. It is almost the same as the Korn Shell built-in command print.

-n   Doesn't print a new line at the end of the arguments. This will cause the *next* line to run on after the end of the echo arguments.

The echo command interprets certain backslash sequences as special. Remember that the backslash is *also* special to the shell, so you'll have to escape the \ in these sequences.

\b   A backspace character.

\c   No ending newline (like the -n option).

\f   Formfeed character.

\n   Newline character (for printing two or more lines of output with a single echo command).

\r   Carriage return.

\t   Tab character.

\\   Backslash.

\0nnn   An ASCII character represented by *nnn*, where *nnn* is an octal character.

## egrep, fgrep, grep—SEARCH FILES FOR REGULAR EXPRESSIONS

```
egrep [-bchilnsv] [eregexp] [file ...]
fgrep [-bchilnvx] [-f file] string [file ...]
grep [-bchilnvw] [regexp] [file ...]
```

The grep commands search files (or standard input) for a pattern. The fgrep command searches for a string, grep searches for a basic regular expression, and egrep command searches for an extended regular expression.

| | |
|---|---|
| -b | Before each matching line, prints the block number (of the disk) where it was found. |
| -c | Prints the number of lines that match instead of printing the lines themselves. |
| -e *pattern* | Searches for *pattern*; this is used only when the string begins with -. |
| -f *file* | Takes the list of strings to match from *file*. |
| -h | Doesn't print the file name when printing the matching line. |
| -i | Ignores the difference between upper- and lowercase letters. |
| -l | Prints (lists) only the names of files that contain matching lines. |
| -n | Before each line that matches, prints its line number (first line is 1). |
| -s | Suppresses error message. |
| -v | Prints all lines *except* the ones that match the pattern. |
| -w | Treats the expression as if it were a word (in vi, as if it were surrounded by \< and \>). Only egrep and grep. |
| -x | Prints only lines that match only the pattern and have no extra characters. Only fgrep. |

## emacs—TEXT EDITOR

```
emacs [-d display] [-nw] [-q] [-u username] [[+n]
file] ... [X-options]
```

Options to Emacs can be multiple letters long, so they can't be grouped.

These are only a few of the startup options available for Emacs. Emacs requires options in a specific order: The Initialization options come first (here, the -d, -nw, -q, and -u options), then other options and file names (the *file* names, possibly preceded by a +n), and, last, any X Window System options (such as -bg).

The initialization options control startup: whether it reads the .emacs startup file in your home directory (or someone else's; even though -u has an argument, it's counted as an initialization option) and whether it runs as an X Window program.

-d *display*   Uses the named *display* when running as an X program.

-nw   Doesn't run as an X program, even if X Window System is available.

-q   Doesn't load a startup file. This option can also be given as -no-init-file.

-u *username*   Loads the startup file (.emacs) from the home directory of *username*.

[+n] *file*   Loads *file* into a buffer. If +n is specified, moves the cursor to line *n* in that buffer.

Emacs commands are command words, possibly with arguments. Any command word can be given by pressing Meta-X and then typing the command word. (If your keyboard does not have a Meta key, the Escape key usually works as the Meta key, and on some systems, Alt is configured to work as the Meta key. They behave differently: when using Escape, press Escape, release it and then press X, but when using Alt, press Alt and keep holding it while you press X.)

The following Emacs commands were discussed in this book.

Basic commands in Emacs:

Quits.                                              Control-X Control-C

Saves file.                                         Control-X Control-S

Cancels command.                                    Control-G

Displays help.                                      Control-H

### Movement Commands in Emacs:

| | |
|---|---|
| Moves cursor down 1 line. | Control-N |
| Moves cursor up 1 line. | Control-P |
| Moves cursor right 1 character. | Control-F |
| Moves cursor left *n* characters. | Control-B |
| Moves cursor to right end of line. | Control-E |
| Moves cursor to first row of line. | Control-A |
| Moves cursor to beginning of next word | Meta-F |
| Moves cursor to word beginning | Meta-B |
| Moves cursor to end of sentence. | Meta-E |
| Moves cursor to beginning of sentence. | Meta-A |
| Moves cursor to end of paragraph. | Meta-} |
| Moves cursor to beginning of paragraph. | Meta-{ |
| Moves cursor forward one screenful. | Control-V |
| Moves cursor backward one screenful. | Meta-V |
| Goes to a specific line, by number. | Meta-X goto-line |
| Redraws screen with cursor in middle. | Control-L |
| Redraws screen so line with cursor is at top. | Meta-1 Control-L |
| Moves cursor to first row of first line on screen. | Meta- - Control-L |

### Emacs Deletion, Change, and Undo Commands:

| | |
|---|---|
| Control-D | Deletes the character under the cursor. |
| Delete | Deletes the character before the cursor. |
| Control-K | Kills text from the cursor to the end of the line. |
| Control-Space | Sets the mark. |
| Control-@ | Sets the mark. |
| Control-W | Kills the text between the mark and the cursor. |
| Control-X u | Undoes the last command that changed the file. |
| Control-_ | Undoes the last command that changed the file. |

### Emacs Commands to Save Files:

| | | |
|---|---|---|
| Saves file. | `save-buffer` | Control-X Control-S |
| Saves file under new name. | `write-file` | Control-X Control-W |
| Saves region as a file. | `write-region` | |
| Replaces file with auto-save file. | `recover-file` | |

### Emacs Search Commands:

| | | |
|---|---|---|
| Searches forward incrementally. | isearch-forward | Control-S |
| Searches backward incrementally. | isearch-backward | Control-B |
| Searches forward for regular expression. | isearch-forward-regexp Meta Control-S | |
| Searches backward for regular expression. | isearch-backward-regexp | Meta Control-R |

### Emacs Search and Replace Commands:

| | | |
|---|---|---|
| Searches and replaces strings with query. | `query-replace` | Meta-% |
| Searches and replaces regular expressions with query. | `query-replace-regexp` | |
| Searches and replaces strings unconditionally. | `replace-string` | |
| Searches and replaces regular expressions unconditionally. | `replace-regexp` | |

### Options in an Emacs Query Search-and-Replace:

| | |
|---|---|
| Displays list of possible responses. | Control-H |
| Displays list of possible responses. | ? |
| Replaces the string. | y |
| Replaces the string. | Space |
| Skips this instance of the string. | n |
| Skips this instance of the string. | Delete |
| Replaces this one and displays the result; then edit replacement with Control-R, accept with Space, or reject with Delete. | , |
| Quits without doing any more replacements. | Enter |
| Replaces this string, then quit. | . |
| Replaces all remaining instances without asking. | ! |

Displays screen and asks again.                    Control-L

Goes back to previous replacement; you can edit           ^
that one with Control-R, accept with Space, or
reject with Delete.

## Some Emacs Text Commands:

Centers the current line.           `center-line`

Enters auto-fill mode.              `auto-fill-mode`

Enters text mode.

Fills (formats) the entire re-      `fill-region-as-paragraph`
gion, ignoring paragraph
breaks, as if it were one
paragraph.

Fills (formats) the paragraph       `fill-paragraph`            Meta-Q
that contains the point.

Fills the entire region,            `fill-individual-`
each paragraph separately,          `paragraphs`
and indents paragraphs to
match their first lines.

Fills the region, each              `fill-region`
paragraph separately.

Sets line length for fill mode      `set-fill-column`          Control-X f
and for centering lines.

Sets the fill prefix to the         `set-fill-prefix`          Control-X .
portion of the current line
preceding the point.

## Emacs Sort Commands:

Sorts the lines in the region by ASCII order.           `sort-lines`

Sorts the paragraphs in the region by ASCII             `sort-paragraphs`
order. A paragraph is separated by blank lines.

Sorts the lines in the region according to some         `sort-fields`
field; the number of the field is specified by the
argument (Meta-*number* or `Control-u` *number*).

Sorts the fields as if they were numbers.               `sort-numeric fields`

## Emacs Spelling Commands:

Asks for a word and then checks its          spell-string
spelling.

| | | |
|---|---|---|
| Checks and corrects spelling of word under point. | spell-word ispell-word | Meta |
| Checks and corrects spelling of words in buffer. | spell-buffer | |
| Checks and corrects spelling of words in region. | spell-region | |
| Completes the word under the point. | ispell-complete-word | Meta-Tab |

### Emacs Abbreviations Commands:

| | | |
|---|---|---|
| Defines global abbreviation for text in buffer. | add-global-abbrev | Control-X a g |
| Defines global expanded text for an abbreviation in the buffer. | inverse-add-global-abbrev | Control-X a I g |
| Defines local abbreviation for text in buffer. | add-mode-abbrev | Control-X a l |
| Defines local expanded text for an abbreviation in the buffer. | inverse-add-mode-abbrev | Control-X a i l |
| Edits current abbreviations. | edit-abbrevs | |
| Lists current abbreviations. | list-abbrevs | |
| Loads the edited abbreviations buffer; the key combination only works in that buffer. | exit-abbrevs-redefine | Control-C Control-C |
| Reads and loads abbreviations from a file. | read-abbrev-file | |
| Saves abbreviations in a file; you are prompted for the file name, but the name ~/.abbrev_defs is common. | write-abbrev-file | |
| Undefines all abbreviations | kill-all-abbrevs | |

### To enter Dired mode, give the command Control-X d. In Dired mode, you may use the following commands:

| | |
|---|---|
| Copies marked files. | C |
| Deletes all files flagged with #, ~, and d. | x |
| Displays brief help information. | ? |
| Deletes all marked files or the file under the cursor. | D |
| Flags all files that match a regular expression to delete them. | %d |

| | |
|---|---|
| Flags auto save files to delete them. | # |
| Flags backup files to delete them. | ~ |
| Flags file to delete it. | d |
| Marks all files that match a regular expression. | %m |
| Marks file for marked operations. | m |
| Moves (renames) this file or all tagged files to a directory. | R |
| Moves cursor down one line to beginning of file name. | n |
| Opens a file or directory and moves the cursor to that window. | o |
| Moves cursor up one line to beginning of file name. | p |
| Opens a file as read-only. | v |
| Removes the mark and moves down one line. | u |
| Removes the mark and moves up one line. | Delete |
| Visits this file in this window. | f |

See Chapter 6, "The Emacs Editor," and Chapter 11, "Advanced Emacs Tricks."

## env—SET AND DISPLAY ENVIRONMENT

```
env [-] [variable=value...] [command]
```

Without arguments, the env command displays the current environment. With arguments, it sets the *variable* to the *value* and runs the *command* with that *variable* added to the environment.

-    Ignores the current environment entirely. Normally, the env command adds the new variables to the current environment. With this option, you cause it to build an entirely new environment for the *command*.

## exec—RUN A COMMAND

```
exec [command]
```

The exec command replaces the current process (usually the shell) with the command given as *command*. Used in this book to try out new shells, it's most often used in shell scripts as a way of manipulating file descriptors such as standard error and standard input. See the exec man page for more details.

## exit—LOGOUT OF A SHELL

```
exit [n]
```

Exit a shell. When used in a shell script, it returns the return code of *n*, where *n* is an integer number. (If you don't provide *n*, the return code is the return code of the last command run in the script before exit.)

## export—MAKE A SHELL VARIABLE VISIBLE TO OTHER PROGRAMS

```
export [variables]
export [name=[value]]
```

This is a shell built-in. Makes the shell variables *variables* (or *name*) visible to other programs, such as subshells. The first form exports variables that have already been set, while the second form assigns a value to *name* and exports it. If no arguments are given, the export command lists all variables that are currently exported.

See Chapter 7, "Customizing Your Environment."

## fc—SHELL HISTORY COMMAND

```
fc [-lnr] [-e editor] [first [last]]
fc -e - [old=new] [command]
```

This is a shell built-in. There are two versions of the command. The first version edits your history file, using the editor named by your FCEDIT environment variable or the editor named after the -e option; if no editor is named, it uses the editor ed. The arguments *first* and *last* are used with the -l option, and can be either command numbers or strings from the beginning of a command.

The second version repeats a command; the second version is usually used as the command r. (See the r command for a description of the second form.)

The shell saves 128 commands by default; this can be changed by setting the HISTFILE environment variable to another number.

-l    Lists the last 16 commands on standard output (as the history command) or the commands specified by the range *first* to *last*. If only *first* is specified, the fc command lists all commands from *first* to the most recent.

-n    Doesn't display command numbers when listing. This is useful if you want to save your most recent commands in a script.

-r    Reverses the order, so the most recent command displays first.

See Chapter 5, "Other Useful Stuff."

## file—GUESS FILE'S TYPE

```
file [-ch] [-flist] [-mfile] file ...
```

The `file` command examines *file* and attempts to determine what type of file it is (executable, data file for a particular program, graphic image, shell script, and so on). It does this by comparing the beginning of the file against a list of "magic numbers" in a database, called the "magic file."

-c        Checks the magic file for errors.

-flist    Takes the list of files to be checked from *file*.

-h        Doesn't follow symbolic links.

-mfile    Uses *file* as the file database.

## find—FIND FILES BY ATTRIBUTES

```
find path... conditions
```

The `find` command searches all files and directories under a specified *path* or *paths* for files that meet certain *conditions*. (The first argument that starts with -, (, or ! is taken to be the beginning of the conditions.) The conditions are tested in the order they occur on the command line.

When there's a time in the `find` command, it's in days. You can specify it as +*n* (more than *n*), *n* (exactly *n*), or -*n* (less than *n*). Condition expressions can be grouped with parentheses ( ), negated with !, joined in a logical and with -a, and joined in a logical or with -o.

-atime *n*        True if the file was accessed *n* days ago.

-cpio device      Always true. Copies the file to *device* in `cpio` format.

-ctime *n*        True if file information was last changed *n* days ago.

| | |
|---|---|
| `-depth` | Always true. Does a depth-first search, doing everything in a directory before doing the directory itself. |
| `-exec` *command* | Always true. Runs the *command* on the file; the placeholder {} can be used to represent the file's name. The command must end with a semi-colon, which may need to be escaped for the shell. |
| `-follow` | Always true. Follows symbolic links. |
| `-fstype` *type* | True if the file system is of the specified *type*. |
| `-group` *name* | True if the file belongs to the group *name*. |
| `-inum` *n* | True if the file has inode number *n*. |
| `-links` *n* | True if the file has *n* links to it. |
| `-local` | True if the file is on a local file system. |
| `-ls` | Always true. Prints the file's name and its statistics (much like `ls -l`). |
| `-mount` | Always true. Doesn't search past a directory containing a mounted file system. |
| `-mtime` *n* | True if the file was last modified *n* days ago. |
| `-name` *pattern* | True if the file's name matches *pattern*. If the pattern contains wild cards, you will have to escape them to avoid interpretation by the shell. |
| `-ncpio` *device* | Always true. Copies the file to *device* in `cpio -c` format. |
| `-newer` *file* | True if the file is newer that the named *file*. |
| `-nogroup` | True if the file belongs to an unknown group (one that isn't in the file `/etc/groups`). |
| `-nouser` | True if the file belongs to an unknown user (one that isn't in the file `/etc/passwd`). |
| `-ok` *command* | Always true. Like `-exec`, this runs *command* on the file, but first it asks you if you want the command run. To run the *command*, type y. |

| | |
|---|---|
| -perm [-]*mode* | True if the file's permissions are the specified *mode*. The *mode* is symbolic. |
| -operm [-]*mode* | True if the file's permissions are the specified numeric *mode*. |
| -print | Always true. Prints the file's name, relative to *path*. |
| -prune | Always true. Doesn't go into subdirectories below *pattern*. Given after a -name *pattern* condition. |
| -size *n*[c] | True if the file is *n* blocks long, or *n* bytes long if the number is followed by a c. |
| -type *c* | True if the file is of the specified *type*. The types are b (block special file), c (character special file), d (directory), l (symbolic link), p (named pipe), or f (plain file). |
| -user *name* | True if the file belongs to the user named *name*. |

## finger—GET INFORMATION ABOUT A USER

```
finger [-bfhilmpqsw] [username ...]

finger [-l] [username@hostname1 [@hostname2 ...@host-
namen ...]]

finger [-l] [@hostname1 [@hostname2 ...@host-
namen...]]
```

The finger command reports on the user named *username*, who may be on another system. Normally, all names that match *username* are displayed; that is, finger john displays all users that have "john" as part of their login name, first name, or last name.

If no *username* is specified, finger displays a list of users currently logged in.

The default format is the "short" output format.

If the *username* is on another system (specified with *@hostname*), only the -l option has an effect.

-b  If long output format is requested, doesn't print the user's shell and home directory.

-f  If long output format is requested, doesn't print the header information.

-h  If long output format is requested, doesn't print the contents of the user's `.project` file.

-i  Prints in the "idle" output format, which shows only login name, terminal, login time, and idle time.

-l  Prints in the long output format, which displays the user's login name, the user's full name, the user's home directory and login shell, the time the user last logged in, the terminal or host the user logged in from, the last time the user received mail, the first line of the user's `$HOME/.project` file, and the contents of the user's `$HOME/.plan` file.

-m  Matches arguments only on user name, not on first name or last name.

-p  If long output format is requested, doesn't print the contents of the user's `.plan` file.

-q  Prints in the "quick" format, which shows only login name, terminal, and login time.

-s  Prints in the "short" format, which displays the user's login name, the user's full name, the terminal name, the idle time, the login time, and the host name if the user is logged in remotely.

-w  If short output format is requested, doesn't display the user's full name.

See Chapter 2, "Electronic Communication."

## for—REPEAT COMMANDS IN A LOOP

```
for variable [in list]
do
    commands
done
```

This is a shell built-in. The `for` command repeats the *commands* for each item in the *list*. The *variable* is given the value of the first item in the *list*, the *commands* are run, and then the shell gives the *variable* the value of the next item in the *list*. It repeats this for each item in the *list*. The `break` command exits a `for` loop. The "in `list`" section is optional only in shell functions and shell scripts; if you don't include a list there, the list is assumed to be the arguments to the function or the script.

See Chapter 8, "Basic Shell Programming."

## ftp—COPY FILES TO AND FROM REMOTE SYSTEM

```
ftp [-dginv] [hostname]
```

The `ftp` command copies files between systems. It is an interactive command.

-d    Enables debugging.

-g    Disables filename globbing (that is, commands will not understand * and ?).

-i    Turns off interactive prompting (similar to the `prompt` command in an FTP session).

-n    Does not automatically login when connecting, even if there is a `.netrc` file.

-v    Be verbose; shows all responses from the remote system.

Some of the commands that can be used in `ftp` are:

| | |
|---|---|
| `append localfile [remotefile]` | Adds the file to the end of the remote file, rather than replacing the remote file. |
| `! [command]` | Runs *command* on the local system. If no *command* is given, the `!` command starts an interactive shell. |
| `ascii` | Sets the transfer type to "network ascii." |
| `binary` | Sets the transfer type to "image." |
| `bye` | Ends the session. |

| | |
|---|---|
| `cd remote-directory` | Changes directories on the remote site to *remote-directory*. |
| `cdup` | Changes directories on the remote site to the parent of the current directory. |
| `delete remotefile` | Deletes the file *file* on the remote system. |
| `get remotefile [localfile]` | Gets the remote file and stores it on the local machine, with the name *localfile*. |
| `help [command]` | Displays help information about *command*. If you don't give a *command*, it lists all the `ftp` internal commands. |
| `lcd [directory]` | Changes your *local* working directory; files you `get` and `put` will go to and come from this directory on the local machine. If you don't specify a *directory*, your home directory becomes your local working directory. |
| `ls [remotedirectory] [localfile]` | Lists the contents of the remote directory. If no remote directory is given, lists the contents of the current directory. If *local-file* is given, stores the contents in the local file by that name instead of displaying them on the terminal. |
| `mget remotefiles` | Gets more than one file. Wildcards can be used |
| `mput localfiles` | Puts more than one file. Wildcards can be used. |
| `prompt` | Turns interactive prompting on and off. |
| `put localfile [remotefile]` | Sends a local file to the remote machine. |

See Chapter 4, "Computer Networks."

## function—CREATE SHELL FUNCTION

```
function name { commands }
```

The `function` defines a shell function. Whenever the *name* is given, the *commands* will be run. The function can accept arguments, like any shell script.

See Chapter 8, "Basic Shell Programming."

## functions—LIST SHELL FUNCTIONS

```
functions
```

The `functions` command lists all of the shell commands currently defined and their definitions. It's a Korn Shell alias for the command `typeset -f`.

For more information about functions, see Chapter 8, "Basic Shell Programming."

## gunzip—UNCOMPRESS FILES

```
gunzip [-cfhlLnNrtvV] [-S suffix] [file ...]
```

This is the same as the command `gzip -d`. For descriptions of the options, see `gzip`. The `gunzip` command decompresses files compressed with `gzip` and files compressed with `compress`. The *file* names on the command line may or may not have the `.gz` or `.Z` extensions; `gunzip` looks for the extensions in either case. The `gzip` and `gunzip` commands are not standard, but they are freely available.

See Chapter 5, "Other Useful Stuff."

## gzip—COMPRESS FILES

```
gzip [-cdfhlLnNrtvV19] [-S suffix] [file ...]
```

The `gzip` command compresses files. Each *file* is replaced by a compressed version that has the extension `.gz` added to the name. To compress entire directories, use the `-r` option. To list the contents of a compressed archive, use `-l`.

The `gzip` and `gunzip` commands are not standard, but they are freely available.

| | |
|---|---|
| -c | Writes compressed file to standard output instead of replacing the *file* named on the command line. |
| -d | "Decompresses" the file; this is the same as gunzip. |
| -f | Forcefully compresses the file, even if a compressed file already exists or if the file has multiple links. |
| -h | Displays a help screen and then quits. |
| -l | Lists information about each compressed *file*. With the -v option, it lists even more information. |
| -L | Displays license information for gzip and then quits. |
| -n | Does not save the original timestamp and file name. |
| -N | Always saves the original timestamp and file name. |
| -r | If any of the *file* arguments is a directory, compresses (or decompresses) the files and subdirectories it contains. |
| -S *suffix* | Uses the specified *suffix* instead of .gz. This option can lead to confusion. |
| -t | Tests that the compressed *file* is good. |
| -v | Be verbose about messages. |
| -V | Displays version information and then quits. |
| -1 | Compresses the file as fast as possible, even if that means it isn't made as small. Values from -2 to -8 represent other tradeoffs between size and speed. |
| -9 | Compresses the file as small as possible, even if that takes longer. Values from -2 to -8 represent tradeoffs between size and speed. |

See Chapter 5, "Other Useful Stuff."

## history—DISPLAY RECENT COMMANDS

```
history [first [last]]
```

Without options, this command displays the last 16 commands. You can also specify a command number or part of a command name as *first* and *last*, to show a range of commands between those two. If you specify only the *first*, history displays all commands from that command to the most recent. In the Korn Shell, history is an alias for fc -l.

See Chapter 5, "Other Useful Stuff."

## hostname—DISPLAY SYSTEM NAME

```
hostname
```

This command may be in the directory /usr/ucb instead. It displays your system's name on the network.

## id—SHOW USER AND GROUP NAMES

```
id [-a] [user]
```

The id command displays the group name, group ID number, and user ID number for the specified *user*. If no *user* is specified, your own information is displayed. The Solaris version supports −a, but the version in /usr/xpg4/bin has different options; see the id man page for details.

−a      Displays all of the groups the *user* belongs to, not just the primary group.

## if—BRANCH BASED ON CONDITION

```
if condition1
then commands1
[elif condition2
    then commands2]
...
[else commands3]
fi
```

The if command allows you to make choices in a command. If the first condition, *condition1*, is true (has a value of 0), then *commands1* will be executed. You can have any number following if conditions using the optional elif commands. If none of those conditions are true, then the *commands3* after the else are executed. The else clause is optional.

The *condition* is usually a `test` command, but it can be any command or even a variable.

See Chapter 8, "Basic Shell Programming."

## ln—LINK FILE

```
ln [-fns] old new
```

The `ln` command creates a new link (name) for the file *old*. Without options, `ln` creates a hard link. Hard links can only be created on a single file system; they can't cross to another drive. Hard links cannot link directories. With the `-s` option, `ln` creates a symbolic link. Symbolic links can cross file systems and they can link directories.

`-f`   Forces the link; doesn't prompt for permission to overwrite a file.

`-n`   Does not overwrite existing files; conflicts with `-f`.

`-s`   Creates a symbolic link.

## ls—LIST FILES

```
ls [-abcCdfFgilLmnopqrRstuvx1] [file …]
```

The `ls` command lists files and directories. If no *files* are given on the command line, `ls` lists the contents of the current directory.

`-a`   Lists all files, including hidden files and the directories dot (.) and dot-dot (..).

`-A`   Lists all entries, including those that begin with a dot but does *not* list dot (.) and dot-dot (..).

`-b`   Shows non-printing characters as octal numbers.

`-c`   Uses the time that the file information (the i-node) was last changed instead of file modification time.

`-C`   Prints multi-column output. When printing to a terminal, this is the default.

`-d`   If the *file* is a directory, prints its name and not its contents.

-f     Forces each argument to be interpreted as a directory. This turns off the -l, -t, -s, and -r options (and turns on -a) and causes files to be listed in the order they appear in the directory, not in ASCII sorted order.

-F     Indicates the file types by printing a character after each file name. A regular character gets no indicator, a directory gets a slash (/), an executable file gets an asterisk (*), and a symbolic link gets an at-sign (@).

-g     Shows long output like -l, but doesn't print the owner's name.

-i     For each file, prints the i-node number.

-l     Shows long listing; see below for the description of the output.

-L     If *file* is a symbolic link, lists the file it points to instead of the name of the link itself.

-m     Lists files on a single line, separated by commas.

-n     Shows long output like -l, but prints the numeric values (UID and GID) for the owner and group.

-o     Shows long output like -l, but doesn't print the group's name.

-p     Indicates directories by a trailing slash (/).

-q     Prints non-printing characters as a question mark (?).

-r     Prints files in reverse order.

-R     Lists recursively, including all subdirectories.

-s     Gives size in blocks, not bytes.

-t     Sorts by time (most recent first) instead of name. By default, modification time is used (but -c and –u change this).

-u     Uses the time the file was last accessed instead of modification time.

-x     Prints multi-column output sorted across the line, not down.

-1     Prints one entry per line in the output.

When the -l option is given, ls prints long-format output.

```
-rwxrwxrwx    2 susan  r+d     80252  Mar 23 13:28 racing_form
```

The first block of 10 characters in a line are the file's *type* and its *permissions*, for the user, group, and other. The following indicate the file types:

d     directory

l     symbolic link

b     block special file

c     character special file

p     fifo (or "named pipe") special file

-     ordinary file

|     FIFO

The permissions are read, write, and execute. The next number is the number of hard *links* to the file (2 in this case). After that come the *owner*'s login name (susan) and *group* (r+d). Following that are the *size* of the file in bytes (80252), the *time* of last modification (March 23, 13:28), and the file's *name*.

See Chapter 4, "Manipulating Files and Directories."

## mailx—SEND AND READ ELECTRONIC MAIL

```
mailx [-BdFintUv~] [-b bcc] [-c cc] [-h n]
[-s subject] recipient ...

mailx [-BdeHiInNUVv~]   [ -f [file|+folder]]
[-T file] [-u user]
```

The first synopsis shown here is for sending mail; the second synopsis is for reading mail.

This lists many but not all of the command line options; some have been omitted from the synopsis. It also does not list all of the internal options in mailx; see the mailx man page for those.

| | |
|---|---|
| -B | Does not buffer stdin or stdout. |
| -b *bcc* | The *bcc* argument is a list of addresses of who should receive blind carbon copies. If the list has more than one address, enclose the entire list in double quotes. The blind carbon copy list can also be set in input mode with the ~b *address-list* command. |
| -c *cc* | The *cc* argument is a list of addresses of who should receive regular carbon copies. If the list has more than one address, enclose the entire list in double quotes. The carbon copy list can also be set in input mode with the ~c *address-list* command. |
| -d | Turns on debugging. |
| -e | Checks for mail and then exits; if there is mail, exits with return value 1 and if there is no mail, exits with return value 0. |
| -F | Records the outgoing mail message in a file with the same name as the first address in the address list. For example, mail to john@wowzers.org would be stored in a file named john. |
| -f *file* | Reads mail from *file* instead of from your system mailbox. |
| -H | Displays the header summary and then exits. |
| -h *n* | Limits the number of network hops to *n*; this is useful in a script that sends mail to another site, since it catches (but doesn't fix) cases where script A sends the mail message to script B, which sends it back to script A, which sends it back to script B… This option will stop that behavior after *n* hops. |
| -I | When displaying the header summary, uses the information in a header line starting with Newsgroups: as the sender. This only works with the -f option, and is intended to display stored articles from Usenet newsgroups. |
| -i | Ignores any interrupt signals while composing mail. |
| -N | Doesn't show the header summary, just goes directly into command mode. |
| -n | Doesn't read system startup files. This can be useful if your system administrator has set options you dislike, although usually a better solution is to unset those options in your .mailrc file. |
| -s *subject* | Uses *subject* as the subject of the mail message. If the subject contains spaces, enclose the entire subject in double quotes. The subject can also be set in command mode with the ~s *subject* command. |

| | |
|---|---|
| -T *file* | For every mail message header that contains a line beginning Article-Id:, extracts the contents of that line and adds it to *file*, one article ID per line. Like -I, this is intended to be used by shell scripts that deal with messages saved from Usenet newsgroups. It also only works with the -f option. |
| -U | Converts UUCP addresses (containing !) to Internet domain-style addresses. |
| -u *user* | Reads from the mailbox of *user* instead of your own mailbox; this option only works if you have permission to read that mailbox. |
| -V | Prints the version number of the program and exits. |
| -v | Passes the -v flag to sendmail (the program that actually sends the mail). |
| -~ | Normally, mailx doesn't read ~ commands in input if the input is a file (not a tty); this option causes it to interpret those commands. |

When composing a message (in send mode or "composition mode"), you can use the following commands. The commands must be given at the beginning of the line.

| | |
|---|---|
| ~~ | Prints a single tilde as the actual first character on this line. |
| ~b *addresses* | Adds *addresses* to "blind" carbon copy list. |
| ~c *addresses* | Adds *addresses* to the carbon-copy (cc) list. |
| ~d | Reads in the contents of the file dead.letter. |
| ~e | Edits the message buffer using the editor specified in the EDITOR environment variable, or ed if no editor is defined. |
| ~f *messages* | Reads in the specified *messages*, where the messages are indicated by the numbers shown in an h display (covered in Lab 3.3). This is only useful if you are reading mail and decide to send or reply to mail. The *messages* are read in, but have no header lines. |
| ~F *messages* | Same as ~f, but keeps all header lines. This is only useful if you are reading mail and decide to send or reply to mail. |
| ~h | Prompts for address (to) list, subject line, and carbon-copy list. |
| ~r *file* | Reads a file into the message. |

| ~p | Prints the message so far. |
|---|---|
| ~m *messages* | Reads in the specified *messages*. This is like ~f, except that the messages are all indented by one tab character. |
| ~M *messages* | Same as ~m, but keeps all header lines. |
| ~s *subject* | Sets subject line. This replaces the current subject line. |
| ~t *addresses* | Adds the specified *addresses* to the list of recipients on the To: line. |
| ~v | Edits the message using the editor specified in your VISUAL environment variable, or vi if that variable is not set. |
| ~w *file* | Writes message onto *file*. This command won't replace or append to an existing file. |
| ~? | Prints help text. |
| ~!*command* | Runs the *command* using the shell; the results of the *command* do not appear in the message, although they may be displayed on the screen. The *command* is a shell command line, and can contain more than one command. |
| ~\|*command* | Pipes the message through the command; the results of the *command* replace the message. For example, if you ran ~\|sort, the message would be replaced by a sorted version. |

Some command-mode commands in mailx:

| Command | Short | Effect |
|---|---|---|
| ! *command* | | Runs *command* in the shell. |
| alias *name address* ... | | Makes the address *name* mean the same as the list of *addresses*. |
| delete *message(s)* | d | Deletes messages. |
| exit | x | Quits without changing system mailbox. |
| from *message(s)* | f | Gives head lines of messages; like h, but lets you specify which messages are summarized. |
| headers | h | Prints out headers of active messages. |
| mail *user(s)* | m | Mails to specified *users*. |
| next | n | Goes to and types next message. |
| preserve *message(s)* | pre | Makes messages go back to incoming mailbox (that is, preserves them). |

| | | |
|---|---|---|
| `quit` | `q` | Quits, saving unresolved messages in mbox. |
| `Reply message(s)` | `R` | Replies to message senders. |
| `reply message(s)` | `r` | Replies to message senders and all recipients. |
| `save message(s) file` | `s` | Appends messages to *file*. |
| `Save message(s)` | `s` | Appends messages to a file with the same name as the sender of the message; if the specified messages contain more than one sender, saves in a file with the same name as the first message in the list. |
| `set` | | Displays current settings (not used in the `.mailrc` file). |
| `set append` | | Normally, new messages are placed at the beginning of the mbox file; setting this option makes mailx add them to the end of the file. |
| `set appenddeadletter` | | Adds new canceled messages to the end of the `dead.letter` file, rather than replacing the existing canceled message. |
| `set asksub` | | Asks for a subject line if the –s option isn't specified on the command line. |
| `set crt=n` | | Uses a pager to display any mail message with more than *n* lines. |
| `set dot` | | Ends input mode by typing a dot alone on a line. This makes pressing Enter, then dot, then Enter, the same as pressing Enter, then ~., then Enter. |
| `set flipr` | | Reverses the meaning of `Reply` and `reply` commands. |
| `set folder=directory` | | When saving mail, treats a path name beginning with + as if it were relative to *directory*. |
| `set hold` | | Keeps mail messages in the incoming mailbox instead of putting read messages in mbox. |
| `set indentprefix=string` | | Uses *string* to indent messages included with ~m instead of using a tab character. |
| `type message(s)` | `t` | Types messages. |
| `undelete message(s)` | | Undeletes messages. |
| `unset setting` | | Unsets one of the values set with `set`; for example, `unset appenddeadletter` would turn off the `appenddeadletter` option. |

| | | |
|---|---|---|
| visual *message(s)* | v | Edits messages with vi or editor specified by VISUAL environment variable. |
| z | z | Scrolls forward through message headers. |

Specifying messages in mailx command mode:

| Specifier | Messages Specified |
|---|---|
| *n* | Message number *n*. |
| . | (A dot.) The current message. |
| * | All messages in the file. |
| ^ | The first undeleted message in the file. |
| $ | The last message in the file. |
| + | The next undeleted message. |
| − | The previous undeleted message. |
| *n-m* | The range of messages from message *n* to message *m*. "9-12" would be messages nine through twelve. |
| *login* | All the messages from the user with that *login* name. |
| /*string* | All the messages that contain the *string* in the subject; case doesn't matter. (To match messages with "FRENCH" in the subject, you can specify with "/french".) |
| :d | All deleted messages. |
| :n | All new messages. |
| :o | All old messages. |
| :i | All read messages. |
| :u | All unread messages. |

## mesg—ACCEPT OR REFUSE MESSAGES

```
mesg [y|n]
```

When given without arguments, `mesg` reports on whether the current terminal will accept ("y") or refuse ("n") a message. The argument `y` causes the terminal to accept messages; the argument n causes the terminal to refuse messages.

The super-user can always send a message, regardless of what `mesg` reports.

See Chapter 2, "Electronic Communication."

## mkdir—CREATE A DIRECTORY

```
mkdir  [-p] [-m mode] dir...
```

The `mkdir` command creates one or more directories.

-m *mode*   Creates the directory with the specified *mode*.

-p        If necessary, creates any intermediate directories in the path name *dir*.

## more—DISPLAY TEXT ONE SCREEN AT A TIME

```
more [-cdflrsuw] [-lines] [+linenumber] [+/pattern]
[file ...]
```

The `more` command is a pager that displays a file or its standard input or standard output, one screen at a time.

*-lines*          Displays only *lines* lines of text.

*+linenumber*    Starts displaying text in the first file at line *linenumber*.

*+/pattern*      Starts displaying text two lines before the first occurrence of the regular expression *pattern*.

-c           Clears the screen before displaying text.

-d           Displays error messages instead of ringing the terminal bell.

-f           Does not fold long lines.

| | |
|---|---|
| -l | Does not treat formfeed characters (Ctrl-L) as page breaks. |
| -r | Displays control characters as a ^ followed by a letter. By default, control characters aren't displayed. |
| -s | Replaces (squeezes) multiple blank lines with a single blank line. |
| -u | Doesn't generate underline sequences; this is used if the terminal can understand underline sequences instead of more generating its own. |
| -w | Waits at the end of the file for some key to be pressed, then exits. By default, more exits as soon as it gets to the end of the file. |

The more command has its own internal commands for movement. Some of the commands are given here. For more, see the official documentation. Most commands can be prefixed by a number of repetitions, shown here by *n*; if no number is given, the command occurs once.

| | |
|---|---|
| *n*Space | Displays another screen of text. |
| *n*Enter | Displays another line of text. |
| *n*b | Moves backward *n* screenfuls and then displays one. |
| *n*d | Moves forward by *n* lines or a half screenful. If *n* is given, that becomes the default for d and u commands. |
| *n*f | Moves forward by *n* screenfuls and then displays one. |
| h | Prints help information. |
| Ctrl-L | Redraws the screen. |
| q | Quits. |
| Q | Quits. |
| = | Displays current line number. |

`n/pattern`    Searches forward for the *n*th occurrence of the regular expression *pattern*. The *pattern* will be displayed on the third line of the screen.

`:f`    Displays current file name and line number.

`n:n`    Shows the *n*th next file. Only has an effect if more than one file was named on the command line.

## mv—MOVE A FILE OR DIRECTORY

```
mv [-fi] oldfile newfile
mv [-fi] file … directory
```

The mv command is used to move or rename a file or directory. There are two forms: The first moves a single file (or directory) to a new name or location. The second moves one or more files into a directory without changing the file names.

`-f`    Forcefully moves files; doesn't ask if a file should be overwritten.

`-i`    Asks before overwriting a file.

## od—DISPLAY FILE IN OCTAL OR OTHER FORMATS

```
od [-bcCDdFfOoSsvXx] [-] [file] [offset_string]

od [-bcCDdFfOoSsvXx] [-A address_base] [-j skip] [-N
count] [-t type_string ... ] [ - ] [file ...]
```

The od command displays the contents of a file in a selected format. The default format displays the file's contents in octal, where each octal number represents two bytes of the file.

The *offset_string* specifies where in the file display begins (it's incompatible with the -A, -j, -N, and -t options). The *offset_string* has one of these formats:

```
[+][0] offset [.][b|B]
[+][0][offset] [.]
[+][0x|x][offset]
[+][0x|x] offset[B]
```

The + sign is required if od is reading from standard input, but can be left off otherwise.

The *offset* is a number; if it starts with 0, it's interpreted as an octal number. If it starts with 0x or x, it's interpreted as a hexadecimal number. If it's followed by a dot (.), it's interpreted as a decimal number; decimal overrides octal, and you can't use both hexadecimal and decimal. A b or a B means the *offset* is units of 512 bytes, and in hexadecimal, you must use B because "b" will be taken as part of the hexadecimal number.

The options are:

| | |
|---|---|
| -A address_base | Each line of output describes how far in the file the bytes are (the offset). Normally, this is displayed in octal, but you can specify the base you want used; the values can be o (octal), d (decimal), x (hexadecimal), or n (don't display an offset). Cannot be used with the *offset_string* operand. |
| -b | Displays unsigned bytes in octal; the same as -t o1. |
| -c | Displays bytes in ASCII. Some characters will appear as names (for example, backspace is "\b"). |
| -C | Displays bytes but interprets characters correctly, whether single-byte or multibyte (depending on the locale). |
| -d | Displays unsigned decimal words of 2 bytes; the same as -t u2. |
| -D | Displays unsigned decimal words of 4 bytes; the same as -t u4. |
| -f | Displays floating point words of 4 bytes; the same as -t f4. |
| -F | Displays floating point words of 8 bytes; the same as -t f8. |
| -j *skip* | Jumps over the first *skip* bytes of the file. The *skip* number is a decimal number, unless you start it with 0x or 0X, in which case it's a hexadecimal number. You can indicate larger chunks than bytes by putting one of the letters b, k, or m after *skip*. A b indicates *skip* units of 512 bytes; the letter k indicates *skip* units of 1024 bytes (or kilobytes), and m indicates *skip* units of 1,048,576 bytes (or megabytes). Cannot be used with the *offset_string* operand. |
| -N *count* | Stops displaying after *count* bytes. The *count* is a decimal number, unless you start it with 0x or 0X, in which case it's hexadecimal. Cannot be used with the *offset_string* operand. |
| -o | Displays in unsigned octal words of 2 bytes; it is the same as -t o2. |

| | |
|---|---|
| -O | Displays in unsigned octal words of 4 bytes; it is the same as -t o4. |
| -s | Displays in signed decimal words of 2 bytes; it is the same as -t d2. |
| -S | Displays in singed decimal words of 4 bytes; it is the same as -t d4. |
| -t *type_string* | Displays according to the specified *type_string*. Many of the other options are short forms for a particular -t option. A *type_string* has a letter that specifies the format and may have a number indicating how many bytes should be displayed, or it may have a letter that stands for a particular number. |

The format letters are:

| | |
|---|---|
| a | Character with a name |
| c | Character |
| d | Decimal |
| f | Floating point number |
| o | Octal number |
| u | Unsigned decimal |
| x | Hexadecimal number |

For example, d2 would be decimal numbers representing 2 bytes. Instead of numbers, letters may be used, representing the sizes of certain types in the C programming language:

| | |
|---|---|
| C | char when used after d, u, o, or x |
| D | double when used after an f |
| F | float when used after an f |
| I | int when used after d, u, o, or x |
| L | long douuble when used after f or long after d, u, o, or x |
| S | short when used after d, u, o, or x |

Cannot be used with the *offset_string* operand.

| | |
|---|---|
| -v | Displays repeated lines; otherwise, od displays a * character when a line is repeatd. |
| -X | Displays in unsigned hexadecimal words of 4 bytes. |
| -x | Displays in unsigned hexadecimal words of 2 bytes. |

## pax—ARCHIVE AND UNARCHIVE FILES

```
pax [-cdnv] [-f archive] [-s replstr] ... [pattern
...]

pax -r [-cdiknuv] [-f archive] [-p string] ...  [-s
replstr] ...  [pattern ...]

pax -w [-adituvX] [-b blocksize] [-f archive] [-s
replstr] ...  [-x format] [file ...]

pax -r -w [-diklntuvX] [-p string] ...  [-s replstr]
...  [file ...]  directory
```

The pax command creates and reads archives of files; it can also be used to copy directory trees. The first option determines what the command does:

- If the first option is -r, pax reads (unarchives) an archive, either from a tape device (the default) or the file specified by the -f option.
- If the option is -w, pax creates an archive.
- If the first two options are -r and -w, pax copies the *files* to the specified *directory*.
- And if the first option is neither -r or -w, pax lists the contents of the archive.

| | |
|---|---|
| -a | Adds the *files* to the end of the archive. This doesn't work for some devices (although it should work for disk files). |
| -b *blocksize* | When writing the archive, uses blocks of *blocksize* bytes. |
| -c | Matches all members of the archive *except* those specified by *file* or *pattern*. |
| -d | When extracting or writing, a directory name causes pax to extract only the directory and not its contents. |
| -f *archive* | Uses the named file *archive* instead of standard input or standard output. |
| -i | Interactively renames files. Every file matching a *file* or *pattern* causes pax to prompt for a new name. |

Pressing Enter causes `pax` to skip the file, a dot (.) causes the file to be processed with its current name, and any other text is a new name for the file.

`-k`                  Doesn't overwrite existing files.

`-1`                  Links files when copying. Whenever possible, hard links will be made between the source and copied files.

`-n`                  Selects the first member of the archive that matches the *pattern*.

`-p string`           Specifies certain file privileges when copying or unpacking a file. The *string* can contain one or more of:

a Doesn't bother to keep the access times the same on the new file.

e Keeps the user ID, group ID, file mode bits, access time, and modification time the same.

m Doesn't keep the file modification time the same on the new file.

o Keeps the user ID and the group ID; normally, the new file gets the user and group IDs of the person running `pax`.

p Keeps the file's mode the same.

`-s replstr`          Changes file names as the file is being unpacked. The *replstring* is a substitute command similar to the one in `vi`, in the form `/old/new/[gp]`. The *old* string is a basic regular expression, and back references are allowed in *new*. More than one `-s` option can be given.

`-t`                  On the archived files' access times, ignores the fact that `pax` had to access the files to archive them. (The access time doesn't get updated in the archived file.)

`-u`                  Updates; ignores older files with the same name.

`-v`                  Be verbose; gives more information than usual.

`-x format`           Writes the archive in the specified *format*. Valid *formats* on Solaris are `cpio` and `ustar` (the default).

## print—WRITE ARGUMENTS TO STANDARD OUTPUT

```
print [-nprRs] [-u[n] [-|—] [arguments...]
```

The `print` command is a Korn Shell built-in command that displays the *arguments*. By default, it displays on standard output, but you can specify a different file descriptor with `-u`. Unless you use the `-r` or `-R` options, it understands the same escape characters as `echo` does, and can be used instead of `echo`.

-n      Doesn't end the *arguments* with a newline.

-p      Sends the *arguments* to a coprocess. This feature is obscure.

-r      Ignores the escape sequences that `echo` understands.

-R      Ignores escape sequences used with `echo` and ignores any options after this one, except for `-n`.

-s      Sends the *arguments* to the history file instead of standard output.

-u*n*   Prints to file descriptor *n*. For example, `-u2` prints to standard error.

-       Ignores all options after this dash. This lets you print arguments that start with a - character.

—       The same as `-`.

See Chapter 8, "Basic Shell Programming."

## r—REPEAT COMMAND

```
r [old=new] [command]
```

The `r` command repeats a command. Without arguments, it repeats the last command executed. If a *command* (either a number or a command name or part of a command name) is given, the most recent matching command is repeated. One feature not described in the book is the *substitution* command: You can substitute one string for another using the *old=new* syntax. For example, if the last `vi` command was `vi myfile` and you want to repeat the command, but edit `yourfile` instead, you can give the command `r my=your vi`. The *first* occurrence of "my" is replaced by "your." (This form replaces only the first occurrence of the string, not all of them.)

In the Korn Shell, the `r` command is an alias for `fc -e -`.

## rcp—COPY FILES TO OR FROM A REMOTE SYSTEM

```
rcp [-p] file1 file2
rcp [-pr] file … directory
```

The `rcp` command behaves like the `cp` command, but the files and directories can be on different systems in the network. The remote system must be one you can use `rsh` on, since `rcp` calls `rsh`. A file on another machine is specified in this way:

```
hostname:path
```

A relative *path* is interpreted as being relative to your home directory on the remote *hostname*.

You can also specify a different user's home directory for relative path names, with the form:

```
username@hostname:path
```

-p  Tries to give the copied file exactly the same permissions, ownership, access times, and so on as the original. This may not be possible, due to differences between machines.

-r  If one of the *file* arguments is a directory, recursively copies all of the files and subdirectories to the destination.

## read—STORE INPUT IN ONE OR MORE VARIABLES

```
read var1 [var2 …]
read [-prs][-u[n] [var1?prompt] [var2…]
```

There are two forms of the `read` command. The first stores a line from standard input in one or more variables. Each word of input is stored in a separate variable, but if there are more words of input than there are variables, all of the remaining words are stored in the last variable. This means if you give one variable, the entire line is stored in that variable.

The second form is specific to the Korn Shell. It lets you specify a *prompt* for the input, and it accepts some options. Otherwise, it behaves as the first form does.

-p    Reads from a coprocess. This feature is obscure.

-r    Reads in raw mode; don't accept \ as a character to continue lines.

-s       Saves input in the history file.

-u[*n*]    Reads from the file descriptor *n*. The default is standard input.

See Chapter 8, "Basic Shell Programming."

## rlogin—LOGIN TO REMOTE SYSTEM

```
rlogin [-L8] [-ec] [-l username] hostname
```

The `rlogin` command logs in to a remote system, *hostname*. When you exit the remote shell, the `rlogin` connection ends.

If there is a `.rhosts` file on the remote system that contains your username and your hostname, you will not be prompted for a password. There are other conditions on the `.rhosts` file; see your system documentation (or Chapter 14).

-8               Sends data in 8-bit mode instead of in 7-bit mode.

-e*c*             Uses *c* as the escape character. The default escape character is ~ (typed at the beginning of a line).

-l *username*   Logs in as user *username*. Without this option, your current username is used.

-L               Runs the command in litout mode.

See Chapter 4, "Computer Networks."

## rm—REMOVE A FILE OR DIRECTORY

```
rm [-fi] file...
rm -rR [-f] [-i] dirname...[file...]
```

The `rm` command removes a link to a file or directory. When all of the links are gone, the file is gone from the system. If the *file* is a symbolic link, the link will be removed but the original (linked) file won't be affected.

To remove a directory, use `rmdir` or the -r or -R options.

-f  Forces the removal of the file; doesn't prompt for confirmation if you do not have write permission on the file.

-i  Prompts for confirmation before removing a file.

-r Recursively removes directories. You cannot use this option to remove a non-empty write-protected directory.

-R Same as -r.

## rmdir—REMOVE A DIRECTORY

    rmdir [-ps] *directory* ...

The rmdir command removes an empty directory. (With the -p option, the directory can contain an empty directory, named in the argument.)

-p Removes the entire path specified by *directory*, if possible. Each child has to be the only child of its parent directory for all of them to be removed. The rmdir command prints a message on the standard error telling whether the whole directory path or only part of it was removed.

-s When -p is used, suppresses messages to the standard error.

## rsh—RUN COMMAND ON REMOTE SYSTEM

    rsh [-n] [-l *username*] *hostname command*
    rsh *hostname* [-n] [-l *username*] *command*

Run the specified *command* on the remote system specified by *hostname*. If you don't specify a command, rsh uses rlogin to log you in to the remote system.

-l *username*   Runs the command as *username*. If this is not specified, your current username is used.

-n              Redirects input of rsh to /dev/null. This may be needed if you're running one rsh in the background and you try to run another.

See Chapter 4, "Computer Networks."

## set—SET SHELL VARIABLES AND OPTIONS

    set [±A *name*] [-aefhkmnpstuvx] [-o [*mode*]] [—] *arg* ...]

Without arguments, the set command displays the current settings for the shell. With arguments, it sets the shell's options. The "positional parameters" are the arguments to the shell, which are stored in $1, $2, $3 and so on up to $9. The set command may also be used in a shell script to get specific behavior. (The `set -x` command is good when trying to get a shell script to work.)

`+A` *name*    Assigns the arguments after this option as the elements of an array name *name*.

`-A` *name*    Like `+A`, but unsets *name* before assigning the arguments.

`-a`    Automatically exports variables after defining or changing them. This is the mode `allexport`.

`-e`    Exits if a command fails (has a non-zero exit status). This is the mode `errexport`.

`-f`    Ignores filename metacharacters (such as * and ?).

`-h`    Creates tracked aliases.

`-i`    Runs as an interactive shell.

`-k`    Assigns environment variables no matter where the assignment appears on the command line. Normally the assignment has to be before the command name.

`-m`    Turns on job control. With job control on, background jobs run as part of a separate process group. This is the mode `monitor`.

`-n`    Reads commands but doesn't execute them. This is a useful option for checking a shell script for errors. This is the mode `noexec`.

`-o` [*mode*]    If no *mode* is given, the command lists the Korn Shell's current modes. Otherwise, it turns on the specified *mode* (although most of the modes can be set by options as well). The modes are:

`allexport` Same as `-a`.

`bgnice` Runs background jobs with lower priority.

`emacs` Uses `emacs` commands for command line editing.

`errexit` Same as `-e`.

ignoreeof Ignores the eof character (normally Ctrl-D). Only exit will exit the shell.

keyword Same as -k.

markdirs Always appends / to the end of directory names.

monitor Same as -m.

noclobber Doesn't overwrite existing files with > redirection, only with >|.

noexec Same as -n.

noglob Same as -f.

nolog Doesn't store function definitions in the history file.

nounset Same as -u.

privileged Same as -p.

trackall Same as -h.

verbose Same as -v.

vi Uses vi commands for command line editing.

viraw Like vi, but processes each character as it's typed.

xtrace Same as -x.

-p      Starts up as a privileged user (doesn't process the file $HOME/.profile).

-s      Sorts the positional parameters (the shell's arguments).

-t      Terminates after a single command is run.

-u      When substituting values for variables, treats an unset variable as an error, not as nothing.

-v      Shows each shell command line when read from input.

-x          Shows commands and arguments when run, preceded by a
            + character. This is useful for debugging shell scripts.

–           Ignores all options after this option. This is useful for giving
            arguments to shell scripts that begin with a - character. If
            there are no arguments after this option, it unsets the posi-
            tional parameters.

See Chapter 7, "Customizing Your Environment."

## stty—SET TERMINAL CHARACTERISTICS

```
stty [-a] [-g]
stty setting ...
```

The stty command displays or sets information about the terminal.
Without arguments, it prints an abbreviated list of the settings.

-a    Displays all settings.

-g    Displays settings in a form that can be used as arguments to the
      stty command.

## sum—CALCULATE A FILE'S CHECKSUM

```
sum [-r] [file…]
```

Like cksum, the sum command calculates a file's checksum and its size in
blocks (units of 512 bytes, or half a kilobyte).

-r    Uses an alternate checksum algorithm (typically it uses the algo-
      rithm of the BSD sum command, but this may not be true on your
      system).

See Chapter 5, "Other Useful Stuff."

## talk—TALK WITH ANOTHER USER

```
talk user [terminal]
```

The talk command opens up a "chat window" with another *user*. You
can name the *terminal* where you want the talk session to take place.
The talk command first prompts the other user to enter a talk command; once the other user has done so, each user is presented with a
split screen.

During a talk session, what you type appears on the screen. Some control characters will affect the display:

| Control Character | Effect |
|---|---|
| Control-G (alert character) | Makes other person's terminal beep. |
| Control-L | Redraws your half of the screen. |
| Backspace (erase) and line kill (normally Control-U) | Backspaces (erases) backspaces, even on the other person's display, and line kill erases from the cursor to the end of the line, even on the other person's display. |
| Control-C (interrupt) or Control-D (end-of-file or EOF) | Ends the `talk` session. Once one person has used the EOF signal (usually Control-D), the `talk` session has been ended on that side, and the person on the other side is notified that the session is over. All the other person can do is exit. According to the documentation, only end-of-file is needed, but on my Solaris system, the second person to exit has to use the interrupt signal. |
| Most printable or space characters | Displays on the other person's terminal. |
| Other non-printable characters | The `talk` program does its best to display other control characters. Most will show up as ^ followed by the appropriate ASCII character. Some characters will appear in "meta" notation, prefixed by an M. |

See Chapter 2, "Electronic Communication."

## tar—ARCHIVE OR UNARCHIVE FILES

```
tar {c|r|t|u|x} [bBefFhilmovwX [0-7]] [device]
[block] [exclude-file ...] [-I include-file] file ...
[-C directory file]
```

The `tar` command creates, lists, and extracts from tape archive files, either on a tape device (the default) or on the file specified by the `f` option.

A `tar` command must have one of the `c`, `r`, `t`, `u`, or `x` subcommands, which can be modified by the other values. (The Solaris version of `tar` treats these as "subcommands" and "modifiers" that don't need a -; other versions may require them to be treated as options.)

- c creates a new tar archive.
- r replaces files in a tar archive.
- t lists the table of contents for a tar archive.
- u updates files if they are newer than the ones already in the tar archive.
- x extracts files from a tar archive.

| | |
|---|---|
| b | Writes or reads information in chunks the size of the *block* argument (a value between 1 and 20). |
| B | Blocks; this is needed to make tar work across Ethernet connections. |
| e | Exits immediately if there is an error. |
| f | Uses the *file* argument as the archive, instead of the default tape device. If more than one *file* is listed, use the first one as the archive. |
| F | Excludes certain files. With one F, doesn't include directories named SCCS and RCS. With two F arguments, excludes those directories, all files with names ending in .o, and all files named errs, core, and a.out. |
| h | Follows symbolic links instead of storing the link file. |
| i | Ignores directory checksum errors. |
| -I *include-file* | Uses the files listed in *include-file* as the *file* arguments. The files must be listed one per line. |
| l | Complains if not all links to a file can be resolved. |
| m | Sets the modification time on an extracted file to the time it was extracted. |
| o | Gives the extracted file the ownership of the person running tar, rather than the value on the archived file. |
| p | Restores all permissions on the files. |
| v | Be verbose in output. |

| | |
|---|---|
| w | Asks for confirmation before performing each action. The user types a word beginning with "y" to confirm. Can't be used with t. |
| X | Excludes any files named in the file *exclude-file*. |
| 0-7 | Uses a different tape drive with the specified number. |

See Chapter 5, "Other Useful Stuff."

## telnet—LOGIN TO REMOTE SYSTEM

```
telnet [-8ELcdr] [-e escape-char] [-l user] [-n file]
[host]
```

The telnet command opens a telnet protocol connection with another machine, named *host*. If no *host* is given, telnet starts in an interactive mode.

Information about remote hosts can be saved in a startup file, .telnetrc.

| | |
|---|---|
| -8 | Uses 8-bit mode instead of 7-bit mode. |
| -c | Doesn't read the .telnetrc file. |
| -d | Turns on debugging. |
| -e escape-char | Uses *escape-char* as the escape character. Default is Ctrl-]; to specify a control character use ^*char*. |
| -E | Doesn't allow escape characters. |
| -l user | Logs in to the remote system as *user*. |
| -L | Uses an 8-bit path on output. |
| -n file | Stores trace information in *file*. |
| -r | Makes the user interface look as much like rlogin as possible, including recognizing the ~ at the beginning of a line as an escape character. |

Some `telnet` commands are given here:

| | |
|---|---|
| z | Suspends the telnet session. |
| ! | Starts a shell. |
| quit | Quits the telnet session. |
| ? | Displays the help information. |

See Chapter 4, "Computer Networks."

## test—TEST A CONDITION

```
test condition
[condition]
```

The `test` command checks a *condition* of some sort. If the condition is true, `test` returns 0; if it is false, `test` returns a non-zero value. Here is a list of almost all conditions supported by the Korn Shell's `test` command. (Some conditions that were not even hinted at in this book are omitted.)

In the following lists, the "true" condition is given.

For testing files and other conditions:

-b *file*    *file* exists and is a block special file.

-c *file*    *file* exists and is a character special file.

-d *file*    *file* exists and is a directory.

-f *file*    *file* exists and is a regular file.

-h *file*    *file* exists and is a symbolic link.

-p *file*    *file* exists and is a named pipe.

-r *file*    *file* exists and is readable.

-s *file*    *file* exists and has a size greater than 0 bytes.

-t [*n*]    The file descriptor indicated by *n* (default standard output) is a terminal.

-w `file`    *file* exists and is writable.

-x `file`    *file* exists and is executable.

For comparing two files:

`file1 -ef file2`    *file1* is the same age as *file2*.

`file1 -nt file2`    *file1* is newer than *file2*.

`file1 -ot file2`    *file1* is older than *file2*.

For comparing strings:

`-n string`              *string* exists and is longer than zero bytes.

`-z string`              *string* is set and is 0 bytes long.

`string1 = string2`      *string1* is the same as *string2*.

`string1 != string2`     *string1* is not the same as *string2*.

`string`                 *string* is not the null string.

For comparing two integer numbers:

`num1 -eq num2`    The first number equals the second number.

`num1 -ge num2`    The first number is greater than or equal to the second number.

`num1 -gt num2`    The first number is greater than the second number.

`num1 -le num2`    The first number is less than or equal to the second number.

`num1 -lt num2`    The first number is less than the second number.

`num1 -ne num2`    The first number is not equal to the second number.

See Chapter 8, "Basic Shell Programming."

## typeset—SET A VARIABLE'S TYPE

```
typeset [-rtx] [-l|-u|-i[n]] [f[c]] [-L[n]|[-R[n]]
[name[=value ...]]
```

The typeset command sets the type of information that can be stored in a variable. How typeset behaves depends on whether you supply a variable *name* or not.

Without any variables, the typeset command displays all variables of a specific type, determined by the options and their values. If you use + before the option instead of -, then typeset displays the names but not the values.

With variables, the typeset command sets the contents of the named variable to the type specified by the options.

-f[c] The *name* represents a function, and the = assignment is not allowed. Without a *name*, the option causes typeset to list all of the current functions. The *c* is flags that are set for the function, and can be one of t (turn on tracing, like set -x), u (the function is undefined), or x (the function is exported to other shells).

-i[n] The variable is an integer of base *n*. (Normal numbers are base 10.)

-L[n] The variable is a flush-left string, *n* characters long.

-l The variable is in lowercase.

-R[n] The variable is a flush-right string, *n* characters long.

-r The variable is read-only.

-t The variable is marked with a user-defined tag.

-u The variable is in uppercase.

-x The variable is automatically exported.

-Z[n] When used with -L, leading 0s are removed. When used alone, it's like -R except that -Z places 0s before numbers and spaces before text values.

See Chapter 8, "Basic Shell Programming."

## umask—SET OR DISPLAY USER FILE MASK

```
umask [-S] [nnn]
```

Without an argument, it displays the current user file creation mask. With an argument, it sets the value to that argument. The argument is a file mode and specifies which bits are turned *off*.

In the Korn Shell, the -S option causes umask to display the current umask symbolically.

See Chapter 9, "More About Files and Permissions."

## unalias—REMOVE A SHELL ALIAS

```
unalias name...
```

Remove the named alias or aliases from the list of aliases.

See Chapter 7, "Customizing Your Environment."

## uname—DISPLAY SYSTEM INFORMATION

```
uname [-aimnprsv]
```

The uname command displays information about the system. If no options are given, uname displays the name of the operating system.

-a Displays all information.

-i Displays hardware platform (implementation).

-m Displays class of machine hardware.

-n Displays node name.

-p Displays processor type.

-r Displays operating system release number.

-s Displays operating system name.

-v Displays the version of the operating system.

## uncompress—EXPAND A COMPRESSED FILE

```
uncompress [-cfv] [file...]
```

The `uncompress` command expands a file that has been compressed with `compress`. If no *file* is specified, it uncompresses standard input.

-c   Writes to standard output.

-f   Does not ask if a file should be overwritten.

-v   Be verbose; writes messages to standard error.

## unset—REMOVE A SHELL SETTING

```
unset [-f] name ...
```

The `unset` command removes the definition of a variable or a function. To remove a function, you must specify -f. (In the Bourne Shell, you do not need to specify -f to `unset` a function.)

-f   The *name* refers to a function.

## uucp—UNIX TO UNIX COPY

```
uucp [-c | -C] [-d | -f] [-ggrade] [-jmr] [-nuser] [-
xdebug] source destination
```

The `uucp` command copies files from one system to another, if they have a UUCP connection. (Use `uuname` to identify systems with a UUCP connection.) Either the *source* or the *destination* is specified in the UUCP format, *hostname!file*. If the *file* is given as a relative path name, it's taken as relative to the `/usr/spool/uucppublic` directory.

-c          Doesn't copy the file to the spool directory. This is the default behavior.

-C          Copies the file to the spool directory.

-d          Makes all directories needed for the copy. This is the default behavior.

-f          Doesn't make intermediate directories.

-ggrade     Sets the priority to the specified *grade*. The *grade* can be a letter, a number, or a string of letters and numbers. (The `uuglist` command on Solaris lists possible grades.)

-j         Prints a job identification number. The `uustat` command uses this number to show the status of a request or to cancel a request.

-m         Sends you mail when your request is completed.

-n*user*   Sends mail to *user* on the remote system when the request is complete.

-r         Queues the job but doesn't start the file transfer.

-x*debug*  Displays debugging information; if *debug* is 0, there's not much information and a value of 9 for *debug* produces lots of information. Values from 1-8 produce intermediate amounts of information.

See Chapter 4, "Computer Networks."

## uuname—DISPLAY NAMES OF KNOWN UUCP SYSTEMS

```
uuname [-l]
```

The `uuname` command displays the names of known systems with UUCP connections.

-l     Displays the UUCP name of the current machine.

See Chapter 4, "Computer Networks."

## vi—TEXT EDITOR

```
vi [- | -s] [-ClLRvV] [-r [filename]] [-t tag] [-wn]
[+command | -c command] filename...
```

The `vi` editor is the standard text editor on most UNIX systems. For your convenience, this summary reproduces information about `vi` from Appendix B of the *UNIX User's Interactive Workbook* and summarizes the information presented in Chapter 10 of this book, "Advanced `vi` Tricks."

-               Runs a script instead of running interactively. The script is provided on standard input.

+*command*      Runs the *command* as soon as `vi` starts. Not all commands can be run, but search and positioning commands can be given.

| | |
|---|---|
| `-c command` | The same as `+command`. |
| `-C` | Encryption option. For security, `vi` asks you for an encryption key and codes all text (even in temporary files) using that key. Very similar to `-x`, except that `-C` assumes the file you're reading in was already encrypted and will give very strange results if it wasn't. |
| `-1` | Sets tabs, auto-indent, and so forth for editing programs written in the LISP programming language. |
| `-L` | Lists the name of all files saved when the system or the editor crashed. |
| `-r [filename]` | Recovers the file *filename* that was being edited when the system or the editor crashed. |
| `-R` | Runs in read-only mode, so the file can't be overwritten. |
| `-s` | Runs a script instead of running interactively, the same as `-`. The script is provided on standard input. |
| `-t tag` | Edits the file that contains the programming construct *tag*. This works for directories containing source code files where the file `ctags` has created an index of source code files. |
| `-v` | Starts in `vi` mode (as opposed to `ex` mode). This is redundant if you typed `vi` to start the command. |
| `-V` | Be verbose. Echo non-terminal input on standard error. This can be useful when running editor scripts with `-s`. |
| `-wn` | Sets the window size to *n* lines high. This is useful when working over slow systems or connections. |
| `-x` | Encryption option. For security, `vi` asks you for an encryption key and codes all text (even in temporary files) using that key. Very similar to `-C`, except that `-x` tries to guess if the file you're reading in was already encrypted, and won't try to "unencrypt" it if the file wasn't encrypted. |

Here are the basic commands:

| Command | Meaning |
| --- | --- |
| Escape | Leaves text input mode and enters command mode. |
| Control-C | Interrupts current command; also leaves text input mode. |
| :quit | Quits if there are no unsaved changes. Can be abbreviated :q. |
| :quit! | Quits even if there are unsaved changes. Can be abbreviated :q!. |
| :write [*name*] | Writes current text into the file *name*. Can be abbreviated :w [*name*]. |
| :write! [*name*] | Writes current text into the file *name*, even if it's not the file you're currently editing. Can be abbreviated :w! [*name*]. |
| :wq | Writes the file and quits. |
| :next | Goes to next file in the argument list if there are no unsaved changes. Can be abbreviated :n. |
| :next! | Goes to the next file in the argument list even if there are no unsaved changes. Can be abbreviated :n!. |

Here are vi commands to enter input mode:

a    Inserts the text after the current cursor position.

A    Inserts the text at the end of the current line.

i    Inserts the text at the current cursor position.

I    Inserts the text at the beginning of the current line.

o    Inserts the text on a new line before the current line.

O    Inserts the text on a new line after the current line.

Movement commands in vi, including contextual movement commands mentioned in Chapter 10, "Advanced vi Tricks," follow:

[*n*]j      Moves cursor down *n* lines (default 1).

[*n*]k      Moves cursor up *n* lines (default 1).

[*n*]l      Moves cursor right *n* characters (default 1).

[*n*]h      Moves cursor left *n* characters (default 1).

[*n*]Enter   Same as j.

[*n*]Space   Same as l.

| | |
|---|---|
| [*n*]Backspace | Same as h. |
| $ | Moves cursor to right end of line. |
| ^ | Moves cursor to first non-blank character on left of line. |
| 0 | Moves cursor to first row of line. |
| [*n*]G | Moves cursor to line *n* of file (default is end of file). |
| [*n*]w | Moves cursor to beginning of *n*th next word (default 1). |
| [*n*]b | Moves cursor to *n*th previous word beginning (default 1). |
| [*n*]) | Moves cursor to beginning of *n*th next sentence (default 1). |
| [*n*] ( | Moves cursor to *n*th previous sentence beginning (default 1). |
| [*n*]} | Moves cursor to beginning of *n*th next paragraph (default 1). |
| [*n*]{ | Moves cursor to *n*th previous paragraph beginning (default 1). |
| [*n*] [ [ | Moves cursor to the *n*th previous section beginning (default 1). |
| [*n*] ] ] | Moves cursor to the *n*th next section beginning (default 1). |
| % | In or on one of a pair of braces, brackets, or parentheses ({ },[ ], ( )), moves the cursor to the matching one of the pair. |
| [*n*]Control-F | Moves cursor forward *n* screenfuls of lines (default 1). |
| [*n*]Control-B | Moves cursor backward *n* screenfuls of lines (default 1). |
| [*n*]Control-E | Moves screen forward *n* lines without moving cursor (default 1). |
| [*n*]Control-Y | Moves screen backward *n* lines without moving cursor (default 1). |
| H | Moves cursor to top line of screen. |
| L | Moves cursor to last line of screen. |
| M | Moves cursor to middle line of screen. |
| z | Redraws screen so line with cursor is at top. |
| m*c* | Marks the line; the mark will be referred to as *c* (a lowercase letter). |
| ' *c* | Moves to the first non-whitespace character on the line marked with bookmark *c*. |
| ' ' | Moves to the first non-whitespace character on the line with the last context. The context is set by insertion, searching, deletion, or ' ' or ` ` commands. |
| ` ` | Moves to the column of the last context. |
| ` *c* | Moves to the same column as when marked on the line marked with bookmark *c*. |

Here are the vi deletion, change, and undo commands:

| | |
|---|---|
| [*n*]dd | Deletes the next *n* lines, starting with the current line (default is 1 line). |
| [*n*]d[*movement*] | Deletes from the current cursor position to the destination of the *movement* command. |
| :*addr*d[elete] | Deletes the lines described in the ex-style *addr*. |
| !!*cmd* | Filters the current line through the named (non-vi) *cmd*. |
| !*mvcmd* | Filters all the text encompassed by the movement command *mv* through the command *cmd*. |
| :*addr*!*cmd* | Filters the lines specified by the ex-style *addr* through the named (non-vi) *cmd*. |
| [*n*]r*c* | Replaces the next *n* characters with the character *c* (default 1). |
| R | Deletes the rest of the line and enters input mode. |
| u | Undoes the last command that changed the file. |
| [*n*]. | Repeats last insertion or deletion *n* times (default 1). |

The vi search commands follow:

| | |
|---|---|
| f*c* | Searches forward in line for character *c*. |
| F*c* | Searches backward in line for character *c*. |
| t*c* | Searches forward in line for character *c*, but puts cursor one character before it. |
| T*c* | Searches backward in line for character *c*, but puts cursor one character before it. |
| /*regexp* | Searches forward for *regexp*. |
| ?*regexp* | Searches backward for *regexp*. |
| /*regexp*/z | Searches forward for *regexp*, and displays screen so matching line is at top. |
| ?*regexp*?z | Searches backward for *regexp*, and displays screen so matching line is at top. |
| / | Searches forward for last *regexp* searched for. |
| ? | Searches backward for last *regexp* searched for. |
| n | Repeats last search. |

Here are the `vi` search-and-replace commands:

| | |
|---|---|
| `:s/`*regexp*`/`*replacement*`/` | Replaces first occurrence of *regexp* on this line with *replacement*. |
| `:s/`*regexp*`/`*replacement*`/g` | Replaces all occurrences of *regexp* on this line with *replacement*. |
| `:%s/`*regexp*`/`*replacement*`/` | Replaces first occurrence of *regexp* on a line throughout file. |
| `:%s/`*regexp*`/`*replacement*`/g` | Replaces all occurrences of *regexp* throughout file. |
| `&` | Repeats last search and replace. |

Here are the `vi` text copying and moving commands:

| | |
|---|---|
| [*n*]`yy` | "Yanks" *n* lines of text for copying. |
| [*n*]`p` | Puts the contents of the buffer *after* the cursor, *n* times (default 1). |
| [*n*]`P` | Puts the contents of the buffer *before* the cursor, *n* times (default 1). |
| `:r` *filename* | Reads in the file *filename* on the line after the cursor. |

The `vi` text buffer commands, where a buffer name is a lowercase letter represented here as *c,* are:

| | |
|---|---|
| `"`*c*`yy` | "Yanks" the line into buffer *c*. If *c* is a capital letter, the line is appended to the current contents of buffer *c*. |
| `"`*c*`ymove` | "Yanks" into buffer *c* all text covered by the *move* command. If *c* is a capital letter, the text is appended to the current contents of buffer *c*. |
| [n]`"`*c*`p` | Puts the contents of buffer *c after* the cursor, *n* times (default 1). |
| [*n*]`"`*c*`P` | Puts the contents of the buffer *before* the cursor, *n* times (default 1). |

Here are the `vi` macro, abbreviation, source, and setting commands:

| | |
|---|---|
| `:ab` | Lists abbreviations. |
| `:ab` *lhs rhs* | Makes the text *lhs* be an abbreviation for the text *rhs*. |
| `:unab` *lhs* | Removes the abbreviation *lhs*. |
| `:map` *lhs rhs* | Defines a macro named *lhs* containing the commands in *rhs* and runs them whenever *lhs* is typed in command mode. |

| | |
|---|---|
| `:map! ` *lhs rhs* | Defines a macro named *lhs* containing the commands in *rhs* and runs them whenever *lhs* is typed in input mode. |
| `@`*c* | Runs the contents of buffer *c* as if they were `ex` commands. |
| `:set [all]` | Displays some or all of the current option settings. |
| `:set ` *option* | Turns on the named *option*. |
| `:set no`*option* | Turns off the named *option*. |
| `:mkexrc[!] ` *file* | Saves the current settings in *file*; if ! is included, overwrites *file* if it exists. |
| `:so[urce] ` *file* | Reads the options from the named *file*. |
| [*n*]`"`*c*`p` | Puts the contents of buffer *c* *after* the cursor, *n* times (default 1). |
| [*n*]`"`*c*`P` | Puts the contents of the buffer *before* the cursor, *n* times (default 1). |

See Chapter 10, "Advanced `vi` Tricks."

## while—REPEAT COMMANDS

```
while condition
do
      commands
done
```

As long as the *condition* is true, the shell will loop through the specified *commands*. The *condition* is often a `read` command. It can also be a `test` command.

## who—DISPLAY USERS ON THE SYSTEM

```
who   [ -abdHlmpqrstTu ]   [ file ]
who -q  [ -n x ]   [ file ]
who am i
who am I
```

The `who` command displays information about the users who are currently using the system. The version of `who` on Solaris is the traditional (System V) version. It has different options than the version found on other systems; a version with the other options is in the directory `/usr/xpg4/bin`.

Some options (such as –b, –d, –p, and –r) are intended for system programmers and administrators.

-a        Runs as if the command had been given all of the options –b, –d, –l, –p, –r, –t, –T, and –u.

-b        Indicates the time and date when the system was last started (rebooted).

-d        Displays processes that have died and have not been restarted by the init process.

-H        Displays headings over the output columns.

-l        Lists lines waiting for someone to log in (displayed with the user name "LOGIN").

-m        Only displays information about the current terminal.

-n *x*     Lists only *x* number of users on a line; *x* must be an integer number (1 or greater). Only valid with –q.

-p        Lists any other process active that was spawned by init.

-q        Displays how many users are logged on and their names. All other options except –n are ignored when –q is given.

-r        Lists current run-level of the init process.

-s        In output, displays only name, terminal line, and time.

-T        In output, displays name, terminal line, state, idle, process ID, comment, and time. The state is one of + (terminal allows messages), – (terminal doesn't allow messages), or ? (who cannot determine if the terminal allows messages).

-t        Indicates the last time the system clock was changed.

-u        Lists only users currently logged in.

See Chapter 2, "Electronic Communication."

## write—SEND A MESSAGE TO ANOTHER USER

```
write user [terminal]
```

The `write` command sends a message to the specified *user* (who must be logged on). You can name a specific *terminal*.

The command reads the message from your standard input; to end the message, send the end-of-file signal (usually Control-D).

The `mesg` command can be used to prevent other users from sending `write` messages to your terminal screen.

See Chapter 2, "Electronic Communication."

## xargs—RUN A COMMAND ON A LONG ARGUMENT LIST

```
xargs [-pt] [-e[eofstr]] [-E eofstr] [-I replstr] [-
i[replstr]] [-L number] [-l[number]] [-n number [-x]]
[-s size] [command [argument...]]
```

The `xargs` command breaks standard input into a set of argument lists, and it runs *command* using each set of arguments until it receives end-of-file on standard input. Only the -n, -s, -t, and -x options are available on BSD systems.

-e[*eofstr*]    Uses *eofstr* character or string as the end-of-file instead of the actual end-of-file. If you don't specify *eofstr*, the _ character is taken to mean the end of the input. If you use -e or -E, a real end-of-file will still end input.

-E *eofstr*    Like -e, except you *must* specify a character or string to be the end-of-file character.

-i[*replstr*]    Substitutes the argument list for *replstr* in the *command*. This allows you to (for example) move files into a directory, because the directory name must come last on the mv command line. If you don't specify *replstr*, `xargs` treats { } as the string to replace.

-I *replstr*    Like -i, except you *must* specify the character or string to be replaced with the argument list.

-l[*number*]    Assuming the input is in lines, runs *command* every *number* of non-empty lines; the default number is 1. The last time the *command* is run can have fewer than *number* lines. Cannot be used with the -L or -n options.

-L *number*    Like -l except that you *must* supply a *number*. Cannot be used with the -l or -n options.

-n *number*    Breaks the input into chunks of *number* arguments, as long as the length of the constructed command isn't longer than specified by -s or the system limit. The last time the *command* is run can have fewer than *number* arguments.

-s *size*    Fits as many arguments into the line as possible without getting longer than *size* characters long. If -n or -l is also given, the shortest command line is constructed.

-t    Writes each generated *command* to standard error before running it.

-x    If the *number* specified by -n or -L won't fit into the space available for a command line, exits without trying to run the command.

See Chapter 5, "Other Useful Stuff."

# INDEX